Building Data-Driven Applications with LlamaIndex

A practical guide to retrieval-augmented generation (RAG) to enhance LLM applications

Andrei Gheorghiu

Building Data-Driven Applications with LlamaIndex

Group Product Manager: Niranjan Naikwadi
Publishing Product Manager: Nitin Nainani
Book Project Manager: Aparna Ravikumar Nair
Content Development Editor: Priyanka Soam
Technical Editor: Rahul Limbachiya
Copy Editor: Safis Editing
Indexer: Pratik Shirodkar
Production Designer: Shankar Kalbhor
DevRel Marketing Coordinator: Vinishka Kalra

First published: May 2024

Production reference: 1150424

Published by
Packt Publishing Ltd.
Grosvenor House
11 St Paul's Square
Birmingham
B3 1RB, UK

ISBN 978-1-83508-950-7

www.packtpub.com

For the past six months, the focus required to create this book has sadly kept me away from the people I love. To my family and friends, your understanding and support have been my harbor in the storm of long hours and endless revisions.

Andreea, your love has been the gentle beacon guiding me through this journey. To my daughter Carla and every young reader out there: never stop learning! Life is a journey with so many possible destinations. Make sure you are the one choosing yours. My dear friends at ITAcademy, you guys rock! Thanks for supporting me along the way. Also, finalizing this book would not have been possible without the dedicated efforts and unwavering commitment of the Packt team. I extend my heartfelt gratitude to everyone involved in this project.

– Andrei Gheorghiu

Contributors

About the author

Andrei Gheorghiu is a seasoned IT professional and accomplished trainer at ITAcademy with over two decades of experience as a trainer, consultant, and auditor. With an impressive array of certifications, including ITIL Master, CISA, ISO 27001 Lead Auditor, and CISSP, Andrei has trained thousands of students in IT service management, information security, IT governance, and audit. His consulting experience spans the implementation of ERP and CRM systems, as well as conducting security assessments and audits for various organizations. Andrei's passion for groundbreaking innovations drives him to share his vast knowledge and offer practical advice on leveraging technology to solve real-world challenges, particularly in the wake of recent advancements in the field. As a forward-thinking educator, his main goal is to help people upskill and reskill in order to increase their productivity and remain relevant in the age of AI.

About the reviewers

Rajesh Chettiar, holding a specialization in AI and ML, brings over 13 years of experience in machine learning, Generative AI, automation, and ERP solutions. He is passionate about keeping up with cutting-edge advancements in AI and is committed to improving his skills to foster innovation.

Rajesh resides in Pune with his parents, his wife, Pushpa, and his son, Nishith. In his free time, he likes to play with his son, watch movies with his family, and go on road trips. He also has a fondness for listening to Bollywood music.

Elliot helped write some of the LlamaIndexTS (Typescript version of LlamaIndex) codebase. He is actively looking to take on new generative AI projects (as of early 2024), he is available on GitHub and Linkedin.

I thank the Lord for everything. Thank you, Dad, Mom, and twin sister for your amazing support. Thank you to my friends who gave me their honest opinions and helped me grow. Thank you Yi Ding at LlamaIndex for helping me start this GenAI journey, and Yujian Tang for introducing me to Yi and always being supportive of open-source. Finally, thank you to everyone who has reached out to talk about generative AI; I learn new things every day from each of you

Srikannan Balakrishnan is an experienced AI/ML professional and a technical writer with a passion for translating complex information into simpler forms. He has a background in data science, including AI/ML, which fuels his ability to understand the intricacies of the subject matter and present it in a way that is accessible to both technical and non-technical audiences. He also has experience in Generative AI and has worked with different clients to solve their business problems with the power of data and AI. Beyond his technical expertise, he is a skilled communicator with a keen eye for detail. He is dedicated to crafting user-friendly documentation that empowers readers to grasp new concepts and navigate complex systems with confidence.

Arijit Das is an experienced Data Scientist with over 5 years of commercial experience, providing data-driven solutions to Fortune 500 clients across the US, UK, and EU. With expertise in Finance, Banking, Logistics, and HR management, Arijit excels in the Data Science lifecycle, from data extraction to model deployment and MLOps. Proficient in Supervised and Unsupervised ML techniques, including NLP, Arijit is currently focused on implementing cutting-edge ML practices at Citi globally.

Table of Contents

Part 1: Introduction to Generative AI and LlamaIndex

1

2

Part 2: Starting Your First LlamaIndex Project

3

Kickstarting Your Journey with LlamaIndex   33

4

Ingesting Data into Our RAG Workflow   61

5

Indexing with LlamaIndex   101

Part 3: Retrieving and Working with Indexed Data

6

7

8

Building Chatbots and Agents with LlamaIndex   223

Part 4: Customization, Prompt Engineering, and Final Words

9

Customizing and Deploying Our LlamaIndex Project   265

10

Prompt Engineering Guidelines and Best Practices   299

11

Conclusion and Additional Resources   319

Preface

Beyond the initial hype that the fast advance of Generative AI and **Large Language Models (LLMs)** has produced, we have been able to observe both the abilities and shortcomings of this technology. LLMs are versatile and powerful tools driving innovation across various fields, serving as the foundation for natural language generation technology. Despite their potential, though, LLMs have limitations such as lacking access to real-time data, struggling to distinguish truth from falsehoods, maintaining context over long documents, and exhibiting unpredictable failures in reasoning and fact retention. **Retrieval-Augmented Generation (RAG)** attempts to solve many of these shortcomings and LlamaIndex is perhaps the simplest and most user-friendly way to begin your journey into this new development paradigm.

Driven by a flourishing and expanding community, this open source framework provides a huge number of tools for different RAG scenarios. Perhaps, that's also why this book is needed. When I first encountered the LlamaIndex framework, I was impressed by its comprehensive official documentation. However, I soon realized that the sheer amount of options can be overwhelming for someone who's just starting out. Therefore, my goal was to provide a beginner-friendly guide that helps you navigate the framework's capabilities and use them in your projects. The more you explore the inner mechanics of LlamaIndex, the more you'll appreciate its effectiveness. By breaking down complex concepts and offering practical examples, this book aims to bridge the gap between the official documentation and your understanding, ensuring that you can confidently build RAG applications while avoiding common pitfalls.

So, join me on a journey through the LlamaIndex ecosystem. From understanding fundamental RAG concepts to mastering advanced techniques, you'll learn how to ingest, index, and query data from various sources, create optimized indexes tailored to your use cases, and build chatbots and interactive web applications that showcase the true potential of Generative AI. The book contains a lot of practical code examples, several best practices in prompt engineering, and troubleshooting techniques that will help you navigate the challenges of building LLM-based applications augmented with your data.

By the end of this book, you'll have the skills and expertise to create powerful, interactive, AI-driven applications using LlamaIndex and Python. Moreover, you'll be able to predict costs, deal with potential privacy issues, and deploy your applications, helping you become a sought-after professional in the rapidly growing field of Generative AI.

Who this book is for

This book has been specifically designed for developers at varying stages of their careers who are eager to understand and exploit the capabilities of Generative AI, particularly through the use of RAG. It aims to serve as a foundational guide for those with a basic understanding of Python development and a general familiarity with Generative AI concepts.

Here are the key audiences who will find this book invaluable:

- **Entry-level developers**: Individuals who have a foundational understanding of Python and are beginning their journey into the world of generative AI will find this book an excellent starting point. It will guide you through the initial steps of using the LlamaIndex framework to create robust and innovative applications. You'll learn the core components, basic workflows, and best practices to kickstart your RAG application development journey.

- **Experienced developers**: For those who are already familiar with the landscape of generative AI and are looking to deepen their expertise, this book offers insight into advanced topics within the LlamaIndex framework. You'll discover how to leverage your existing skills to develop and deploy more complex RAG applications, enhancing the capabilities of your projects and pushing the boundaries of what's possible with AI.

- **Professionals seeking to harness the full power of LLMs**: If you're looking to improve your productivity by building quick solutions for data-driven problems, this book will teach you the basic concepts and provide you with powerful abilities. If you're a natural learner and want to experiment with this wonderful technology, this book will provide you with the tools to solve complex problems with greater efficiency and creativity.

What this book covers

Chapter 1, Understanding Large Language Models, serves as an introduction to generative AI and LLMs. It explains what LLMs are, their role in modern technology, and their strengths and weaknesses. The chapter aims to provide you with a foundational understanding of the capabilities of LLMs that LlamaIndex builds upon.

Chapter 2, LlamaIndex: The Hidden Jewel - An Introduction to the LlamaIndex Ecosystem, introduces the LlamaIndex ecosystem and how it can augment LLMs. It explains the general structure of the book – starting with basic concepts and gradually introducing more complex elements of the LlamaIndex framework. The chapter also introduces the **PITS – Personalized Intelligent Tutoring System** project, which will be used to apply the concepts studied in the book and covers the preparation of the development environment.

Chapter 3, Kickstarting Your Journey with LlamaIndex, covers the basics of starting your first LlamaIndex project. It explains the essential components of a RAG application in LlamaIndex, such as documents, nodes, indexes, and query engines. The chapter provides a typical workflow model and a simple hands-on example, where readers will begin building the PITS project.

Chapter 4, Ingesting Data into Our RAG Workflow, focuses on importing our proprietary data into LlamaIndex, emphasizing the usage of the LlamaHub connectors. We learn how to break down and organize documents by parsing them into coherent, indexable chunks of information. The chapter also covers ingestion pipelines, important data privacy considerations, metadata extraction, and simple cost estimation methods.

Chapter 5, Indexing with LlamaIndex, explores the topic of data indexing. It provides an overview of how indexing works, comparing different indexing techniques to help readers choose the most suitable one for their use cases. The chapter also explains the concept of layered indexing and covers persistent index storage and retrieval, cost estimation, embeddings, vector stores, similarity search, and storage contexts.

Chapter 6, Querying Our Data, Part 1 – Context Retrieval, explains the mechanics of querying data and various querying strategies and architectures within LlamaIndex, with a deep focus on retrievers. It covers advanced concepts such as asynchronous retrieval, metadata filters, tools, selectors, retriever routers, and query transformations. The chapter also discusses fundamental paradigms such as dense retrieval and sparse retrieval, along with their strengths and weaknesses.

Chapter 7, Querying Our Data, Part 2 – Postprocessing and Response Synthesis, continues the query mechanics topic, explaining the role of node post-processing and response synthesizers in the RAG workflow. It presents the overall query engine construct and its usage, as well as output parsing. The hands-on part of this chapter focuses on using LlamaIndex to generate personalized content in the PITS application.

Chapter 8, Building Chatbots and Agents with LlamaIndex, introduces the essentials of chatbots, agents, and conversation tracking with LlamaIndex, applying this knowledge to the hands-on project. You will learn how LlamaIndex facilitates fluid interaction, retains context, and manages custom retrieval/ response strategies, which are essential aspects for building effective conversational interfaces.

Chapter 9, Customizing and Deploying Our LlamaIndex Project, provides a comprehensive guide to personalizing and launching LlamaIndex projects. It covers tailoring different components of the RAG pipeline, a beginner-friendly tutorial on deploying with Streamlit, advanced tracing methods for debugging, and techniques for evaluating and fine-tuning a LlamaIndex application.

Chapter 10, Prompt Engineering Guidelines and Best Practices, explains the essential role of prompt engineering in enhancing the effectiveness of a RAG pipeline, highlighting how prompts are used "under the hood" of the LlamaIndex framework. It guides readers on the nuances of customizing and optimizing prompts to harness the full power of LlamaIndex and ensure more reliable and tailored AI outputs.

Chapter 11, Conclusion and Additional Resources, serves as a comprehensive conclusion, highlighting other projects and pathways for extended learning and summarizing the core insights from the book. It offers an overview of the main features of the framework, provides a curated list of additional resources for further exploration, and includes an index for quick terminology reference.

To get the most out of this book

You will need to have a basic understanding of Python development. General experience in using Generative AI models is also recommended. All the examples provided in the book have been specifically designed to run in a local Python environment, and because several libraries will be required along the way, it is recommended that you have a minimum of 20 GB of storage space available on your computer.

Software/hardware covered in the book	Operating system requirements
Python >= 3.11	Windows or Linux
LlamaIndex >= 0.10	

Because most of the examples presented in the book rely on the OpenAI API, you'll also need to obtain an OpenAI API key.

If you are using the digital version of this book, we advise you to type the code yourself or access the code from the book's GitHub repository (a link is available in the next section). Doing so will help you avoid any potential errors related to the copying and pasting of code.

As many of the code examples rely on the OpenAI API, keep in mind that running them will incur costs. Everything has been optimized for minimum cost but neither the author nor the publisher are responsible for these costs. You should also be advised of the security implications when using a public API such as the one provided by OpenAI. If you choose to use your own proprietary data to experiment with different examples, make sure you consult OpenAI's privacy policy in advance.

Download the example code files

You can download the example code files for this book from GitHub at `https://github.com/PacktPublishing/Building-Data-Driven-Applications-with-LlamaIndex`. The repository is organized in different folders. There is one corresponding folder for each chapter titled *ch<x>*, where *<x>* represents the chapter number. The folder called *PITS_APP* contains the source code of the main project presented throughout the book. If there's an update to the code, it will be updated in the GitHub repository.

We also have other code bundles from our rich catalog of books and videos available at `https://github.com/PacktPublishing/`. Check them out!

Conventions used

There are a number of text conventions used throughout this book.

`Code in text`: Indicates code words in text, database table names, folder names, filenames, file extensions, pathnames, dummy URLs, user input, and Twitter handles. Here is an example: "[...] using the `download_llama_pack()` method and specifying a download location such as [...]"

A block of code is set as follows:

```
from llama_index.llms.openai import OpenAI
llm = OpenAI(
    api_base='http://localhost:1234/v1',
    temperature=0.7
)
```

When we wish to draw your attention to a particular part of a code block, the relevant lines or items are set in bold:

```
from llama_index.llms.openai import OpenAI
llm = OpenAI(
    api_base='http://localhost:1234/v1',
    temperature=0.7
)
```

Any command-line input or output is written as follows:

```
$ pip install llama-index-llms-neutrino
```

Bold: Indicates a new term, an important word, or words that you see onscreen. For instance, words in menus or dialog boxes appear in **bold**. Here is an example: "Select **System info** from the **Administration** panel."

> **Tips or important notes**
> Appear like this.

Get in touch

Feedback from our readers is always welcome.

General feedback: If you have questions about any aspect of this book, email us at customercare@packtpub.com and mention the book title in the subject of your message.

Errata: Although we have taken every care to ensure the accuracy of our content, mistakes do happen. If you have found a mistake in this book, we would be grateful if you would report this to us. Please visit www.packtpub.com/support/errata and fill in the form.

Piracy: If you come across any illegal copies of our works in any form on the internet, we would be grateful if you would provide us with the location address or website name. Please contact us at copyright@packt.com with a link to the material.

If you are interested in becoming an author: If there is a topic that you have expertise in and you are interested in either writing or contributing to a book, please visit authors.packtpub.com.

Share Your Thoughts

Once you've read *Building Data-Driven Applications with LlamaIndex*, we'd love to hear your thoughts! Scan the QR code below to go straight to the Amazon review page for this book and share your feedback.

https://packt.link/r/1-835-08950-X

Your review is important to us and the tech community and will help us make sure we're delivering excellent quality content.

Download a free PDF copy of this book

Thanks for purchasing this book!

Do you like to read on the go but are unable to carry your print books everywhere?

Is your eBook purchase not compatible with the device of your choice?

Don't worry, now with every Packt book you get a DRM-free PDF version of that book at no cost.

Read anywhere, any place, on any device. Search, copy, and paste code from your favorite technical books directly into your application.

The perks don't stop there, you can get exclusive access to discounts, newsletters, and great free content in your inbox daily

Follow these simple steps to get the benefits:

1. Scan the QR code or visit the link below

https://packt.link/free-ebook/9781835089507

2. Submit your proof of purchase
3. That's it! We'll send your free PDF and other benefits to your email directly

Part 1:
Introduction to
Generative AI and LlamaIndex

This first part begins by introducing generative AI and **Large Language Models (LLMs)**, discussing their ability to produce human-like text, their limitations, and how **Retrieval-Augmented Generation (RAG)** can address these issues by enhancing accuracy, reasoning, and relevance. We then progress to understand how LlamaIndex leverages RAG to bridge the gap between LLMs' extensive knowledge and proprietary data, elevating the potential of interactive AI applications.

This part has the following chapters:

- *Chapter 1, Understanding Large Language Models*
- *Chapter 2, LlamaIndex: The Hidden Jewel - An Introduction to the LlamaIndex Ecosystem*

1

Understanding
Large Language Models

If you are reading this book, you have probably explored the realm of **large language models (LLMs)** and already recognize their potential applications as well as their pitfalls. This book aims to address the challenges LLMs face and provides a practical guide to building data-driven LLM applications with LlamaIndex, taking developers from foundational concepts to advanced techniques for implementing **retrieval-augmented generation (RAG)** to create high-performance interactive **artificial intelligence (AI)** systems augmented by external data.

This chapter introduces **generative AI (GenAI)** and LLMs. It explains how LLMs generate human-like text after training on massive datasets. We'll also overview LLM capabilities, limitations such as outdated knowledge potential for false information, and lack of reasoning. You'll be introduced to RAG as a potential solution, combining retrieval models using indexed data with generative models to increase fact accuracy, logical reasoning, and context relevance. Overall, you'll gain a basic LLM understanding and learn about RAG as a way to overcome some LLM weaknesses, setting the stage for utilizing LLMs practically.

In this chapter, we will cover the following main topics:

- Introducing GenAI and LLMs
- Understanding the role of LLMs in modern technology
- Exploring challenges with LLMs
- Augmenting LLMs with RAG

Introducing GenAI and LLMs

Introductions are sometimes boring, but here, it is important for us to set the context and help you familiarize yourself with GenAI and LLMs before we dive deep into LlamaIndex. I will try to be as concise as possible and, if the reader is already familiar with this information, I apologize for the brief digression.

What is GenAI?

GenAI refers to systems that are capable of generating new content such as text, images, audio, or video. Unlike more specialized AI systems that are designed for specific tasks such as image classification or speech recognition, GenAI models can create completely new assets that are often very difficult – if not impossible – to distinguish from human-created content.

These systems use **machine learning** (**ML**) techniques such as **neural networks** (**NNs**) that are trained on vast amounts of data. By learning patterns and structures within the training data, generative models can model the underlying probability distribution of the data and sample from this distribution to generate new examples. In other words, they act as big prediction machines.

We will now discuss LLMs, which are one of the most popular fields in GenAI.

What is an LLM?

One of the most prominent and rapidly advancing branches of GenAI is **natural language generation** (**NLG**) through **LLMs** (*Figure 1.1*):

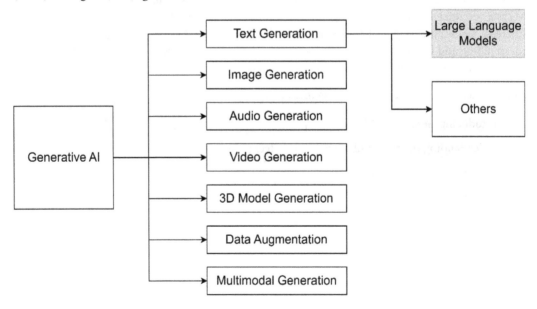

Figure 1.1 – LLMs are a sub-branch of GenAI

LLMs are NNs that are specifically designed and optimized to understand and generate human language. They are *large* in the sense that they are trained on massive amounts of text containing billions or even trillions of words scraped from the internet and other sources. Larger models show increased performance on benchmarks, better generalization, and new emergent abilities. In contrast with earlier, rule-based generation systems, the main distinguishing feature of an LLM is that it can produce novel, original text that reads naturally.

By learning patterns from many sources, LLMs acquire various language skills found in their training data – from nuanced grammar to topic knowledge and even basic common-sense reasoning. These learned patterns allow LLMs to extend human-written text in contextually relevant ways. As they keep improving, LLMs create new possibilities for automatically generating **natural language** (**NL**) content at scale.

During the training process, LLMs gradually learn probabilistic relationships between words and rules that govern language structure from their huge dataset of training data. Once trained, they are able to generate remarkably human-like text by predicting the probability of the next word in a sequence, based on the previous words. In many cases, the text they generate is so natural that it makes you wonder: aren't we humans just a similar but more sophisticated prediction machine? But that's a topic for another book.

One of the key architectural innovations is the **transformer** (that is the *T* in *GPT*), which uses an **attention mechanism** to learn contextual relationships between words. Attention allows the model to learn long-range dependencies in text. It's like if you're listening carefully in a conversation, you pay **attention** to the context to understand the full meaning. This means they *understand* not just words that are close together but also how words that are far apart in a sentence or paragraph relate to each other.

Attention allows the model to selectively focus on relevant parts of the input sequence when making predictions, thus capturing complex patterns and dependencies within the data. This feature makes it possible for particularly large transformer models (with many parameters and trained on massive datasets) to demonstrate surprising new abilities such as in-context learning, where they can perform tasks with just a few examples in their prompt. To learn more about transformers and **Generative Pre-trained Transformer** (**GPT**), you can refer to *Improving Language Understanding with unsupervised learning*– Alec Radford, Karthik Narasimhan, Tim Salimans and Ilya Sutskever (`https://openai.com/research/language-unsupervised`).

The best-performing LLMs such as GPT-4, Claude 2.1, and Llama 2 contain trillions of parameters and have been trained on internet-scale datasets using advanced **deep learning** (**DL**) techniques. The resulting model has an extensive vocabulary and a broad knowledge of language structure such as grammar and syntax, and about the world in general. Thanks to their unique traits, LLMs are able to generate text that is coherent, grammatically correct, and semantically relevant. The outputs they produce may not always be completely logical or factually accurate, but they usually read convincingly like being written by a human. But it's not all about size. The quality of data and training algorithms – among others – can also play a huge role in the resulting performance of a particular model.

Many models feature a user interface that allows for response generation through prompts. Additionally, some offer an API for developers to access the model programmatically. This method will be our primary focus in the upcoming chapters of our book.

Next up, we'll talk about how LLMs are making big changes in tech. They're helping not just big companies but everyone. Curious? Let's keep reading.

Understanding the role of LLMs in modern technology

Oh! What good times we are living in. There has never been a more favorable era for small businesses and entrepreneurs. Given the enormous potential of this technology, it's a real miracle that, instead of ending up strictly under the control of large corporations or governments, it is literally within everyone's reach. Now, it's truly possible for almost anyone – even a non-technical person – to realize their ideas and solve problems that until now seemed impossible to solve without a huge amount of resources.

The disruptive potential that LLMs have – in almost all industries – is enormous.

It's true: there are concerns that this technology could replace us. However, technology's role is to make lives easier, taking over repetitive activities. As before, we'll likely do the same things, only much more efficiently and better with LLMs' help. We will do more with less.

I would dare say that LLMs have become the foundation of NLG technology. They can already power chatbots, search engines, coding assistants, text summarization tools, and other applications that synthesize written text interactively or automatically. And their capabilities keep advancing rapidly with bigger datasets and models.

And then, there are also the **agents**. These automated wonders are capable of perceiving and interpreting *stimuli* from the digital environment – and not just digital – to make decisions and act accordingly. Backed by the power of an LLM, intelligent agents can solve complex problems and fundamentally change the way we interact with technology. We'll cover this topic in more detail throughout *Chapter 8, Building Chatbots and Agents with LlamaIndex*.

Despite their relatively short existence, LLMs have already proven to be remarkably versatile and powerful. With the right techniques and prompts, their output can be steered in useful directions at scale. LLMs are driving innovation in numerous fields as their generative powers continue to evolve. Their capabilities keep expanding from nuanced dialog to multimodal intelligence. And, at the moment, the LLM-powered wave of innovation across industries and technologies shows no signs of slowing down.

The Gartner Hype Cycle model serves as a strategic guide for technology leaders, helping them evaluate new technologies not just on their merits but also in the context of their organization's specific needs and goals (`https://www.gartner.com/en/research/methodologies/gartner-hype-cycle`).

Judging by current adoption levels, LLMs are currently well into the **Slope of Enlightenment** stage, ready to take off into the **Plateau of Productivity** – where mainstream adoption really starts to take off (*Figure 1.2*). Companies are becoming more pragmatic about their application, focusing on specialized use cases where they offer the most value:

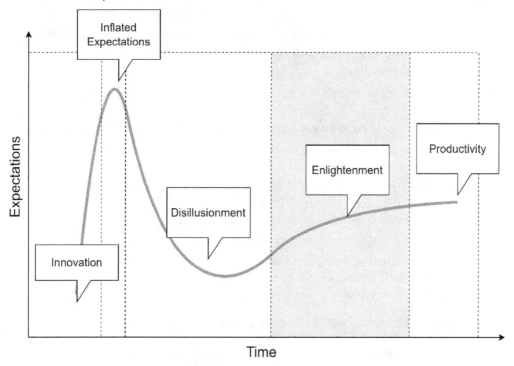

Figure 1.2 – The Gartner Hype Cycle

But, unlike other more specific technologies, LLMs are rather a new form of infrastructure – a kind of ecosystem where new concepts will be able to manifest and, undoubtedly, revolutionary applications will be born.

This is their true potential, and this is the ideal time to learn how to take advantage of the opportunities they offer.

Before we jump into innovative solutions that could maximize LLMs' capabilities, let's take a step back and look at some challenges and limitations.

Exploring challenges with LLMs

Not all the news is good, however. It's time to also discuss the *darker* side of LLMs.

These models do have important limitations and some collateral effects too. Here is a list of the most important ones, but please consider it non-exhaustive. There may be others not included here, and the order is arbitrarily chosen:

- They lack access to real-time data.

    - LLMs are trained on a static dataset, meaning that the information they have is only as up to date as the data they were trained on, which might not include the latest news, scientific discoveries, or social trends.

    - This limitation can be critical when users seek real-time or recent information, as the LLMs might provide outdated or irrelevant responses. Furthermore, even if they cite data or statistics, these numbers are likely to have changed or evolved, leading to potential misinformation.

> **Note**
> While recent features introduced by OpenAI, for example, allow the underlying LLM to integrate with Bing to retrieve fresh context from the internet, that's not an inherent feature of the LLM but rather an augmentation provided by the ChatGPT interface.

    - This lack of real-time updating also means that LLMs – by themselves – are not suited for tasks such as live customer service queries that may require real-time access to user data, inventory levels, or system statuses, for example.

- They have no intrinsic way of distinguishing factual truth from falsehoods.

    - Without proper monitoring, they can generate convincing misinformation. And trust me – they don't do it on purpose. In very simple terms, LLMs are basically just looking for words that fit together.

    - Check out *Figure 1.3* for an example of how one of the previous versions of the GPT-3.5 model would produce false information:

Figure 1.3 – Screenshot from a GPT 3.5-turbo-instruct playground

- As these models stochastically (randomly) generate text, their outputs are not guaranteed to be completely logical, factual, or harmless. Also, the training data inherently biases the model, and LLMs may generate toxic, incorrect, or nonsensical text without warning. Since this data sometimes includes unsavory elements of online discourse, LLMs risk amplifying harmful biases and toxic content present in their training data.

> **Note**
>
> While this kind of result may be easily achieved in a playground environment, using an older AI model, OpenAI's ChatGPT interface uses newer models and employs additional guardrails, thus making these kinds of responses much less probable.

- They also cannot maintain context and memory over long documents.

  - An interaction with a vanilla-flavor, standard LLM can prove to be a charm for simple topics or a quick question-and-answer session. But go beyond the context window limit of the model, and you'll soon experience its limitations as it struggles to maintain coherence and may lose important details from earlier parts of the conversation or document. This can result in fragmented or incomplete responses that may not fully address the complexities of a long-form interaction or in-depth analysis, just like a human suffering from *short-term memory loss*.

> **Note**
>
> Although recently released AI models such as Anthropic's Claude 2.1 and Google's Gemini Pro 1.5 have dramatically raised the bar in terms of context window limit, ingesting an entire book and running inference on such a large context may prove to be prohibitive from a cost perspective.

- LLMs also exhibit unpredictable failures in reasoning and fact retention. Take a look at *Figure 1.4* for a typical logic reasoning problem that proves to be challenging even for newer models such as GPT-4:

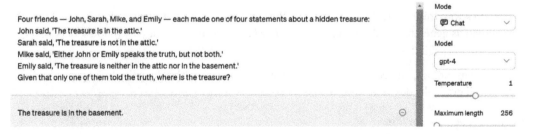

Figure 1.4 – Screenshot from a GPT-4 playground

- In this example, the answer is wrong because the only scenario that fits is if Emily is the one telling the truth. The treasure would then be neither in the attic nor in the basement.

- Their capabilities beyond fluent text generation remain inconsistent and limited. Blindly trusting their output without skepticism invites errors.

- The complexity of massive LLMs also reduces transparency into their functioning.

  - The lack of interpretability makes it hard to audit for issues or understand exactly when and why they fail. All you get is the output, but there's no easy way of knowing the actual decision process that led to that output or the documented fact in which that particular output is grounded. As such, LLMs still require careful governance to mitigate risks from biased, false, or dangerous outputs.

- As with many other things out there, it turns out we cannot really call them sustainable. At least not yet.

  - Their massive scale makes them expensive to train and environmentally costly due to huge computing requirements. And it's not just the training itself but also their usage. According to some estimates, *"the water consumption of ChatGPT has been estimated at 500 milliliters for a session of 20-50 queries"* – AMPLIFY, VOL. 36, NO. 8: *Arthur D. Little's Greg Smith, Michael Bateman, Remy Gillet, and Eystein Thanisch* (`https://www.cutter.com/article/environmental-impact-large-language-models`). This is not negligible by any means. Think about the countless failed attempts to get an answer from an LLM, then multiply that with the countless users exercising their prompt engineering skills every minute.

- And here's some more bad news: as models advance in complexity and training techniques, LLMs are rapidly becoming a huge source of machine-generated text.

  - So huge, in fact, that according to predictions, it will end up almost entirely replacing human-generated text (*Brown, Tom B. et al. (2020). Language Models are Few-Shot Learners. arXiv:2005.14165 [cs.CL].* `https://arxiv.org/abs/2005.14165`).

  - In a way, this means they may become the victims of their own success. As more and more data is generated by AI, it gradually *contaminates* the training of new models, decreasing their capabilities.

  - As in biology, any ecosystem that cannot maintain a healthy diversity in its genetic pool will gradually degrade.

I saved the good news for last.

What if I told you there is at least one solution that can partially address almost all these problems?

In many ways, a language model is very similar to an operating system. It provides a foundational layer upon which applications can be built. Just as an operating system manages hardware resources and provides services for computer programs, LLMs manage linguistic resources and provide services for various **NL processing** (NLP) tasks. Using prompts to interact with them is much like writing code using an Assembly Language. It's a low-level interaction. But, as you'll soon find out, there are more sophisticated and practical ways of using LLMs to their full potential.

It's time to talk about RAG.

Augmenting LLMs with RAG

Coined for the first time in a 2020 paper, *Lewis, Patrick et al. (2005). "Retrieval-Augmented Generation for Knowledge-Intensive NLP Tasks". arXiv:2005.11401 [cs.CL]* (https://arxiv.org/abs/2005.11401), published by several researchers from Meta, RAG is a technique that combines the powers of retrieval methods and generative models to answer user questions. The idea is to first retrieve relevant information from an indexed data source containing proprietary knowledge and then use that retrieved information to generate a more informed, context-rich response using a generative model (*Figure 1.5*):

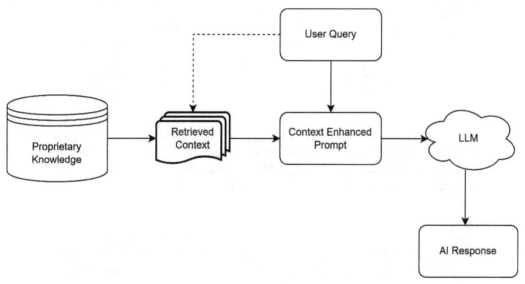

Figure 1.5 – A RAG model

Let's have a look at what this means in practice:

- **Much better fact retention**: One of the advantages of using RAG is its ability to pull from specific data sources, which can improve fact retention. Instead of relying solely on the generative model's own *knowledge* – which is mostly generic – it refers to external documents to construct its answers, increasing the chances that the information is accurate.

- **Improved reasoning**: The retrieval step allows RAG models to pull in information that is specifically related to the question. In general, this would result in more logical and coherent reasoning. This could help overcome limitations in reasoning that many LLMs face.

- **Context relevance**: Because it pulls information from external sources based on the query, RAG can be more contextually accurate than a standalone generative model, which has to rely only on its training data and might not have the most up-to-date or contextually relevant information. Not only that, but you could also get an actual *quote* from the model regarding the source of the actual knowledge used in the answer.

- **Reduced trust issues**: While not foolproof, the hybrid approach means that RAG could, in principle, be less prone to generating completely false or nonsensical answers. That means an increased probability of receiving a valid output.

- **Validation**: It's often easier to validate the reliability of the retrieved documents in an RAG setup by setting up a mechanism to provide a reference to the original information used for generating a response. This could be a step toward more transparent and trustworthy model behavior.

A word of caution

Even if RAG makes LLMs better and more reliable, it doesn't completely fix the issue of them sometimes giving wrong or confusing answers. There is no silver bullet that will completely eliminate all the issues mentioned previously. It's still a good idea to double-check and evaluate their outputs, and we'll talk about ways of doing that later in the book. Because, as you may already know or you've probably guessed by now, LlamaIndex is one of the many ways of augmenting LLM-based applications using RAG. And a very effective one, I should add.

While some LLM providers have started introducing RAG components into their API, such as OpenAI's **Assistants** feature, using a standalone framework such as LlamaIndex provides many more customization options. It also enables the usage of local models, enabling self-hosted solutions and greatly reducing costs and privacy concerns associated with a hosted model.

Summary

In this chapter, we covered a quick introduction to GenAI and LLMs. You learned how LLMs such as GPT work and some of their capabilities and limitations. A key takeaway is that while powerful, LLMs have weaknesses – such as the potential for false information and lack of reasoning – that require mitigation techniques. We discussed RAG as one method to overcome some LLM limitations.

These lessons provide useful background on how to approach LLMs practically while being aware of their risks. At the same time, you learned the importance of techniques such as RAG to address LLMs' potential downsides.

With this introductory foundation in place, we are now ready to dive into the next chapter where we will explore the LlamaIndex ecosystem. LlamaIndex offers an effective RAG framework to augment LLMs with indexed data for more accurate, logical outputs. Learning to leverage LlamaIndex tools will be the natural next step to harness the power of LLMs in a proficient way.

2

LlamaIndex: The Hidden Jewel – An Introduction to the LlamaIndex Ecosystem

Now that you've got a solid understanding of what **large language models** (**LLMs**) are and what they can (and cannot) do. It's time to discover how **LlamaIndex** can take your interactive AI applications to the next level. We'll explore how **retrieval-augmented generation** (**RAG**) using LlamaIndex can provide the missing link between the vast knowledge of LLMs and your proprietary data.

In this chapter, we will cover the following main topics:

- Optimizing language models – The symbiosis of fine-tuning, RAG, and LlamaIndex
- Discovering the advantages of progressively disclosing complexity
- Introducing **personalized intelligent tutoring system** (**PITS**) – our hands-on LlamaIndex project
- Preparing our coding environment
- Familiarizing ourselves with the structure of the LlamaIndex code repository

Technical requirements

The following elements will be required for this chapter:

- *Python 3.11* (`https://www.python.org/`)
- *Git* (`https://git-scm.com/`)
- *LlamaIndex* (`https://github.com/run-llama/llama_index`)
- *OpenAI account* and an *API key*
- *Streamlit* (`https://github.com/streamlit/streamlit`)
- *PyPDF* (`https://pypi.org/project/pypdf/`)
- *DOC2Txt* (`https://github.com/ankushshah89/python-docx2txt/blob/master/docx2txt/docx2txt.py`)

All the sample code snippets presented throughout this book as well as the entire project code base can be found in this GitHub repository: `https://github.com/PacktPublishing/Building-Data-Driven-Applications-with-LlamaIndex`.

Optimizing language models – the symbiosis of fine-tuning, RAG, and LlamaIndex

In the previous chapter, we saw that vanilla LLMs have some limitations right outside of the box. Their knowledge is static and they occasionally spit out nonsense. We also learned about RAG as a potential way to mitigate these issues. Blending **prompt engineering** techniques with programmatic methods, RAG can elegantly solve many of the LLM shortcomings.

> **What is prompt engineering?**
>
> Prompt engineering involves crafting text inputs designed to be effectively processed by a **generative AI (GenAI)** model. Composed in natural language, these prompts describe the specific tasks to be carried out by the AI. We'll have a much deeper conversation on this topic during *Chapter 10, Prompt Engineering Guidelines and Best Practices*.

Is RAG the only possible solution?

Of course not. Another approach is to fine-tune the AI model, which involves additional training on proprietary data to adapt the LLM and embed new data. It takes a model that is pre-trained on a general collection of data and continues its training on a more specialized dataset. This specialized dataset can be tailored to a particular domain, language, or set of tasks that you are interested in. The result is a model that maintains its broad knowledge base while gaining expertise in a specific area.

Take a look at *Figure 2.1* for a graphical explanation of the process.

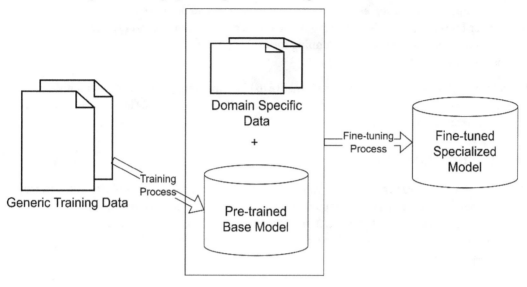

Figure 2.1 – An illustration of the LLM fine-tuning process

Fine-tuning can improve performance but has drawbacks, such as being expensive, requiring large datasets, and being difficult to update with fresh information. It also has the disadvantage of permanently altering the original AI model, which makes it inappropriate for personalizing purposes. Think of the original AI model as a classic recipe for a beloved dish. Fine-tuning this model is akin to modifying the traditional recipe to suit specific tastes or requirements. While these changes can make the dish more suitable for some, they also fundamentally alter the original recipe.

> **Note**
>
> Not all fine-tuning methods permanently alter the base AI model. Take **Low-Rank Adaptation (LoRA)** for example. LoRA is a fine-tuning method for LLMs that offers a more efficient approach compared to traditional **full fine-tuning**. In full fine-tuning, all layers of a neural network are optimized, which, while effective, is resource-intensive and time-consuming. LoRA, on the other hand, involves fine-tuning only two smaller matrices that approximate the larger weight matrix of the pre-trained LLM. In the LoRA method, the original weights of the model are *frozen*, meaning they are not directly updated during the fine-tuning process. The changes to the model's behavior are achieved by the addition of these low-rank matrices. This approach allows for the original model to be preserved, while still enabling it to be adapted for new tasks or improved performance. You can find more information on this method here: `https://ar5iv.labs.arxiv.org/html/2106.09685`.

Even though LoRA is more efficient in terms of memory usage compared to full fine-tuning, it still requires computational resources and expertise to implement and optimize effectively, which might be a barrier for some users. Using fine-tuning to create a more personalized experience for a large number of different users requires re-running the tuning process for every user, which is definitely not cost-effective.

I'm not trying to say that RAG is a better alternative to LLM fine-tuning. In fact, RAG and fine-tuning are complementary techniques that are often used together. However, to rapidly incorporating changing data and personalization, RAG is preferable.

What LlamaIndex does

With LlamaIndex, you can rapidly create *smart* LLMs that can adapt to your specific use case. Instead of relying only on their generic pre-trained knowledge, you can inject targeted information so that they give you accurate, relevant answers. It provides an easy way to connect external datasets to LLMs such as GPT-4, Claude, and Llama. LlamaIndex builds a bridge between your custom knowledge and the vast capabilities of LLMs.

> **Note**
>
> Created in 2022 by Princeton University graduate and entrepreneur Jerry Liu, the *LlamaIndex framework* has quickly become very popular in the developer community. LlamaIndex allows you to take advantage of the computational power and language understanding capabilities of LLMs while focusing their responses on specific, reliable data. This unique combination enables businesses and individuals to get the most out of their AI investments, as they can use the same underlying technology for a wide array of specialized applications.

For example, you could index a collection of your company's documents. Then, when you ask questions related to your business, the LLM augmented with LlamaIndex provides responses based on real data rather than just making up vague answers!

The result is that you get all the expressive power of LLMs while greatly reducing the amount of incorrect or irrelevant information. LlamaIndex guides the LLM to pull from trusted sources you provide, and these sources could contain both *structured* and *unstructured* data. In fact, as we will see in the next chapters, the framework can ingest data from pretty much *any* data source available. That's pretty cool, right?

If you are not already thinking about the many possible uses for this framework, let me give you some quick ideas. With LlamaIndex, you could do the following:

- **Build a search engine for your document collection**: One of its most powerful applications is the ability to index all your documents – they could be PDFs, Word files, Notion documents, GitHub repos, or other formats. Once indexed, you can query the LLM to search for specific information, making it a powerful search engine tailored specifically for your resources

- **Create a company chatbot with customized knowledge**: If your business has specific jargon, policies, or expertise, you can make the LLM *understand* these nuances. The chatbot could then handle a range of queries, from basic customer service questions to more specialized interactions that would typically require human expertise

- **Generate summaries of large reports or papers**: If your organization deals with lengthy documents or reports, LlamaIndex can be used to feed the LLM with their contents. Then, you can ask the LLM to generate concise summaries, capturing the most important points

- **Develop a smart assistant for complex workflows**: By training the LLM on the nuances of multi-step tasks or procedures unique to your organization, you can transform it into a smart assistant data agent that provides valuable insights and guidance

And these are just the tip of the iceberg.

In addition, *Figure 2.2* shows how implementing smart RAG strategies can offset some of the costs associated with fine-tuning the model on a specific domain.

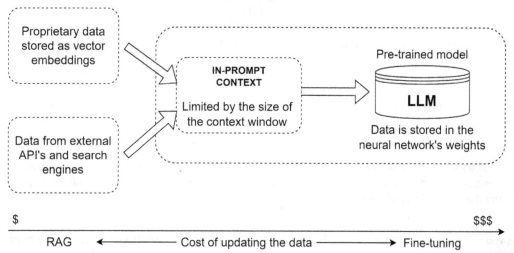

Figure 2.2 – The relative costs of updating data in a pre-trained LLM

Before we dive deeper into the applications and use cases of the LlamaIndex framework, let's talk a bit about the architecture and the design principles behind it!

Discovering the advantages of progressively disclosing complexity

The creator of LlamaIndex wanted to make it accessible to everyone – from beginners just getting started with LLMs all the way to expert developers building complex systems. That's why LlamaIndex uses a design principle called **progressive disclosure of complexity**. Don't worry about the fancy name – it just means that the framework starts simple and gradually reveals more advanced features when you need them.

When you first use LlamaIndex, it feels like magic! With just a few lines of code, you can connect data and start querying the LLM. Under the hood, LlamaIndex converts the data into an efficient index that the LLM can use.

Have a look at this very simple example that first loads a set of text documents from a local directory. It then builds an index over the documents and queries that index to get a summarized view of the documents based on a natural language query:

```
from llama_index.core import VectorStoreIndex, SimpleDirectoryReader
documents = SimpleDirectoryReader('files').load_data()
index = VectorStoreIndex.from_documents(documents)
query_engine = index.as_query_engine()
response = query_engine.query(
    "summarize each document in a few sentences"
)
print(response)
```

It's that simple. Just six lines of code!

> **Note**
> Don't try to run the code just yet. It's more for illustration purposes, There is a bit of environmental preparation we need to handle before that. Don't worry, we'll cover that a bit later in this chapter and then you'll be ready to go.

As you use LlamaIndex more, you will uncover its more powerful capabilities. There are plenty of parameters you can tweak. You can select specialized index structures optimized for different uses, carry out detailed cost analyses for different prompt strategies, customize query algorithms, and much more.

But LlamaIndex always starts you off gently before getting into more detailed workings, and for quick and simple projects, you don't need to go much deeper than that. This way, both beginners and experts can benefit from its versatility and capabilities.

Now, let's go on a quick tour of our hands-on project and then start prepping for the fun part: writing the code.

An important aspect to consider

As you go further through this book, and you will most likely want to experiment based on the examples it gives, you need to keep one very important point in mind. By default, the LlamaIndex framework is configured to use AI models provided by OpenAI. Although these models are extremely powerful and versatile, they incur costs. Many of the LlamaIndex functionalities presented in this book, be it metadata extraction, indexing, retrieval, or response synthesis, are based on either LLMs or embedding models. I have tried to use as simple examples as possible with small sample datasets in an attempt to limit these costs as much as possible.

> **Note**
>
> I strongly advise you to keep a close eye on the OpenAI API consumption. In case you don't already have it, the link where you can monitor the API usage is here: `https://platform.openai.com/usage`. I also advise you to be careful from a privacy perspective. These issues are discussed in more detail in *Chapters 4* and *5*.

Alternatively, if you want to avoid both the costs of using an external LLM and the potential privacy risks, you can apply the methods described in *Chapter 9, Customizing and Deploying Our LlamaIndex Project*. It is important to note, however, that all examples provided in the book are written and tested using the default models provided by OpenAI. There is a (quite likely) possibility that some examples may not work as well – or at all – running on locally hosted alternatives.

Introducing PITS – our LlamaIndex hands-on project

Nothing beats learning by doing.

So, I've cooked up a fun and useful project for us to start using LlamaIndex!

Here, we will introduce PITS. Wouldn't it be cool to have an AI tutor that helps you learn new concepts interactively? Well, we're going to build one together!

Here's how it will work

First, you will introduce yourself to PITS. You'll have the chance to describe the topic you want to learn about and specify any personal learning preferences you may have.

Then, you will be able to upload any existing study materials you may have on the topic. PITS will accept and ingest any PDFs, Word documents, or text files you may provide.

Based on the documents provided, the tutor will first build a quiz. You'll have the option to complete the quiz. That way, the tutor will be able to gauge your current knowledge of the topic and adjust the learning experience.

Our nifty tutor will then build learning material for you. This will consist of slides and narration for each slide. The training material will be divided into chapters.

Then, your learning journey begins. During each learning session, PITS you will advance through the chapters, presenting each topic in your preferred style and adapting to your knowledge level.

After each concept is explained, you'll have a chance to ask for more explanations or examples to learn more about the topic. It will answer your questions, create quizzes, explain concepts, and adapt responses based on your needs.

The best part is that your entire conversation with the agent will be recorded. It will remember both your questions and its own answers so it won't repeat itself or lose the conversation context.

Too tired to continue in one session? Not a problem. When you're ready to start another lesson, it will just resume from where you left off and give you a summary of the previous discussion.

But, hey! They say a picture's worth a thousand words, right?

You'll find an overview in *Figure 2.3*.

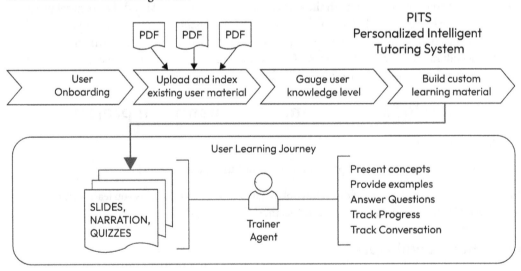

Figure 2.3 – An overview of the PITS workflow

It doesn't really get more customized than this. This is the ultimate learning experience.

As you can imagine, PITS needs to be smart on several fronts. It needs to be able to do the following:

- Understand and index the study materials we provide

- Converse fluently with users and retain the context

- Teach effectively based on the indexed knowledge

LlamaIndex will help with the first part by ingesting the study material. The user will be able to upload any relevant training material such as manuals, slides or even student notes, and sample questions.

For the second part, we'll mostly use the capabilities of GPT-4 to power the actual teaching interactions.

However, the foundation will be the knowledge augmentation capabilities of LlamaIndex. Pretty neat, right? We'll have a personally customized tutor!

> **Note**
>
> I'm not sure whether you've read my biography, but I work as a trainer. The moment I first learned of the power of GenAI and discovered GPT-3, I knew exactly that a few years from now, systems such as PITS would emerge sooner or later. I was thrilled about their potential to provide free, quality education to people around the world, regardless of their location, background, or financial status. Later, when I discovered RAG and tools such as LlamaIndex, I became convinced that they would appear rather sooner than later.

Okay, enough daydreaming – let's start setting up the pieces.

Preparing our coding environment

Before we embark on the LlamaIndex coding journey, it's essential to set up our development environment properly. This setup is the first step toward ensuring that we can smoothly run through the examples and exercises I've prepared for you.

> **Note**
>
> To maintain simplicity and ensure consistency across all examples, I've designed the sample code to be run in a local Python environment. I'm aware that many of you are fond of using web-based coding environments such as Google Colab and Jupyter Notebooks for your coding projects, so I kindly ask for your understanding if these examples do not directly translate to or run in these platforms. My goal was to keep our setup straightforward, allowing us to focus on the learning experience without compatibility concerns. Thank you for your understanding and happy coding!

Let's quickly get our computer set up for some cool LlamaIndex coding.

Installing Python

You'll need a Python 3.7+ environment. I recommend Python 3.11 if possible.

If you don't have Python, install it from `https://www.python.org`. If you already have an older version, you can upgrade or install a newer Python version side by side.

For a coding environment, my personal preference is **NotePad++** (`https://notepad-plus-plus.org/`), which is not quite an IDE but is very fast. However, you can also use Microsoft's **VSCode** (`https://code.visualstudio.com/`), **PyCharm** (`https://www.jetbrains.com/pycharm/`), or anything else you prefer.

Installing Git

Before we proceed, it's important to have Git installed. Git is a version control system that lets you manage changes to your code and collaborate with others. It's also essential for cloning code repositories, like the one we'll be using in this book.

Head over to the official Git website (`https://git-scm.com/book/en/v2/Getting-Started-Installing-Git`) and download the installer for your operating system.

Follow the installation steps, and you should have Git up and running in no time.

All the sample code snippets presented throughout the book as well as the entire project code base can be found in this GitHub repository: `https://github.com/PacktPublishing/Building-Data-Driven-Applications-with-LlamaIndex`.

So, if you want to download the project files locally, once you have finished installing Git, you can simply follow these steps:

1. **Navigate to the desired directory**: Open a new command prompt or terminal window. Use the `cd` command to navigate to the directory where you'd like to store the project. Here is an example:

    ```
    cd path/to/your/directory
    ```

2. **Clone the repository**: Run the following command to clone the GitHub repository:

    ```
    git clone https://github.com/PacktPublishing/Building-Data-
    Driven-Applications-with-LlamaIndex
    ```

    This will download a copy of the project to your local machine.

3. **Enter the project directory**: Navigate into the newly created project folder:

    ```
    cd Building-Data-Driven-Applications-with-LlamaIndex
    ```

As we move forward with our project, you have two options:

- You can either write the code on your own and then compare it with what's in the repository
- Or you can directly explore the code files in the repository to get a better understanding of the code structure

If you correctly performed all of the preceding steps, listing the contents of the current folder should return several subfolders called chX – where X is the chapter number, and a separate subfolder called PITS_APP. The chapter folders contain all sample source files corresponding to each chapter. The PITS_APP folder contains the source code for our main project.

Installing LlamaIndex

Next, let's get the LlamaIndex library installed. At your command prompt, run the following:

```
pip install llama-index
```

This will include a LlamaIndex package that contains the core LlamaIndex components as well as a selection of useful integrations. For the most efficient deployment possible, there is also the option of installing just the minimum core components and only the necessary integrations, but for the purpose of this book, the presented option will do just fine.

> **Note**
> In case you're already running a version older than v0.10, it is recommended that you start with a fresh install in a virtual environment to avoid any conflicts with the legacy version. You can find detailed instructions here: https://pretty-sodium-5e0.notion.site/v0-10-0-Migration-Guide-6ede431dcb8841b09ea171e7f133bd77.

We're now ready to import and start using it.

Signing up for an OpenAI API key

Since we'll be using OpenAI's GPT models via LlamaIndex, you'll need an API key to authenticate. Head to https://platform.openai.com and sign up. Once logged in, you can create a new secret API key. Make sure to keep it safe!

LlamaIndex will use this key every time it interacts with OpenAI's models. Because it has to be kept secret, it's a good idea to store it in an environment variable on your local machine.

A short guide for Windows users

On Windows, you can accomplish that by following these steps:

1. Open **Environment Variables**: Open the Start menu and search for **Environment Variables** or right-click on **This PC** or **My Computer** and select **Properties**.

2. Then, click on **Advanced system settings** followed by the **Environment Variables** button in the **Advanced** tab as shown in *Figure 2.4*:

Figure 2.4 – Editing Windows environment variables

3. **Create a new environment variable**: In the **Environment Variables** window, under the **User variables** section, click the **New** button.

4. **Enter the variable details**: For the **Variable name**, enter OPENAI_API_KEY. For **Variable value**, paste the secret API key you received from OpenAI. See *Figure 2.5* for an illustration.

Figure 2.5 – Creating the OPENAI_API_KEY environment variable

5. **Confirm and apply**: Click **OK** to close all of the dialog boxes. You will need to restart your computer for the changes to take effect.

6. **Verify the environment variable**: To ensure the variable is set correctly, open a new command prompt, and run the following:

```
echo %OPENAI_API_KEY%
```

This should display the API key you just stored.

A short guide for Linux/Mac users

On Linux/Mac, you can accomplish Signing up for an OpenAI API key by following these steps:

1. Run the following command in your terminal, replacing `<yourkey>` with your API key:

```
echo "export OPENAI_API_KEY='yourkey'" >> ~/.zshrc
```

2. Update the shell with the new variable:

```
source ~/.zshrc
```

3.   Make sure that you have set your environment variable with the following command:

```
echo $OPENAI_API_KEY
```

Your OpenAI API key is now securely stored in an environment variable and can be easily accessed by LlamaIndex when needed, without exposing it in your code or system.

> **Note**
>
> While OpenAI provides a free trial option for their GPT models through their API, you'll only receive a limited number of free credits. Currently, the free credit is limited to $5 and expires after 3 months. That should be more than enough to experiment for the purpose of our project and for reading the book. However, If you wish to get serious about building LLM-based applications, you'll have to sign up for a paid account on their platform. Alternatively, you can always choose to use another AI model for LlamaIndex. We will discuss customizing the AI model in more detail in *Chapter 10, Prompt Engineering Guidelines and Best Practices.*

OK. The backend is all set up. Let's talk about the rest of the stack.

Discovering Streamlit – the perfect tool for rapid building and deployment!

Before we can build cool apps such as PITS, we need somewhere to … well, build and run them! That's where Streamlit comes in. Streamlit is an awesome open-source Python library that makes it super easy to create and deploy web apps and dashboards.

With just a few lines of Python code, you can build complete web interfaces and see the results instantly. The best part is that Streamlit apps can be deployed nearly anywhere – on servers, on platforms such as Heroku, or even directly from GitHub!

I love Streamlit because it lets me focus on the fun stuff – such as creating PITS with LlamaIndex – rather than fussing over complex web development. For AI experimentation, it's perfect!

We'll primarily use it to create the interface for uploading study guides and interacting with our PITS tutor. For the purpose of the next chapters, we'll be using Streamlit for running and testing our app locally. However, in *Chapter 9, Customizing and Deploying Our LlamaIndex Project*, we will also discover how we can easily deploy our app using **Streamlit Share** or any other hosting service you prefer.

Streamlit has tons of cool capabilities such as data frames, charts, and widgets – but don't worry about learning it all now. As we build up features, I'll explain the relevant parts so you can gain Streamlit skills along the way!

Installing Streamlit

Lastly, we need to install the Streamlit library:

```
pip install streamlit
```

Great! We have our backend tool (LlamaIndex), our frontend layer (Streamlit), and our goal (PITS). It's time for a final touch.

Finishing up

Because our project should be able to ingest PDF and DOCX documents, we will also need to install two additional libraries:

```
pip install pypdf
pip install docx2txt
```

That's it! Our environment is LlamaIndex ready.

Let's recap what we have:

- Python 3.11

- Git

- LlamaIndex package

- OpenAI account and an API key

- Streamlit for app building

- PyPDF and DOC2Txt libraries

One final check

To verify that everything was installed correctly, open a new command prompt or terminal window, and run the following commands:

```
python --version
git --version
pip show llama-index
echo %OPENAI_API_KEY%
pip show streamlit
pip show pypdf
pip show docx2txt
```

A simple way to check whether your environment is ready is to try navigating into the ch2 subfolder of your local git folder and run the file called sample1.py:

```
python sample1.py
```

You should get a nice summary of the two sample documents provided in the ch2/files subfolder if everything has been properly installed.

If anything is missing, please go back and retake the necessary steps before proceeding further. Trust me, you'll avoid a lot of pain and frustration further down the line.

We're all set to start ingesting data, constructing indices with LlamaIndex, and building our PITS tutor app! I don't know about you, but I'm *kid-in-a-candy-store* excited to start experimenting.

In the next chapters, we'll get hands-on with our first LlamaIndex program. This is where the real fun begins! We'll explore ingesting data, constructing indexes, executing queries, and more.

I'll explain each concept and line of code in simple terms along the way. In no time, you'll be implementing the basics like a LlamaIndex pro! Once we've got these fundamentals down, we can start expanding the capabilities of our tutor app.

But first, let's clarify the overall code structure of the framework's GitHub repository.

Familiarizing ourselves with the structure of the LlamaIndex code repository

Because you'll probably spend a lot of time browsing the official code repository of the LlamaIndex framework, it's good to have an overall image of its general structure. You can always consult the repository here: `https://github.com/run-llama/llama_index`.

Starting with version 0.10, the code has been thoroughly reorganized into a more modular structure. The purpose of this new structure is to improve efficiency, by avoiding loading any unnecessary dependencies, while also improving readability and overall user experience for developers.

Figure 2.6 describes the main components of the code structure:

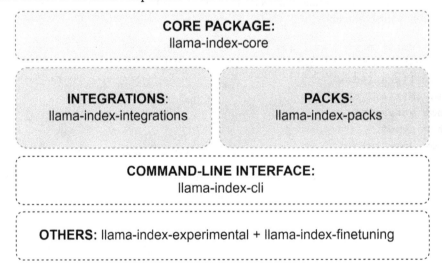

Figure 2.6 – The LlamaIndex GitHub repository code structure

The `llama-index-core` folder serves as the foundational package for LlamaIndex, enabling developers to install the essential framework and then selectively add from over 300 integration packages and different Llama-packs to tailor functionality for their specific application needs.

The `llama-index-integrations` folder of LlamaIndex consists of various add-on packages that extend the functionality of the core framework. These allow developers to customize their build with specific elements such as custom LLMs, data loaders, embedding models, and vector store providers to best fit their application's requirements. We'll cover some of these integrations later in our book, starting with *Chapter 4, Ingesting Data into Our RAG Workflow*.

The `llama-index-packs` folder contains more than 50 Llama packs. Developed and constantly improved by the LlamaIndex developer community, these packs serve as ready-made templates designed to kickstart a user's application. We'll talk about them in more detail during *Chapter 9, Customizing and Deploying Our LlamaIndex Project*.

The `llama-index-cli` folder is used by the LlamaIndex command-line interface, which we will also cover briefly during *Chapter 9, Customizing and Deploying Our LlamaIndex Project*.

The last section, called **OTHERS** in *Figure 2.6*, consists of two folders that currently contain fine-tuning abstractions and some experimental features that we will not cover in this book.

Note

The subfolders in `llama-index-integrations` and `llama-index-packs` represent individual packages. The folder name corresponds to the package name. For example, the `llama-index-integrations/llms/llama-index-llms-mistralai` folder corresponds to the `llama-index-llms-mistralai` PyPI package.

Following this example, there is something you need to do before you import and use the `mistralai` package in your code like this:

```
from llama_index.llms.mistralai import MistralAI
```

You'll have to first install the corresponding PyPI package by running the following:

```
pip install llama-index.llms.mistralai
```

Don't worry too much about missing any necessary packages for the examples included in the book, as you will find them nicely listed at the beginning of each chapter under the *Technical requirements* heading.

Summary

In this chapter, we introduced LlamaIndex, a framework for connecting LLMs to external datasets. We discovered how LlamaIndex allows LLMs to incorporate real-world knowledge into their responses.

The chapter discussed the benefits of LlamaIndex over fine-tuning, such as easier updating and personalization. It introduced the concept of progressive disclosure of complexity, where LlamaIndex starts simple but reveals advanced capabilities when needed.

The chapter then presented an overview of the hands-on project PITS, a personalized intelligent tutoring system. It covered setting up the required tools such as Python, Git, and Streamlit, and getting an OpenAI API key. The chapter finished by verifying that the environment is ready for building LlamaIndex apps.

We're now ready to continue our journey and proceed with a more technical understanding of the inner workings of the LlamaIndex framework. See you in the next chapter!

Part 2:
Starting Your First
LlamaIndex Project

In this part, we explore the detailed aspects of LlamaIndex, including data ingestion through LlamaHub connectors, text-chunking tools, metadata infusion, data privacy, and efficient ingestion pipelines, before moving on to a comprehensive guide to the indexing functionality within LlamaIndex, detailing types of indexes, customization, and strategies for building scalable RAG systems.

This part has the following chapters:

- *Chapter 3, Kickstarting Your Journey with LlamaIndex*
- *Chapter 4, Ingesting Data into Our RAG Workflow*
- *Chapter 5, Indexing with LlamaIndex*

3

Kickstarting Your Journey with LlamaIndex

It's time to dive deeper and gain a more technical understanding of how LlamaIndex works its magic under the hood. In this chapter, we'll explore some of the key concepts and components that make up LlamaIndex's architecture. We'll learn about the core building blocks used by the framework to ingest, structure, and query our data. Understanding these fundamentals will provide a solid foundation before we start applying them hands-on. We'll go through the theoretical aspects of each concept and then connect the dots between the theory and practical application.

Here are the main topics covered in this chapter:

- Uncovering the essential building blocks of LlamaIndex – **Documents**, **Nodes**, and **indexes**
- Building our first interactive, augmented **large language model (LLM)** application
- Starting our **personalized intelligent tutoring system (PITS)** project – a hands-on exercise

Technical requirements

You will need to install the following Python libraries in your environment to be able to run the examples included in this chapter:

- *PYYAML* (https://pyyaml.org/wiki/PyYAMLDocumentation)
- *Wikipedia* (https://wikipedia.readthedocs.io/en/latest/)

Two LlamaIndex integration packages will also be required:

- *Wikipedia reader* (`https://pypi.org/project/llama-index-readers-wikipedia/`)

- *OpenAI LLMs* (`https://pypi.org/project/llama-index-llms-openai/`)

All code samples from this chapter can be found in the `ch3` subfolder of the book's GitHub repository: `https://github.com/PacktPublishing/Building-Data-Driven-Applications-with-LlamaIndex`.

Uncovering the essential building blocks of LlamaIndex – documents, nodes, and indexes

As we're getting started with LlamaIndex, it's time to understand some of the key concepts and components that make up its architecture. You may consider this chapter as a quick introduction to the typical **retrieval-augmented generation** (**RAG**) architecture with LlamaIndex and an overview of the most important tools provided by this framework. It should give you a basic understanding of how to build a simple RAG application. In the next chapters, we'll take it step by step and explore in detail each one of the components presented here.

At a high level, LlamaIndex helps connect external data sources to LLMs. To do this effectively, it needs to ingest, structure, and organize your data in a way that allows for efficient retrieval and querying. In this first part of our chapter, we'll explore the core elements that enable LlamaIndex to augment LLMs – Documents, Nodes, and indexes.

Documents

It all begins with the data.

Now, trying to handle raw data directly can be as tricky as holding water in your hands. It's often all over the place without any set structure. This is where we need to step in and give it some shape. That's exactly what we do in LlamaIndex with something called Documents. A Document is how we capture and contain any kind of data, whether you enter it manually or load it over from an external source. It's like putting the data in a nice bottle so it's easier to handle.

Imagine you've got a bunch of your company's procedures saved as PDFs and you want to make sense of them using a powerful language model such as GPT-4. In LlamaIndex, each of these procedures would be turned into its `Document` object – and it's not just about files. Say you have data sitting in a database or coming through an API – those can be Documents, too. Check out *Figure 3.1* for a visual overview:

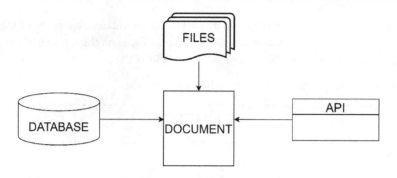

Figure 3.1 – Documents can come from multiple sources

Think of the Document class as a container. It holds not just the raw text or data from wherever it originated but also any extra bits of information you decide to tag along. This extra info, called **metadata**, is a game changer when you start searching through your Documents because it lets you get really specific with your queries.

Here is a basic example of how a Document can be created manually:

```
from llama_index.core import Document
text = "The quick brown fox jumps over the lazy dog."
doc = Document(
    text=text,
    metadata={'author': 'John Doe','category': 'others'},
    id_='1'
)
print(doc)
```

In this example, after importing the Document class, we create a Document object called doc. The object contains the actual text, a document ID, and some additional metadata of our choice that is provided as a dictionary.

Here are some of the most important attributes of a Document object:

- text: This attribute stores the text content of the document

- metadata: This attribute is a dictionary that can be used to include additional information about the document, such as the file name or categories. The keys in the metadata dictionary must be strings and the values can be strings, floats, or integers

- id_: This is a unique ID for each Document. You can set this manually if you want, but if you don't specify an ID, LlamaIndex will automatically generate one for you

There are also other attributes that you can find by consulting the GitHub repository of LlamaIndex. However, to keep things simple, at this moment we will only focus on these three. These attributes provide various ways to customize and enhance the functionality of the Document class in LlamaIndex.

Figure 3.2 presents the basic structure of a LlamaIndex Document.

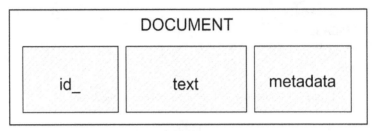

Figure 3.2 – The basic structure of a document

The LlamaIndex Documents contain data in its unprocessed, or **raw**, form. Although the given example illustrates how we can manually create one, typically, in practical applications, these Documents are generated in bulk by sourcing them from various data sources. This bulk ingestion of data uses predefined **data loaders** – sometimes called **connectors** or simply **readers** – from an extensive library known as **LlamaHub** (`https://llamahub.ai/`).

> **Note**
>
> Developed primarily by the LlamaIndex community, these plug-and-play packages extend the functionality of the core components of the framework. They provide different LLMs, agent tools, embedding models, vector stores, and data loaders. These data ingestion tools offer compatibility with a wide range of data file formats, databases, and API endpoints. There are more than 130 different data readers in LlamaHub already and the list keeps growing. We'll cover the topic of LlamaHub in much more detail in the next chapter. For now, we'll focus on the data loaders.

Here is a basic example of automated data ingestion using one of the predefined LlamaHub data loaders. Before you can run the example, make sure you install the libraries mentioned in the *technical requirements* section and complete all the necessary environment preparations mentioned in *Chapter 2* if you haven't already:

```
pip install wikipedia
pip install llama-index-readers-wikipedia
```

The first library allows for easy access and parsing of data from Wikipedia while the second one is the LlamaIndex integration for the Wikipedia data loader.

Once you have installed the two libraries, you'll be able to run the following example:

```
from llama_index.readers.wikipedia import WikipediaReader
loader = WikipediaReader()
documents = loader.load_data(
    pages=['Pythagorean theorem','General relativity']
)
print(f"loaded {len(documents)} documents")
```

The `WikpediaReader` loader extracts the text from Wikipedia articles using the Wikipedia Python package. Apart from `WikipediaReader`, there are many more specialized data connectors available in the LlamaHub.

So, creating Documents is a very straightforward process. But how do the raw `Document` objects get converted into a format that LLMs can efficiently process and reason over? This is where Nodes come in.

Nodes

While Documents represent the raw data and can be used as such, Nodes are smaller chunks of content extracted from the Documents. The goal is to break down Documents into smaller, more manageable pieces of text. This serves a few purposes:

- **Allows our proprietary knowledge to fit within the model's prompt limits**: Imagine that if we had an internal procedure that is 50 pages long, we would definitely run into size limit problems when trying to feed that in the context of our prompt. However, most likely, in practice, we wouldn't need to feed the entire procedure in one prompt. Therefore, selecting just the relevant Nodes can solve this problem.

- **Creates semantic units of data centered around specific information**: This can make it easier to work with and analyze the data, as it is organized into smaller, more focused units.

- **Allows the creation of relationships between Nodes**: This means that Nodes can be linked together based on their relationships, creating a network of interconnected data. This can be useful for understanding the connections and dependencies between different pieces of information within the Documents.

Take a look at *Figure 3.3* for a visual representation of this concept:

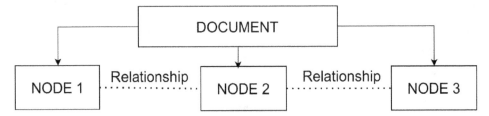

Figure 3.3 – Relationships between Nodes extracted from a Document

In LlamaIndex, Nodes can also store images but we won't focus on that functionality in this book. Our main protagonist from now on will be the `TextNode` class.

Here's a list of some important attributes of the `TextNode` class:

- `text`: The chunk of text derived from an original Document.

- `start_char_idx` and `end_char_idx` are optional integer values that can store the starting and ending character positions of the text within the Document. This could be helpful when the text is part of a larger Document, and you need to pinpoint the exact location.

- `text_template` and `metadata_template` are template fields that define how the text and metadata are formatted. They help produce a more structured and readable representation of `TextNode`.

- `metadata_seperator`: This is a string field that defines the separator between metadata fields. When multiple metadata items are included, this separator is used to maintain readability and structure.

- Any useful `metadata` such as the parent Document ID, relationships to other Nodes, and optional tags. This metadata can be used for storing additional context when necessary. We'll talk about it in more detail in *Chapter 4, Ingesting Data into Our RAG Workflow*.

Just like in the case of Documents, if you want to see a full list of the `TextNode` attributes, you can find them described on the LlamaIndex GitHub repository: `https://github.com/run-llama/llama_index/blob/main/llama-index-core/llama_index/core/schema.py`.

You should know that the Nodes will automatically inherit any metadata already present at the Document level but their metadata can also be individually customized.

There are several ways in which Nodes can be created in LlamaIndex, which we will discuss in upcoming subsections. Let's start with the manual creation of Nodes.

Manually creating the Node objects

Here is a simple example of how we can manually create Node objects:

```
from llama_index.core import Document
from llama_index.core.schema import TextNode
doc = Document(text="This is a sample document text")
n1 = TextNode(text=doc.text[0:16], doc_id=doc.id_)
n2 = TextNode(text=doc.text[17:30], doc_id=doc.id_)
print(n1)
print(n2)
```

In this example, we're using the text-slicing capabilities of Python to manually extract the text for the two Nodes. This manual approach can be very handy when you really want to have full control of both the text of the Nodes and the accompanying metadata.

To understand what's happening backstage, let's have a look at the output of this code:

```
Node ID: 102b570f-5b22-48b5-b9b6-6378597e920d
Text: This is a sample
Node ID: 0ad81b09-bf12-4063-bfe4-6c5fd3c36cd4
Text: document text
```

> **Note**
>
> As you can see, the two Nodes contain a randomly generated ID and the segments of text that we have sliced from the original Document. The TextNode constructor automatically generated an ID for each node using the Python UUID module. But we can customize that identifier after creating the Nodes if we want to employ a different identification scheme.

Automatically extracting Nodes from Documents using splitters

Because **Document chunking** is very important in an RAG workflow, LlamaIndex comes with built-in tools for this purpose. One such tool is TokenTextSplitter.

As an example of how we can automatically generate Nodes, TokenTextSplitter attempts to split the Document text into chunks that contain whole sentences. Each chunk will include one or more sentences and there's also a default overlap between the chunks to maintain more context.

Under the hood, there are a number of parameters that we can customize on `SimpleNodeParser` such as `chunk_size` and `chunk_overlap` but we will talk about them more and how this text splitter works in the next chapter. For now, let's have a look at a simple example of how to use `TokenTextSplitter` with its default settings on a `Document` object:

```python
from llama_index.core import Document
from llama_index.core.node_parser import TokenTextSplitter
doc = Document(
    text=(
    "This is sentence 1. This is sentence 2. "
    "Sentence 3 here."
    ),
    metadata={"author": "John Smith"}
)
splitter = TokenTextSplitter(
    chunk_size=12,
    chunk_overlap=0,
    separator=" "
)
nodes = splitter.get_nodes_from_documents([doc])
for node in nodes:
    print(node.text)
    print(node.metadata)
```

Here is the code output this time:

```
Metadata length (6) is close to chunk size (12). Resulting chunks are
less than 50 tokens. Consider increasing the chunk size or decreasing
the size of your metadata to avoid this.
This is sentence 1.
{'author': 'John Smith'}
This is sentence 2.
{'author': 'John Smith'}
Sentence 3 here.
{'author': 'John Smith'}
```

> **Note**
>
> Given that chunk size is how much content can be processed at a time, if the metadata is too large, it will take up most of the space in each chunk, leaving less room for the actual content text. This can lead to chunks that are mostly metadata with very little actual content. In our example, the warning is triggered because the effective chunk size (the chunk size minus the space taken up by the metadata) results in chunks that would be less than 50 tokens. This is considered too small for efficient processing.

This was just a basic example meant to illustrate an automatic method for chunking the data in separated Nodes. If you look at the metadata of each node, you'll also notice that it was automatically inherited from the originating Document.

> **Are there any other ways to create Nodes?**
>
> Yes, there are a few other methods. In the next chapter, we'll go more in-depth with the text-splitting and node-parsing techniques available in LlamaIndex. You will also have the opportunity to understand how they work under the hood and what kind of customization options they provide.

But wait, there's more to understand about Nodes.

Nodes don't like to be alone – they crave relationships

Now that we've covered some basic examples of how to create simple Nodes, how about adding some relationships between them?

Here's an example that manually creates a simple relationship between two Nodes:

```
from llama_index.core import Document
from llama_index.core.schema import (
    TextNode,
    NodeRelationship,
    RelatedNodeInfo
)
doc = Document(text="First sentence. Second Sentence")
n1 = TextNode(text="First sentence", node_id=doc.doc_id)
n2 = TextNode(text="Second sentence", node_id=doc.doc_id)
n1.relationships[NodeRelationship.NEXT] = n2.node_id
n2.relationships[NodeRelationship.PREVIOUS] = n1.node_id
print(n1.relationships)
print(n2.relationships)
```

In this example, we've manually created two Nodes and defined a **previous** or **next** relationship between them. The relationship tracks the order of Nodes within the original Document. This code tells LlamaIndex that the two Nodes belong to the initial Document and they also come in a particular order.

Figure 3.4 shows exactly what LlamaIndex understands now after we ran the code:

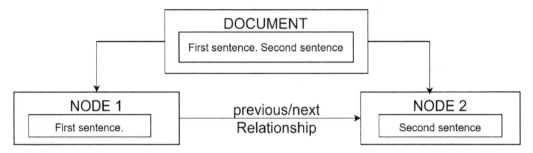

Figure 3.4 – Previous or next relationship between two Nodes

> **Note**
> You should know that LlamaIndex contains the necessary tools to *automatically* create relationships between the Nodes. For example, when using the automated node parsers discussed previously, in their default configuration, LlamaIndex will automatically create previous or next relationships between the Nodes it generates.

There are other types of relationships that we could define. In addition to simple relationships such as previous or next, Nodes can be connected using the following:

- SOURCE: The **source relationship** represents the original source Document that a node was extracted or parsed from. When you parse a Document into multiple Nodes, you can track which Document each node originated from using the source relationship.

- PARENT: The **parent relationship** indicates a hierarchical structure where the node with this relationship is one level higher than the associated node. In a tree structure, a parent node would have one or more children. This relationship is used to navigate or manage nested data structures where you might have a main node and subordinate Nodes representing sections, paragraphs, or other subdivisions of the main node.

- CHILD: This is the opposite of PARENT. A node with the **child relationship** is a subordinate of another node – the parent. Child Nodes can be seen as the leaves or branches in a tree structure stemming from their parent node.

But why are relationships important? Let's discuss why they are useful.

Why are relationships important?

Creating relationships between Nodes in LlamaIndex can be useful for several reasons:

- **Enables more contextual querying**: By linking Nodes together, you can leverage their relationships during querying to retrieve additional relevant context. For example, when querying a node, you could also return the previous or next Nodes to provide more context.

- **Allows tracking provenance**: Relationships encode provenance – where source Nodes originated and how they are connected. This is useful when you need to identify the original source of a node for example.

- **Enables navigation through nodes**: Traversing Nodes by their relationships enables new types of queries. For example, finding the next node that contains some keyword. Navigation along relationships provides another dimension for searching.

- **Supports the construction of knowledge graphs**: Nodes and relationships are the building blocks of knowledge graphs. Linking Nodes into a graph structure allows for constructing knowledge graphs from text using LlamaIndex. We'll talk more about knowledge graphs during *Chapter 5, Indexing with LlamaIndex*.

- **Improves the index structure**: Some LlamaIndex indexes, such as trees and graphs, utilize node relationships to build their internal structure. Relationships allow the construction of more complex and expressive index topologies. We will discuss this more in *Chapter 5, Indexing with LlamaIndex*.

In summary, relationships augment the Nodes with additional contextual connections. This supports more expressive querying, source-tracking knowledge graph construction, and complex index structures.

With raw data ingested as Documents and structured into Nodes that can be queried, the last step is to organize Nodes into efficient indexes.

Indexes

Our third important concept – the index – refers to a specific data structure used to organize a collection of Nodes for optimized storage and retrieval.

A simplified analogy

Getting your data into shape for RAG is kind of like getting your clothes ready for a big trip – you have to make sure everything is organized and accessible! Let's say you're packing for an important business trip. You could just throw everything into your suitcase, but your shirts, socks, pants, and other stuff would get mixed up! The problem is that when you want to grab what you need quickly, you may pull out the wrong item and end up inventing an entirely new dress code.

That's exactly why indexing your data is so crucial when prepping for LLM augmentation. Without indexing, your data is a messy pile of disorganized facts and files, and it's like digging through a bursting suitcase for a matching pair of socks.

Proper indexing neatly sorts information into categories that make sense. For example, our sales records are in one index, and support tickets in another. It's just like packing related items together. This transforms messy data into neatly organized knowledge that AI can make use of. You go from randomly hunting through a suitcase to grabbing exactly what you need from custom pockets.

So, remember – to avoid frustration and wasted time down the road, put in the work early to index and structure your data. It will make your job much easier down the line.

LlamaIndex supports different types of indexes, each with its strengths and trade-offs. Here is a list of some of the available index types:

- `SummaryIndex`: This is very similar to a box for recipes – it keeps your Nodes in order, so you can access them one by one. It takes in a set of documents, chunks them up into Nodes, and then concatenates them into a list. It's great for reading through a big Document.

- `DocumentSummaryIndex`: This constructs a concise summary for each document, mapping these summaries back to their respective nodes. It facilitates efficient information retrieval by using these summaries to quickly identify relevant documents.

- `VectorStoreIndex`: This is one of the more sophisticated types of indexes and probably the workhorse in most RAG applications. It converts text into vector embeddings and uses math to group similar Nodes, helping locate Nodes that are alike.

- `TreeIndex`: The perfect solution for those who love order. This index behaves similarly to putting smaller boxes inside bigger ones, organizing Nodes by levels in a tree-like structure. Inside, each parent node stores summaries of the children nodes. These are generated by the LLM, using a general summarization prompt. This particular index can be very useful for summarization.

- `KeywordTableIndex`: Imagine you need to find a dish by the ingredients you have. The keyword index connects important words to the Nodes they're in. It makes finding any node easy by looking up keywords.

- `KnowledgeGraphIndex`: This is useful when you need to link facts in a big network of data stored as a knowledge graph. This one is good for answering tricky questions about lots of connected information.

- `ComposableGraph`: This allows you to create complex index structures in which Document-level indexes are indexed in higher-level collections. That's right: you can even build an index of indexes if you want to access the data from multiple Documents in a larger collection of Documents.

We'll talk more about the inner workings of these indexes and other variations in *Chapter 5, Indexing with LlamaIndex*. This is just an overview of the topic.

All the index types in LlamaIndex share some common core features:

- **Building the index**: Each index type can be constructed by passing in a set of Nodes during initialization. This builds the underlying index structure.

- **Inserting new Nodes**: After an index is built, new Nodes can be manually inserted. This adds to the existing index structure.

- **Querying the index**: Once built, indexes provide a query interface to retrieve relevant Nodes based on a specific query. The retrieval logic varies by index type.

The specifics of index structure and querying differ across index types. But this building, inserting, and querying pattern is consistent. Understanding the particular features of each index type is really important if you want to exploit their full potential. During *Chapter 5, Indexing with LlamaIndex*, we will cover this topic in much more detail and I will give you specific examples for each type of index.

For now, let's consider a simple example to illustrate the creation of `SummaryIndex`:

```
from llama_index.core import SummaryIndex, Document
from llama_index.core.schema import TextNode
nodes = [
    TextNode(
        text="Lionel Messi is a football player from Argentina."
    ),
    TextNode(
        text="He has won the Ballon d'Or trophy 7 times."
    ),
    TextNode(text="Lionel Messi's hometown is Rosario."),
    TextNode(text="He was born on June 24, 1987.")
]
index = SummaryIndex(nodes)
```

This is very simple to follow. We first defined a set of Nodes containing the data and then created `SummaryIndex` based on these Nodes. This index is a simple list-based data structure.

Think of `SummaryIndex` as a little notepad where you jot down points from lots of stories. When it's getting set up, it takes a big bunch of stories, breaks them into smaller bits, and lines them up in a list. The best part? LlamaIndex doesn't even need to use the LLM when it builds this type of index.

Are we there yet?

Almost. Indexes are great for organizing data, but how do we get answers from them? That's where **retrievers** and **response synthesizers** come in!

Let's use the Lionel Messi index we just created as an example. Say you ask, "What is Messi's hometown?" See the following:

```
query_engine = index.as_query_engine()
response = query_engine.query("What is Messi's hometown?")
print(response)
```

This is the output:

```
Messi's hometown is Rosario.
```

The summary index organizes all Nodes sequentially in a list.

When queried, it retrieves all Nodes, allowing the synthesis of a response with full context.

How does this actually work under the hood?

QueryEngine contains a retriever, which is responsible for retrieving relevant Nodes from the index for the query. The retriever does a lookup to fetch and rank relevant Nodes from the index for that query. It grabs Nodes from the index that are likely to contain information about Messi's hometown.

But just getting back a list of Nodes isn't very useful. Another part of QueryEngine called the **node postprocessor** comes into play at this point. This part enables the transformation, re-ranking, or filtering of Nodes after they've been retrieved and before the final response is crafted. There are many types of postprocessors available, and each can be configured and customized depending on the use case.

The QueryEngine object also contains a response synthesizer, which takes the retrieved Nodes and crafts the final response using the LLM by performing the following steps:

1. The response synthesizer takes the Nodes selected by the retriever and processed by the node postprocessor and formats them into an LLM prompt.
2. The prompt contains the query along with context from the Nodes.
3. This prompt is given to the LLM to generate a response.
4. Any necessary postprocessing is done on the raw response using the LLM to return the final natural language answer.

So, index.as_query_engine() is creating a full query engine for us, containing a default version of the three elements: retriever, node postprocessor, and response synthesizer.

We'll get into a lot more detail on these three elements in *Chapters 6* and *7*.

The final result of running this engine will be a natural language answer such as Messi's hometown is Rosario.

> **Remember**
>
> This is just a basic example using a particular type of index called `SummaryIndex`. Each index type behaves differently as we will discuss in *Chapter 5*. For example: a `TreeIndex` arranges Nodes in a hierarchy, allowing for summarization and a `KeywordIndex` maps keywords for fast lookup. The index structure impacts performance and determines its best use cases. By itself, the index structure defines the data management logic. As we have seen, the index needs to be combined with a retriever, postprocessor, and response synthesizer to form a complete query pipeline, allowing applications to leverage the indexed data.

More details will be added in the upcoming chapters. But, at this point, you should have a high-level idea of Indexes and their role.

Let's have a look at *Figure 3.5* for an overview of the complete flow.

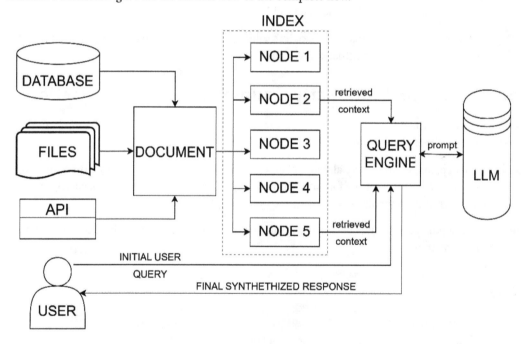

Figure 3.5 – The complete RAG workflow with LlamaIndex

As shown in *Figure 3.5*, the process involves the following steps:

1. Loading data as Documents
2. Parsing Documents into coherent Nodes
3. Building an optimized index from Nodes
4. Running queries over the index to retrieve relevant Nodes
5. Synthesizing the final response

Too much to remember? Let's recap the building blocks of LlamaIndex.

A quick recap of the key concepts

Here is a quick rundown of what we have covered so far:

- **Documents**: The raw data ingested
- **Nodes**: Logical chunks extracted from Documents
- **Indexes**: Data structures organizing Nodes based on use case
- **QueryEngine**: This contains a retriever, node postprocessor, and response synthesizer

Understanding these building blocks is crucial for working with LlamaIndex. They allow you to effectively structure and connect external data to LLMs.

Now, you have a conceptual foundation. Next, let's solidify this knowledge by looking at a simplified workflow model and building an actual application.

Building our first interactive, augmented LLM application

It's time to connect the dots and do something practical with all this knowledge. If we put all the previous code together, we can now build our first LlamaIndex application.

For this next step, make sure you've already taken care of the technical requirements mentioned at the beginning of the chapter. For the following code example, we'll need the Wikipedia package to be able to parse a certain Wikipedia article and extract our sample data from there.

Once the Wikipedia package has been successfully installed, the sample app should run without issues. Here is the code:

```
from llama_index.core import Document, SummaryIndex
from llama_index.core.node_parser import SimpleNodeParser
from llama_index.readers.wikipedia import WikipediaReader
loader = WikipediaReader()
documents = loader.load_data(pages=["Messi Lionel"])
parser = SimpleNodeParser.from_defaults()
nodes = parser.get_nodes_from_documents(documents)
index = SummaryIndex(nodes)
query_engine = index.as_query_engine()
print("Ask me anything about Lionel Messi!")
while True:
    question = input("Your question: ")
    if question.lower() == "exit":
```

```
        break
    response = query_engine.query(question)
    print(response)
```

It should be noted that this does not function as a genuine chat system because it does not retain the context of the conversation. It could be more accurately described as a simple Q&A system.

Here's a quick walk-through for the code:

1. We start by loading a Wikipedia page on Lionel Messi as a Document using the `WikipediaReader` data loader. This ingests the raw text data

2. Next, we parse the Document into smaller Node chunks using `SimpleNodeParser`. This splits the text into logical segments

3. We then build `SummaryIndex` from the Nodes. This organizes the Nodes sequentially for full context retrieval

4. We define `QueryEngine`, forming a complete query pipeline

5. Finally, we create a loop that queries the index, passing our question to `QueryEngine`. This handles retrieving relevant Nodes, prompting the LLM, and returning the final response

Again, you can have a look at *Figure 3.5* to visualize the overall workflow – ingesting data, parsing it into Nodes, building an index, and querying it to retrieve and synthesize the final answer.

But what if we want to know exactly what happens behind the scenes?

Using the logging features of LlamaIndex to understand the logic and debug our applications

When you run code like in our previous example, you might feel like there's some *magic* happening behind the scenes. You pass in some text, call a simple indexing method, and boom – you can start querying an AI assistant powered by your own data.

But as your applications get more complex, you'll want to understand exactly how LlamaIndex is doing its thing under the hood. This is where **logging** becomes important. LlamaIndex provides tons of helpful log statements that show you step-by-step what's going on during indexing and querying. It's like having a little debug narrator describing each action.

Enabling basic logging is as simple as adding this code:

```
import logging
logging.basicConfig(level=logging.DEBUG)
```

With debug logging enabled, you'll see how LlamaIndex does things, such as the following:

- Parses your Documents into Nodes
- Decide which indexing structure to use
- Formats prompts for the LLM
- Retrieves relevant Nodes based on your queries
- Synthesizes a response from the Nodes

As we'll see in the next chapters, logging also reveals useful data such as the following:

- The number of tokens used for API calls
- Latency information
- Any warnings or errors

> **Note**
> When things aren't working as expected, don't panic! Just check the logs. They provide crucial clues for identifying issues. For now, using the basic logging feature should do fine. With this feature enabled, most of the backstage activities will now be displayed during run time so you'll be able to monitor the flow of your app step by step. We'll talk more about advanced debugging during *Chapter 9, Customizing and Deploying Our LlamaIndex Project*.

Now, how about some tweaking?

Customizing the LLM used by LlamaIndex

Let's say we would like to configure the framework to use another LLM. By default, LlamaIndex uses the OpenAI API with the **GPT-3.5-Turbo** model. Here's an overview of the key features of GPT-3.5-Turbo:

- It's faster and cheaper to run compared to **GPT-4**
- While not as advanced as other models, such as GPT-4, it's still a very capable generative and conversational model
- It can perform very well on a variety of **natural language processing** (NLP) tasks such as classification, summarization, or translation

You can see why the creators of LlamaIndex have chosen this model. All things considered, it provides a good balance of performance and cost for most use cases. For most applications, it's probably sufficient. As you have seen already if you've tested the application, it handles the questions about Lionel Messi pretty well.

But what if we need to customize that for a more specific case? Let's say we need the best possible performance of GPT-4, the larger context provided by **Claude-2**, or maybe we want to use an open-source AI for our purposes.

Easy as 1-2-3

We only need to add three lines of code at the beginning of our app:

```
from llama_index.llms.openai import OpenAI
from llama_index.core.settings import Settings
Settings.llm = OpenAI(temperature=0.8, model="gpt-4")
```

Make sure you add the `Settings.llm` line immediately after your imports so that it applies to all the other operations. Here's the explanation for each step:

1. The first line imports the OpenAI class from `llama_index.llms.openai` so that we can use it to initialize an OpenAI LLM

2. The second import is responsible for the `Settings` class. We'll use it to customize the LLM

3. Next, we configure `Settings` with an OpenAI LLM instance using the GPT-4 model and set the `temperature` to `0.8`, overriding the default LLM

We just configured LlamaIndex to use GPT-4 for all operations instead of the default GPT-3.5-Turbo model. The next part of the code will build an index and run a simple query using the newly configured LLM:

```
from llama_index.core.schema import TextNode
from llama_index.core import SummaryIndex
nodes = [
    TextNode(text="Lionel Messi's hometown is Rosario."),
    TextNode(text="He was born on June 24, 1987.")
]
index = SummaryIndex(nodes)
query_engine = index.as_query_engine()
response = query_engine.query(
    "What is Messi's hometown?"
)
print(response)
```

Next, we need to talk about the `temperature` parameter.

The temperature parameter

On OpenAI models such as GPT-3.5 and GPT-4, this parameter controls the randomness and creativity of the AI's responses. Check out *Figure 3.6* for an overview:

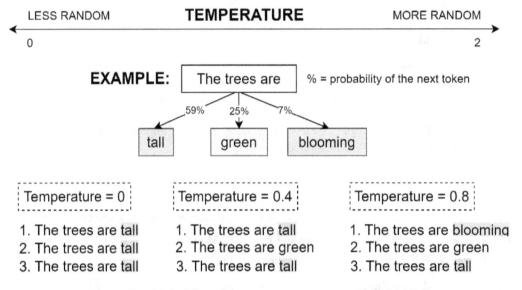

Figure 3.6 – Effect of temperature on output variability

The temperature values for the OpenAI models range from 0 to 2. Higher values produce more random, creative output. Lower values produce more focused, deterministic output.

A temperature value of 0 will produce almost the same output every time for the same input prompt. You noticed that I've used the word "almost." That is because even with the 0 setting, most models will probably still produce slight answer variations given the same prompt. This is caused by inherent randomness in the model's initialization or subtle variations in the model's internal state that can occur due to factors such as floating-point precision limitations or the stochastic nature of certain operations within the neural network. Even with a temperature value of 0, which aims to minimize randomness, these small variations can lead to slightly different outputs for identical inputs.

Setting the right temperature depends on your use case – whether you want responses strongly based on factual data or more imaginative ones. For code generation or data analysis tasks, a temperature value of 0.2 would be appropriate, while more creativity-focused tasks such as writing or chatbot responses would benefit from a setting of 0.5 and higher.

> **Note**
> If you have a use case that really requires consistent responses for multiple iterations using the same prompt, here's some practical advice. In my experimental research, I have achieved the most consistent results using the GPT-3.5-Turbo-1106 model with a temperature value of 0.

Apart from `temperature`, there are several other parameters you can tune by passing them as a dictionary to the `additional_kwargs` argument. If you plan on using OpenAI models in your RAG workflow, I advise you to familiarize yourself with these LLM settings, as they can be very important in an RAG scenario. Apart from `temperature`, the `top_p` and `seed` parameters are particularly useful as they can be leveraged to control the randomness of the outputs. For a detailed list, you can consult the official OpenAI documentation here: `https://platform.openai.com/docs/models`.

Here's a simple playground that you could use for experimenting with different LLM settings:

```
from llama_index.llms.openai import OpenAI
llm = OpenAI(
    model="gpt-3.5-turbo-1106",
    temperature=0.2,
    max_tokens=50,
    additional_kwargs={
        "seed": 12345678,
        "top_p": 0.5
    }
)
response = llm.complete(
    "Explain the concept of gravity in one sentence"
)
print(response)
```

Using the previous code, you can experiment with different settings, examining the output and finding the best configuration for your particular use case.

If you are wondering what different LLMs available right now can do for your RAG purposes, here is a side-by-side comparison extracted from the LlamaIndex documentation. This list was built by the LlamaIndex community by testing various LLMs: `https://docs.llamaindex.ai/en/stable/module_guides/models/llms.html`.

Understanding how Settings can be used for customization

You've probably noticed that I have used something called `Settings` to customize the AI model in the previous section. A brief explanation is in order.

`Settings` is a key component in LlamaIndex that allows you to customize and configure the *elements* used during indexing and querying. It contains common objects needed across LlamaIndex such as the following:

- LLM: This allows for the overriding of the default LLM with a custom one as we've seen in the previous example

- `Embedding model`: This is used for generating vectors for text to enable semantic search. These vectors are called **embeddings** and we'll talk about them in much more detail during *Chapter 5, Indexing with LlamaIndex*

- `NodeParser`: This is used for setting the default node parser

- `CallbackManager`: This handles callbacks for events within LlamaIndex. As we will see later, this is used for debugging and tracing our apps

There are also other parameters that can be tweaked in `Settings`. We'll dive much deeper into different customization options during *Chapter 9, Customizing and Deploying Our LlamaIndex Project*. Regardless of what you want to change, the customization will be done like in the previous example. Once you've defined your custom `Settings`, all subsequent operations will use this configuration.

OK. We've covered enough concepts for one chapter. How about some coding?

Starting our PITS project – hands-on exercise

Are you ready for a bit of hands-on practice? It's time to start building our PITS project. We have enough theoretical groundwork laid out and, in this chapter, we'll begin the preparation for the more advanced elements to come.

I've tried to build the project in a modular structure. I believe it helps a lot with code clarity and will enable us to go through some of the important concepts from LlamaIndex one by one. As I mentioned in the previous chapter, you can either write the code alongside reading the book or download and study it in full using the GitHub repository that I've made available to you.

Disclaimer

There are many aspects that can be improved in the existing code base, and quite a few features are missing from it for PITS to be considered a production-ready application. For example, in my implementation, there is no authentication and the application is a single user. Also, to keep the code short, I've not dealt much with error handling. But, of course, these are not bugs but features. This way, you can continue the story of PITS, adding the missing elements and transforming it into a commercial-grade application. Why not?

Before we start, I'd like to briefly explain the code structure that will underpin our application. Here's a list of Python source code files used by our PITS along with brief descriptions for each:

- `app.py`: The main entry point for the Streamlit app. This handles the initialization of the application and manages the navigation between different screens based on the application logic

- `document_uploader.py`: This interfaces with LlamaIndex to ingest and index uploaded Documents

- `training_material_builder.py`: This constructs the learning materials (slides and narration) based on the user's current knowledge. It utilizes uploaded and indexed materials to generate the learning content

- `training_interface.py`: This is where the actual teaching will take place. It displays the slides and the tutor narration together with the conversational side panel for user interactions

- `quiz_builder.py`: This generates quizzes based on the ingested materials and the user's current knowledge

- `quiz_interface.py`: This administers quizzes and evaluates the user's knowledge level depending on the results – what everyone hated in high school

- `conversation_engine.py`: This manages the conversational side panel, responding to user queries and providing explanations. It also keeps track of the context of conversations with the tutor to avoid repetition and ensure relevant assistance. It also retrieves summaries of previous discussions and ensures the tutor picks up where it left off

- `storage_manager.py`: This handles all file operations, such as saving and loading session states and user uploads. It manages local file storage and can be later adapted for cloud storage solutions

- `session_functions.py`: This handle storing and retrieving session information locally – and eventually in the cloud

- `logging_functions.py`: This handles the logging of all user interactions with the app. Writes descriptive log statements with timestamps to track the user's actions throughout the app. Stores and retrieves application logs locally – and eventually in the cloud

- `global_settings.py`: This contains application settings, configurations, and eventually Streamlit's secrets for deployment. It centralizes parameters for easy management and updates

- `user_onboarding.py`: This module takes care of the user onboarding steps

- `index_builder.py`: This module builds the indexes used throughout the application

Keep in mind that, currently, the application is designed to run locally. During *Chapter 9*, *Customizing and Deploying Our LlamaIndex Project*, we will discuss the deployment options available with Streamlit apps in more detail. Before continuing, make sure you have installed the second package mentioned at the beginning of the chapter – the YAML package for Python.

This one will be required by PITS for its `session_functions` module. I will explain it in a few moments.

To install it, use the following code:

```
pip install pyyaml
```

For now, we will focus on three of the PITS modules:

- `global_settings.py`
- `session_functions.py`
- `logging_functions.py`

Let's have a look at the source code

We will first start with the global settings in `global_settings.py`:

```
LOG_FILE = "session_data/user_actions.log"
SESSION_FILE = "session_data/user_session_state.yaml"
CACHE_FILE = "cache/pipeline_cache.json"
CONVERSATION_FILE = "cache/chat_history.json"
QUIZ_FILE = "cache/quiz.csv"
SLIDES_FILE = "cache/slides.json"
STORAGE_PATH = "ingestion_storage/"
INDEX_STORAGE = "index_storage"

QUIZ_SIZE = 5
ITEMS_ON_SLIDE = 4
```

This is where we will store our global configurations. We'll use the different parameters here to customize the experience of PITS and adjust some of its internal settings.

For now, the only two parameters I would like to emphasize are `LOG_FILE` and `SESSION_FILE`. They are used to define the storage location for "our log file" and session-related data. The `log` file will be used to remember all user interactions and maintain conversational context. The `session` file will allow resuming existing sessions while maintaining the session state.

Now, let's move on to `session_functions.py`.

The `session_functions.py` module contains functions that handle the saving, loading, and deleting of a user's session state:

```
from global_settings import SESSION_FILE
import yaml
import os
def save_session(state):
    state_to_save = {key: value for key, value in state.items()}
    with open(SESSION_FILE, 'w') as file:
        yaml.dump(state_to_save, file)
```

The `save_session` function takes the current state as an argument, which includes all the necessary information about the user's session and writes it to a file named `SESSION_FILE`. The state is converted into YAML format before saving, which ensures that it can be easily reloaded later.

```python
def load_session(state):
    if os.path.exists(SESSION_FILE):
        with open(SESSION_FILE, 'r') as file:
            try:
                loaded_state = yaml.safe_load(file) or {}
                for key, value in loaded_state.items():
                    state[key] = value
                return True
            except yaml.YAMLError:
                return False
    return False
```

This function attempts to read `SESSION_FILE`, if it exists, and loads the stored session data into the provided state object. If the file is read successfully and the YAML content is correctly parsed, it returns `True`, indicating that the session state has been restored. Otherwise, it returns `False`.

```python
def delete_session(state):
    if os.path.exists(SESSION_FILE):
        os.remove(SESSION_FILE)
    for key in list(state.keys()):
        del state[key]
```

When a session needs to be cleared, this function deletes `SESSION_FILE` and removes all the keys from the passed state object, effectively resetting the session.

> **Why YAML?**
>
> I've used YAML as the format for serialization instead of Streamlit own persistence format because it's human readable and platform independent. YAML works well with hierarchical data structures, making it easy to read and edit outside of the application if necessary. It allows the session state to be stored in a structured, standard format that can easily be transferred or modified as needed. YAML is often used for configuration files, but it's also suitable for storing simple data structures such as, in our case, the session state.

We also need to create `logging_functions.py`. Here is the code:

```python
from datetime import datetime
from global_settings import LOG_FILE
import os
def log_action(action, action_type):
```

```
        timestamp = datetime.now().strftime('%Y-%m-%d %H:%M:%S')
        log_entry = f"{timestamp}: {action_type} : {action}\n"
        with open(LOG_FILE, 'a') as file:
            file.write(log_entry)
    def reset_log():
        with open(LOG_FILE, 'w') as file:
            file.truncate(0)
```

The `logging_functions.py` module is responsible for recording events, user actions, and other significant occurrences during the execution of the application into a log file. I've designed it to keep track of user actions and system events mainly to provide context for the PITS agent during its interactions with the user but also for monitoring and debugging purposes.

Here's what the functions in the module do:

- `log_action(action, action_type)`: This function records an action or event. It accepts two arguments: `action`, which is a string describing what occurred, and `action_type`, which categorizes the action. The function gets the current `timestamp`, formats it with the action and type, and appends this entry to `LOG_FILE`. This helps maintain a chronological record of actions and events

- `reset_log()`: In the current implementation, when the users return to an existing session, they have the option to start a new one. When that happens, we clear the log file to avoid collecting too much data. This function opens `LOG_FILE` and truncates its content, effectively deleting all the logged entries. This is usually not a common thing to do in production environments, as logs are valuable for historical data analysis, but in our case, it simplifies the flow

I know I've promised we'll have fun writing the code for PITS, and I am perfectly aware that logging seems less *ha-ha* and more *ho-hum*, but trust me, there's no fun if you can't debug your app. We needed to lay the foundations here and we'll continue with the rest of the modules in the next chapters.

Summary

This chapter covered foundational concepts such as Documents, Nodes, and indexes – the core building blocks of LlamaIndex. I've demonstrated a simple workflow to load data as Documents, parse it into coherent Nodes using parsers, build an optimized index from the Nodes, and then query the index to retrieve relevant Nodes and synthesize a response.

The logging features of LlamaIndex were introduced as an important tool for understanding the underlying logic and debugging applications. Logs reveal how LlamaIndex parses, indexes, prompts the LLM, retrieves Nodes, and synthesizes responses. Customizing the LLM and other services used by LlamaIndex was shown using the `Settings` class.

We've also started to build our PITS tutoring application, laying the groundwork with session management and logging functions. This modular structure will enable the exploration of LlamaIndex's capabilities incrementally as the app is built up.

With the foundational knowledge established, it's time to move on to more advanced LlamaIndex features. The journey continues!

4

Ingesting Data
into Our RAG Workflow

We've taken a good look at the overall structure of LlamaIndex from afar. It's now time to get much closer and understand the small details of this framework. It's bound to get more technical but also more intriguing as we go further.

Ready to go deeper down the rabbit hole? Follow me!

In this chapter, we will learn about the following:

- Using the LlamaHub connectors to ingest our data
- Taking advantage of the many text-chunking tools in LlamaIndex
- Infusing our nodes with metadata and relationships
- Keeping our data private and our budget safe
- Creating ingestion pipelines for better efficiency and lower costs

Technical requirements

You will need to install the following Python libraries in your environment to be able to run the examples included in this chapter:

- **LangChain**: `https://www.langchain.com/`
- **Py-Tree-Sitter**: `https://pypi.org/project/tree-sitter/`

In addition, several LlamaIndex Integration packages will be required:

- **Entity extractor**: `https://pypi.org/project/llama-index-extractors-entity/`

- **Hugging Face LLMs**: `https://pypi.org/project/llama-index-llms-huggingface/`

- **Database reader**: `https://pypi.org/project/llama-index-readers-database/`

- **Web reader**: `https://pypi.org/project/llama-index-readers-web/`

All the code examples in this chapter can be found in the *ch4* subfolder of this book's GitHub repository: `https://github.com/PacktPublishing/Building-Data-Driven-Applications-with-LlamaIndex`.

Ingesting data via LlamaHub

As we saw in *Chapter 3, Kickstarting Your Journey with LlamaIndex*, one of the first steps in a RAG workflow is to ingest and process our proprietary data. We already discovered the concepts of documents and nodes, which are used to organize the data and prepare it for indexing. I've also briefly introduced the LlamaHub data loaders as a way to easily ingest data into LlamaIndex. It's time to examine these steps in more detail and gradually learn how to infuse LLM applications with our own, proprietary knowledge. Before we continue, though, I'd like to emphasize some very common challenges encountered at this step:

1. No matter how effective our RAG pipeline is, at the end of the day, the quality of the final result will largely depend on the quality of the initial data. To overcome this challenge, make sure you start by cleaning up your data first. Eliminate potential duplicates and errors. While not exactly duplicates, redundant information can also clutter your knowledge base and confuse the RAG system. Be on the lookout for ambiguous, biased, incomplete, or outdated information. I've seen many cases of poorly structured and insufficiently maintained knowledge repositories that were completely useless for users looking for quick and accurate answers. Ask yourself this question: *If I were to manually search through this data, how easy would it be to find the information I need?* Before moving on with building the pipeline, do yourself a favor and prepare your data thoroughly until you're satisfied with the answer to that question.

2. Our data is dynamic. An organizational knowledge repository is rarely a static, permanent data source. It evolves with the business, reflecting new insights, discoveries, and changes in the external environment. Recognizing this fluid nature is key to maintaining a relevant and effective system. To overcome this challenge, in a production RAG application, you'll have to implement a systematic method for periodically reviewing and updating the content, ensuring that new information is incorporated and outdated or incorrect data is removed.

3. Data comes in many flavors, shapes, and sizes. Sometimes, it's structured, sometimes not. A well-built RAG system should be able to properly ingest all kinds of formats and document types. While LlamaIndex provides a huge number of data loaders for many different APIs, databases, and document types, building an automated ingestion system can still prove to be challenging. To overcome this particular challenge, later in this section, we'll cover **LlamaParse** – an innovative hosted service designed to automatically ingest and process data from different data sources.

Now that we know what kind of problems await along the way, let's start our journey by first discussing the simplest ways of ingesting the data into the RAG pipeline – by using the available LlamaHub data loaders.

An overview of LlamaHub

LlamaHub is an extensive library of integrations that augments the capabilities of the core framework. Among many other types of integrations, LlamaHub contains numerous **connectors** – also known as **data readers** or **data loaders** – specially built to allow seamless integration of external data with LlamaIndex. There are over 180 readily available data readers spanning a wide range of data sources and formats, and the list is constantly increasing.

These connectors act as a standard way to ingest data, extracting data from sources such as databases, APIs, files, and websites and converting it into LlamaIndex `Document` objects. This relieves you from the burden of writing customized parsers and connectors for every new data source. But of course, if you're not satisfied with the existing connectors, you can always build your own and contribute to the collection.

LlamaHub empowers you to tap into diverse data sources with just a few lines of code. The resulting `Document` objects can then be parsed into nodes and indexed as required by your application. The unified output as LlamaIndex `Document` objects means your core business logic does not have to worry about handling various data types. The complexity is abstracted by the framework.

Why do we need so many integrations?

In *Chapter 2, LlamaIndex: The Hidden Jewel - An Introduction to the LlamaIndex Ecosystem*, in the *Familiarizing ourselves with the structure of the LlamaIndex code repository* section, I explained the motives behind the framework's modular architecture. Because of this modular architecture, many RAG components provided by LlamaIndex are not included in the core elements that are installed together with the rest of the framework. This means that before using any data loader for the first time, we have to install the corresponding integration package. Once the package has been installed, we'll be able to import the reader into our code and use its functionality. Some readers also utilize specialized libraries and tools tailored to each data type. For example, `PDFReader` leverages Camelot and Tika for parsing PDF content. `AirbyteSalesforceReader` uses the Salesforce API client, and so on. This allows us to efficiently adapt to the format and interface of each source but may require us to install additional packages in our development environment.

All available readers are listed on the LlamaHub website and usually come with detailed documentation and usage samples. Therefore, I'll briefly cover just a few examples to give a general idea of how you can use them in your applications.

I strongly encourage you to take your time and go through the entire list of data readers when building your LlamaIndex apps instead of spending valuable time building one from scratch. Chances are you'll just be reinventing the wheel.

If you're looking to consult the source code for the readers, you'll find them all included in the Llama-index GitHub repository, under the `llama-index-integrations/readers` subfolder: `https://github.com/run-llama/llama_index/tree/main/llama-index-integrations/readers`.

The LlamaHub documentation for each data reader lists its installation requirements and usage guidance, so before trying to use them, make sure you also install any additional dependencies required by specific connectors you want to use.

Using the LlamaHub data loaders to ingest content

Apart from the *Wikipedia* reader that we discussed in the previous chapter, to get a better understanding of how data readers work, let's look at a few more examples of LlamaHub readers that we can use to ingest data.

Ingesting data from a web page

`SimpleWebPageReader` can extract text content from web pages.

To use it, we must first install the corresponding integration:

```
pip install llama-index-readers-web
```

Once installed, it's really easy to use:

```
from llama_index.readers.web import SimpleWebPageReader
urls = ["https://docs.llamaindex.ai"]
documents = SimpleWebPageReader().load_data(urls)
for doc in documents:
    print(doc.text)
```

This loads and displays the text content of the specified web pages into documents.

At its core, `SimpleWebPageReader` serves as a bridge between the vast, unstructured world of the internet and the structured environment of the LlamaIndex RAG pipeline. To better understand its inner workings, let's explore what happens under the hood when it extracts text content from web pages.

When loading the data, `SimpleWebPageReader` iterates over a list of URLs provided by the user. For each URL, it performs a web request to fetch the page content. The response, initially in HTML format, can be transformed into plain text if the `html_to_text` flag is set to `True`. This transformation strips away the HTML tags and converts the web page content into a more digestible text format. However, remember what I've said about external dependencies for these readers? In this case, the HTML-to-text conversion feature requires the `html2text` package, which has to be installed first.

Another significant aspect of this reader is its ability to attach metadata to the scraped documents. Through the `metadata_fn` parameter, we can pass a custom function that takes a URL as input and returns a dictionary of metadata. This flexibility allows for the enrichment of documents with additional information or any relevant tags that might be useful in categorizing and understanding the context of the data better. Should the user provide a `metadata_fn` parameter, the reader then applies this function to the current URL to extract metadata, enriching the final `Document` object with this additional layer of information.

> **A practical use case for the metadata_fn function**
>
> We could, for example, use a function that simply returns the current date and time. That way, we could ingest the same URL at different moments and build a chronological timeline highlighting different versions of that page at various points in time. This could prove useful in scenarios such as browsing a code repository or answering questions about a developing news story.

Finally, each web page's content, along with its URL and optionally added metadata, is encapsulated in a `Document` object. These objects are then collected into a list, providing a structured representation of the text content and metadata extracted from each web page.

> **One thing to keep in mind**
>
> As its name suggests, this reader is a simple tool. While it can be effective for reading simple web pages, for more advanced cases such as pages requiring interaction (for example, navigating a login process or handling JavaScript-rendered content), `SimpleWebPageReader` might not be sufficient. Websites that dynamically generate content based on user interactions or rely heavily on client-side scripting can pose challenges that this basic scraper is not designed to handle.

Through `SimpleWebPageReader`, the task of ingesting and structuring basic web content is simplified. The great thing about these readers is that they allow us to focus on building and enhancing the logic of our RAG applications instead of spending precious time on building compatible ingestion tools for each type of data in our knowledge base.

Ingesting data from a database

Using databases is not only a common practice but also a highly efficient method for managing and retrieving structured information. Databases offer a robust platform for storing a vast array of data types, from simple text to complex relationships between entities, making them an indispensable asset in data management.

The `DatabaseReader` connector allows querying many database systems. First, we need to install the necessary integration package:

```
pip install llama-index-readers-database
```

Here's an example of how you can easily fetch the contents of an SQLite database:

```
from llama_index.readers.database import DatabaseReader
reader = DatabaseReader(
    uri="sqlite:///files/db/example.db"
)
query = "SELECT * FROM products"
documents = reader.load_data(query=query)
for doc in documents:
    print(doc.text)
```

Under the hood, `DatabaseReader` connects to various databases to fetch data and transform it into a format usable by the RAG pipeline. It supports connection through a `SQLDatabase` instance, a **SQLAlchemy Engine**, a connection URI, or a set of database credentials – provided through the `scheme`, `host`, `port`, `user`, `password`, and `dbname` arguments. Once set up, it executes a provided SQL query to retrieve data. After connecting to the database, the reader executes the provided `query`. The resulting rows are then converted into Document objects, with each row from the query result forming a single Document. The conversion process involves concatenating each column-value pair into a string, which is then assigned as the text of a document.

The example I have provided executes the SQL query against an SQLite database stored in the `ch4/files/db` folder, loads each returned row as a Document, and displays the results. You can find a more general example on the official project documentation website: `https://docs.llamaindex.ai/en/stable/examples/data_connectors/DatabaseReaderDemo.html`.

Alright – I think you understand the workflow now. As you've probably noticed, the approach for using LlamaHub readers is very straightforward. In all the examples, first, we install the required integration package, as described on LlamaHub, and then use it to import and load data from the reader. Apart from the examples I have provided, you'll find a huge number of data readers available on LlamaHub. From Office documents, Gmail accounts, videos and images, YouTube videos, and RSS feeds to GitHub repositories and Discord chats, pretty much every popular data format is supported.

But apart from reading individual files using dedicated data readers, in the next section, we will also explore more efficient methods that can be used for ingesting multiple documents at once.

Bulk-ingesting data from sources with multiple file formats

Loading data into LlamaIndex is a crucial first step. But sifting through the wide range of data loaders in LlamaHub and figuring out how to configure each one can feel overwhelming early on. That's why I'm going to show you two different methods that can greatly simplify and reduce the burden of data ingestion for your RAG systems.

We'll start with the simple method first.

Using SimpleDirectoryReader to ingest multiple data formats

When you just want to get started fast or have a simple use case, `SimpleDirectoryReader` comes to the rescue. Think of this reader as your trusty pocketknife for bulk data ingestion. It's easy to use, requires minimal setup, and automatically adapts to different file types. To load data, you simply point the reader to a folder or list of files. Loading a folder containing PDFs, Word docs, plain text files, and CSVs is very straightforward. Here's a demonstration:

```
from llama_index.core import SimpleDirectoryReader
reader = SimpleDirectoryReader(
    input_dir="files",
    recursive=True
)
documents = reader.load_data()
for doc in documents:
    print(doc.metadata)
```

> **Under the hood**
>
> `SimpleDirectoryReader` has built-in methods to determine which reader works best for each file type. You don't need to worry about those details. It will automatically detect formats such as PDF, DOCX, CSV, plain text, and others based on the file extensions. Then, it chooses the best tool to extract the content into Document objects. For plain text files, it simply reads the text content. For binary files such as PDFs and Office docs, it uses libraries such as PyPDF and Pillow to extract the text.

`SimpleDirectoryReader` effortlessly handles the different files and returns the parsed content as documents. By default, it only processes files in the directory's top level. To include subdirectories, you can set the `recursive` parameter to `True`.

You can also pass in a list of specific files to load, like this:

```
files = ["file1.pdf", "file2.docx", "file3.txt"]
reader = SimpleDirectoryReader(files)
documents = reader.load_data()
```

The result is a batch of Document objects ready for indexing in just a few lines of code. No headaches setting up separate data readers for each file type. When you want quick and easy data ingestion without the complexity, let `SimpleDirectoryReader` handle the hard work! It's versatile and automated.

Parsing like a pro with the help of LlamaParse

While `SimpleDirectoryReader` is great for quick and easy data ingestion, sometimes, you need more advanced parsing capabilities, especially for complex file formats. Most of the time, we have to deal with complex file structures containing a mix of data. For example, a PDF file may include images, charts, code snippets, mathematical formulas, and other elements alongside its text content. The naive readers included in the LlamaHub integration library will be overwhelmed by such cases. They would most probably fail to extract the entire content or – even worse – mess up the extracted data and complicate its further processing.

This is where LlamaParse shines. Provided through the LlamaCloud enterprise platform (`https://cloud.llamaindex.ai/parse`), this reader is implemented through a cutting-edge hosted service that integrates seamlessly with the other components of the framework. It uses multi-modal capabilities and LLM intelligence under the hood to provide industry-leading document parsing, including exceptional support for tricky formats such as PDFs containing tables, figures, and equations.

One of the standout features of `LlamaParse` is that it allows you to provide natural language instructions to guide the parsing by using the `parsing_instruction` parameter. Since you know your documents best, you can tell `LlamaParse` exactly what kind of output you need and how that information should be extracted from the files.

> **For instance:**
> When parsing a technical whitepaper, you could instruct it to extract all the section headings, ignore the footnotes, and output any code snippets in markdown format. `LlamaParse` will follow your instructions to parse the document accurately.

In addition to the instruction-guided parsing mode, `LlamaParse` also offers a JSON output mode that provides rich structured data about the parsed document, including marking tables, headings, extracting images, and more. Also, for bulk-ingesting entire folders in one go, `LlamaParse` can be used in combination with `SimpleDirectoryReader`, as you will see in the next example. This gives you full flexibility to build custom RAG applications over a complex collection of documents. You could also accomplish this manually by using specialized data readers for each file format in your collection of data. However, using `LlamaParse` will greatly simplify this process, improve the overall quality, and save you a lot of time.

`LlamaParse` supports a wide and expanding range of file types beyond just PDFs, including Word docs, PowerPoint, RTF, ePub, and many more. It offers a generous free tier to get started.

The necessary `LlamaParse` integration package should already be installed along with the LlamaIndex components, so no additional installation is required to run the code example in this section.

The next step is to create a free account on `https://cloud.llamaindex.ai` and obtain an API key. Once you have obtained the key, you can use it directly in your code, but for a more secure approach, I strongly encourage you to follow the same steps we followed in *Chapter 2, LlamaIndex: The Hidden Jewel - An Introduction to the LlamaIndex Ecosystem*, and add the key as a variable in your local environment under the name `LLAMA_CLOUD_API_KEY`. To demonstrate the capabilities of this tool, I've designed a sample PDF with a more complex structure, as can be seen in *Figure 4.1*:

ARTICLE 1

In ancient Rome, the city of Rome itself was the heart of the vast Roman Empire. It was known for its grand architecture, including iconic structures like the Colosseum (Figure 1) and the Pantheon. The Romans were skilled engineers and builders, creating an extensive network of roads, aqueducts, and bridges that connected their far-reaching territories.

Figure 1: An AI-generated sketch of the Colosseum

Rank	Breed	Size
1	French Bulldog	Small
2	Poodle (Toy or Mini)	Small-Medium
3	German Shepherd	Large
4	Golden Retriever	Large
5	Labrador Retriever	Large

Table 2: A list of popular dog breeds

ARTICLE 2

Many people consider dogs to be their loyal companions. These furry creatures come in various breeds (Table 2), each with its own unique traits and personalities.

Figure 4.1 – A sample PDF containing multiple articles, images, and tables

Here's a basic code example that uses `LlamaParse` to ingest this PDF:

```
from llama_parse import LlamaParse
from llama_index.core import SimpleDirectoryReader
from llama_index.core import VectorStoreIndex
```

The first part of the code imported the necessary modules. Next, we'll configure `LlamaParse` and pass it to `SimpleDirectoryReader` as a `file_extractor` argument:

```
parser = LlamaParse(result_type="text")
file_extractor = {".pdf": parser}
reader = SimpleDirectoryReader(
    "./files/pdf",
    file_extractor=file_extractor
)
docs = reader.load_data()
```

Once the PDF content has been ingested into a new Document object, it's time to build an index and run a query against our data:

```
index = VectorStoreIndex.from_documents(docs)
qe = index.as_query_engine()
response = qe.query(
    "List all large dog breeds mentioned in Table 2 "
)
print(response)
```

The output of this script should be similar to the following:

```
Started parsing the file under job_id <…>
German Shepherd, Golden Retriever, Labrador Retriever
```

> **Important note**
>
> One important consideration with using a hosted service such as `LlamaParse` is data privacy. Before submitting your proprietary data through the API, be sure to carefully review their privacy policy to ensure it aligns with your data protection requirements. While the service offers powerful parsing capabilities, it's crucial to safeguard sensitive information.

Keep in mind that this is a paid service. The great news, however, is that you can take advantage of their generous **free tier**. For higher volume needs, the current pricing can be found on the website. If you want to unlock the full potential of `LlamaParse` to build advanced document retrieval systems or deploy it on your private cloud for maximal data security, that option is available as well.

For professional, production-ready applications, `LlamaParse` is a powerful tool that puts you in full control of parsing your data to maximize the quality of your knowledge base and RAG applications.

Now that we've got the data, let's make it easier to handle by breaking it down into smaller pieces.

Parsing the documents into nodes

As we saw in *Chapter 3, Kickstarting Your Journey with LlamaIndex*, the next step is to split the documents into nodes. In many cases, documents tend to be very large, so we need to break them down into smaller units called nodes. Working at this granular level allows for better handling of our content while maintaining an accurate representation of its internal structure. This is the basic mechanism that LlamaIndex uses to manage our proprietary data content more easily.

Now is the time to understand how nodes can be generated in LlamaIndex and what customization opportunities we have along the way. In the previous chapter, we talked about how to manually create nodes. But that was merely a way to simplify the explanation and help you better understand their mechanics. In a real application, most likely, we will want to use some automatic methods to generate them from the ingested documents. So, that's what we'll focus on going forward.

In this section, we will discover different ways of chunking a document. We'll start by understanding simple **text splitters** – which operate on raw text – and then we'll cover the more advanced **node parsers** – which are capable of interpreting more complex formats and following the document structure when extracting the nodes.

Understanding the simple text splitters

Text splitters *break down* the document into smaller pieces operating at the raw text level. They are useful when the content has a *flat* structure and does not come in a specific format.

To run the following examples, make sure you add the necessary imports and the document reading logic, using `FlatReader`, at the beginning of your code for all examples:

```
from llama_index.core.node_parser import <Splitter_Module>
from llama_index.readers.file import FlatReader
from pathlib import Path
reader = FlatReader()
document = reader.load_data(Path(<file_name>))
```

Also, if you want to see the actual nodes generated by the code, you can add something like this *after* running the parsers:

```
for node in nodes:
    print(f"Metadata {node.metadata} \nText: {node.text}")
```

Alright. Let's see what's in store in the *text splitter* category.

SentenceSplitter

This one splits text while maintaining sentence boundaries, providing nodes containing groups of sentences. You saw an example of using this parser in *Chapter 3, Kickstarting Your Journey with LlamaIndex*, in the *Automatically extracting nodes from documents using splitters* section.

TokenTextSplitter

This splitter breaks down text while respecting sentence boundaries to create suitable nodes for further natural language processing. It operates at the token level.

A typical usage in code would look like this:

```
splitter = TokenTextSplitter(
    chunk_size = 70,
    chunk_overlap = 2,
    separator = " ",
    backup_separators = [".", "!", "?"]
)
nodes = splitter.get_nodes_from_documents(document)
```

Here are some notes on the parameters of this splitter:

- `chunk_size`: This sets the maximum number of tokens for each chunk
- `chunk_overlap`: This defines the overlap in tokens between consecutive chunks
- `separator`: This is used to determine the primary token boundary
- `backup_separators`: These can be used for additional splitting points if the primary separator doesn't split the text sufficiently

CodeSplitter

This smart splitter knows how to interpret source code. It splits text based on programming language and is ideal for managing technical documentation or source code. Before running the example, make sure you install the necessary libraries:

```
pip install tree_sitter
pip install tree_sitter_languages
```

Let's have a look at an example of how to use this splitter in your code:

```
code_splitter = CodeSplitter.from_defaults(
    language = 'python',
    chunk_lines = 5,
    chunk_lines_overlap = 2,
    max_chars = 150
)
nodes = code_splitter.get_nodes_from_documents(document)
```

As you can see, there are several parameters you can tune with this splitter:

- `language`: This specifies the language of the code
- `chunk_lines`: This defines the number of lines per chunk
- `chunk_lines_overlap`: This defines the lines overlap between chunks
- `max_chars`: This defines the maximum characters per chunk

> **Quick side note on CodeSplitter**
>
> This splitter is cleverly built around a concept called **abstract syntax tree** (**AST**). An AST is a key idea in computer science that's mainly used in creating programs that translate or interpret code. It's like a branching diagram that shows the basic structure of the code written in a programming language. Each point on the diagram represents a different part or piece of the code. Because of this splitter's awareness of AST, when you're splitting code, you keep related statements together as much as possible, which is vital when you need to maintain the logical flow of code to understand or process it later.

Using more advanced node parsers

Text splitters only provide basic logic for breaking down text, mostly by using simple rules. We also have more advanced tools for chunking text into nodes. These are designed to process various standard file formats or can be used for more specific types of content.

Before we continue, keep in mind that all the node parsers that we will discuss here are derived from the generic class called `NodeParser`. Each parser has various parameters that can be configured according to the use case, but at the base, three common elements can be customized for all parsers:

- `include_metadata`: This determines whether the parser should take into account the metadata or not. By default, this is set to `True`

- `Include_prev_next_rel`: This determines whether the parser should automatically include **prev/next** type relationships between nodes. Again, the default value is `True`

- `Callback_manager`: This can be used to define a specific **callback function**. These functions can be used for debugging, tracing, and cost analysis, among other functions. We will talk more about them in *Chapter 10, Prompt Engineering Guidelines and Best Practices*

Apart from these three general options, each parser provides specific parameters to customize. You can get a complete list of configurable parameters for each parser by consulting the official documentation.

Let's explore the node parsers available in LlamaIndex.

SentenceWindowNodeParser

Based on the simple **SentenceSplitter**, this parser splits text into individual sentences and also includes a *window* of surrounding sentences in the metadata of each node. It is useful for building more context around each sentence. During the querying process, that context will be fed into the LLM and allow for better responses. We can use it like this:

```
parser = SentenceWindowNodeParser.from_defaults(
    window_size=2,
    window_metadata_key="text_window",
    original_text_metadata_key="original_sentence"
)
nodes = parser.get_nodes_from_documents(document)
```

For this parser, three specific parameters can be customized:

- `Window_size`: This defines the number of sentences on each side to include in the window

- `window_metadata_key`: This defines the metadata key for the window sentences

- `original_text_metadata_key`: This defines the metadata key for the original sentence

LangchainNodeParser

If you prefer using the LangChain splitters, this parser allows using any text splitter from the Langchain collection, extending the parsing options offered by LlamaIndex.

As a prerequisite for the next example, you'll have to install the `LangChain` library:

```
pip install langchain
```

Here's a simple example of how to use this parser:

```
from langchain.text_splitter import CharacterTextSplitter
from llama_index.core.node_parser import LangchainNodeParser
parser = LangchainNodeParser(CharacterTextSplitter())
nodes = parser.get_nodes_from_documents(document)
```

> **A quick note on LangChain**
>
> The LangChain framework is similar in purpose to LlamaIndex and provides a versatile toolkit specialized in advanced natural language processing capabilities. Its collection of text segmentation, summarization, and language understanding models assist in splitting and digesting textual data into coherent chunks ready for indexing in a similar way to LlamaIndex. When dealing with large data sources requiring nuanced linguistic analysis, LangChain empowers users to finely control the breakdown and ingestion of text - ensuring context and clarity are retained for downstream retrieval and querying. As you can see, the two can complement each other in a RAG scenario. Want to know more? Check out `https://www.langchain.com/`.

Let's see what other parsers we have available.

SimpleFileNodeParser

This one automatically decides which of the following three node parsers should be used based on file types. It can automatically handle these file formats and transform them into nodes, simplifying the process of interacting with various types of content:

```
parser = SimpleFileNodeParser()
nodes = parser.get_nodes_from_documents(documents)
```

You can simply rely on `FlatReader` to load the file into your `Document` object; `SimpleFileNodeParser` will know what to do from there.

HTMLNodeParser

This parser uses **Beautiful Soup** to parse HTML files and convert them into nodes based on selected HTML tags. This parser simplifies the HTML file by extracting text from standard text elements and merging adjacent nodes of the same type. The parser can be used like this:

```python
my_tags = ["p", "span"]
html_parser = HTMLNodeParser(tags=my_tags)
nodes = html_parser.get_nodes_from_documents(document)
print('<span> elements:')
for node in nodes:
    if node.metadata['tag']=='span':
        print(node.text)
print('<p> elements:')
for node in nodes:
    if node.metadata['tag']=='p':
        print(node.text)
```

As you can see, you have the option to customize the HTML `tags` from where you want to retrieve content.

MarkdownNodeParser

This parser processes raw *markdown* text and generates nodes reflecting its structure and content. The markdown node parser divides the content into nodes for each header encountered in the file and incorporates the header hierarchy into the metadata. Here's how to use `MarkdownNodeParser`:

```python
parser = MarkdownNodeParser.from_defaults()
nodes = parser.get_nodes_from_documents(document)
```

JSONNodeParser

This parser is specialized in processing and querying structured data in JSON format. In a similar way to the Markdown parser, the JSON parser can be used like this:

```python
json_parser = JSONNodeParser.from_defaults()
nodes = json_parser.get_nodes_from_documents(document)
```

Using relational parsers

Relational parsers parse information into nodes that are linked to each other through relationships. Relationships add a whole new dimension to our data and allow for more advanced retrieval techniques in our RAG workflow.

HierarchicalNodeParser

This parser organizes the nodes into hierarchies across multiple levels. It will generate a hierarchy of nodes, starting with top-level nodes with larger section sizes, down to child nodes with smaller section sizes, where each child node has a parent node with a larger section size (*Figure 4.1*). By default, the parser uses `SentenceSplitter` to chunk text. The node hierarchy looks like this:

- *Level 1*: Section size 2,048
- *Level 2*: Section size 512
- *Level 3*: Section size 128

The top-level nodes, with larger sections, can provide high-level summaries, while the lower nodes can allow for a more detailed analysis of text sections. Have a look at *Figure 4.2* for a visual representation of this concept:

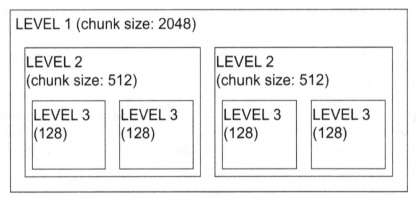

Figure 4.2 – Hierarchical nodes of 2,048, 512, and 128 chunk sizes

In this way, the different node levels can be used to adjust the accuracy and depth of search results, allowing users to find information at different granularity levels. Here's an example of how to use this parser in your code:

```
hierarchical_parser = HierarchicalNodeParser.from_defaults(
    chunk_sizes=[128, 64, 32],
    chunk_overlap=0,
)
nodes = hierarchical_parser.get_nodes_from_documents(document)
```

There are two specific parameters to customize for this parser:

- `chunk_sizes`: The values in this list define your hierarchy levels based on content size
- `chunk_overlap`: This defines the overlap size between chunks

UnstructuredElementNodeParser

I left this one last because it is used for more special situations. Sometimes, our documents may include a mix of text and data tables, which can make parsing inefficient by conventional methods.

This parser can process and split these documents into interpretable nodes, distinguishing between text sections and other embedded structures such as tables. We'll talk about it in more detail toward the end of this chapter.

Confused about node parsers and text splitters?

You may have noticed that I use the two terms quite loosely. Categorizing parsing modules into these two groups might initially cause some confusion. To simplify, a node parser is a more sophisticated mechanism than a simple splitter. While both serve the same basic function and operate at different levels of complexity, they differ in their implementations.

Text splitters such as `SentenceSplitter` can divide long flat texts into nodes, based on certain rules or limitations, such as **chunk_size** or **chunk_overlap**. The nodes could represent lines, paragraphs, or sentences, and may also include additional metadata or links to the original document.

Node parsers are more sophisticated and can involve additional data processing logic. Beyond simply dividing text into nodes, they can perform extra tasks, such as analyzing the structure of HTML or JSON files and producing nodes enriched with contextual information.

Understanding chunk_size and chunk_overlap

As you have probably understood by now, text splitters are a basic but important component. They control how text in documents gets split into nodes during parsing. For each text splitter type, LlamaIndex provides several parameters to customize the text splitting behavior.

Probably two of the most important parameters for a text splitter are `chunk_size` and `chunk_overlap`. The text splitters themselves, such as `SentenceSplitter`, `TokenTextSplitter`, `TextSplitter`, and others, take in the `chunk_size` and `chunk_overlap` arguments to control how they break text into smaller chunks during node creation. `chunk_size` controls the maximum length of text chunks in nodes. This is useful for ensuring nodes don't take long for the LLM to process. Note that in LlamaIndex, the default `chunk_size` is 1,024, while the default `chunk_overlap` is 20.

chunk size is an important setting when building an RAG system. If chunks are too small, important context may be lost and the quality of the LLM response will be lower. On the other hand, large chunks increase the size of the prompts, increasing both computational cost and response generation time. An experimental approach was used when the default values were selected for LlamaIndex: `https://blog.llamaindex.ai/evaluating-the-ideal-chunk-size-for-a-rag-system-using-llamaindex-6207e5d3fec5`.

`chunk_overlap` creates overlapping nodes by re-including some tokens from the previous Node. This helps provide context so that the LLM can understand the continuity of ideas when processing adjacent Nodes.

Figure 4.3 provides a visual representation of this concept:

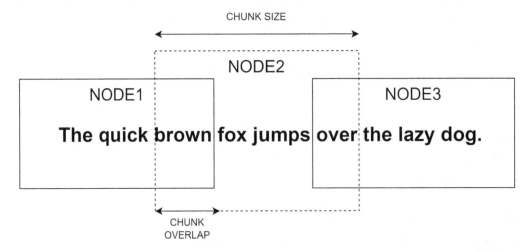

Figure 4.3 – chunk_size and chunk_overlap explained

The concept is similar to the way `SentenceWindowNodeParser` works – that is, it extracts a *window* of context for each sentence. For example, with `chunk_size=100` and `chunk_overlap=10`, let's say we had the following text:

Gardening is not only a relaxing hobby but also an art form. Cultivating plants, designing landscapes, and nurturing nature bring a sense of accomplishment. Many find it therapeutic and rewarding, especially when they see their garden flourish.

It would get split into the following areas:

- *Node 1 (first 100 characters)*: "Gardening is not only a relaxing hobby but also an art form. Cultivating plants, designing landscapes, an"

- *Node 2 (starts from the 75th character, next 100 characters)*: "designing landscapes, and nurturing nature bring a sense of accomplishment. Many find it therapeutic and re"

- *Node 3 (starts from the 150th character to the end of the text)*: "Many find it therapeutic and rewarding, especially when they see their garden flourish."

In this setup, the overlap between node 1 and node 2 is "`designing` landscapes, an," whereas the overlap between node 2 and node 3 is "Many find it therapeutic and re."

These overlaps mean that one node re-includes parts of the previous node. This mechanism ensures continuity and context between the chunks, making each part more meaningful when read in sequence. Of course, choosing the right values for these two parameters is very important. The biggest impact will be on creating vector indexes. We'll talk about them later, during *Chapter 5, Indexing with LlamaIndex*.

Next, let's have a quick overview of node relationships.

Including relationships with include_prev_next_rel

Let's talk a bit about another important parameter that can dictate the behavior of our parsers: the `include_prev_next_rel` option. When set to `True`, this option makes the parser automatically add `NEXT` and `PREVIOUS` relationships between consecutive nodes. Here's an example:

```
node_parser = SentenceWindowNodeParser.from_defaults(
    include_prev_next_rel=True
)
```

This helps capture the sequencing between nodes. Then, later when querying, you can optionally retrieve previous or next nodes for more context using features such as `PrevNextNodePostprocessor`. More on that in *Chapter 6, Querying Our Data, Part 1 – Context Retrieval*.

The relationships get added to the `.relationships` dictionary on each node.

So, node 1 would now be as follows:

```
node1.relationships[PREVIOUS] = RelatedNodeInfo(node_id=node0.node_id)
```

Node 2 would be as follows:

```
node2.relationships[NEXT] = RelatedNodeInfo(node_id=node3.node_id)
```

Capturing these sequences helps provide contextual continuity in long documents and brings a lot of other benefits that I listed in more detail in the previous chapter.

Among other things, having a previous-next relationship enables *cluster retrieval*: you can get a cluster of related nodes by following the relationships to fetch nearby connected nodes. This provides a more focused context instead of randomly scattered nodes. Maintaining a cohesive narrative thread through the content when following a story or a dialogue is another good reason for having these relationships between nodes.

Next, let's have a look at how to use these parsers and splitters in our workflow.

Practical ways of using these node creation models

How you implement the node parsers or text splitters in your code depends on how much you want to customize the process but, in the end, it all comes down to three main options:

1. Using them standalone by calling `get_nodes_from_documents()`, like in this example:

    ```
    from llama_index.core import Document
    from llama_index.core.node_parser import
    SentenceWindowNodeParser
    doc = Document(
        text="Sentence 1. Sentence 2. Sentence 3."
    )
    parser = SentenceWindowNodeParser.from_defaults(
        window_size=2 ,
        window_metadata_key="ContextWindow",
        original_text_metadata_key="node_text"
    )
    nodes = parser.get_nodes_from_documents([doc])
    ```

    This code will produce three nodes. If we look at the second node, for example, by running `print(nodes[1])`, we'll get the following output:

    ```
    Node ID: 0715876a-61e6-4e77-95ba-b93e10de1c67
    Text: Sentence 2.
    ```

    As you can see, the parser extracted the second sentence and allocated a random ID to the node. But if we take a peek at the node's metadata by running `print(nodes[1].metadata)`, we'll also see the context it gathered, using the keys we specified:

    ```
    {'ContextWindow': 'Sentence 1.  Sentence 2.  Sentence 3.',
    'node_text': 'Sentence 2. '}
    ```

    This metadata can later be used when building queries to provide more context for each sentence and improve the LLM responses.

    We'll explore this in more detail during *Chapter 6, Querying Our Data, Part 1 – Context Retrieval.*

2. Configuring them in `Settings`.

    The second option is a bit more general and convenient when you need to automatically use the same parser for multiple purposes in your app:

    ```
    from llama_index.core import Settings, Document,
        VectorStoreIndex
    from llama_index.core.node_parser import
        SentenceWindowNodeParser
    doc = Document(
        text="Sentence 1. Sentence 2. Sentence 3."
    )
    ```

```
text_splitter = SentenceWindowNodeParser.from_defaults(
    window_size=2  ,
    window_metadata_key="ContextWindow",
    original_text_metadata_key="node_text"
)
Settings.text_splitter = text_splitter
index = VectorStoreIndex.from_documents([doc])
```

This time, after we define and configure our custom `text_splitter`, we pre-load it in `Settings`. From this point forward, whenever we call any function that relies on text splitting, our custom `text_splitter` will be used by default.

Of course, this actual example is a bit of overkill. You've probably noticed that I've used a node parser in place of a simple text splitter. The index we're building with the nodes won't benefit in any way from the additional context metadata created by the parser. I just wanted to emphasize my previous point regarding parsers and splitters.

3. Defining the parsers as a **transformation** step in an **ingestion pipeline**.

   An ingestion pipeline is an automatic and structured process for ingesting data. It's running the data through a series of steps (called **transformations**) one by one.

   I will explain how this works and what it can be used for later in this chapter, in the *Using the ingestion pipeline to increase efficiency* section. You'll also get to see the code for implementing the parser as a transformation in the pipeline.

Next, we'll talk about metadata and how metadata can be used to improve our RAG application.

Working with metadata to improve the context

What is **metadata**? It's simply additional information we can attach to our documents and nodes. This extra context helps LlamaIndex better understand our data. It provides additional context about data and can be customized in terms of visibility and format.

For example, let's say you've *ingested* some PDF reports as documents. You could then simply add some metadata like this:

```
document.metadata = {
    "report_name": "Sales Report April 2022",
    "department": "Sales",
    "author": "Jane Doe"
}
```

This metadata gives vital clues when querying the data later. In this example, we can use it to locate reports by department or author. You can store anything useful as metadata – categories, timestamps, locations, and more.

And here's a neat trick – any metadata you set on a document automatically flows down to child nodes! So, if I set an `author` field on a document, all nodes derived from that document will inherit the `author` metadata. This propagation saves time and prevents duplicating metadata across nodes.

There are multiple ways of defining metadata:

1. Setting the metadata values directly in the `Document` constructor as follows:

    ```
    document = Document(
        text="...",
        metadata={"author": "John Doe"}
    )
    ```

2. Adding the metadata after document creation:

    ```
    document.metadata = {"category": "finance"}
    ```

3. Automatically setting metadata in the ingestion process, when using data connectors such as `SimpleDirectoryReader`:

    ```
    def set_metadata(filename):
        return {"file_name": filename}
    documents = SimpleDirectoryReader(
        "./data",
        file_metadata=set_metadata("file1.txt")
    ).load_data()
    ```

4. Using standalone, dedicated extractors provided by LlamaIndex. **Metadata extractors** are a powerful way to generate relevant metadata from text using the power of LLMs. This extracted metadata can then be attached to documents and nodes to provide additional context

5. Defining the extractor as a *transformation* step in an ingestion pipeline. Just like in the case of node parsers, extractors can also become part of the pipeline. We'll cover this approach later in this chapter in the *Using the ingestion pipeline to increase efficiency* section

But first, let's put our magnifying glass on these specialized metadata extractors to better understand how they work.

Before you go further, if you want to run the following code examples, make sure to include the necessary imports, document ingestion, and node parsing logic at the beginning of your code by adding the following lines:

```
From llama_index.core import SimpleDirectoryReader
from llama_index.core.node_parser import SentenceSplitter
reader = SimpleDirectoryReader('files')
documents = reader.load_data()
parser = SentenceSplitter(include_prev_next_rel=True)
nodes = parser.get_nodes_from_documents(documents)
```

This boilerplate code prepares your data – ingested from the `files` subfolder – and puts everything you need into `Nodes`. We'll store our metadata in a variable called `metadata_list`. I've added `print(metadata_list)` at the end of each example so that we'll see an output of the extracted metadata. Apart from describing their logic, I've also highlighted practical uses for each one of the extractors.

SummaryExtractor

This extractor generates summaries of the text contained by the node. Optionally, it can generate summaries for the previous and next adjacent nodes. Here's an example:

```
from llama_index.core.extractors import SummaryExtractor
summary_extractor = SummaryExtractor(summaries=["prev", "self",
    "next"])
metadata_list = summary_extractor.extract(nodes)
print(metadata_list)
```

This extractor generates concise summaries for each node or adjacent node. These are essential during the retrieve phase in an RAG architecture. This ensures that the search can consider the summary of the documents without having to process the entirety of their content.

> **Practical use case**
>
> Imagine a customer support knowledge base on which `SummaryExtractor` can provide summaries of customer issues and resolutions. Then, when a new support request comes in, our app can retrieve the most relevant past cases to help generate a detailed and contextual solution.

You can customize the type of `summaries` to generate by setting the values in the summaries list and the actual prompt that will be used with the LLM by defining the prompt in the `prompt_template` parameter.

QuestionsAnsweredExtractor

This extractor generates a specified number of questions the node text can answer.

The following example should give you a usage guideline:

```
from llama_index.core.extractors import QuestionsAnsweredExtractor
qa_extractor = QuestionsAnsweredExtractor(questions=5)
metadata_list = qa_extractor.extract(nodes)
print(metadata_list)
```

This extractor identifies questions that the text is uniquely positioned to answer, allowing the retrieval process to focus on nodes that explicitly address specific inquiries.

> **Practical use case**
>
> For an FAQ system, the extractor identifies unique questions answered by articles, making it easier to find precise answers to user queries.

You can customize the number of questions it generates but also the actual prompt that will be used with the LLM – by setting the `prompt_template` parameter. There is also an `embedding_only` Boolean parameter that – if set to `True` – will make the metadata available only for embeddings. More on that in *Chapter 5, Indexing with LlamaIndex*.

TitleExtractor

This one extracts a title for the text. Here's an example:

```
from llama_index.core.extractors import TitleExtractor
title_extractor = TitleExtractor ()
metadata_list = title_extractor.extract(nodes)
print(metadata_list)
```

`TitleExtractor` specializes in pulling out meaningful titles from larger texts, assisting in the quick identification and retrieval of documents. In digital libraries, for example, `TitleExtractor` can help categorize documents by extracting titles from untitled texts, making retrieval more efficient when titles are used as search keywords. There are several parameters you can tweak for this extractor:

- `nodes`: This sets the number of nodes to use for title extraction
- `node_template`: This changes the default prompt template that's used for extracting the titles
- `combine_template`: This changes the prompt template for combining multiple node-level titles in a document-wide title

Now, let's look at `EntityExtractor`.

EntityExtractor

This will extract entities such as people, locations, organizations, and more from the node text by using the **span-marker** package. This package is installed automatically together with the `EntityExtractor` integration, so no additional installations are required. It provides the ability to perform **named entity recognition** (**NER**) and relies on a tokenizer provided by the **Natural Language Toolkit** (**NLTK**) package: https://www.nltk.org/.

> **A quick note on NER**
>
> NER is a technique that's used by computers to identify and label specific entities in text, such as people's names, company names, places, and dates. This helps the computer to better understand the content and provides useful context in an RAG scenario.

Here's a code example for using this extractor:

```
from llama_index.core.extractors import EntityExtractor
entity_extractor = EntityExtractor (
    label_entities = True,
    device = "cpu"
)
metadata_list = entity_extractor.extract(nodes)
print(metadata_list)
```

The extractor identifies named entities from the text, labels them, and adds them to the metadata, enabling a retrieval system to focus on nodes with specific references.

> **Practical use case**
>
> Imagine a legal document archive having this metadata attached to each node. This extractor could ease the retrieval of documents mentioning particular people, locations, or organizations, thus providing the best context for our query.

There's a long list of parameters that you can tune for this extractor:

- `model_name`: This sets the name of the model to be used by `SpanMarker`
- `prediction_threshold`: This changes the default 0.5 minimum prediction threshold for named entities. As you may have guessed, entity recognition is usually not a 100% accurate process. However, you can experiment with different values here until you find the best compromise
- `span_joiner`: This changes the default string used to join the spans
- `label_entities`: If set to `True`, it will make the extractor label every entity name with an entity type. This could be useful later, in the retrieval and querying phase. By default, this is set to `False`
- `device`: This controls the device on which the model runs. It defaults to `cpu`, but if your system allows, it can be set to `cuda`
- `entity_map`: This allows you to customize the labels for each entity type. The extractor comes with a predefined entity map that includes labels for people, organizations, places, events, and many others
- `Tokenizer`: This allows you to change the default tokenizer function – which defaults to the NLTK tokenizer

Now, let's discuss how to extract keywords with `KeywordExtractor`.

KeywordExtractor

This extractor extracts important keywords from the text. Let's have a look at an example:

```
from llama_index.core.extractors import KeywordExtractor
key_extractor = KeywordExtractor (keywords=3)
metadata_list = key_extractor.extract(nodes)
print(metadata_list)
```

This one identifies important words or phrases, making it an invaluable tool for retrieving the most relevant nodes based on user queries.

> **Practical use case**
>
> Integrating KeywordExtractor into a content recommendation engine can significantly enhance its effectiveness. By aligning the keywords extracted from content nodes with the terms used in user searches, the engine can more accurately match and recommend content that aligns with user interests. This keyword-based matching ensures that recommendations are not only relevant but also tailored to the specific inquiries or topics users are exploring.

You can customize the number of keywords it generates by changing the keywords parameter to a specific value.

PydanticProgramExtractor

This extractor extracts metadata using a **Pydantic** structure. Have a look here for a complete example of using this extractor: https://docs.llamaindex.ai/en/stable/examples/ metadata_extraction/PydanticExtractor.html#pydantic-extractor.

This *Swiss Army knife* enables the creation of complex and structured metadata schemas with a single LLM call by making use of Pydantic models. One of the main advantages it has over other extractors is that it can pull multiple fields of data using a single LLM call making it a very efficient way to extract metadata. This data will be nicely organized in a model of our design.

> **A quick introduction to Pydantic models**
>
> A **Pydantic model** is like a blueprint or a set of rules that you define as a class in a Python program. It helps you make sure that the data you receive or work with follows certain rules and is in the right format. Think of it as a way to define how your data should look – Pydantic helps you enforce those rules and make sure the data fits in your desired structure.

For example, imagine you have a program that deals with user data such as names, ages, and email addresses. You can create a Pydantic model that specifies that a user's name should be a string, their age should be a number, and their email address should be a valid email format. If input data doesn't follow these rules, Pydantic will raise an error, telling you that the data is not correct. LlamaIndex embraces this mechanism whenever it needs to ensure the consistency and correctness of the data it handles, especially as it often works with complex structures and interrelated data.

MarvinMetadataExtractor

This extractor extracts metadata using the **Marvin AI engineering framework** (`https://www.askmarvin.ai/`). Taking advantage of the Marvin AI engineering framework, this extractor is capable of trustworthy and scalable metadata extraction and augmentation. Its sophistication lies in providing type-safe schemas for text – similar to Pydantic models - but also supporting business logic transformations. You can find a detailed example here: `https://docs.llamaindex.ai/en/stable/examples/metadata_extraction/MarvinMetadataExtractorDemo.html`.

Defining your custom extractor

Just in case none of these ready-made extractors satisfies your needs, you can always define your own extractor function. Here is a simple example of how to define a custom extractor:

```
from llama_index.core.extractors import BaseExtractor
from typing import List, Dict
class CustomExtractor(BaseExtractor):
    async def aextract(self, nodes) -> List[Dict]:
        metadata_list = [
            {
                "node_length":  str(len(node.text))
            }
            for node in nodes
        ]
        return metadata_list
```

This basic extractor measures the length in characters for each node and saves these values in the metadata. Of course, you could replace that with any logic required by your app.

Having so many tools and methods available at our disposal is a great thing. But then a new question arises: *do we need that much metadata?* Let's find out the answer.

Is having all that metadata always a good thing?

Not necessarily. A key detail is that metadata gets injected into the text that's sent to the LLM and embedding model. This can potentially induce some bias in the models. This means that sometimes, you may not want all metadata to be visible. For example, filenames may help embeddings but may *distract* the LLM because the LLM might not understand them as filenames but as other entities instead, and also because the filenames may have no relevance in the context of the prompt. You can selectively hide metadata with the following command:

```
document.excluded_llm_metadata_keys = ["file_name"]
```

This hides `file_name` from the LLM. You can also hide metadata from embeddings if you want:

```
document.excluded_embed_metadata_keys = ["file_name"]
```

Also, you can customize the metadata format like this:

```
document.metadata_template = "{key}::{value}"
```

Here is a pro tip when dealing with metadata mode. LlamaIndex has an enum called `MetadataMode` that controls metadata visibility:

- `MetadataMode.ALL`: Shows all metadata
- `MetadataMode.LLM`: Only metadata visible to the LLM
- `MetadataMode.EMBED`: Only metadata visible to embeddings

You can test the visibility of metadata with the following command:

```
print(document.get_content(metadata_mode=MetadataMode.LLM))
```

So, in summary, metadata gives your data much-needed context. You have full control over its format and visibility to different models. These customizations let you mold metadata to match your use case!

With that topic exhausted, it's time to talk about money.

Estimating the potential cost of using metadata extractors

A key consideration when utilizing the various metadata extractors in LlamaIndex is the associated LLM compute costs. As mentioned earlier, most of these extractors rely on LLMs under the hood to analyze text and generate descriptive metadata.

Repeatedly calling LLMs to process large volumes of text can quickly add up in charges. For example, if you are extracting summaries and keywords from thousands of document nodes using `SummaryExtractor` and `KeywordExtractor`, those constant LLM invocations will carry a significant cost.

Follow these simple best practices to minimize your costs

Let's talk about some common best practices for minimizing your LLM costs:

- Batch content into fewer LLM calls instead of individual calls per node. This amortizes the overhead because you consume fewer tokens compared to multiple separate calls. Using the

Pydantic extractor is very useful for this purpose since it generates multiple fields in a single LLM call

- Use cheaper LLM models with lower compute requirements if full accuracy is not necessary. However, be careful – you may introduce errors in your data, and these errors have the bad habit of propagating and amplifying downstream

- Cache previous extractions and reuse them without having to re-invoke LLMs every time. I'm going to show you how to accomplish that using *ingestion pipelines* later in this chapter, in the *Using the ingestion pipeline to increase efficiency* section

- Restrict metadata extraction only to select subsets of critical nodes rather than full coverage. This may be difficult to implement in an automated scenario

- Consider offline LLMs to eliminate cloud costs. Depending on your hardware, this may or may not be a solution

While these guidelines should help you greatly reduce the extraction costs, it's still a good idea to make sure you run some estimates before processing large datasets.

Estimate your maximal costs before running the actual extractors

Here is a basic example of how we can estimate LLM costs by using a **MockLLM** before running the extractor on the real one:

```
from llama_index.core import
ettings
from llama_index.core.extractors import QuestionsAnsweredExtractor
from llama_index.core.llms.mock import MockLLM
from llama_index.core.schema import TextNode
from llama_index.core.callbacks import (
    CallbackManager,
    TokenCountingHandler
)
llm = MockLLM(max_tokens=256)
counter = TokenCountingHandler(verbose=False)
callback_manager = CallbackManager([counter])
Settings.llm = llm
Settings.callback_manager = CallbackManager([counter])
sample_text = (
    "LlamaIndex is a powerful tool used "
    "to create efficient indices from data."
)
nodes= [TextNode(text=sample_text)]
extractor = QuestionsAnsweredExtractor(
    show_progress=False
```

```
)
Questions_metadata = extractor.extract(nodes)
print(f"Prompt Tokens: {counter.prompt_llm_token_count}")
print(f"Completion Tokens: {counter.completion_llm_token_count}")
print(f"Total Token Count: {counter.total_llm_token_count}")
```

You'll notice that we're using some specialized tools to run the actual estimation. Let's have a quick overview of the code. `MockLLM` – as its name implies – is a stand-in LLM that simulates the behavior of an LLM without any actual API calls.

When you create a `MockLLM` instance, you have the option to set a `max_tokens` parameter. This parameter represents the maximum number of tokens that the mock model is supposed to generate for any given prompt, mirroring the behavior you'd expect from a real language model – but without actually generating any meaningful content.

How does the max_token parameter work?

The goal here is to predict a *worst-case* scenario, but your actual cost will vary depending on the LLM response size and in most regular scenarios should be lower than the `max_tokens` value. It's still a very useful tool because it helps you understand how different metadata extraction strategies applied to different datasets can affect your total cost. For metadata extraction, this total cost will depend on the prompt and response size multiplied by the total number of calls the extractor performs.

CallbackManager is a debugging mechanism that's implemented in LlamaIndex that we will cover in more detail in *Chapter 10, Prompt Engineering Guidelines and Best Practices*. In our example, `CallbackManager` is used in combination with the **TokenCountingHandler** module, which is specialized in counting the tokens that are used for various operations involving an LLM. When defining `TokenCountingHandler`, you can also specify a `tokenizer` parameter.

What is the tokenizer and why do we need it?

The **tokenizer** is responsible for *tokenization* of the text – that is, converting it into tokens – since LLMs work with tokens and also measure their usage using tokens. When running a cost prediction for a specific prompt on a specific LLM, it's important to use a tokenizer that is compatible with that specific LLM. Each LLM is often trained with a particular tokenizer, which determines how the text is split into tokens. Using the correct tokenizer is important if you want to make more accurate cost predictions. By default, LlamaIndex uses the `CL100K` tokenizer, which is specific for GPT-4. So, if you plan on using other LLMs, you may want to customize the tokenizer. More on this topic and on how we can optimize the costs of our RAG app will be covered in *Chapter 10, Prompt Engineering Guidelines and Best Practices*.

Going back to our example, what happens under the hood is that when we run the extractor, it uses `MockLLM` – so, everything stays locally. Then, `TokenCountingHandler` *intercepts* both the prompt and the response from this `MockLLM` and counts the actual number of tokens used.

We will discuss a similar mechanism that can be used for estimating the costs of generating certain types of Indexes and running queries later in *Chapters 5* and *6*.

In this example, I've shown you how to estimate the cost for only one type of extractor, `QuestionsAnsweredExtractor`. If you need to estimate the individual cost for more than one extractor in the same run, you can use the `token_counter.reset_counts()` method to reset the counters to zero before running the next extraction round.

> **The main lesson of this section**
>
> While rich metadata unlocks many capabilities, overuse without conscious optimization can negatively impact operating costs and ruin your day. Make sure you take that into account. Apply best practices to minimize the costs and always estimate before running extractors on large datasets.

Next, let's talk about another very important aspect to consider data privacy.

Preserving privacy with metadata extractors, and not only

Augmenting LLMs with your proprietary data – which, by the way, may belong to your customers in many instances – can prove to be a challenging task in terms of **data privacy**. While a cloud based LLM solution can enrich your proprietary data and offer numerous advantages, *uncontrolled data sharing with external parties can quickly turn into a legal, security, and regulatory nightmare.*

Although the topic of data privacy is more stringent in the case of indexing and querying, utilizing metadata extractors can also raise potential privacy concerns to be aware of. Therefore, I believe a brief warning is required already.

Since most extractors rely on processing content via LLMs to generate metadata, this means your actual data gets transmitted to and analyzed by external cloud services.

There is a risk of exposure or mishandling of any personal or confidential information contained in this data, whether due to security lapses, insider risks at the LLM vendor, or malicious activities.

> **It's not just OUR privacy at stake here**
>
> Speaking of privacy issues, remember the example LlamaHub connectors we discussed earlier? Ingesting messages with `DiscordReader` transfers data from Discord servers. Given that Discord messages may contain private conversations, there is a potential privacy concern, especially if Discord's terms of service and the expectations of the message senders are not taken into account. So, if your data includes private identities, healthcare details, financial information, and so on, allowing unrestrained extraction workflows could be problematic.

Here are some ways to mitigate privacy risks:

- Scrubbing personal data before ingestion into LlamaIndex using, for example, `PIINodePostprocessor` in combination with a local LLM. Check out the next section for a simple implementation guideline for this option

- Restricting metadata extraction to only non-sensitive subsets of nodes. Of course, this assumes that you manually classify the sensitivity of each Node. That would be impractical for automated processing pipelines

- Running LLMs locally instead of in the cloud where possible to limit external exposure. That depends, of course, on your available hardware and model choice

- Enabling encryption mechanisms if such features are available with certain LLM vendors. If privacy is a big concern in your implementation, you might want to consider and read more about **fully homomorphic encryption** (**FHE**): `https://huggingface.co/blog/encrypted-llm`

These concerns and best practices apply to any type of interaction with an LLM. This subject has been discussed and analyzed in many available lectures and articles, so I'm not going to go into further detail here. But that doesn't mean it's not important!

> **Key message**
> What you should understand is that using an LLM already poses a privacy risk for your data. Augmenting that LLM with an additional framework such as LlamaIndex means also augmenting the privacy risks involved.

In essence, additional diligence is needed when dealing with private data to ensure convenience does not override security requirements.

Scrubbing personal data and other sensitive information

In a world filled with nosy onlookers and data rulebooks, it's crucial to be as cautious with your data as a squirrel guarding its acorns in a crowded park! The good news is that there are solutions for ensuring privacy. And a convenient one is already provided by the LlamaIndex framework.

Node post-processors can solve this problem for us.

In the previous chapter, we discovered how node post-processors are used in a query engine. They are applied to the nodes that are returned from a retriever, before the response synthesis step, to apply different transformations on the nodes or node data itself. This is, at least, their most common use case.

> **But there's also another reason to use them**
>
> It turns out we can also use node processors outside of the query engine. Among other things, they can be used to clean up any sensitive data before extracting metadata using external LLMs, for example.

There are two methods available: `PIINodePostprocessor` and `NERPIINodePostprocessor`. The first one is designed to work with any local LLM that you may have on hand, while the other is customized for using a specialized NER model. In case you're not familiar with the acronym, **PII** stands for **Personally Identifiable Information**.

Here's a simple example of using `NERPIINodePostprocessor` to clean up the data. This method uses a NER model from **Hugging Face** to do the job. Because I wanted to keep it simple, I didn't specify a particular model. Therefore, you may expect a warning and the HuggingFaceLLM will probably default to using the `dbmdz/bert-large-cased-finetuned-conll03-english` model, as documented here: `https://huggingface.co/dbmdz/bert-large-cased-finetuned-conll03-english`.

Make sure you install the corresponding integration package first:

```
pip install llama-index-llms-huggingface
```

Also, on the first run, the code will download the model from Hugging Face and you'll need to make sure you have at least 1.5 GB of free space available on your machine.

Here is the code:

```
from llama_index.core.postprocessor import NERPIINodePostprocessor
from llama_index.llms.huggingface import HuggingFaceLLM
from llama_index.core.schema import NodeWithScore, TextNode
original = (
    "Dear Jane Doe. Your address has been recorded in "
    "our database. Please confirm it is valid: 8804 Vista "
    "Serro Dr. Cabo Robles, California(CA)."
)
node = TextNode(text=original)
processor = NERPIINodePostprocessor()
clean_nodes = processor.postprocess_nodes(
    [NodeWithScore(node=node)]
)
print(clean_nodes[0].node.get_text())
```

The output should be similar to this:

```
Dear [PER_5]. Your address has been recorded in our database.
Please confirm it is valid: 8804 [LOC_95] Dr. [LOC_111], [LOC_124]
([LOC_135]).
```

Looking at the results, we can see that the names have been replaced with placeholders so that the data can now be safely passed to any external LLM. The beauty of this method is that, on return, the answer can be processed back and the placeholders can be replaced with the original data, resulting in a seamless user experience.

The actual mapping between placeholders and real data will be stored in `clean_nodes[0].node.metadata`. This metadata will not be sent to the LLM and can later be used to produce the original names during response synthesis.

Next, we'll discuss how to improve the efficiency of the ingestion pipeline.

Using the ingestion pipeline to increase efficiency

Starting with `version 0.9`, the LlamaIndex framework introduced a really neat concept: the so-called **ingestion pipeline**.

> **A simple analogy**
>
> An ingestion pipeline is a bit like a conveyor belt in a factory. In the context of LlamaIndex, it's a setup that takes your raw data and gets it ready to be integrated into your RAG workflow. It does this by running the data through a series of steps – called **transformations** – one by one. The key idea is to break the ingestion process into a series of reusable transformations that are applied to input data. This helps standardize and customize ingestion flows for different use cases. Think of transformations as different workstations along this conveyor belt. As your raw data moves along, it hits different stations where something specific happens. It might be split into sentences at one station – that's your `SentenceSplitter` – and have a title extracted at another – such as using `TitleExtractor`.

If the factory's default workstations don't quite cut it for you, no worries! Let's say you have this special tool you want to use on your raw data. LlamaIndex makes it easy to plug in your custom tool – **custom transformation**. Just say what your tool does – for example, replacing acronyms with complete names using a dictionary – and LlamaIndex will happily add it to your pipeline. *Figure 4.4* provides an ingestion pipeline schematic:

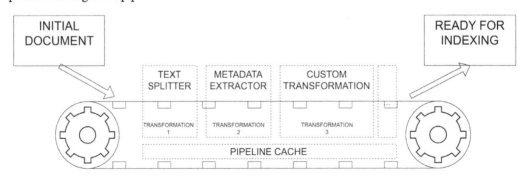

Figure 4.4 – An ingestion pipeline at work

The most important thing about the ingestion pipeline is that *it remembers the data it has already processed*. It runs a hashing function on the combination of each node data and each transformation run. On any future runs of the same transformation on the same nodes, the hashes will be identical, so the cached, already processed data will be used instead of re-running the transformation.

> **What does this mean for me?**
>
> If you send the same document through the pipeline again, it's like having a fast-track lane where it skips the line because it's already been handled. This is cool because it saves you both time and money by avoiding useless multiple processing of the same data.

By default, the cache is stored locally but you can customize the storage options and use any external database provider you prefer. Let's cover an example of how the pipeline could be implemented. I will explain the code section by section to make it easier to follow.

Let's start with the first section of the code:

```
from llama_index.core import SimpleDirectoryReader
from llama_index.core.extractors import
SummaryExtractor,QuestionsAnsweredExtractor
from llama_index.core.node_parser import TokenTextSplitter
from llama_index.core.ingestion import IngestionPipeline,
IngestionCache
from llama_index.core.schema import TransformComponent
class CustomTransformation(TransformComponent):
    def __call__(self, nodes, **kwargs):
        # run any node transformation logic here
        return nodes
```

After taking care of the required imports, to show you how to customize your pipeline, I have defined a class called `CustomTransformation`. This will be fed into the pipeline later. In my example, no actual processing takes place, so this will return the nodes unchanged.

Let's continue with the second section:

```
reader = SimpleDirectoryReader('files')
documents = reader.load_data()
try:
    cached_hashes = IngestionCache.from_persist_path(
"./ingestion_cache.json"
)
    print("Cache file found. Running using cache...")
except:
    cached_hashes = ""
    print("No cache file found. Running without cache...")
```

The preceding code is responsible for fetching all content of the `files` subfolder into documents. Next, the code checks if the cache file already exists and attempts to load it into memory. Remember, the cache file contains the hashes and the results generated by the previous runs. The first time you run the code, there will be no file, so the code won't load any cached values.

Let's move on to the third section:

```
pipeline = IngestionPipeline(
    transformations = [
        CustomTransformation(),
        TokenTextSplitter(
            separator=" ",
            chunk_size=512,
            chunk_overlap=128),
        SummaryExtractor(),
        QuestionsAnsweredExtractor(
            questions=3
        )
    ],
    cache=cached_hashes
)
```

This is the part where we define our pipeline. As you can see, it will contain four transformations. The first is our `CustomTransformation`, followed by `TokenTextSplitter`, which is responsible for breaking each document into smaller chunks and generating nodes. The third transformation extracts the summaries metadata and the last one extracts a set of questions that each node can answer.

If you want to take a peek at the result, you could add `print(nodes[0])` at the end of the entire script. Notice that, in the `cache` parameter, we also specify the source of the cache for the pipeline. If that is empty, it will be ignored; otherwise, it will be used to avoid any unnecessary processing by retrieving values from the cache.

And now, the final part:

```
nodes = pipeline.run(
    documents=documents,
    show_progress=True,
)
pipeline.cache.persist("./ingestion_cache.json")
print("All documents loaded")
```

This is where we run the pipeline with the `show_progress` option set to `True`. This will make the pipeline's progress visible and help you better understand what's happening in the background. In the end, we save the results in the cache file to avoid re-processing in the next run.

> **A quick side note:**
> Even if you saved a cache file, any changes you make in your pipeline logic will not be cached and will have to be processed at the next run.

You should also know there is an alternative to manually defining and running the pipeline every time you want to ingest more data. Just like with the node parsers, we can define the transformations inside `Settings` like this:

```
from llama_index.core import Settings
Settings.transformations = [
    CustomTransformation(),
    TokenTextSplitter(
        separator=" ",
        chunk_size=512,
        chunk_overlap=128
    ),
    SummaryExtractor(),
    QuestionsAnsweredExtractor(
        questions=3
    )
]
```

In conclusion, an ingestion pipeline is a super-efficient way to get your data automatically prepped and polished by running it through customizable sets of transformations until it's just right for your app or database.

As we build up the PITS tutoring app, we'll leverage ingestion pipelines and you'll get the opportunity to experiment more with this concept.

Next, let's talk about more complex scenarios.

Handling documents that contain a mix of text and tabular data

Data is not always simple. Many real-world documents, such as research papers, financial reports, and others, contain a mix of unstructured text, as well as structured tabular data in tables. Ingesting such heterogeneous documents presents an additional challenge - we need to not only extract text but also identify, parse, and process tables embedded within the text. Because, sometimes you get tables, sometimes you get text and sometimes you have to deal with a mix of both.

LlamaIndex provides `UnstructuredElementNodeParser` to tackle such documents containing both free-form text as well as tables and other structured elements. It leverages the `Unstructured` library to analyze the document layout and delineate text sections from tables.

This parser works exclusively on HTML files and can extract two types of nodes:

- **Text nodes**: Containing the text chunks

- **Table nodes**: Containing the table data and metadata, such as coordinates

Storing these elements as separate nodes allows more modular and meaningful processing later in the RAG workflow. The text can be indexed and searched normally with elements like keywords. The tables can be loaded into a **pandas DataFrame** or any structured database for SQL-based access. So, in complex cases involving mixed data types, leveraging `UnstructuredElementNodeParser` before ingestion enables better data organization.

You can find a complete demo for using `UnstructuredElementNodeParser` in the official LlamaIndex documentation: `https://docs.llamaindex.ai/en/stable/examples/query_engine/sec_tables/tesla_10q_table.html`.

With these new concepts in our toolbox, let's continue building our tutoring project.

Hands-on – ingesting study materials into our PITS

It's time for some practice. We now have everything we need to continue building our project. Let's write the `documend_uploader.py` module.

This module will take care of ingesting and preparing our available study material. The user can upload any available books, technical documentation, or existing articles to provide more context to our tutor.

1. First, we have the imports:

   ```
   from global_settings import STORAGE_PATH, CACHE_FILE
   from logging_functions import log_action
   from llama_index import SimpleDirectoryReader, VectorStoreIndex
   from llama_index.ingestion import IngestionPipeline,
   IngestionCache
   from llama_index.text_splitter import TokenTextSplitter
   from llama_index.extractors import SummaryExtractor
   from llama_index.embeddings import OpenAIEmbedding
   ```

2. Next, we must define the main function that's responsible for handling the ingestion process. You'll notice that it uses an ingestion pipeline to both streamline the code but also benefit from caching:

   ```
   def ingest_documents():
       documents = SimpleDirectoryReader(
           STORAGE_PATH,
           filename_as_id = True
       ).load_data()
   ```

```
for doc in documents:
    print(doc.id_)
    log_action(
        f"File '{doc.id_}' uploaded user",
        action_type="UPLOAD"
    )
```

- The function loads all readable documents available in STORAGE_PATH, which was defined in global_settings.py.

- For each document processed, a new event is stored in our log file using log_action from logging_functions.py.

3. Next, the function checks if there's already cached pipeline data to use:

```
try:
    cached_hashes = IngestionCache.from_persist_path(
        CACHE_FILE
    )
    print("Cache file found. Running using cache...")
except:
    cached_hashes = ""
    print("No cache file found. Running without...")
```

4. The next step is to define and run the pipeline. If hashes from the cache file correspond, no operations should be processed; instead, the values will be directly loaded from the cache:

```
pipeline = IngestionPipeline(
    transformations=[
        TokenTextSplitter(
            chunk_size=1024,
            chunk_overlap=20
        ),
        SummaryExtractor(summaries=['self']),
        OpenAIEmbedding()
    ],
    cache=cached_hashes
)
nodes = pipeline.run(documents=documents)
pipeline.cache.persist(CACHE_FILE)
return nodes
```

We run three transformations in the pipeline:

I.   Basic chunking using `TokenTextSplitter`.

II.   A metadata extractor that summarizes each node.

III. Embedding generation using `OpenAIEmbedding`. Don't worry about this step for now. I will explain it thoroughly in *Chapter 5, Indexing with LlamaIndex*.

5. In the end, the function saves the current data in the cache file and returns the processed nodes.

That's it for now. We have now uploaded and prepared the study materials for future processing. We'll continue with the indexing part in the next chapter.

Summary

LlamaHub offers a variety of pre-built data loaders, streamlining the process of importing data from various sources as documents. This eliminates the need for creating unique parsers for different data formats.

After data is imported, it undergoes further processing into nodes, and we discussed various customization options available.

There's a broad range of options for metadata extraction, and the parsing process can be tailored to meet specific requirements.

Developing pipelines for data ingestion is an invaluable tool for enhancing the efficiency, both in terms of cost and time, of our RAG applications. It's also vital to keep privacy considerations in mind.

With data ingestion completed, let's continue our journey and discover the indexing powers of LlamaIndex.

5

Indexing with LlamaIndex

This chapter provides an in-depth look at the different types of indexes available in LlamaIndex. It explains how indexes work, and their key capabilities, customization options, underlying architectures, and use cases. Overall, this chapter serves as a guide for leveraging the indexing functionality within LlamaIndex to build performant and scalable RAG systems. Let's get started!

Throughout this chapter, we'll cover the following topics:

- Indexing data – a bird's-eye view
- Understanding the Vector Store Index
- Understanding embeddings
- Persisting and re-using Indexes
- Exploring other Index types in LlamaIndex
- Building Indexes on top of other Indexes with ComposableGraph
- Estimating the potential cost of building and querying Indexes

Technical requirements

For this chapter, you will need to install the following package in your environment:

- *ChromaDB*: `https://www.trychroma.com/`

In addition, there are two integration packages that will be required by the sample code:

- *Chroma Vector Store*: `https://pypi.org/project/llama-index-vector-stores-chroma/`
- *Hugging Face embeddings*: `https://pypi.org/project/llama-index-embeddings-huggingface/`

All code samples from this chapter can be found in the `ch5` subfolder of the book's GitHub repository: `https://github.com/PacktPublishing/Building-Data-Driven-Applications-with-LlamaIndex`

Indexing data – a bird's-eye view

We briefly discussed the importance and general functioning of Indexes in a RAG application in *Chapter 3*, in the section titled *Uncovering the essential building blocks of LlamaIndex – documents, nodes, indexes*. Now, it is time to have a closer look at the different indexing methods available in LlamaIndex with their advantages, disadvantages, and specific use cases.

In principle, data can be accessed even without an Index. But it's like reading a book without a table of contents. As long as it's about a story that has continuity and can be read sequentially, section by section, and chapter by chapter, reading will be a pleasure. However, things change when we need to quickly search for a specific topic in that book. Without a table of contents, the search process will be slow and cumbersome.

In LlamaIndex, however, **Indexes** represent more than just a simple table of contents. An Index provides not only the necessary structure for navigation but also the concrete mechanisms to update or access it. That includes the logic for the **retrievers** and the mechanisms used for fetching data, which we will discuss in detail during *Chapter 6*, *Querying Our Data, Part 1 – Context Retrieval*.

In this book, I've kept things simple, giving you the basics of how Indexes work and providing some examples to help you understand their usage. Exploring every possible way to use and mix these Indexes would be a huge task and that's not what we're about here.

We'll talk later about what makes each type of Index unique, but first, let's see what they all have in common.

Common features of all Index types

Each type of Index in LlamaIndex has its own characteristics and functions, but because all of them inherit the `BaseIndex` class, there are certain features and parameters they share, which can be customized for any kind of Index:

- **Nodes**: All Indexes are based on nodes and we can choose which Nodes are included in the Index. Plus, all Index types provide methods to insert new Nodes or delete existing ones, allowing for dynamic updates to the Index as your data changes. We can either build an Index from pre-existing Nodes by providing the Nodes directly to the Index constructor like this `vector_index = VectorStoreIndex(nodes)` or we can provide a list of documents as an input using `from_documents()` and let the Index extract the Nodes by itself. Keep in mind that we can use `Settings` – before actually building the Index – to customize its underlying mechanics. As we discussed during *Chapter 3* in the *Understanding how settings can be used for customization* section, this simple class allows for different settings such as changing the LLM, embedding model, or default Node parser used by an Index.

- **The storage context**: The storage context defines how and where the data (documents and nodes) for the Index is stored. This customization is crucial for managing data storage efficiently, depending on the application's requirements.

- **Progress display**: The `show_progress` option lets us choose whether to display progress bars during long-running operations such as building the Index. Implemented using the `tqdm` Python library, this feature can be useful for monitoring the progress of large indexing tasks.

- **Different retrieval modes**: Each Index allows for different pre-defined retrieval modes, which can be set to match the specific needs of your application. And you can also customize or extend the Retriever classes to change how queries are processed and how results are retrieved from the Index. More on that during *Chapter 6, Querying Our Data, Part 1 – Context Retrieval.*

- **Asynchronous operations**: The `use_async` parameter implemented by some of the Indexes determines whether certain operations should be performed asynchronously. Asynchronous processing allows the system to manage multiple operations concurrently, rather than waiting for each operation to be completed sequentially. This can be important for performance optimization, especially when dealing with large datasets or complex operations.

> Quick note
>
> An important thing to consider before diving further and starting to tinker with the sample code is that indexing often relies on LLM calls for summarizing or embedding purposes. Just like in the case of metadata extraction, which we covered in *Chapter 4, Ingesting Data into Our RAG Workflow*, indexing in LlamaIndex may also raise cost and privacy concerns. Make sure you read the cost-related section at the end of this chapter before running any large-scale experiments to test your ideas.

Let's start with our first and most frequently used Index type.

Understanding the VectorStoreIndex

In LlamaIndex, the `VectorStoreIndex` stands out as the workhorse, being the most commonly utilized type of Index.

For most RAG applications, a `VectorStoreIndex` might be the best solution because it facilitates the construction of Indexes on collections of Documents where **embeddings** for the input text chunks are stored within the **Vector Store** of the Index. Once constructed, this Index can be used for efficient querying because it allows for **similarity searches** over the embedded representations of the text, making it highly suitable for applications requiring fast retrieval of relevant information from a large collection of data. Don't worry if you're not yet familiar with terms such as embeddings, vector store, or similarity searching, because we'll cover them in the following sections. The `VectorStoreIndex` class in LlamaIndex supports these operations by default and also allows for asynchronous calls and progress tracking, which can improve performance and user experience in typical RAG scenarios.

A simple usage example for the VectorStoreIndex

Here's the most basic way of constructing a `VectorStoreIndex`

```
from llama_index.core import VectorStoreIndex, SimpleDirectoryReader
documents = SimpleDirectoryReader("files").load_data()
index = VectorStoreIndex.from_documents(documents)
print("Index created successfully!")
```

As you can see, in just a few lines of code, we have ingested the Documents and the `VectorStoreIndex` took care of everything. Note that using this approach, we have skipped the Node parsing step entirely, because the Index did that by itself by using the `from_documents()` method.

There are several parameters that we can customize for the `VectorStoreIndex`:

- `use_async`: This parameter enables asynchronous calls. By default, it is set to `False`.

- `show_progress`: This parameter shows progress bars during Index construction. The default value is `False`.

- `store_nodes_override`: This parameter forces LlamaIndex to store Node objects in the Index store and document store, even if the vector store keeps text. This can be useful in scenarios where you need direct access to Node objects, even if their content is already stored in the vector store. We'll talk in more detail about the Index store, document store, and vector store later in this chapter. The default setting for this parameter is `False`.

Let's have a look at *Figure 5.1* for a visual representation of this type of Index:

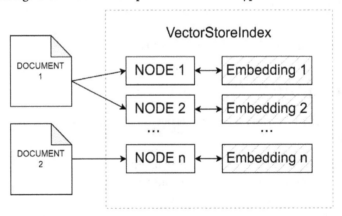

Figure 5.1 – The structure of a VectorStoreIndex

The `VectorStoreIndex` took the ingested Documents, breaking them down into Nodes. It used the default parameters for text splitter, chunk size, chunk overlap, and so on. Of course, we could have customized all these parameters if we wanted to.

> **Note**
> **Fixed-size chunking** simply splits text into same-sized chunks, optionally with some overlap. Although computationally cheap and simple to implement, this simple chunking may not always be the best approach. Performance testing various chunk sizes is key to optimizing for an application's particular needs.

The nodes containing chunks of the original text were then *embedded* into a high-dimensional vector space using a language model. The embedded vectors were stored within the vector store component of the Index. Next, when a query is made, the query text will be similarly embedded and compared against the stored vectors using a **similarity measure** identified with a method called **cosine similarity**. The most similar vectors – and thus the most relevant document chunks – will be returned as the query result. This process enables rapid, semantically aware retrieval of information, leveraging the mathematical properties of vector spaces to find the documents that best answer the user's query.

Sounds a bit confusing? Let's go through these concepts together in the next section.

Understanding embeddings

In simple terms, **vector embeddings** represent a machine-understandable data format. They capture meaning and may conceptually represent a word, an entire document, or even non-textual information such as images and sounds. In a way, embeddings represent a standard language of thought for an LLM. In the context of an LLM, they serve as a foundational representation through which the model understands and processes information. They transform diverse and complex data into a uniform, high-dimensional space where the LLM can perform operations such as comparison, association, and prediction more effectively. *Figure 5.2* provides an illustration of the process of embedding data:

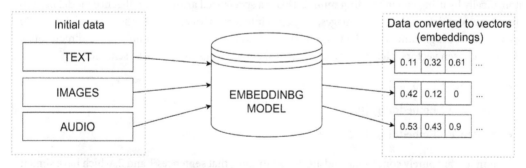

Figure 5.2 – How an embedding model converts data into numerical representations

Because it's all about math under the hood. And math works well with numbers – more precisely, large lists of floating-point numbers, where each number represents a dimension in a hypothetical vector space. The LLM can work with these arrays of numbers to understand, interpret, and generate responses based on the input it receives. Essentially, these numbers in the vector embeddings allow the LLM to *see* and *think* about the data in a way that's meaningful and structured.

The beauty of this system lies in its ability to handle ambiguity and complexity. The model can understand semantic relationships between words, such as synonyms, antonyms, and more complex linguistic patterns. In the case of polysemous words, the same word can have different meanings in different contexts. For example, the word *bank* can refer to the side of a river or a financial institution. Vector embeddings help the LLM understand these nuances by providing context-sensitive representations. So, in one situation, *bank* might be closely associated with words such as *river* and *shore*, while in another, it's more closely linked to *money* and *account*.

> **Quick note**
>
> An important factor to consider is that the size of text chunks being embedded impacts precision – too small and context is lost; too large and all that additional detail may dilute the meaning.

In case you're not very familiar with embeddings yet, the following example could be useful to get a better grasp of the concept. Let's assign some *arbitrary* vector embeddings to three randomly chosen sentences:

- **Sentence 1**: The quick brown fox jumps over the lazy dog
- **Sentence 2**: A fast dark-colored fox leaps above a sleepy canine
- **Sentence 3**: Apples are sweet and crunchy

In a real-world scenario, the embeddings associated with each of these sentences would be calculated automatically by using an **embedding model**. This is a specialized artificial intelligence model used to convert complex data such as text, images, or graphs into a numerical format. The embeddings would also normally be high-dimensional, but for the sake of explanation, I'll use simple, three-dimensional, arbitrarily chosen vectors. Here are the hypothetical embeddings for the three sentences:

- **Sentence 1 Embedding**: [0.8, 0.1, 0.3]
- **Sentence 2 Embedding**: [0.79, 0.14, 0.32]
- **Sentence 3 Embedding**: [0.2, 0.9, 0.5]

These numbers are purely conceptual and are meant to show that sentences 1 and 2, which have similar meanings, have embeddings that are closer to each other in vector space. *Sentence 3*, which has a different meaning, has an embedding that is farther away from the first two. Have a look at *Figure 5.3* for a straightforward visual comparison of the three embeddings:

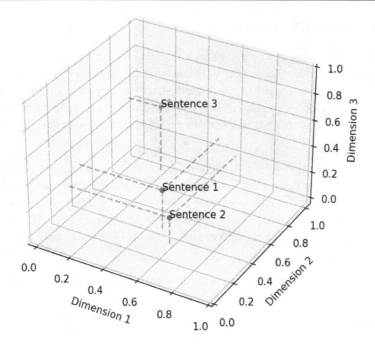

Figure 5.3 – A comparison of the three embedded sentences in a 3D space

When we visualize them in a three-dimensional space, sentences 1 and 2 are plotted near each other, while sentence 3 will be plotted at a distance. This spatial representation is what allows machine learning models to determine semantic similarity.

When you search using a query on a vector store Index in order to retrieve useful context, LlamaIndex converts your search terms into a similar embedding and then finds the closest matches among the pre-computed embeddings of your text chunks.

We call this process **similarity** or **distance search**. So, when you encounter the term **top-k similarity search**, you should know that it relies on an algorithm that calculates the similarity between vector embeddings. It takes a vector embedding as an input and returns the most similar k number of vectors found in the vector store. Because the initial vector and the *top-k* returned neighbors are similar to each other, we can consider their meanings to be conceptually similar. Now you understand why I have previously called embeddings a *standard language of thought* for an LLM. It doesn't really matter anymore whether they represent text, images, or any other types of information. We measure their similarity in numbers.

The only thing that may be implemented differently, depending on our use case, is the actual formula for defining that distance or similarity.

Spoiler alert: a bit of mathematical concepts up next.

Understanding similarity search

In the realms of machine learning and deep learning, the concept of similarity search is very important. It forms the backbone of many applications, from recommendation systems and information retrieval to clustering and classification tasks. As models and systems interact with high-dimensional data, identifying patterns and relationships between data points becomes essential. This involves measuring how *close* or *similar* data elements are, a task that often takes place in a vector space where each item is represented as a vector.

Locating points in this space that are near each other enables machines to assess similarity and, by extension, to make decisions, draw inferences, or, in our case, retrieve information based on that assessment of closeness. With the advent of embeddings in deep learning, the need for effective similarity search has grown. As embeddings capture the semantic meaning of the data they represent, performing similarity searches on these vectors allows machines to understand content at a level approaching human cognition.

Let's explore the methods that LlamaIndex currently employs to measure the similarity between vectors, each with its unique advantages and applicability.

Cosine similarity

This method measures the cosine of *the angle* between two vectors. Imagine two arrows pointing in different directions; the smaller the angle between them, the more similar they are.

Have a look at *Figure 5.4*, which depicts a cosine similarity comparison between two vectors:

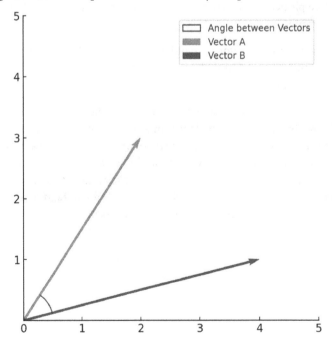

Figure 5.4 – How a cosine similarity comparison would look

In terms of embeddings, a small angle (or a high cosine similarity score, close to 1) indicates that the content they represent is similar. This method is particularly useful in text analysis because it is less affected by the length of the documents and focuses more on their direction or orientation in the vector space.

> **Note**
>
> Cosine similarity is also the default method used by LlamaIndex for calculating similarity between embeddings.

Dot product

Also called the **scalar product**, because it is represented by a single value, this is another method of calculating how well two vectors align with each other. To calculate the scalar product of two vectors, the algorithm multiplies the corresponding elements of the vectors and then sums these products.

Let's take a simple example of *vector A*: [2,3] and *vector B*: [4,1]. The **dot product** is calculated by multiplying their corresponding elements: (2×4) + (3×1), which gives us 8 + 3 = 11. Thus, the dot product of these two vectors is 11.

Figure 5.5 exemplifies this concept:

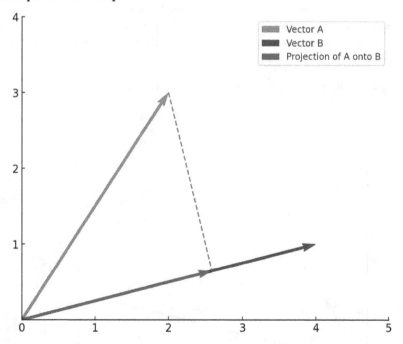

Figure 5.5 – Calculating similarity using the dot product method

In the preceding diagram, the dot product is visualized by projecting one vector onto the other. This projection illustrates the geometric interpretation of the dot product. It's calculated by projecting the components of one vector in the direction of the other and then multiplying these projected components by the corresponding components of the second vector. The sum of these products gives us the dot product. This visualization helps us understand that the dot product is not just a measure of how vectors point in the same direction; it also incorporates their lengths.

Higher values of the dot product mean higher similarities between vectors. In contrast with the cosine method, the dot product is sensitive both to the length of the two vectors compared and their relative direction. Unlike the dot product, cosine similarity normalizes the dot product by the magnitudes of the vectors. This normalization makes cosine similarity solely a measure of the directional alignment between vectors, independent of their lengths.

The longer the vectors, the higher the result, and this is an important thing to consider in a RAG scenario. Longer vectors, which might represent longer documents or more detailed information, could dominate the retrieved results due to their inherently larger dot product values. This could bias the system toward retrieving longer documents, even if they are not the most relevant.

Euclidean distance

This method is different from the dot product and cosine similarity methods. While those methods look at the angle or alignment between vectors, **Euclidean distance** is all about how close the actual values of the vectors are to each other. This can be especially useful when the values in the vectors represent actual counts or measurements, especially where the vector dimensions have real-world physical interpretations.

Take a look at *Figure 5.6* for a visual representation of Euclidean distance:

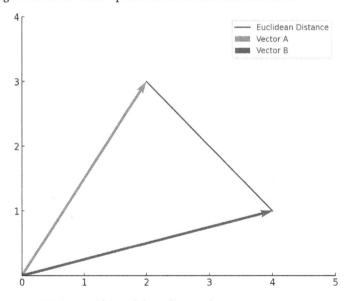

Figure 5.6 – The Euclidean distance between two vectors

You should now have a foundational understanding of embeddings, how vector similarity works, and, in particular, how they are implemented in LlamaIndex. If you want to familiarize yourself better with this concept, you can find more information on the web.

Here are some suggested additional reading resources you could start with: `https://developers.google.com/machine-learning/clustering/similarity/measuring-similarity`

OK, but how does LlamaIndex generate these embeddings?

The short answer is, *however, you prefer*. By default, the framework is configured to rely on OpenAI's `text-embedding-ada-002` model. This model has been trained to produce embeddings that effectively capture semantic meanings of the text, enabling applications such as semantic search, topic clustering, anomaly detection, and others. It provides a very good balance between quality, performance, and cost. LlamaIndex uses this model by default to embed documents during Index construction as well as for query embeddings.

Sometimes, though, when you may want to index large volumes of data, the cost associated with a hosted model such as this one may be too high for your budget. In other instances, you might be concerned about the privacy of your proprietary data and prefer to use a local model instead. Or maybe, in some cases, you may want to use more specialized models for a particular topic or technical domain.

The great news is that LlamaIndex also supports a variety of other embedding models. For example, if you wish to use local models, you can set the service context to use a local embedding, which uses a well-balanced default model provided by *Hugging Face* (`https://huggingface.co/BAAI/bge-small-en-v1.5`). This can be particularly useful if you aim to reduce costs or have requirements to process data locally.

A brief introduction to Hugging Face

Hugging Face is a very important resource in the AI field, primarily known for its extensive collection of pre-trained machine learning models, especially in **natural language processing** (**NLP**). Its importance lies in democratizing access to state-of-the-art AI models, tools, and techniques, enabling developers and researchers to implement advanced AI functionalities with relative ease. Similar to GitHub, Hugging Face embraces a community-driven approach, where users can share, collaborate on, and improve AI models, much like developers share and contribute to code repositories on GitHub. This community-centric model accelerates innovation and dissemination of AI advancements.

Before running the next sample, make sure you install the necessary integration:

```
pip install llama-index-embeddings-huggingface
```

This example will show you how to set up a local embedding model:

```
from llama_index.embeddings.huggingface import HuggingFaceEmbedding
embedding_model = HuggingFaceEmbedding(
    model_name="WhereIsAI/UAE-Large-V1"
)
embeddings = embedding_model.get_text_embedding(
    "The quick brown fox jumps over the lazy cat!"
)
print(embeddings[:15])
```

On the first run, the code will download the `Universal AngIE Embedding` model from Hugging Face. This is one of the best-performing embedding models at the moment, offering great overall performance and quality balance.

More info is available here: `https://huggingface.co/WhereIsAI/UAE-Large-V1`.

After downloading and initializing the embedding model, the script calculates the embeddings for the sentence and displays the first 15 values of the vector.

For advanced users or specific applications, LlamaIndex makes it easy to integrate custom embedding models. You can simply extend the `BaseEmbedding` class provided by LlamaIndex and implement your own logic for generating embeddings.

Here, you can find an example of how to define your custom embedding class: `https://docs.llamaindex.ai/en/stable/examples/embeddings/custom_embeddings.html`.

Apart from OpenAI and local models, there are integrations with Langchain, enabling you to use any embedding model they offer. You also have the option to use embedding models from Azure, CohereAI, and other providers through additional integrations offered by LlamaIndex. This great flexibility ensures that no matter your needs or constraints, you can configure LlamaIndex to use an embedding model that is suitable for your application.

How do I decide which embedding model I should use?

The choice of embedding model can significantly affect the performance, quality, and cost of your RAG app. Here are some key points to consider when choosing a particular model:

- **Qualitative performance**: Different embedding models may encode the semantics of the text in different ways. While embeddings of models such as OpenAI's Ada are designed to have a broad understanding of text, other models might be fine-tuned on specific domains or tasks and would outperform in those scenarios. Domain-specific models could lead to more accurate representations of specialized topics

- **Quantitative performance**: This includes factors such as how well the model captures semantic similarity, its performance on benchmarks, and generalization to unseen data. This can vary considerably between different models and domains of application. For a general benchmark of the most popular models, you can consult the **Massive Text Embedding Benchmark (MTEB)** Leaderboard (`https://huggingface.co/spaces/mteb/leaderboard`) on the Hugging Face website.

- **Latency and throughput**: For applications with real-time constraints or large volumes of data, the speed of the embedding model could be a deciding factor. Also consider the maximum input chunk sizes that models can handle, which impacts how text is divided for embedding. Keep in mind that your Nodes will have embeddings computed during ingestion, so that will not affect your overall application performance. However, during retrieval, each query will have to be embedded in real time so that similarity can be measured and the relevant nodes can be retrieved. This is where latency and throughput become important.

  To get an idea of how different embedding models may perform, have a look at this article: `https://blog.getzep.com/text-embedding-latency-a-semi-scientific-look/`.

- **Multilingual support**: Embedding models can be multilingual or trained for a specific language. Depending on your use case, this can also become an important decision factor. For example, smaller models such as `Mistral` could provide excellent results on par with hosted models such as GPT 3.5 for English data, but their performance in other languages is clearly inferior

- **Resource requirements**: Embedding models can vary greatly in size and computational expense. Large models might provide more accurate embeddings but may require substantially more computational resources and thus lead to higher costs.

- **Availability**: Some embedding models may only be available through certain APIs or require specific software to be installed, which could affect ease of integration and usage. Fortunately, you have a high degree of customization available in LlamaIndex.

- **On-device or local usage**: You may prefer to use a local model when data privacy is a concern or when operating in an environment with limited or no internet access.

- **Usage cost**: Consider the cost associated with API calls for cloud-based, hosted embedding models versus the computational and storage costs of local embedding models.

The good news is that LlamaIndex supports many out-of-the-box embedding models and provides flexibility to use various embeddings.

By the way, a complete list of supported models can be found here: `https://docs.llamaindex.ai/en/stable/module_guides/models/embeddings.html#list-of-supported-embeddings`

For most use cases, though, OpenAI's default embedding model – text-embedding-ada-002 – will provide you with a good balance between all the parameters we've discussed. However, if you have specific needs or constraints, you might benefit from exploring and benchmarking different models to see which provides the best outcomes for your particular application.

Now that we know about embeddings, let us shift our focus to how to store and reuse them.

Persisting and reusing Indexes

An important question arises – where exactly can we store the vector embeddings generated during the indexing process?

Storing them is important for multiple reasons:

- Avoid the computational cost of re-embedding documents and rebuilding Indexes in every session. Generating high-quality embeddings for large document collections requires significant processing that can become costly over time. Persisting Indexes preserves these precomputed artifacts

- Enable low-latency processing. Avoiding runtime embedding and indexing by loading the already computed embeddings allows applications to get up and running much faster

- Maintain query consistency and accuracy. Reloading an Index guarantees we reuse the exact vectors and structure used in the previous sessions. This promises consistent and accurate query execution

If we want to avoid regenerating them on each run, these vector embeddings need to reside somewhere – a repository, if you will – that allows for efficient storage and retrieval.

This is the job of a vector store within LlamaIndex.

By default, LlamaIndex uses an in-memory vector store, but for persistence, it offers a straightforward approach using the .persist() method available for any type of Index. This method writes all data to disk at a specified location, ensuring persistence.

Let's see how we can persist and then load the vector embeddings. First, we create our Index, which handles the embedding of documents:

```
from llama_index.core import VectorStoreIndex, SimpleDirectoryReader
documents = SimpleDirectoryReader("data").load_data()
index = VectorStoreIndex.from_documents(documents)
```

To persist this data, we use the persist() method:

```
index.storage_context.persist(persist_dir="index_cache")
print("Index persisted to disk.")
```

This saves the entire Index data to disk. In future sessions, we can easily reload the data:

```
from llama_index.core import StorageContext, load_index_from_storage
storage_context = StorageContext.from_defaults(
    persist_dir="index_cache")
index = load_index_from_storage(storage_context)
print("Index loaded successfully!")
```

By rebuilding a `StorageContext` from the persisted directory and using `load_index_from_storage`, we can effectively reconstitute our Index without needing to re-index our data.

Understanding the StorageContext

The `StorageContext` serves as the unifying custodian over configurable storage components used during indexing and querying. Its key components are as follows:

- The **Document store** (`docstore`): This manages the storage of documents. The data is locally stored in a file named `docstore.json`.

- The **Index Store** (`index_store`): This manages the storage of Index structures. Indexes are stored locally in a file called `index_store.json`.

- **Vector Stores** (`vector_stores`): This is a dictionary managing multiple vector stores, each potentially serving a different purpose. The vector stores are stored locally in `vector_store.json`.

- The **Graph Store** (`graph_store`): This manages the storage of graph data structures. A file named `graph_store.json` is automatically created by LlamaIndex for storing the graphs.

The `StorageContext` class encapsulates document, vector, index, and graph data stores under one umbrella. The files mentioned in the previous list for locally storing the data are automatically created by LlamaIndex when we invoke the `persist()` method. If we prefer not to save them in the current folder, we can provide a specific persistence location from where we can load them in future sessions.

Out-of-the-box, LlamaIndex offers basic local stores, but we can swap them with more capable persistence solutions such as *AWS S3*, *Pinecone*, *MongoDB*, and others.

As an example, let's explore customizing vector storage using ChromaDB, an efficient open source vector engine.

First, make sure you install `chromadb` using pip:

```
pip install chromadb
```

The first part of the code takes care of the necessary imports:

```
import chromadb
from llama_index.vector_stores.chroma import ChromaVectorStore
from llama_index.core import (
    VectorStoreIndex, SimpleDirectoryReader, StorageContext)
```

We then continue by initializing the Chroma client and creating a collection within Chroma to store our data:

```
db = chromadb.PersistentClient(path="chroma_database")
chroma_collection = db.get_or_create_collection(
    "my_chroma_store"
)
```

In ChromaDB, we create **collections** to store data. These are similar to *tables* in relational databases. The my_chroma_store collection will hold our embeddings.

Next, we initialize a tailored vector store using ChromaVectorStore and wire it into the StorageContext:

```
vector_store = ChromaVectorStore(
    chroma_collection=chroma_collection
)
storage_context = StorageContext.from_defaults(
    vector_store=vector_store
)
```

We're now ready to ingest our documents and build the Index:

```
documents = SimpleDirectoryReader("files").load_data()
index = VectorStoreIndex.from_documents(
    documents=documents,
    storage_context=storage_context
)
```

We can now use the get() method to display the entire contents of the Chroma collection:

```
results = chroma_collection.get()
print(results)
```

Subsequently, restoring this Index in future sessions is also very simple:

```
index = VectorStoreIndex.from_vector_store(
    vector_store=vector_store,
    storage_context=storage_context
)
```

We just rebuilt our original Index.

By wrapping **vector databases** such as ChromaDB, LlamaIndex makes enterprise-scale vector storage accessible through a simple storage abstraction. The complexity is concealed, enabling you to focus on your application logic while still leveraging industrial-strength data infrastructure.

In summary, LlamaIndex provides flexibility in vector storage – from a simple in-memory store for testing to cloud-hosted databases for large, real-world deployments. And through storage integrations, swapping any component is a breeze!

The difference between vector stores and vector databases

The terms vector store and vector database are often used in the context of managing and querying large sets of vectors, which are commonly used in machine learning, particularly in applications involving NLP, image recognition, and similar tasks. You may have already noticed that I'm using them quite often in this chapter, sometimes implying they are similar concepts. However, there is a subtle distinction between the two:

- **Vector store**: This generally refers to a storage system or repository where vectors are stored. The vectors are high-dimensional and represent complex data such as text, images, or audio in a format that can be processed by machine learning models. A vector store focuses primarily on the efficient storage of these vectors. It might not have advanced capabilities for querying or analyzing the data and its main purpose is to maintain a large repository of vectors that can be retrieved and used for various machine learning tasks

- **Vector database**: A vector database, on the other hand, is a more sophisticated system that not only stores vectors but also provides advanced functionalities for querying and analyzing them. This includes the ability to perform similarity searches and other complex operations that are useful in machine learning and data analysis. A vector database is designed to handle the nuances of vector data, such as their high dimensionality and the need for specialized indexing techniques to enable efficient search and retrieval. In a nutshell

While a vector store is more about the storage aspect, a vector database encompasses both storage and the complex querying capabilities required for vector data. This makes vector databases particularly important in applications where it's necessary to search through large volumes of vectorized data quickly and accurately.

One distinguishing feature usually representative of a vector database and less often provided by vector stores is the support for CRUD (`create`, `read`, `update`, `delete`) functions. Whether or not a vector store offers CRUD functions can vary depending on the specific implementation and design of the store. However, in general, a vector store, especially if it's a simplified or basic form of storage for vector data, might not support all the CRUD operations in the same way a traditional database system would. Let's break down the typical operations:

- **Create**: The ability to add new vectors to the store is usually a fundamental feature. This is essential for building up the vector repository.

- **Read**: Reading or retrieving vectors based on some form of identifier or criterion is also a common feature. In a basic vector store, this might be limited to simple retrieval rather than complex queries.

- **Update**: Updating existing vectors in a vector store might not be as straightforward or as commonly supported as in traditional databases. This is because vector data, often used in machine learning and similar applications, is usually generated in a fixed form and not frequently updated.

- **Delete**: The capability to delete vectors may be supported, but like updating, it may not be a primary feature, depending on the use case of the vector store.

In many machine learning and AI applications, once vectors are created and stored, they are not frequently updated or deleted, which is why some vector stores might focus more on efficient storage and retrieval (create and read operations) rather than full CRUD functionality.

In contrast to a simple vector store, a vector database, which is more sophisticated, is more likely to offer complete CRUD capabilities, allowing for more dynamic and flexible management of the vector data.

Here's a good starting point in your journey toward a better understanding of vector databases: `https://learn.microsoft.com/en-us/semantic-kernel/memories/vector-db`.

Exploring other index types in LlamaIndex

While the `VectorStoreIndex` may be the star of the show in most of our RAG scenarios, LlamaIndex provides many other useful indexing tools. They all have specific features and use cases and the following section will explore them in more detail.

The SummaryIndex

The `SummaryIndex` offers a straightforward yet powerful way of indexing data for retrieval purposes. Unlike the `VectorStoreIndex`, which focuses on embeddings within a vector store, the `SummaryIndex` is based on a simple data structure where nodes are stored in a sequence. You'll find a simple depiction of the structure of the `SummaryIndex` in *Figure 5.7*:

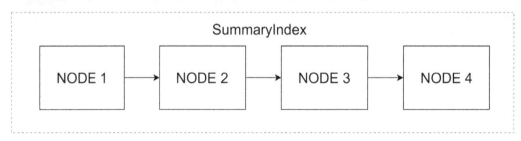

Figure 5.7 – The structure of a SummaryIndex

When building the Index, it ingests a collection of documents, splits them into smaller chunks, and then compiles these chunks into a sequential list. Everything runs locally, without involving an LLM or any embedding model.

Practical use case

Imagine we would create a documentation search tool within a software development project. Often, software projects accumulate extensive documentation over time, including technical specifications, API documentation, user guides, and developer notes. Keeping track of this information can become challenging, especially when the team needs to quickly reference specific details. Implementing a SummaryIndex for the project's documentation repository allows developers to perform quick searches across all documents. For example, a developer could query *What are the error handling procedures for the payment gateway API?* The SummaryIndex would scan through the indexed documentation to retrieve relevant sections where error handling is discussed, without the need for complex embedding models or intensive computational resources. This Index would be particularly useful in environments where maintaining an extensive vector store would not be viable due to resource constraints or where simplicity and speed are prioritized.

The SummaryIndex is particularly effective for applications where a linear scan through data is sufficient or where complex embedding-based retrieval is not required. It's a more basic form of indexing but still versatile enough for various use cases, especially in scenarios where you need a simple way to index your data.

A simple usage model for the SummaryIndex

Creating a SummaryIndex is a straightforward process:

```
from llama_index.core import SummaryIndex, SimpleDirectoryReader
documents = SimpleDirectoryReader("files").load_data()
index = SummaryIndex.from_documents(documents)
query_engine = index.as_query_engine()
response = query_engine.query("How many documents have you loaded?")
print(response)
```

Here, Nodes are created from our sample files and the SummaryIndex is instantiated with these Nodes. This simple model enables quick setup without the complexity of embedding or using vector storage.

If you have correctly cloned the structure of our book's GitHub repository and have a files subfolder containing two text files, the output of the previous code snippet should be the following:

```
I have loaded two documents.
```

Understanding the inner workings of the SummaryIndex

Internally, the `SummaryIndex` operates by storing each node in a list-like structure. When a query is executed, the Index iterates through this list to find relevant nodes. While this process is less complex than embedding-based searches in `VectorStoreIndex`, it's still effective for many applications.

The Index can be used with various retrievers such as `SummaryIndexRetriever`, `SummaryIndexEmbeddingRetriever`, and `SummaryIndexLLMRetriever`, each providing different mechanisms for searching and retrieving data. During queries, the `SummaryIndex` employs a *create and refine* approach to formulate responses. Initially, it assembles a preliminary answer based on the first chunk of text. This initial response is subsequently refined by incorporating additional text chunks as contextual information. The refinement process involves either maintaining the initial answer, slightly modifying it, or entirely rephrasing the original response. We'll cover the retrieval part in detail during *Chapter 6, Querying Our Data, Part 1 – Context Retrieval.*

The DocumentSummaryIndex

LlamaIndex's arsenal of indexing tools extends beyond its well-regarded `VectorStoreIndex`, encompassing a variety of specialized Indexes designed for diverse applications. Among these, the `DocumentSummaryIndex` stands out for its unique approach to document management and retrieval.

At its core, the `DocumentSummaryIndex` is designed to optimize information retrieval by summarizing Documents and mapping these summaries to their corresponding Nodes within the Index. This process facilitates efficient data retrieval, using the summaries to quickly identify relevant Documents.

Figure 5.8 provides a visual representation of this mechanism:

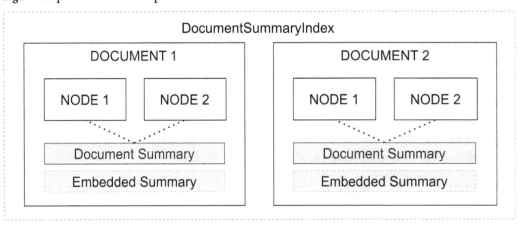

Figure 5.8 – The DocumentSummaryIndex

This Index operates by first creating a summary for each ingested Document. These summaries are then linked to the Document's Nodes, forming a structured Index that enables fast and accurate data retrieval.

The `DocumentSummaryIndex` is particularly useful for handling queries where a succinct overview of the document content can significantly narrow down the search space, making it a great tool for applications requiring quick access to specific Documents in a large and diverse dataset.

For example, a practical use case for the `DocumentSummaryIndex` is in the development of a knowledge management system within a large organization. In such an environment, employees often need quick access to a vast array of documents, including reports, research papers, policy documents, and technical manuals. These documents are typically stored across different departments and may be extensive in length, making it challenging to quickly find specific information relevant to a user's query. In addition, multiple documents may contain similar chunks of text, making a simple embedding-based retrieval impractical over the entire dataset.

Several parameters can be customized for this particular Index:

- `response_synthesizer`: This parameter allows you to specify a response synthesizer that is responsible for generating summaries. By customizing this parameter, you can control the summarization process, adjusting it to fit specific needs or preferences in how summaries are generated.

- `summary_query`: This parameter is used to define the query that guides the summarization process. Essentially, it tells the response synthesizer what kind of summary to generate for each Document. The default query asks for a summary that describes what the Document is about and what questions it can answer. Adjusting this query allows you to tailor the focus and style of the summaries, making them more relevant to the specific use cases of the Index.

- `show_progress`: This Boolean parameter determines whether to display progress bars during operations that can take a significant amount of time. Setting this to `True` provides visual feedback on the progress of these operations.

- `embed_summaries`: When set to `True` – which is the default – this parameter indicates that the summaries should be embedded. Embedded summaries can then be used for similarity comparisons and retrieval in an embedding-based search. This is particularly useful for scenarios where you want to retrieve Nodes based on the similarity between the Document summary content and the user query. We'll cover this in more detail during *Chapter 6, Querying Our Data, Part 1 – Context Retrieval*.

Let's now see how to use the `DocumentSummaryIndex`.

A simple usage model for the DocumentSummaryIndex

Creating a `DocumentSummaryIndex` involves a series of steps, starting with the aggregation of Documents and their subsequent summarization. The following code snippet demonstrates the basic setup for creating this Index:

```
from llama_index.core import (
    DocumentSummaryIndex, SimpleDirectoryReader)
documents = SimpleDirectoryReader("files").load_data()
index = DocumentSummaryIndex.from_documents(
    documents,
    show_progress=True
)
```

This process involves reading documents from a directory, parsing them into Nodes, summarizing the Documents, and then associating the corresponding Nodes with these summaries for quick retrieval. Next, let's observe the summaries that were generated in the process:

```
summary1 = index.get_document_summary(documents[0].doc_id)
summary2 = index.get_document_summary(documents[1].doc_id)
print("\n Summary of the first document: " + summary1)
print("\n Summary of the second document: " + summary2)
```

The second part of the code sample displays the summaries that were generated for each Document. These summaries were associated with the underlying Nodes for each Document. During retrieval, this association will allow extracting only the relevant Nodes, based on the user query and the summary of each Document.

Internally, the `DocumentSummaryIndex` supports both embedding-based and LLM-based retrievers, allowing for flexible retrieval mechanisms that cater to different needs. By default, the Index also generates embeddings for each summary in order to facilitate embedding-based retrieval, which is particularly useful for similarity searches.

The KeywordTableIndex

The `KeywordTableIndex` in LlamaIndex implements a clever architecture – similar to a glossary of terms – for rapidly matching queries to relevant nodes based on important terms. Unlike complex embedding spaces, this structure relies on a straightforward keyword table, yet proves highly effective for targeted factual lookup. This Index extracts keywords from documents and constructs a keyword-to-node mapping, offering a highly efficient search mechanism.

It's particularly useful in scenarios where precise keyword matching is vital for retrieving relevant information. These keywords become the reference keys in a central lookup table, each one pointing to associated nodes such as a glossary definition. During retrieval, just like scanning a glossary for entries of interest, relevant nodes containing a particular keyword are identified and returned. See *Figure 5.9* for a visual representation:

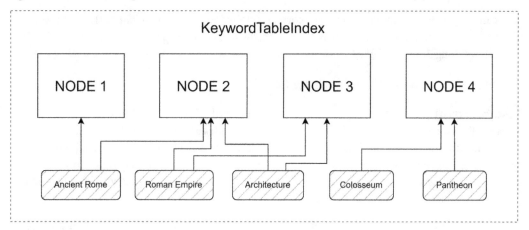

Figure 5.9 – The structure of a KeywordTableIndex

The customizable parameters for the `KeywordTableIndex` are as follows:

- `keyword_extract_template`: This is an optional prompt template used for keyword extraction. Custom prompts can be specified to change how keywords are extracted from text, allowing for tailored keyword extraction strategies. We'll talk more about prompt customization during *Chapter 10*.

- `max_keywords_per_chunk`: This sets the maximum number of keywords to extract from each text chunk. By using this parameter, we can make sure the keyword table remains manageable and focused on the most relevant keywords. The default value is `10`.

- `use_async`: This determines whether to use asynchronous calls. This can improve performance, especially when handling large datasets or complex operations. Its default setting is `False`.

Next up, we will create the `KeywordTableIndex`.

A simple usage model for the KeywordTableIndex

Creating a `KeywordTableIndex` is very straightforward:

```
from llama_index.core import KeywordTableIndex, SimpleDirectoryReader
documents = SimpleDirectoryReader("files").load_data()
index = KeywordTableIndex.from_documents(documents)
query_engine = index.as_query_engine()
response = query_engine.query("
    What famous buildings were in ancient Rome?")
print(response)
```

Here, the Index automatically extracts keywords from your data and sets up a keyword table, streamlining the process of setting up a keyword-based retrieval system.

Just like in the previous example, if you have correctly cloned the structure of our GitHub repository and have a `files` subfolder containing two text files, the output of the previous code snippet should be something along the lines of *The Colosseum and the Pantheon were famous buildings in ancient Rome.*

How does the KeywordTableIndex operate?

The `KeywordTableIndex` builds and operates a keyword table, akin to a glossary, where each keyword is linked to relevant nodes. The Index initially processes a collection of documents, breaking them down into smaller chunks. For each chunk, the Index uses the LLM with a specially designed prompt to identify and extract relevant keywords. These keywords, which may range from simple terms to short phrases, are subsequently cataloged in the keyword table. Each keyword in this table is directly linked to the chunk of text from which it was derived.

Upon receiving a query, the Index identifies keywords within it and matches them with the table entries, enabling rapid and accurate retrieval of related chunks containing those keywords. It supports various retrieval modes, including simple keyword matching and advanced techniques such as **RAKE** or LLM-based keyword extraction and matching. We'll talk more about these retrieval modes during *Chapter 6, Querying Our Data, Part 1 – Context Retrieval.*

> **Quick note on the RAKE extraction method**
>
> This method is particularly effective in identifying phrases or keywords that are significant within a body of text. The key idea behind RAKE is that keywords often consist of multiple words but rarely include punctuation, stop words, or words with minimal lexical meaning. The `KeywordTableIndex` has two similar alternatives that are designed to operate without the assistance of an LLM: `SimpleKeywordTableIndex`, which uses a simple regex extractor, and `RAKEKeywordTableIndex`, which relies on a RAKE keyword extractor based on the `rake_nltk` (Natural Language Toolkit) Python package.

You should know that, just like the `SummaryIndex`, the `KeywordTableIndex` also uses a *create and refine* approach when synthesizing the final response. The adaptability of the `KeywordTableIndex` makes it a versatile tool for diverse applications where keyword precision is key.

The TreeIndex

The `TreeIndex` introduces a hierarchical approach to information organization and retrieval. Unlike a simple list, this structure organizes data in a hierarchical tree format.

Have a look at *Figure 5.10* for a diagram depicting the structure of the `TreeIndex`:

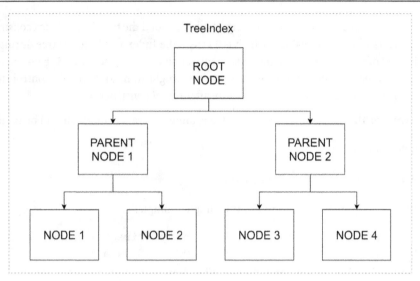

Figure 5.10 – The structure of a TreeIndex

Each node in this tree can represent a piece of data or information, similar to a branch or leaf on a real tree. This structural formation allows for efficient handling and querying of data. The TreeIndex first takes in a set of documents as input. It then builds up a tree in a bottom-up fashion; each parent node is able to summarize the child nodes using a general summarization prompt, and each intermediate node contains text summarizing the components below it. This summary is generated using an LLM based on a prompt template that can be customized with the summary_prompt parameter. TreeIndex acts like an organizer and summarizer, taking lots of individual pieces of data, grouping them together, and creating a summary that captures their essence.

Customizable parameters for the TreeIndex

Apart from the general customization inherited from the BaseIndex class, the TreeIndex provides the following parameters:

- summary_template: This is a prompt for summarization, used during Index construction. This prompt can be customized for better control of the summarization process.

- insert_prompt: This is a prompt used by the Index for tree insertion, facilitating Index construction. This prompt facilitates the insertion of nodes into the tree. It guides how new information is integrated into the existing tree structure. We'll cover details about prompt customization during *Chapter 10, Prompt Engineering Guidelines and Best Practices*.

- num_children: This defines the maximum number of child nodes each node should have. This parameter controls the breadth of the tree, impacting its level of detail at each node. By default, this is set to 10.

- `build_tree`: This is a Boolean indicating whether to build the tree during Index construction. If we don't use the default value – which is `True` – the Index will build its tree during query time instead of building it during the Index construction. Setting the `build_tree` parameter to `False` could be useful in scenarios where you might want to manually control the tree-building process or modify the tree structure after initial construction.

- `use_async`: This determines whether asynchronous operation mode should be used.

Next, let's create a simple `TreeIndex`.

A simple usage model for the TreeIndex

To implement a `TreeIndex`, you can follow this simple example:

```
from llama_index.core import TreeIndex, SimpleDirectoryReader
documents = SimpleDirectoryReader("files").load_data()
index = TreeIndex.from_documents(documents)
query_engine = index.as_query_engine()
response = query_engine.query("Tell me about dogs")
print(response)
```

This process involves the `TreeIndex` taking in documents, structuring them hierarchically, and then allowing for queries that leverage this structure for efficient data retrieval.

The inner mechanics of the TreeIndex

The index-building process is recursive. After the first level of parent nodes is created, the builder can repeat the process, summarizing these parent nodes into higher-level nodes, and so on. This creates multiple levels in the tree, with each level abstracting and summarizing the information from the level below it. Also, for large datasets, the Index can handle data asynchronously with `use_async`. This means it can process multiple parts of the data simultaneously, making the building process faster and more efficient.

By using LLMs for summaries, the `TreeIndex` can encapsulate a nuanced understanding of the data. This is particularly useful for complex datasets where relationships and context matter.

For example, in organizations

In organizations with complex hierarchical data such as reports, memos, and research papers, a `TreeIndex` can organize this information efficiently, allowing for quick retrieval of specific data points within their knowledge management systems.

`TreeIndex` operates by building a tree where each node is a summarized representation of its children, offering a clear and organized view of the data.

This Index supports several retrieval modes:

- `TreeSelectLeafRetriever`: This traverses the tree to find leaf nodes that can best answer a query. It involves choosing a specific number of child nodes at each level for traversal.

- `TreeSelectLeafEmbeddingRetriever`: This utilizes embedding similarity between the query and node text to traverse the tree, selecting leaf nodes based on this similarity.

- `TreeRootRetriever`: This directly retrieves answers from the root nodes of the tree. This method assumes the graph already stores the answer, so it doesn't parse information down the tree.

- `TreeAllLeafRetriever`: This builds a query-specific tree from all leaf nodes to return a response. It rebuilds the tree for each query, making it suitable for scenarios where the tree structure doesn't need to be built during initialization.

During query time, the tree Index operates in the following way:

1. First, the provided query string is processed to extract relevant keywords
2. Beginning from the root Node, the Index navigates through the tree structure
3. At each Node, it determines whether the keywords are found in the Node's summary
4. If keywords are found, the Index proceeds to explore the Node's child Nodes
5. If the keywords are absent, the Index advances to the subsequent Node
6. This process persists until a leaf Node is encountered or all Nodes in the tree have been examined

The reached leaf Nodes represent the context with the highest likelihood of relevance to the given query.

We'll cover the retrievers in more detail during *Chapter 6, Querying Our Data, Part 1 – Context Retrieval*.

Some potential drawbacks of using the TreeIndex

Using a `TreeIndex` in our RAG workflow can potentially be less advantageous compared to simpler retrieval methods. Here are a few reasons why:

- *Increased computation*: Building and maintaining a `TreeIndex` requires additional computational resources. During the Index construction phase, the tree structure needs to be created by recursively summarizing and organizing the Nodes. This process involves applying summarization using LLM calls and constructing the hierarchical structure, which can be computationally intensive, especially for large datasets.

- *Recursive retrieval*: When querying the Index, the retrieval process involves traversing the tree structure from the root nodes down to the relevant leaf nodes. This recursive traversal can require multiple steps and computations, especially if the tree is deep or if multiple branches need to be explored. Each step in the traversal may involve comparing the query with the Node summaries and making decisions on which branches to follow. This recursive process can be more computationally expensive compared to retrieving from a flat Index.

- *Summarization overhead*: This Index relies on summarizing the content of each node to provide a concise representation of its child Nodes. The summarization process needs to be performed during Index construction and potentially during updates or insertions, adding to the overall computational overhead.

- *Storage requirements*: Storing a `TreeIndex` requires additional storage compared to a flat Index. The Index needs to store the tree structure, Node summaries, and metadata associated with each Node. This extra storage overhead can increase storage costs, especially for large-scale datasets.

- *Maintenance and updates*: Maintaining a `TreeIndex` requires regular updates and re-organization as new data is added or existing data is modified. Inserting new nodes or updating existing nodes in the tree structure may trigger a cascading effect, requiring updates to the parent nodes and their summaries. This maintenance process can be more complex and time-consuming compared to other Indexes.

However, it's important to note that the higher costs associated with using a `TreeIndex` can be justified in certain scenarios. If the RAG application deals with a large-scale dataset and requires efficient and context-aware retrieval, the benefits of using this type of Index may outweigh the additional costs. Its hierarchical structure and summarization capabilities can lead to improved retrieval performance, reduced search space, and better response generation quality. By traversing the tree from the root Nodes and selectively exploring relevant branches, the model can quickly narrow down the search to the most promising Nodes. This can lead to faster retrieval times and improved efficiency compared to searching through a flat Index structure.

The key is to assess the specific requirements, scale, and constraints of the RAG scenario to determine whether the benefits of using a `TreeIndex` justify the potential increase in costs. Careful evaluation and benchmarking can help in making an informed decision based on the trade-offs between retrieval efficiency, generation quality, and computational and storage costs.

The KnowledgeGraphIndex

The `KnowledgeGraphIndex` enhances query processing by constructing a **knowledge graph (KG)** from extracted **triplets**. This type of Index primarily relies on the LLM to extract triplets from text, but it also provides flexibility to use custom extraction functions if needed.

KG Indexes excel in scenarios where understanding complex, interlinked relationships and contextual information is important. They are very good at capturing intricate connections between entities and concepts, thus offering better insights and context-aware responses to queries. Among other use cases, KGs are ideal for answering multifaceted questions that require an understanding of the relationships between different entities. *Yes, I'm talking about our tutor project, PITS, here.*

Let's get a visual of how KGs work in *Figure 5.11*:

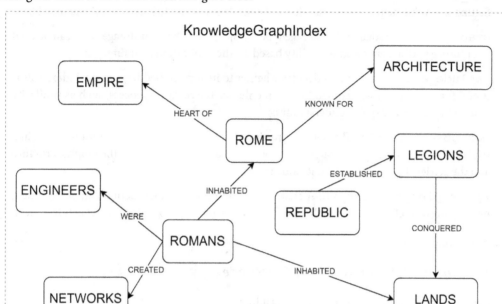

Figure 5.11 – The structure of a KnowledgeGraphIndex

Practical use case

An interesting use case for a KG could be, for example, a news aggregation app, where large volumes of text are ingested every day from various sources such as newspapers, blogs, and social media platforms. In such a scenario, KGs could be used to represent entities such as people, organizations, locations, and so on, and their relationships over time. This would allow users to explore historical trends, breaking news events, and related entities based on the graph structure and traversal algorithms.

Sounds good, right? We will now take a look at how you can work with KnowledgeGraphIndex.

Customizable parameters for the KnowledgeGraphIndex

You can customize the following parameters:

- kg_triple_extract_template: This is a prompt template for extracting triplets. It can be customized to change how triplets (subject-predicate-object) are identified, enabling tailored extraction strategies based on specific use cases.

- `max_triplets_per_chunk`: This limits the number of triplets extracted per text chunk. Setting this value helps manage the size and complexity of the KG. The default value is `10`.

- `graph_store`: This defines the storage type for the graph. Different storage types can be used to optimize performance and scalability based on the application's requirements.

- `include_embeddings`: This decides whether to include embeddings in the Index. This is useful for scenarios where embeddings can enhance the retrieval process, such as similarity searches or advanced query understanding.

- `max_object_length`: This sets the maximum length – in characters – for the object in a triplet. It prevents overly long or complex objects that could complicate the graph's structure and the retrieval process. Its default value is `128`.

- `kg_triplet_extract_fn`: A custom function for triplet extraction can be provided, offering the flexibility to use specialized or proprietary methods for extracting triplets from text.

Let's create a simple KG next.

A basic usage model for KnowledgeGraphIndex

Here's a simple way of constructing and querying a KG:

```
from llama_index.core import (
    KnowledgeGraphIndex, SimpleDirectoryReader)
documents = SimpleDirectoryReader("files").load_data()
index = KnowledgeGraphIndex.from_documents(
    documents, max_triplets_per_chunk=2, use_async=True)
query_engine = index.as_query_engine()
response = query_engine.query("Tell me about dogs.")
print(response)
```

In this setup, the Index builds a KG by extracting triplets from documents, enabling complex relationship queries. Notice that we configured the Index to run the build process in asynchronous mode by setting `use_async` to `True`. Of course, for the two small documents that we're using as an example in our case, this won't make too much difference in the total execution time. However, when working with large datasets, enabling asynchronous operation for this Index may provide an important performance boost.

How does the KnowledgeGraphIndex build its structure?

`KnowledgeGraphIndex` operates by extracting subject-predicate-object triplets from text data, forming a KG.

There are two main ways in which this Index can build its structure:

- *The default, built-in approach*: In its default implementation, the Index uses an internal method to extract triplets from text. This method takes the text content of each Node and passes it through a pre-defined prompt template – `DEFAULT_KG_TRIPLET_EXTRACT_PROMPT` or a custom template provided during initialization through the `kg_triple_extract_template` argument. The prompt template is designed to instruct the LLM to extract knowledge triplets from the given text. The LLM's response is then parsed by a specialized internal method to extract the subject, predicate, and object of each triplet. This method extracts knowledge triplets in the format of *subject, predicate, object*. It applies various checks and string manipulations to ensure the validity and consistency of the extracted triplets. Finally, the method returns a list of cleaned and well-formatted triplets that can be added to the KG Index.

- *The second approach involves a custom triplet extraction function*: If a custom `kg_triplet_extract_fn` function is provided during initialization, it will be used instead of the LLM-based method. This allows us to define our own function to extract triplets from text based on their specific requirements or domain knowledge.

Regardless of whether we're using the first or the second approach to generate the triplets, the inner components of the Index are responsible for building the actual KG from the given Nodes. They iterate over each Node, extract triplets using either the LLM-based method or the custom extraction function and add the triplets to the Index structure.

If the `include_embeddings` flag is set to `True`, the Index will also generate embeddings for each triplet using the specified embedding model. These embeddings are stored in the `embedding_dict` of the Index structure.

The `upsert_triplet()` method allows the manual insertion of triplets into the KG. It adds the triplet to the graph store and also optionally generates embeddings for the triplet if `include_embeddings` are set to `True`.

During querying, the Index leverages the KG to retrieve relevant data and help provide context-rich responses. There are three distinct retrievers available for this Index: `KGTableRetriever` for keyword-focused queries, `KnowledgeGraphRAGRetriever` for retrieving sub-graphs based on extracted entities and synonyms, and a hybrid mode that combines both keyword and embedding strategies for a comprehensive approach. More details about these retrieval capabilities will be explored during *Chapter 6, Querying Our Data, Part 1 – Context Retrieval*.

Building Indexes on top of other Indexes with ComposableGraph

The `ComposableGraph` in LlamaIndex represents a sophisticated way to structure information by **stacking Indexes** on top of each other.

Figure 5.12 provides an overview of a `ComposableGraph`:

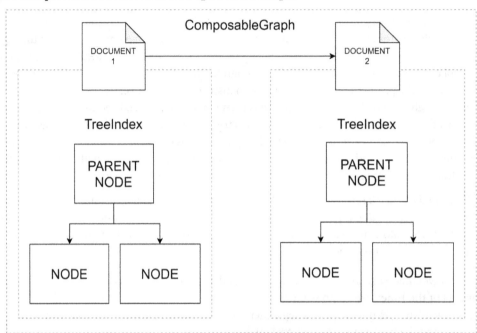

Figure 5.12 – The structure of a ComposableGraph

This approach allows for the construction of Indexes within individual documents – lower-level Indexes – and the aggregation of these Indexes into higher-order ones over a collection of documents. For example, you can build a `TreeIndex` for the text within each document and a `SummaryIndex` that encompasses each `TreeIndex` in a collection.

How to use the ComposableGraph

Here's a simple code example demonstrating the usage of `ComposableGraph`:

```
from llama_index.core import (
    ComposableGraph, SimpleDirectoryReader,
    TreeIndex, SummaryIndex)
documents = SimpleDirectoryReader("files").load_data()
index1 = TreeIndex.from_documents([documents[0]])
index2 = TreeIndex.from_documents([documents[1]])
summary1 = "A short introduction to ancient Rome"
summary2 = "Some facts about dogs"
graph = ComposableGraph.from_indices(
    SummaryIndex, [index1, index2],
    index_summaries=[summary1, summary2]
```

```
)
query_engine = graph.as_query_engine()
response = query_engine.query("What can you tell me?")
print(response)
```

In this example, the `ComposableGraph` facilitates the organization of detailed information within Documents and the summarization across Documents.

We first load our two test Documents: one related to ancient Rome and the other one describing dogs. We then create a `TreeIndex` for each Document.

We also define the summaries of the two Documents.

Pro tip

As an alternative to manually defining the summaries, we could have also queried each individual Index to automatically generate the content summary or used `SummaryExtractor` to accomplish the same purpose.

In the next step, we build a `ComposableGraph` containing the two tree Indexes along with their summaries. For this example, the output of the code should be something similar to the following: *I can tell you about the ancient Roman civilization and dogs and their various breeds, traits, and personalities.*

Once the `ComposableGraph` has been built, the root `SummaryIndex` will have an overview of the contents of the individual Indexes for each document.

A more detailed description of this concept

Under the hood, a `ComposableGraph` enables the creation of hierarchical structures by stacking Indexes on top of each other. This allows for the organization of detailed information within individual Documents using lower-level Indexes and the aggregation of these Indexes into higher-order ones over a collection of Documents.

The process begins by creating individual Indexes for each Document to capture the detailed information within the Documents. Additionally, summaries are defined for each Document.

The `ComposableGraph` is then constructed using the `from_indices()` class method. It takes the root Index class (in our example, the `SummaryIndex`), the child Indexes (in our example, the two `TreeIndex` instances), and their corresponding summaries as input. The method creates `IndexNodes` instances for each child Index, associating the summary with the respective Index. These `IndexNodes` instances are then used to construct the root Index.

During a query, the `ComposableGraph` starts with the top-level summary Index, where each Node corresponds to an underlying lower-level Index. The query is executed recursively, starting from the root Index, and traversing through the sub-Indexes. The `ComposableGraphQueryEngine` is responsible for this recursive querying process.

The query engine retrieves relevant Nodes from the root Index based on the query. For each relevant Node, it identifies the corresponding child Index using the `index_id` stored in the Node's relationships. It then queries the child Index with the original query to obtain more detailed information. This process continues recursively until all relevant sub-Indexes have been queried.

Custom query engines can be configured for each Index within the `ComposableGraph`, allowing for tailored retrieval strategies at different levels of the hierarchy. This enables a deep, hierarchical understanding of complex datasets by seamlessly integrating information from various levels of Indexes.

Overall, the `ComposableGraph` allows for the efficient retrieval of relevant information from both high-level summaries and detailed, low-level Indexes, enabling a comprehensive understanding of the underlying data.

Now that we have covered the Indexes available for our RAG implementation, it's time to address the elephant in the room – **cost**.

Estimating the potential cost of building and querying Indexes

In a similar manner to metadata extractors, Indexes pose issues related to costs and data privacy. That is because, as we have seen in this chapter, most Indexes rely on LLMs to some extent – during building and/or querying.

Repeatedly calling LLMs to process large volumes of text can quickly break your budget if you're not paying attention to your potential costs. For example, if you are building a `TreeIndex` or `KeywordTableIndex` from thousands of documents, those constant LLM invocations during Index construction will carry a significant cost. Embeddings can also rely on calls to external models; therefore, the `VectorStoreIndex` is another important source of costs. In my experience, prevention and prediction are the best ways to avoid nasty surprises and keep your expenses low.

Just like with metadata extraction, I'd start first by observing and applying some best practices:

- Use Indexes with no LLM calls during building where possible, such as `SummaryIndex` or `SimpleKeywordTableIndex`. This eliminates Index building costs.

- Use cheaper LLM models. If full accuracy isn't critical, cheaper LLM models with lower computational demands can be used but be aware of possible quality trade-offs.

- Cache and reuse Indexes. Avoid rebuilding Indexes by caching and reusing previously constructed ones.

- Optimize query parameters to minimize LLM calls during your search. For example, reducing `similarity_top_k` in `VectorStoreIndex` will reduce your query cost.

- Use local models. To further manage costs and maintain data privacy when using Indexes in LlamaIndex, consider utilizing local LLM and embedding models instead of relying on hosted services. This approach not only offers more control over data privacy but also helps in reducing the dependency on external services, which can be costly. Using local models can significantly cut down on expenses, particularly when handling large volumes of data or when operating within strict budget constraints.

> **Important side note regarding local AI models**
>
> Always remember that RAG introduces additional knowledge and contextual information into the model's processing, effectively bridging the gap caused by a smaller training dataset. So, even for models that haven't been trained on extensive or diverse data, RAG allows them to access a broader range of information beyond their initial training set, thus enhancing their performance and output quality.

These guidelines will definitely help you reduce costs, but it's still a good idea to estimate before indexing larger datasets.

Here is a basic example of how we can estimate the LLM costs of building a `TreeIndex` using a `MockLLM`:

```python
import tiktoken
from llama_index.core import (
    TreeIndex, SimpleDirectoryReader, Settings)
from llama_index.core.llms.mock import MockLLM
from llama_index.core.callbacks import (
    CallbackManager, TokenCountingHandler)
```

In the previous part, we first took care of the necessary imports. If you're unfamiliar with the reasons to use `tiktoken` as a tokenizer here, head back to *Chapter 4, Ingesting Data into Our RAG Workflow* where we discussed estimating the potential cost of using metadata extractors. Let's set up the `MockLLM` next:

```python
llm = MockLLM(max_tokens=256)
token_counter = TokenCountingHandler(
    tokenizer=tiktoken.encoding_for_model("gpt-3.5-turbo").encode
)
callback_manager = CallbackManager([token_counter])
Settings.callback_manager=callback_manager
Settings.llm=llm
```

We just created a `MockLLM` instance with a specified maximum token limit acting as a worst-case maximal cost. We then initialized `TokenCountingHandler` with a tokenizer that matches our real LLM model using the following:

```
tiktoken.encoding_for_model("gpt-3.5-turbo").encode).
```

This handler will track token usage. This construct simulates an LLM without actually calling the `gpt-3.5-turbo` API:

```
documents = SimpleDirectoryReader(
    "cost_prediction_samples").load_data()
```

We've loaded our documents and are now ready to build the `TreeIndex`:

```
index = TreeIndex.from_documents(
    documents=documents,
    num_children=2,
    show_progress=True)
print("Total LLM Token Count:", token_counter.total_llm_token_count)
```

After building the Index, the script displays the `total_llm_token_count` value stored in the `TokenCountingHandler`.

In this example, we're only using the `MockLLM` class because there are no embeddings used for building the `TreeIndex`. This allows us to estimate the worst-case LLM token cost before actually building the Index and invoking the real LLM. The same method can be applied to estimate query costs.

> **The main lesson here?**
> While Indexes unlock many capabilities, overuse without optimization can greatly impact costs. Always estimate token usage before indexing larger datasets.

Here is a second example. It's similar to the previous one, but this time, we're first estimating the embedding costs of building a `VectorStoreIndex` and after that, the total cost of querying the Index:

```
import tiktoken
from llama_index.core import (
    MockEmbedding, VectorStoreIndex,
    SimpleDirectoryReader, Settings)
from llama_index.core.callbacks import (
    CallbackManager, TokenCountingHandler)
from llama_index.core.llms.mock import MockLLM
```

The first part took care of the imports. Next, we set up the MockEmbedding and MockLLM objects:

```
embed_model = MockEmbedding(embed_dim=1536)
llm = MockLLM(max_tokens=256)
token_counter = TokenCountingHandler(
    tokenizer=tiktoken.encoding_for_model("gpt-3.5-turbo").encode
)
callback_manager = CallbackManager([token_counter])
Settings.embed_model=embed_model
Settings.llm=llm
Settings.callback_manager=callback_manager
```

After initializing the MockEmbedding and MockLLM objects, we defined a TokenCountingHandler and a CallbackManager and wrapped them into the custom Settings. It's now time to load our sample documents and build the VectorStoreIndex using the custom Settings:

```
documents = SimpleDirectoryReader(
    "cost_prediction_samples").load_data()
index = VectorStoreIndex.from_documents(
    documents=documents,
    show_progress=True)
print("Embedding Token Count:",
    token_counter.total_embedding_token_count)
```

If you have successfully cloned the book's GitHub repo, the cost_prediction_samples subfolder in the ch5 folder should contain a file with a fictional story about Fluffy the cat. The VectorStoreIndex uses an embedding model to encode document text into vectors during indexing. In our second example, we estimated the token costs of those embedding calls by using MockEmbedding and TokenCountingHandler. The embedding token count provides an indication of how expensive it will be to build this Index per document based on the text lengths.

To have a complete view, we can take this a step further and also estimate search costs:

```
query_engine = index.as_query_engine(service_context=service_context)
response = query_engine.query("What's the cat's name?")
print("Query LLM Token Count:", token_counter.total_llm_token_count)
print("Query Embedding Token Count:",
    token_counter.total_embedding_token_count)
```

This shows the potential search fees as well by counting tokens for embedding lookups and synthesizing the response. We also had to use MockLLM to catch the LLM tokens hypothetically consumed during response synthesis.

So, in summary, follow preventive best practices and always forecast your Index build and query expenses before unleashing them on your full document collection!

It's time to make some progress with our project. Let's revisit our PITS project.

Indexing our PITS study materials – hands-on

With a solid understanding of how indexing works in LlamaIndex, we're now ready to implement the indexing logic in our tutoring application.

Let's create the `index_builder.py` module. This module takes care of Index creation. In the current implementation, it creates two Indexes: a `VectorStoreIndex` and a `TreeIndex`. As you can see, this is a very basic implementation and there is definitely room for improvement. Let's handle the imports first:

```
from llama_index.core import (
    VectorStoreIndex, TreeIndex, load_index_from_storage)
from llama_index.core import StorageContext
from global_settings import INDEX_STORAGE
from document_uploader import ingest_documents
```

Next, we'll implement our Index building function:

```
def build_indexes(nodes):
    try:
        storage_context = StorageContext.from_defaults(
            persist_dir=INDEX_STORAGE
        )
        vector_index = load_index_from_storage(
            storage_context, index_id="vector"
        )
        tree_index = load_index_from_storage(
            storage_context, index_id="tree"
        )
        print("All indices loaded from storage.")
```

We first check to see whether the Indexes have already been persisted to disk. If affirmative, then we leverage persistence to avoid the additional cost of rebuilding them.

Note on: Notice the usage of index_id

Because we have persisted more than one Index in the same storage folder – INDEX_STORAGE – when using `load_index_from_storage`, we need to specify their individual IDs so that LlamaIndex can identify the correct Index.

If we cannot find them in the INDEX_STORAGE folder, we proceed to build them from the nodes. We also set an ID for each Index using set_index_id so that we can load them correctly in future sessions:

```
    except Exception as e:
        print(f"Error occurred while loading indices: {e}")
        storage_context = StorageContext.from_defaults()
        vector_index = VectorStoreIndex(
            nodes, storage_context=storage_context
        )
        vector_index.set_index_id("vector")
        tree_index = TreeIndex(
            nodes, storage_context=storage_context
        )
        tree_index.set_index_id("tree")
        storage_context.persist(
            persist_dir=INDEX_STORAGE
        )
        print("New indexes created and persisted.")
    return vector_index, tree_index
```

The build_indexes function returns the two Index objects that we'll use later in our application.

That's it for now. We'll take the next steps during *Chapter 6, Querying Our Data, Part 1 – Context Retrieval.*

Summary

In this chapter, we explored various indexing strategies and architectures within LlamaIndex. Indexes provide essential capabilities for building performant RAG systems.

Throughout the chapter, we looked at the VectorStoreIndex, which is the most commonly used Index type. We also gained an understanding of embeddings, vector stores, similarity search, and storage contexts. These are key concepts related to the VectorStoreIndex.

We also covered other Index types such as SummaryIndex for simple linear scans, KeywordTableIndex for keyword search, TreeIndex for hierarchical data, and KnowledgeGraphIndex for relationship-based queries. ComposableGraph was introduced as a tool for building multi-level Indexes, and cost estimation techniques were discussed together with best practices.

Overall, this chapter provided an overview of indexing capabilities in LlamaIndex, laying the foundation for building sophisticated and efficient RAG applications.

See you in *Chapter 6*, where we'll discuss methods for querying our data in LlamaIndex.

Part 3:
Retrieving and Working with Indexed Data

This part progresses from exploring LlamaIndex's querying capabilities within a RAG workflow, focusing on retrieval mechanisms, query mechanics, and advanced retrieval strategies, to refining these queries through post-processing techniques and integrating them into comprehensive query engines. It culminates in a practical examination of building chatbots and intelligent agents, covering various engine modes, agent architectures, and the implementation of conversational features, thereby equipping you with the knowledge to create dynamic, conversational RAG interfaces.

This part has the following chapters:

- *Chapter 6, Querying Our Data, Part 1 – Context Retrieval*
- *Chapter 7, Querying Our Data, Part 2 – Postprocessing and Response Synthesis*
- *Chapter 8, Building Chatbots and Agents with LlamaIndex*

Querying Our Data, Part 1 – Context Retrieval

The focus of this chapter will be on understanding the querying capabilities of LlamaIndex in an RAG workflow. We'll be covering the overall working of the querying system, mostly focusing on the retrieval capabilities of the framework.

Here are the main sections that will be covered in this chapter:

- Learning about query mechanics – an overview
- Understanding the basic retrievers
- Building more advanced retrieval mechanisms
- Increasing efficiency with asynchronous retrieval
- Working with metadata filters, tools, and selectors
- Transforming queries and generating sub-queries
- Understanding the concepts of dense and sparse retrieval

Technical requirements

For this chapter, you will need to install the `Rank-BM25` package in your environment. You can find it at `https://pypi.org/project/rank-bm25/`.

Two additional integration packages are required to run the sample code:

- *OpenAI Question Generator*: `https://pypi.org/project/llama-index-question-gen-openai/`
- *BM25 Retriever*: `https://pypi.org/project/llama-index-retrievers-bm25/`
- All the code samples for this chapter can be found in the ch6 subfolder of this book's GitHub repository: `https://github.com/PacktPublishing/Building-Data-Driven-Applications-with-LlamaIndex`.

Learning about query mechanics – an overview

In this chapter, we will finally begin to reap the fruits of our work so far. Document ingestion, parsing and segmenting, metadata extraction, and index building were all just preparatory steps for what we are about to discuss: **querying**. At the heart of any RAG workflow is the idea of being able to bring relevant context into the prompt we use in the LLM query. So far, we have been concerned with constructing and organizing this context, but now, it is time to use it and extract the best possible answers from our interactions with LLMs. In the following sections, we will discuss various techniques that LlamaIndex provides us for the query part. As usual, we will start with the simplest query methods – called *naive* methods in jargon – and then discuss more advanced query variants.

First, we need to understand the typical steps in the query process: **retrieval**, **postprocessing**, and **response synthesis**.

In *Chapter 3, Kickstarting Your Journey with LlamaIndex*, in the *Indexes* section, we discussed the simplest way to go through the three steps – using `QueryEngine` but built very simply by running `index.as_query_engine()`. This is very simple but not necessarily always effective as this *naive* way of querying an index is just the tip of the iceberg. We will now explore the three mechanisms individually and understand how they work and the customizable options they offer.

First, we'll focus on **retrievers**.

Understanding the basic retrievers

Retrieval mechanisms are a central element in any RAG system. Although they work in different ways, all types of retrievers are based on the same principle: they browse an index and select the relevant nodes to build the necessary context. Each index type offers several retrieval modes, each providing different features and customization options. Regardless of the retriever type, the result that will be returned is in the form of a `NodeWithScore` object – a structure that combines a node with an associated score. The score can be useful further in the RAG flow because it allows us to sort the returned nodes according to their relevance. However, keep in mind that while all retrievers return `NodeWithScore`, not all of them associate a specific node score.

As usual, LlamaIndex offers multiple alternatives to accomplish a task, so a retriever can be constructed in several ways. The simplest path is direct construction from an `Index` object. Assuming that we have already dealt with document ingestion, the following code builds an index and then builds a retriever based on the structure of the index:

```
from llama_index.core import SummaryIndex, SimpleDirectoryReader
documents = SimpleDirectoryReader("files").load_data()
summary_index = SummaryIndex.from_documents(documents)
retriever = summary_index.as_retriever(
```

```
    retriever_mode='embedding'
)
result = retriever.retrieve("Tell me about ancient Rome")
print(result[0].text)
```

In the previous example, the generated retriever is of the `SummaryIndexRetriever` type. This is the default retriever for this index.

The second option is direct instantiation, as shown in the following example:

```
from llama_index.core import SummaryIndex, SimpleDirectoryReader
from llama_index.core.retrievers import SummaryIndexEmbeddingRetriever
documents = SimpleDirectoryReader("files").load_data()
summary_index = SummaryIndex.from_documents(documents)
retriever = SummaryIndexEmbeddingRetriever(
    index=summary_index
)
result = retriever.retrieve("Tell me about ancient Rome")
print(result[0].text)
```

In the next section, we'll go through a list of retrieval options that are available for each index type. Next to each retriever type, I've specified how it can be instantiated from the corresponding index. I warn you now that a lot of information has been condensed in the next section. However, it is useful information that you can bookmark and come back to later when you start building real applications with the LlamaIndex framework.

So, here's the list of retrievers for each type of index.

The VectorStoreIndex retrievers

We have two retriever options available for this index. Let's have a look at how they work and how to customize them for different use cases.

VectorIndexRetriever

The default retriever that's used by `VectorStoreIndex` is `VectorIndexRetriever`. It can easily be constructed using the following command:

```
VectorStoreIndex.as_retriever()
```

As expected, since `VectorStoreIndex` is one of the most sophisticated and widely used indexes, this retriever is also complex.

Figure 6.1 exemplifies its operating mode:

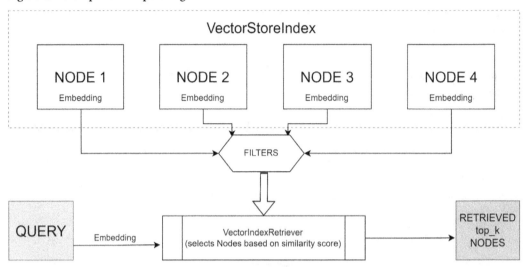

Figure 6.1 – Node retrieval using VectorIndexRetriever

This retriever operates by converting queries into vectors and then performing *similarity-based* searches in the vector space. Several parameters can be customized for different use cases:

- `similarity_top_k`: This defines the number of *top (k)* results returned by the retriever. This determines how many of the most similar results are returned for each query. For example, if we want a broader search, we can change the default value, which is 2.

- `vector_store_query_mode`: This sets the query mode of the vector store. Different variants of external vector stores, such as *Pinecone* (`https://www.pinecone.io/`), *OpenSearch* (`https://opensearch.org/`), and others, support different query modes. This is the mechanism by which we can make best use of their search capabilities.

- `filters`: Remember that in *Chapter 3*, in the *Nodes* section, we saw how to add metadata to our nodes? Well, we can use this metadata to narrow down the search scope of the retriever. We will see a practical example of this in this chapter, where we will use metadata filters to implement a simple system for filtering nodes returned by an index.

- `alpha`: This one is useful when using a hybrid search mode (a combination of sparse and **dense search**). We will discuss the difference between sparse and dense search in more detail later in this chapter.

- `sparse_top_k`: The number of top results for the **sparse search**. This is relevant in hybrid search modes. The previous mention applies here also.

- `doc_ids`: Similar to metadata filters, but slightly coarser, `doc_ids` can be used to restrict the search to a specific subset of documents. For example, suppose the organization uses a common knowledge base that is shared by all departments. At the same time, however, the organization has a clear naming convention for documents. If the department's name or code is found in the document name, we could use this parameter to limit a user's query to documents in their department only.

- `node_ids`: This parameter is similar to `doc_ids` but refers to node IDs within the index. This can give us even more granular control over the information that's returned by the retriever.

- `vector_store_kwargs`: This parameter can pass additional arguments that are specific to each vector store so that they can be sent at query time.

As a secure design principle, security should be implemented as early as possible in the life cycle of an application. This is also true for an RAG application. For example, if we want to better control access to information, we should filter the information that's processed by the application as early as possible. In an RAG flow, which means from the moment it is retrieved – if not earlier. There are ways to filter the information later in the query engine – for example, in post-processing or even in response synthesis – but it is much easier not to introduce risks in the first place by introducing information into the flow that is outside the user's security context. There is also a cost issue. Since much of the processing in an RAG flow is based on LLM ingestion, the less information we process, the lower the cost.

VectorIndexAutoRetriever

All the parameters we discussed earlier regarding `VectorIndexRetriever` are very useful when we know exactly what we are looking for and understand the structure of the data very well. Unfortunately, in some situations, we will be dealing with complex structures or ambiguities in the indexed data.

`VectorIndexAutoRetriever` is a more advanced form of retriever that can use an LLM to automatically set query parameters in a vector store based on a natural language description of the content and supporting metadata. This is particularly useful when users are unfamiliar with the structure of the data or do not know how to formulate an effective query. In these situations, this retriever can transform vague or unclear queries into more structured queries and better leverage the capabilities of the vector store, thus increasing the chances of finding relevant results. Since a detailed discussion of this mechanism would take several pages and I am probably digressing too much from the main topic, if you want to learn more about how it works, I suggest that you consult the official documentation at `https://docs.llamaindex.ai/en/stable/examples/vector_stores/elasticsearch_auto_retriever.html`.

The SummaryIndex retrievers

There are three retriever options available for this index. Let's take a look.

SummaryIndexRetriever

This retriever can be built using the following command:

```
SummaryIndex.as_retriever(retriever_mode = 'default')
```

This is the default retriever for `SummaryIndex`. As seen in *Figure 6.2*, it has a very simple approach – it returns all nodes in the index without applying any filtering or sorting:

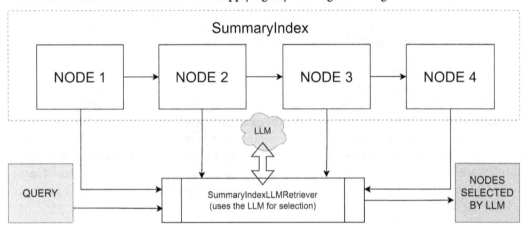

Figure 6.2 – Retrieving nodes using SummaryIndexRetriever

This is useful when we want to get a complete view of the data in the index, without having to filter or sort the results. No relevance score is returned for the nodes.

SummaryIndexEmbeddingRetriever

We can build this one with the following command:

```
SummaryIndex.as_retriever(retriever_mode='embedding')
```

This retriever relies on embeddings to retrieve nodes from SummaryIndex. While SummaryIndex itself stores nodes in plain text, this retriever uses an embedding model to convert these plain text nodes into embeddings when a query is made. Have a look at *Figure 6.3* to get a better view of its operating mode:

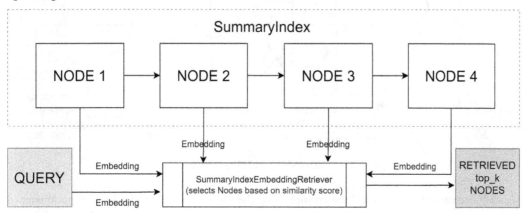

Figure 6.3 – Inner workings of SummaryIndexEmbeddingRetriever

The embeddings are created dynamically as needed for retrieval, rather than being stored persistently with the index. The `similarity_top_k` parameter determines the number of nodes to return, based on their similarity to the query. This retriever is useful for finding the most relevant nodes concerning a given query by using similarity computation.

For each selected node, the retriever calculates a similarity score – based on embeddings – which is then returned alongside the node as `NodeWithScore`. This score is a reflection of the extent to which each node corresponds to the query.

SummaryIndexLLMRetriever

This retriever can be built using the following command:

```
SummaryIndex.as_retriever(retriever_mode='llm')
```

As its name suggests, this retriever uses an LLM to retrieve nodes from SummaryIndex. It uses a prompt to select the most relevant nodes. Check out *Figure 6.4* for an overview of its approach:

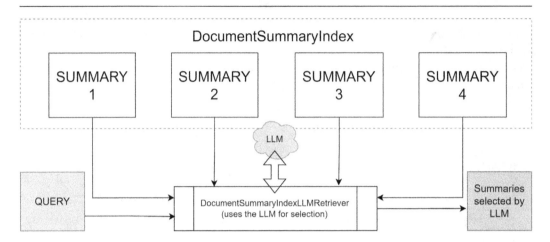

Figure 6.4 – SummaryIndexLLMRetriever in action

If we wish, we can override the default prompt using the `choice_select_prompt` parameter. Queries are processed in batches; the size of each batch is determined by the `choice_batch_size` parameter. Optionally, we can also provide the `format_node_batch_fn` and `parse_choice_select_answer_fn` functions as parameters. These are used to format the batch of nodes and parse the LLM responses. The `parse_choice_select_answer_fn` function is also responsible for calculating node-specific relevance scores. The scores are determined by parsing the LLM responses. These scores are then associated with the corresponding nodes and returned as `NodeWithScore`. If we don't want to use the default LLM, that's not a problem: the retriever accepts `service_context` as a parameter. In Chapter 3, we saw how to customize the default LLM using `ServiceContext`.

This type of retriever is useful in complex search systems where LLMs can provide contextual and detailed answers to queries.

Next, we'll talk about retrievers for `DocumentSummaryIndex`.

The DocumentSummaryIndex retrievers

For this index, we only have two retrieval options. Let's take a look.

DocumentSummaryIndexLLMRetriever

We can build this with the following command:

```
DocumentSummaryIndex.as_retriever(retriever_mode='llm')
```

This retriever uses an LLM to select relevant summaries from an index of document summaries. You can get a better understanding of how it works by looking at *Figure 6.5*:

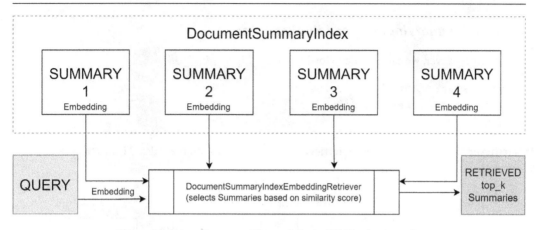

Figure 6.5 – How DocumentSummaryIndexLLMRetriever works

This retriever processes queries in batches, with each batch containing a specified number of nodes to send to the LLM for evaluation. The `choice_batch_size` parameter can be used to specify the size of a batch. The retriever can use a custom prompt provided via the `choice_select_prompt` parameter to determine the relevance of the abstracts to the query. Results are sorted by relevance and returned according to the number specified by `choice_top_k`. The `format_node_batch_fn` and `parse_choice_select_answer_fn` functions can also be specified as parameters. The first function, `format_node_batch_fn`, prepares the information from nodes in a format suitable for the LLM. This may include combining text from multiple nodes, structuring the information in a particular way, or adding contextual elements to help the LLM understand and evaluate the content. The second function, `parse_choice_select_answer_fn`, can, for example, determine which nodes are most relevant to the query and extract relevance scores or other metrics associated with each node. By analyzing the LLM response, this function allows the retriever to decide which nodes are most relevant to the user's query. To summarize, `DocumentSummaryIndexLLMRetriever` is useful for retrieving useful data from a large number of documents using the natural language processing power of LLMs. As a useful side note, it is good to know that this retriever also returns the relevance score that is associated with each of the nodes.

> **Additional observation**
>
> During my experimentation with this type of retriever, I noticed that the relevance scores that are assigned to each node by the LLM were consistently high, often reaching the maximum value of 10 (tested using GPT3.5-Turbo). For applications where nuanced differentiation between degrees of relevance is crucial, it might be beneficial to adjust the prompt or apply post-processing to the LLM's responses to achieve a more balanced and nuanced distribution of relevance scores. This issue also underscores the importance of tailoring LLM prompts and response handling to suit the specific needs and contexts of different applications. We'll talk more about prompt customization in *Chapter 10*.

DocumentSummaryIndexEmbeddingRetriever

To build this retriever, we can use the following code:

```
DocumentSummaryIndex.as_retriever(
    retriever_mode='embedding'
)
```

This retriever relies on embeddings to retrieve summary nodes from the index. *Figure 6.6* exemplifies its operation:

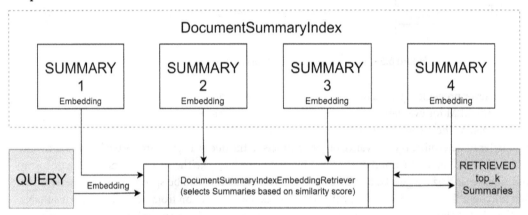

Figure 6.6 – DocumentSummaryIndexEmbeddingRetriever

It computes the embeddings for the query and then finds the summaries with the highest similarity to the query. For this method to work, the index should have been built with the `embed_summaries` parameters set to `True`. The `similarity_top_k` parameter specifies the number of summary nodes to return based on similarity. The retriever does not return a relevance score associated with each node.

It is effective for finding the most relevant summaries relative to a given query, using similarity calculation techniques based on embeddings.

The TreeIndex retrievers

This is a more complex index type that constructs a tree graph of nodes, as we saw in *Chapter 5, Indexing with LlamaIndex*, in the *Other index types in LlamaIndex* section.

Important note

`TreeIndex`, by its very nature, is designed to reflect hierarchical relationships within data, making it a great tool for scenarios where data is naturally organized in a tree-like structure, such as filesystems, organizational charts, or product categories. That being said, the LlamaIndex implementation of this structure is a tree of summaries about the data. Regardless of any existing structure in the initial document, this index builds a parallel hierarchical structure by chunking it down and creating summaries at each level of the tree. Because of the recursive nature of `TreeSelectLeafRetriever` and `TreeSelectLeafEmbeddingRetriever`, navigating this structure at query time could be more computationally expensive than with other types of indexes. This recursive process adds computational overhead, especially for deep trees or large datasets.

That being said, we have several ways to query `TreeIndex`.

TreeSelectLeafRetriever

We can construct this retriever like this:

```
TreeIndex.as_retriever(retriever_mode='select_leaf').
```

This is also the default retriever that's used by `TreeIndex`. Its purpose is to recursively navigate the index structure and identify the leaf nodes that are most relevant to the query being formulated. This can be seen in *Figure 6.7*:

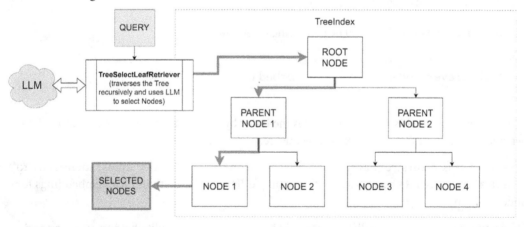

Figure 6.7 – TreeSelectLeafRetriever configured with a child_branch_factor argument value of 1

The `child_branch_factor` argument specifies the number of child nodes to be considered at each level of the tree. Setting a higher value can result in a more exhaustive search and increase the chance of finding the most relevant nodes. However, this has the disadvantage of increasing the computational cost and processing time. If no value is specified, the retriever defaults to a value of `1`. Another very useful parameter is `Verbose`, which, when set to `True`, causes the detailed selection process to be displayed. This is a very good way to understand how the retriever works or troubleshoot possible execution problems. The nodes that are returned by this retriever do not contain an associated relevance score. As this retriever uses an LLM for node selection, several parameters can be used to customize the prompts:

- `query_template`: This is a prompt template that we can use to customize queries for the LLM
- `text_qa_template`: This is another template that's used for text-based Q&A queries. It is used to get specific answers from text nodes
- `refine_template`: This template is used to refine or enhance the initial answers that are obtained from the LLM. It can be used to add additional context or clarify answers
- `query_template_multiple`: An alternative prompt template that allows queries to be formulated for multiple nodes simultaneously. It is useful when using a `child_branch_factor` argument that's higher than 1

We'll talk about `TreeSelectEmbeddingRetriever`.

TreeSelectLeafEmbeddingRetriever

This particular kind of retriever can be built using the following code:

```
TreeIndex.as_retriever(
    retriever_mode='select_leaf_embedding'
)
```

As its name suggests, this retriever navigates the index by using the similarity of the embeddings between the query and the node text to select the relevant nodes.

This process is recursive, navigating all levels of the tree. It works almost identically to `TreeSelectLeafRetriever`, with the only difference being that it uses embeddings for node selection.

The parameters we discussed earlier are also valid here, but there is an additional parameter: `embed_model`. This can be used to specify a preferred embedding model. As with the previous retriever, the nodes that are returned by this retriever do not contain an associated relevance score.

TreeAllLeafRetriever

Here's the fastest way to construct this retriever:

```
TreeIndex.as_retriever(retriever_mode='all_leaf')
```

You can find an explanatory diagram in *Figure 6.8*:

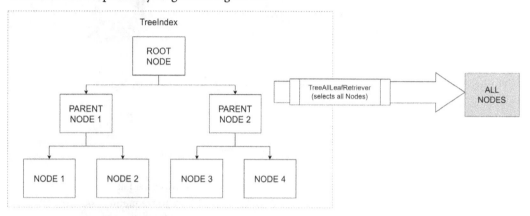

Figure 6.8 – Retrieving all nodes by using TreeAllLeafRetriever

This retriever is useful for its ability to analyze a large amount of data, ensuring that no potentially relevant information is missed in the response generation process. In a similar way to `SummaryIndexRetriever`, this retriever extracts all nodes from the index and sorts them, regardless of their position in the hierarchy. This is akin to a bulk retrieval but without it returning any relevance score.

TreeRootRetriever

We can build this with the following command:

```
TreeIndex.as_retriever(retriever_mode='root')
```

Unlike `TreeAllLeafRetriever`, this retriever focuses on retrieving responses directly from the root nodes of the tree. It assumes that the index tree already stores the response. Unlike other methods that might parse information down the tree to extract relevant nodes, `TreeRootRetriever` relies on the fact that the answer is already at the root level. *Figure 6.9* provides a visual explanation:

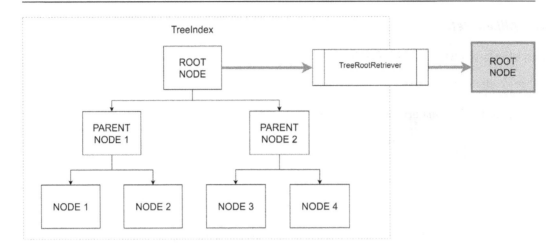

Figure 6.9 – Retrieving from the root of the tree

It is effective in cases where essential information is aggregated or synthesized at the top level of the data structure, such as data summaries, general conclusions, or answers to frequently asked questions. This retriever also does not return relevance scores associated with nodes.

> **Practical use case**
>
> A practical example would be a **clinical decision support system** (**CDSS**) in the medical field. Imagine such a system having a `TreeIndex` retriever in which each root node represents a specific medical question and the corresponding answers or clinical advice are pre-computed and stored in these root nodes. For example, the root nodes may store a pre-computed answer such as *Common symptoms of COVID-19 include fever, dry cough, tiredness, and so on*. In this scenario, when a doctor or patient interrogates the system with the *Symptoms of a COVID-19 infection* query, this retriever will look at the appropriate root node and return the pre-computed answer without any additional processing or having to traverse the tree to find information.

The KeywordTableIndex retrievers

The retrieval process from `KeywordTableIndex` starts by extracting the relevant keywords from the query given to the retriever. Extraction can be done in several ways, depending on the retriever being used. Once the keywords have been extracted, the retriever counts their frequency in the different indexed. All retrievers that are available for this index operate as described in *Figure 6.10*. The only difference is the method that's used to extract the keywords:

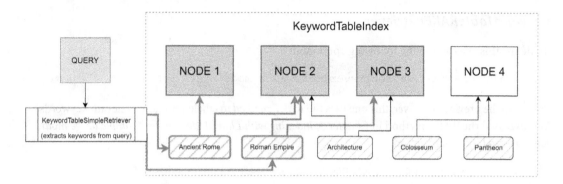

Figure 6.10 – KeywordTableIndex

The nodes are sorted by the number of matching keywords, usually in descending order of relevance, and returned as a `NodeWithScore` response.

It's worth noting that queries against this type of index do not return a relevance score associated with the nodes.

Let's have a look at the available retrievers for this Index.

KeywordTableGPTRetriever

We can build this type of retriever with the following command:

```
KeywordTableIndex.as_retriever(retriever_mode='default')
```

It uses an LLM query to identify relevant keywords in a query and then returns the nodes associated with those keywords.

KeywordTableSimpleRetriever

This retriever can be built as follows:

```
KeywordTableIndex.as_retriever(retriever_mode='simple')
```

This is a simpler method that does not use the LLM and is faster. However, it may be less efficient at identifying complex or contextual keywords. It uses a regular expression-based keyword extractor.

KeywordTableRAKERetriever

To define this, we can use the following command:

```
KeywordTableIndex.as_retriever(retriever_mode='rake')
```

Similar to the previous retriever, this one uses the *RAKE method* to efficiently extract relevant keywords. We discussed the RAKE method in *Chapter 5, Indexing with LlamaIndex,* i*n the A simple usage model for KeywordTableIndex* section.

There are also several common arguments that we can use to set up the retrievers of `KeywordTableIndex`:

- `query_keyword_extract_template`: This is used to change the default prompt that's used to extract keywords from the text of a query. This can only be applied to the default mode.

- `max_keywords_per_query`: This specifies the maximum number of keywords that can be extracted from a single query. This parameter is important to control query complexity and to avoid overloading the system with too many keywords.

- `num_chunks_per_query`: This specifies the maximum number of chunks that can be retrieved in a query. This parameter helps limit the amount of data that can be processed in a single query, optimizing system performance and efficiency.

Next, we'll talk about how to retrieve data from knowledge graphs.

The KnowledgeGraphIndex retrievers

As discussed in the previous chapter, this type of Index constructs a graph made up of *triplets*. Each **triplet** consists of a subject, a predicate, and an object. The **subject** is the entity or concept about which a statement is being made. The **predicate** is the relationship or verb that links the subject to the object, describing how the two are related, and the object is the entity or concept that is linked to the subject by the predicate. At the core of this index, there are two retrievers, `KGTableRetriever` and `KnowledgeGraphRAGRetriever`, both of which extract relevant nodes from a knowledge graph based on queries.

`KGTableRetriever` is the default retriever for `KnowledgeGraphIndex` and can be configured in three retrieval modes: using keywords only, using embeddings only, or a combination of both – in hybrid mode. All modes operate as described in *Figure 6.11*:

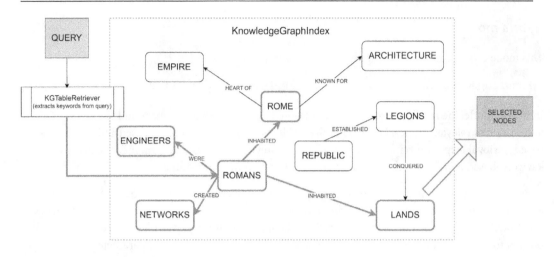

Figure 6.11 – The inner workings of KGTableRetriever

Let's look at how they work under the hood.

Keyword mode

The retriever can be built in this mode using the following command:

```
KnowledgeGraphIndex.as_retriever(retriever_mode='keyword')
```

When configured in keyword mode, the retriever uses keywords extracted from the query to find relevant nodes containing those keywords.

Keywords are evaluated in case-sensitive mode. This means that on a hypothetical index, a query of the form *where is the Colosseum?* will return a correct result, while *where is the colosseum?* will return no nodes.

Embedding mode

We can set it to this mode using the following code:

```
KnowledgeGraphIndex.as_retriever(
    retriever_mode='embedding'
)
```

In this mode, the retriever turns the query into an embedding and the system finds nodes in the graph whose vector representation is similar to the embedding of the query, even if the same keywords are not used.

Hybrid mode

This mode can be configured using the following command:

```
KnowledgeGraphIndex.as_retriever(retriever_mode='hybrid')
```

In hybrid mode, the retriever uses both the keywords extracted from the query and the embeddings to find a set of relevant Nodes. It combines the results from both the keyword-based and embedding-based retrieval steps and removes any duplicated results. This approach combines the precision of keyword-based search with the semantic understanding of the embeddings.

There are several customizable parameters for this type of retriever. For example, `query_keyword_extract_template`, `refine_template`, and `text_qa_template` can be used to change the default prompt for keyword extraction, the default prompt for query refinement, and the default prompt for text queries and answers, respectively. Here are some other useful parameters:

- `max_keywords_per_query`: This limits the number of keywords to avoid overloading the search process. The default value is `10`.

- `num_chunks_per_query`: This determines how many text fragments can be parsed in a single query. The default is `10` and any change must take into account the performance impact and limitations of the LLM used.

- `include_text`: The default value is `True`. This argument indicates whether the text of the source document should be used in queries in each relevant triplet. This can enrich the query with additional context but inevitably increases the computational cost.

- `similarity_top_k`: When the retriever is configured in embedding or hybrid mode, this parameter specifies the number of similar embeddings to be considered in the retrieval process. The default value is `2`.

- `graph_store_query_depth`: This parameter controls how deep into the graph structure to search for relevant information. The default value is `2`.

- `use_global_node_triplets`: When set to `True`, the retriever will not limit itself to keywords extracted directly from the user query; instead, it will search for other keywords or entities in the text fragments that have already been identified as relevant to the initial keywords. This process helps bring an additional layer of knowledge to the query. By exploring the relationships and connections between different nodes in the graph, the retriever can access richer and more contextual information than would be possible by limiting itself to the original keywords. However, this approach is more costly in terms of computing resources and search time as it involves analyzing a greater number of nodes and relationships in the graph. For this reason, the option is disabled by default – that is, it's set to `False`.

- `max_knowledge_sequence`: This parameter provides a balance between the quality and quantity of information presented. For example, if a query can theoretically generate 100 sequences of relevant knowledge, but `max_knowledge_sequence` is set to 30, only the most relevant 30 sequences will be presented as answers. This is also the default. Setting a limit ensures that the answer does not become too long or difficult to interpret, while still retaining enough information to be useful

Although they return `NodeWithScore` objects, the knowledge graph retrievers do not provide any score for the actual nodes. Instead, they simply return a default value of `1000` for each retrieved node.

If the retrievers do not find any nodes in the index based on the configured mode and search parameters, they will first try to identify nodes based on the provided keywords only. If they do not find any relevant nodes, they will return a single placeholder node with the text *No relationships found* and a score of 1.

KnowledgeGraphRAGRetriever

This additional retriever is a bit more special in that it operates by identifying key entities within a query and leveraging these to navigate the knowledge graph. It utilizes functions and templates for entity extraction (`extraction entity_extract_fn` and `entity_extract_template`) and synonym expansion (`synonym_expand_fn` and `synonym_expand_template`) to enrich the query with a broader context of related terms and concepts. The retriever traverses the graph to a specified depth – `graph_traversal_depth` – based on these entities and their synonyms, constructing a knowledge sequence relevant to the query.

This retriever can operate in various modes and can be configured by setting `retriever_mode`, allowing for flexibility in its approach to finding relevant nodes.

Just like `KGTableRetriever`, this retriever has three operating modes: `keyword`, `embedding`, and `keyword_embedding`.

> **A note regarding retrieval modes**
> As of January 2024, in LlamaIndex v0.9.25, only the keyword retrieval mode was implemented.

In addition, the retriever features the `with_nl2graphquery` option, which, when enabled, combines **Natural Language to Graph Query** (**NL2GraphQuery**) capabilities, enhancing its ability to interpret and respond to complex queries. NL2GraphQuery is a process that converts natural language queries into graph-based query languages. This is achieved via a combination of entity extraction, synonym expansion, and graph traversal techniques. This parameter is set to `False` by default.

Here are some other parameters that we may wish to customize:

- `max_knowledge_sequence`: Sets a limit on the number of knowledge sequences included in the response, balancing detail with clarity

- `max_entities`: Specifies the maximum number of entities to extract from the query, defaulting to 5

- `max_synonyms`: Determines the maximum number of synonyms to expand for each entity, with a default value of 5

- `synonym_expand_policy`: Controls the policy for synonym expansion, either *union* or *intersection*, with *union* as the default

- `entity_extract_policy`: Sets the policy for entity extraction, also either *union* or *intersection*, defaulting to *union*

- `verbose`: As usual, this is used to enable or disable the printing of debug information, aiding in the understanding of the Retriever's operation

- `graph_traversal_depth`: Determines the depth of the traversal within the knowledge graph. By default, this is set to 2

> **A quick note**
>
> There's something important to highlight for all retrievers that use LLMs and accept parameters for customization prompts: All of these parameters are of the `BasePromptTemplate` type. We will talk more about the structure of this class and how to use it in *Chapter 10, Prompt Engineering Guidelines and Best Practices*.

With that, we've covered the differences between each type of retriever. Now, let's see what they all have in common.

Common characteristics shared by all retrievers

All retrievers accept either a query directly or a `QueryBundle` object as a parameter. `QueryBundle` is a universal mechanism that can be used for more advanced use cases, such as searching based on embeddings or searching for images and/or text in a multimodal scenario.

In addition, all retrievers accept the `callback_manager` argument. We will discuss this mechanism in more detail in *Chapter 10, Prompt Engineering Guidelines and Best Practices*.

These are the basic building blocks for the retrieval logic of our RAG applications. If we want a generic and easy-to-build solution, we can use them directly. However, for more complex cases, there are several advanced retrieval modules in LlamaIndex that either combine the functionality of the basic retrievers or add new features to the mix. We will discuss some of them later in this chapter.

As we have seen, some retrievers use either embedding models or LLM queries to identify the most relevant nodes. However, at their core, all of the retriever types listed here are subclasses of `BaseRetriever`. This means that they all inherit the main `retrieve()` method, as well as `aretrieve()`, for asynchronous operation.

We will discuss the asynchronous operation next.

Efficient use of retrieval mechanisms – asynchronous operation

For the sake of simplicity, all the code examples we have discussed so far have used **synchronous methods**. Although the synchronous – or **serialized** – mode of operation is linear, easy to understand, and predictable, in modern applications, performance and low latency are very important to provide a great user experience.

The good news is that LlamaIndex already offers – in most cases – **asynchronous execution** alternatives. Here's a simple example of asynchronous execution for two Retrievers defined over KeywordTableIndex:

```python
import asyncio
from llama_index.core import KeywordTableIndex
from llama_index.core import SimpleDirectoryReader
async def retrieve(retriever, query, label):
    response = await retriever.aretrieve(query)
    print(f"{label} retrieved {str(len(response))} nodes")
async def main():
    reader = SimpleDirectoryReader('files')
    documents = reader.load_data()
    index = KeywordTableIndex.from_documents(documents)
    retriever1 = index.as_retriever(
retriever_mode='default'
)
    retriever2 = index.as_retriever(
        retriever_mode='simple'
)
    query = "Where is the Colosseum?"
    await asyncio.gather(
        retrieve(retriever1, query, '<llm>'),
        retrieve(retriever2, query, '<simple>')
    )
asyncio.run(main())
```

The preceding code executes the two retrievals in parallel. Of course, being a trivial example with a very small dataset, the performance benefits of **asynchronous operation** will not be significant in this case.

However, in the context of a commercial application that frequently calls retrievers and operates numerous complex queries over many indexed nodes, the benefits will be substantial. Asynchronous operation improves performance, uses resources more efficiently, reduces latency, and generally provides a more natural user experience by reducing waiting times.

Now, it's time to talk about the more advanced retrieval methods.

Building more advanced retrieval mechanisms

Now we understand the basic components offered by LlamaIndex, we can build increasingly sophisticated solutions. On one hand, the retrievers we have discussed already provide efficient solutions for knowledge base querying and context enhancement in an RAG flow. On the other hand, we'll see that there are many more advanced retrieval methods that either use specific techniques or ingeniously combine the retrievers already discussed.

The naive retrieval method

LlamaIndex provides fast query methods by default. As we have seen, in just a few lines of code, we can ingest documents, create nodes and, for example, build a `VectorStoreIndex` retriever, which we can then just as easily query to return the most relevant parts using a retriever that uses similarity measurement techniques.

The method is very simple and easy to implement. However, it is not an ideal method in all situations. More often than not, the **naive method**, as it is usually called, produces mediocre rather than **state-of-the-art** (SOTA) solutions.

> **To use an analogy…**
>
> It's pretty much like using a hammer for all kinds of repairs in a house. The hammer is an essential and easy-to-use tool, but it is not always the best solution for every problem. Similarly, using a simplified method of questioning may be effective for basic situations but will not be as effective for more complex situations or specific needs that require a greater degree of finesse and adaptation.

In these more complex cases, it is necessary to explore more advanced and tailored solutions, which may involve adapting the retrieval algorithms or combining them in different ways.

Also, for large datasets, naive methods can be inefficient, either returning too many irrelevant results or missing important information. They can also underperform in terms of response time and resource consumption.

In addition, in a real-world situation, data can vary significantly in terms of quality, structure, and format. Simple methods are not always able to manage this diversity and extract valuable information.

For example, if the specific information we are looking for is scattered in small chunks that are randomly distributed throughout the document, the results will be below expectations. In the next few sections, we'll discuss some more advanced retrieval methods that can provide much better results in various specific situations.

Implementing metadata filters

A very simple but also effective retrieval mechanism is filtering the retrieved nodes by **metadata**. We'll tackle a practical problem that's usually encountered in an organization and for which the retrieval functions in LlamaIndex can provide a solution.

We will see how to implement a retrieval system that filters the returned nodes according to the user's department. Similar to the concept of polymorphism in object-oriented programming, it often happens that the same concept has different definitions, depending on the area of use.

In our example, the user is looking for the definition of an incident in an organizational knowledge base. However, the term *incident* may have a different definition for those who deal with information security than for those who deal with IT service operations. Let's have a look at how we can implement a form of polymorphism in a retrieval mechanism.

1. First, we must take care of the necessary imports and define a mapping of users to departments:

    ```
    from llama_index.core.vector_stores.types import MetadataFilter,
    MetadataFilters
    from llama_index.core import VectorStoreIndex
    from llama_index.core.schema import TextNode
    user_departments = {"Alice": "Security", "Bob": "IT"}
    ```

2. Then, we must define two nodes that both store the definition of the concept of incident. The difference is in the metadata, which specifies the department where the definition applies:

    ```
    nodes = [
        TextNode(
            text=(
                "An incident is an accidental or malicious event
    that has the potential to cause unwanted effects on the security
    of our IT assets."),
            metadata={"department": "Security"},
        ),
        TextNode(
            text=("An incident is an unexpected interruption or
                degradation of an IT service."),
            metadata={"department": "IT"},
        )
    ]
    Next, we must define the function that's responsible for
    filtering and retrieval:
    def show_report(index, user, query):
        user_department = user_departments[user]
        filters = MetadataFilters(
            filters=[
                MetadataFilter(key="department",
                    value=user_department)
    ```

```
        ]
    )
    retriever = index.as_retriever(filters=filters)
    response = retriever.retrieve(query)
    print(f"Response for {user}: {response[0].node.text}")
```

3. Now, if we run the same query in the context of each user, we will get different answers, depending on the department each user belongs to:

```
index = VectorStoreIndex(nodes)
query = "What is an incident?"
show_report(index, "Alice", query)
show_report(index, "Bob", query)
```

The output will look like this:

```
Response for Alice: An incident is an accidental or malicious
event that has the potential to cause unwanted effects on the
security of our IT assets.
Response for Bob: An incident is an unexpected interruption or
degradation of an IT service.
```

See how simple that was? The same mechanism can be used, for example, to control access to information and define security rules.

For example, in a knowledge base system shared by several clients on a multi-tenancy model, we can restrict access by implementing MetadataFilters.

The code you saw earlier only does simple filtering: it restricts the search to nodes for which the value of the department key is equal to the user's department. But there are also more complex filtering variants that use operators based on the FilterOperator class. Unfortunately, the default vector store in LlamaIndex only supports the EQ (equal) operator – that is, it can only apply filters where the value of a key is equal to a certain parameter. If we use a more sophisticated version of vector store (such as Pinecone or ChromaDB), we can use the full range of operators available in FilterOperator, as listed in the following table:

Symbolic Operator	Programming Equivalent	Description
EQ	==	Equal (default)
GT	>	Greater than
LT	<	Less than
NE	!=	Not equal to
GTE	>=	Greater than or equal to
LTE	<=	Less than or equal to
IN	in	In array
NIN	nin	Not in array

Table 6.1 – A complete list of operators available for FilterOperator

Here is an example where we use filter operators and filter aggregation conditions to implement more complex scenarios:

```
from llama_index.core.vector_stores.types import (
    FilterOperator, FilterCondition)
filters = MetadataFilters(
    filters=[
        MetadataFilter(
            key="department",
            value="Procurement"
        ),
        MetadataFilter(
            key="security_classification",
            value=<user_clearance_level>,
            operator=FilterOperator.LTE
        ),
    ],
    condition=FilterCondition.AND
)
```

In the previous example, we implemented a very simple access control mechanism based on clearance level and security classification. Only nodes that belong to a particular department and have a classification level less than or equal to the user's access level will be returned. We'll talk about another method next.

Using selectors for more advanced decision logic

In an advanced user interaction system, the user may employ a wide variety of queries. For example, they may ask a very specific question, looking for a precise definition. At other times, the user may be looking for more general information or may be asking the system to summarize or compare two documents.

In these complex situations, which retriever should be used? It becomes clear that the best implementation is based on the combined strength of many retrieval systems. But this implicitly means that the RAG application must have an internal selection mechanism to choose the most appropriate retriever according to the query. This brings us to the topic of this section: the use of **selectors**.

In LlamaIndex, they come in five different flavors: `LLMSingleSelector`, `LLMMultiSelector`, `EmbeddingSingleSelector`, `PydanticSingleSelector`, and `PydanticMultiSelector`.

The way they work is slightly different. As the name suggests, some rely on the decision capabilities of an LLM, others select a particular option from a list of options based on a similarity calculation, and others use Pydantic objects to return a selection. Some return a single option from a list; others may return multiple selections from a list of options. In the end, however, their result is more or less the same: they help us implement advanced conditional logic in the applications we develop.

That is because they can evaluate complex conditions and decide which logic branch the application should follow – just like an *IF...THEN* decision block, but able to handle more complex scenarios.

The following diagram can help us better understand the role a selector plays in the logic of an RAG application. *Figure 6.12*, provides a visual representation of how `LLMSingleSelector` works:

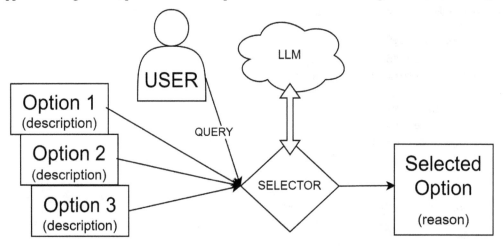

Figure 6.12 – Visualizing LLMSingleSelector

Here is a very simple implementation of a selector that uses an LLM to return a single option from a list of predefined options:

```
from llama_index.core.selectors.llm_selectors import LLMSingleSelector
options = [
    "option 1: this is good for summarization questions",
    "option 2: this is useful for precise definitions",
    "option 3: this is useful for comparing concepts",
]
selector = LLMSingleSelector.from_defaults()
```

In the first part of the code, we defined the options as a list of strings to be sent to the LLM via the `.select()` method:

```
decision = selector.select(
    options,
    query="What's the definition of space?"
).selections[0]
print(decision.index+1)
print(decision.reason)
```

The `.select()` method takes the defined options and the user query as arguments. Under the hood, the selector uses a specially constructed prompt to ask the LLM to choose the best option from the list based on the query.

As a response, the selector returns a `SingleSelection` object containing the number of the selected option and a justification for the selection made. As you can see, the selector is not something specific to retrievers. We haven't even defined a retriever in this example.

This is because I wanted to show that the mechanism is generic and can be used for absolutely any conditional logic we want to implement in the application. The returned option number could help us to choose from a list of parsers, indexes, retrievers, and so on. In this simple version, the selector simply chooses from a list of strings defining the available options. However, there is a more advanced form of selection that involves the use of the `ToolMetadata` class. But to understand this concept, we first need to clarify what a **tool** is.

Understanding tools

An essential element in any **agentic functionality**, where the application decides which method to use depending on the context, is a generic container. It may contain different functionalities that can be called by the application at runtime.

There is a rich collection of tools already developed and available in LlamaHub: `https://llamahub.ai/?tab=tools`. They can perform various specific functions, from composing and sending emails to querying various APIs or interacting with the computer's filesystem. We will talk much more about the use of tools in implementing **agents** in *Chapter 8, Building Chatbots and Agents with LlamaIndex*, where we will build our PITS chatbot.

For now, I want to show you how we can encapsulate a retriever in a tool container, and then use selectors to implement an adaptive retrieval mechanism. We will focus on the `RetrieverTool` class, which takes two important arguments: a retriever and a textual description of the retriever. Based on the description, the selector decides, for example, whether to use one retriever or another for a particular query. We define a `RouterRetriever` object on top of each retriever we build. This `RouterRetriever` is a complex decision mechanism that uses the selector to decide which retriever to use depending on the situation. The most important arguments to give it are the selector and the options to choose from – in the form of `RetrieverTool` objects. Let's see how we can implement this in code:

```
from llama_index.core.selectors import PydanticMultiSelector
from llama_index.core.retrievers import RouterRetriever
from llama_index.core.tools import RetrieverTool
from llama_index.core import (
    VectorStoreIndex, SummaryIndex, SimpleDirectoryReader)
documents = SimpleDirectoryReader("files").load_data()
vector_index = VectorStoreIndex.from_documents([documents[0]])
```

```
summary_index = SummaryIndex.from_documents([documents[1]])
vector_retriever = vector_index.as_retriever()
summary_retriever = summary_index.as_retriever()
```

First, we took the two sample files from the `files` subfolder. The first file contains information about ancient Rome and the second is a generic text about dogs. Then, we created an index for each file and from each index, we created a retriever. Now, we must define the tools:

```
vector_tool = RetrieverTool.from_defaults(
    retriever=vector_retriever,
    description="Use this for answering questions about Ancient Rome"
)
summary_tool = RetrieverTool.from_defaults(
    retriever=summary_retriever,
    description="Use this for answering questions about dogs"
)
```

As you can see, we have wrapped each retriever into `RetrieverTool` and added a clear description for the selector to use. Next, we must build `RouterRetriever`:

```
retriever = RouterRetriever(
    selector=PydanticMultiSelector.from_defaults(),
    retriever_tools=[
        vector_tool,
        summary_tool
    ]
)
response = retriever.retrieve(
    "What can you tell me about the Ancient Rome?"
)
for r in response:
    print(r.text)
```

That's all we need to do. From this point on, every time we query this dynamic retriever, the selector will determine which individual retriever to use to return the context. Here's an example:

```
retriever.retrieve("What can you tell me about the Ancient Rome?")
```

This will use `vector_tool` for retrieval. Now, take a look at the following code:

```
retriever.retrieve("Tell me all you know about dogs")
```

This will call `summary_tool`. Because we used `PydanticMultiSelector`, we can also handle situations where both retrievers should be used, like so:

```
retriever.retrieve("Tell me about dogs in Ancient Rome")
```

Unlike `PydanticSingleSelector`, `PydanticMultiSelector` can simultaneously select multiple options from the selector list, covering multiple use cases. Similarly, we can also define more complex routers at the query engine level by using `RouterQueryEngine`. We will discuss this in more detail in *Chapter 7*.

First, we need to cover a few other advanced forms of retrievers.

Transforming and rewriting queries

In the previous section, we saw how we can use selectors and the router concept to let the application decide which retriever to use.

Another very powerful tool that our RAG application can use is the `QueryTransform` construct. This allows us to rewrite and modify a query before using it to interrogate the index, as shown in *Figure 6.13*:

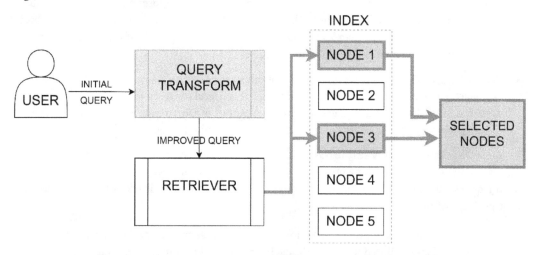

Figure 6.13 – QueryTransform improving the retrieval process

Let's imagine a scenario where we might need the functionality provided by `QueryTransform`.

Practical example

A chatbot designed to provide technical support for complex software: Users often describe their problems in vague or non-technical terms. `QueryTransform` can interpret these descriptions, break them down into more specific sub-queries, or enrich them with technical terms that better match the documentation. For example, a query of the form *My computer keeps freezing* could be transformed into a more specific query, such as *Troubleshooting steps for operating system freezes*.

There are several variations of `QueryTransform` that we can use. Each has its specific role in augmenting the information retrieval process. Let's look at each one:

- `IdentityQueryTransform`: This is a basic transform that does not modify the query. It returns the query as it was received, without any transformation. It's useful for maintaining default or basic behavior where no specific transformations are required

- `HyDEQueryTransform`: **Hypothetical Document Embeddings** (**HyDE**) transforms the query into a hypothetical document generated by an LLM. The idea is to generate hypothetical query answers and use them as embedding strings. This can help improve the relevance of the results. This method filters out inaccurate details while grounding the generated response in the actual content. You can read more about the benefits of using this technique here: *Gao, Luyu; Ma, Xueguang; Lin, Jimmy; Callan, Jamie (2022). "Precise Zero-Shot Dense Retrieval without Relevance Labels". arXiv:2212.10496v1 [cs.IR].* `https://arxiv.org/abs/2212.10496`

- `DecomposeQueryTransform`: This type of transform decomposes a complex query into a simpler and more focused subquery. This can be useful to make queries easier for the index to process and increase the chances of finding relevant nodes, especially if the index structure is not optimized for complex or ambiguous queries

- `ImageOutputQueryTransform`: This method adds instructions for formatting results as images, such as generating HTML *<img>* tags. It is useful for cases where query results are expected to be displayed as images or when the output is just an intermediate step in more complex logic and has to be further processed in a particular format

- `StepDecomposeQueryTransform`: This is similar to `DecomposeQueryTransform` but it adds an extra layer by taking previous reasoning or context into account when decomposing the query. This can help to continually refine the query based on feedback or previous results, thus improving retrieval accuracy

Each of these transformations improves a system's ability to process and respond to queries in a more efficient way that is better tailored to the user's specific needs or the nature of the data.

Let's have a look at a practical example to better understand how they work:

```
from llama_index.core.indices.query.query_transform.base import
DecomposeQueryTransform
decompose = DecomposeQueryTransform()
query_bundle = decompose.run(
    "Tell me about buildings in ancient Rome"
)
print(query_bundle.query_str)
```

Once we run the code, `DecomposeQueryTransform` takes in our original – and otherwise very ambiguous – query. It then uses a specially designed prompt to generate a more precise query using the LLM. In our example, the output should look something like this:

```
What were some famous buildings in ancient Rome?
```

You can immediately see that the new query is much clearer and greatly increases the chances of the retriever generating a correct context from the index.

Creating more specific sub-queries

Another useful approach to augmenting a query is to generate sub-queries. Sometimes, an ambiguous or very complex question becomes much clearer when it is split into several specific questions. LlamaIndex comes to our rescue this time too. `OpenAIQuestionGenerator` is a mechanism that's designed exactly for this operation. Here is the code we used as an example earlier when we talked about selectors and routers. This time, we will adapt it a bit to demonstrate how `OpenAIQuestionGenerator` works:

```
from llama_index.question_gen.openai import OpenAIQuestionGenerator
from llama_index.core.tools import RetrieverTool, ToolMetadata
from llama_index.core import (
    VectorStoreIndex, SummaryIndex,
    SimpleDirectoryReader, QueryBundle)
documents = SimpleDirectoryReader("files").load_data()
vector_index = VectorStoreIndex.from_documents(
    [documents[0]]
)
summary_index = SummaryIndex.from_documents([documents[1]])
```

So far, the code is identical to the earlier example. We read the two files from the `files` subfolder and then create an index for each document:

```
vector_tool_metadata = ToolMetadata(
    name="Vector Tool",
    description="Use this for answering questions about Ancient Rome"
)
summary_tool_metadata = ToolMetadata(
    name="Summary Tool",
    description="Use this for answering questions about dogs"
)
```

For each index, we define a name and a description in a `ToolMetadata` structure. This information will be used by `OpenAIQuestionGenerator` to *understand* what role each retriever has and what type of questions it might answer. Next, we will define the two retrievers:

```
vector_tool = RetrieverTool(
    retriever=vector_index.as_retriever(),
    metadata=vector_tool_metadata
)
summary_tool = RetrieverTool(
    retriever=summary_index.as_retriever(),
    metadata=summary_tool_metadata
)
```

Now follows the generation of sub-queries. First, we initialize an `OpenAIQuestionGenerator` object with the default settings. Then, we build a `QueryBundle` object that will contain the original query received from the user. This `QueryBundle` will be sent as an argument to the question generator:

```
question_generator = OpenAIQuestionGenerator.from_defaults()
query_bundle = QueryBundle(
    query_str="Tell me about dogs and Ancient Rome")
sub_questions = question_generator.generate(
    tools=[vector_tool.metadata, summary_tool.metadata],
    query=query_bundle
)
```

As you can see, the subquery generator takes two arguments – a list of tools at its disposal, and the original query from which it can build more specific queries:

```
for sub_question in sub_questions:
    print(f"{sub_question.tool_name}: {sub_question.sub_question}")
```

In the end, the generated questions might look something like this:

```
Summary Tool: What are the different breeds of dog?
Summary Tool: What was the role of dogs in ancient Rome?
Vector Tool: What were the most important events in Ancient Rome?
Vector Tool: What were the most famous buildings in ancient Rome?
```

`OpenAIQuestionGenerator` took the initial query and, using the LLM, returned a list of more specific questions.

The answer that's returned in the `sub_questions` variable is a list of `SubQuestion` items - a simple class with two attributes: `tool_name` and `sub_question`. We can now iterate through all the items in the list and get the tools and questions we are looking for.

In practice, using more specific queries, as in the preceding example, is likely to generate more context with the retriever and therefore likely to get a better-quality answer from `QueryEngine`.

As an alternative to `OpenAIQuestionGenerator`, it is good to know that there is also `LLMQuestionGenerator`, which, as its name suggests, allows us to use any LLM. Another difference between the two is that `LLMQuestionGenerator` uses a special parser to structure the output, unlike `OpenAIQuestionGenerator`, which relies on the generation of Pydantic objects.

The same collection of question generators also includes `GuidanceQuestionGenerator`. This mechanism uses an LLM to create helper questions to guide the query engine. It can be extremely useful when you're dealing with complex queries that need to be broken down and processed in a particular order.

Once these sub-queries have been generated, they can be used in a specially constructed query engine. We will discuss this step in more detail in *Chapter 7*, *Querying Our Data, Part 2 – Postprocessing and Response Synthesis*, when we talk about `SubQuestionQueryEngine`.

Next, we'll talk about two important concepts related to information retrieval.

Understanding the concepts of dense and sparse retrieval

As we have seen, retrieval methods are a critical component of RAG systems. They enable the identification and ranking of relevant content for queries, which is the first step in generating useful answers from an LLM. During your journey into RAG application development, you're likely to encounter two dominant retrieval paradigms – **dense retrieval** and **sparse retrieval**. Because it is important to understand these concepts, this section will focus on their characteristics, trade-offs, and the benefits of combining them.

Dense retrieval

The dense retrieval method relies on embedding vectors to represent text in a continuous, high-dimensional space. Using embedding models, texts are **encoded** into fixed-length numerical vectors that are intended to capture semantic meaning. Queries are also encoded so that the similarity between them and the node vectors can be measured using geometric operations. In dense retrieval, nodes are embedded in vectors and stored in a specialized index such as `VectorStoreIndex`.

We call them **dense** because these vectors are typically densely populated with non-zero values, representing rich and nuanced semantic information in a compact form. During retrieval, incoming queries are dynamically embedded and used to retrieve the top-k nodes using similarity search algorithms, such as those discussed in *Chapter 5*.

This approach has several advantages, particularly in terms of semantic understanding, speed, and scalability. Nodes that convey similar meanings tend to cluster closer together. Also, the words themselves do not have to match perfectly. Synonyms and polysemous words don't affect precision as much.

Specialized indexing solutions, such as those provided by a Pinecone vector database (`https://www.pinecone.io/product/`), also allow lightning-fast similarity searches over millions of vectors. Latencies range from milliseconds to less than a second and scaling is easily achieved.

There are, however, several drawbacks associated with dense search:

- **Computational cost**: Embedding and indexing large volumes of data can be computationally expensive and time-consuming.
- **A trade-off between precision and recall**: Dense retrieval systems can sometimes favor recall over precision or vice versa, depending on how the embedding model is tuned. Finding the right balance between retrieving all relevant documents and not retrieving too many irrelevant documents can be difficult.

- **Difficulty in dealing with long documents**: Dense models that generate fixed-length vectors can sometimes struggle with very long content, where important information can be diluted or lost in the embedding process.

- **Logical reasoning gaps**: While these methods are excellent at capturing semantic similarity, they typically lack logical reasoning capabilities. This means that they can identify documents that are semantically similar to the query but may struggle to understand context or logical relationships that require reasoning beyond this pattern matching. As a result, they may retrieve documents that are superficially related to the query but not truly relevant to the user's intent, especially in cases where the query requires an understanding of complex relationships or nuanced reasoning.

- **Dependence on model quality**: The effectiveness of a dense retrieval system is highly dependent on the quality of the underlying embedding model. Poorly trained models can result in suboptimal retrieval performance.

Next, we'll talk about sparse retrieval.

Sparse retrieval

Sparse retrieval methods associate documents with keywords. These methods are based on exact keyword matching or overlaps between the query and the documents.

The general process involves indexing documents by analyzing them for important terms. These keywords are then recorded in inverted indexes, which are data structures used to quickly retrieve documents containing a given keyword.

During the retrieval phase, queries are searched against these inverted indexes to find documents that share keywords with the query. Documents are ranked based on the number of common terms identified between the query and each indexed document. One of the most common techniques used in sparse retrieval is the **Term Frequency – Inverse Document Frequency (TF-IDF)** method.

TF-IDF in sparse retrieval

TF-IDF is a numerical statistic that reflects how important a word is to each document in a collection of documents. This method transforms text into a numerical representation that captures the significance of words in documents, taking into account both their frequency in individual documents and across the entire collection of documents.

- **Term Frequency (TF)** measures how often a term occurs in a document, normalized by the total number of terms in the document. It's calculated by dividing the number of times a particular term – that is, a word – appears in a document by the total number of words in that document. This indicates the importance of the term within the specific document.

- **Inverse Document Frequency (IDF)** assesses the importance of the term across the collection. It is calculated by taking the logarithm of the ratio of the total number of documents to the number of documents containing the term. This helps to downplay the importance of terms that occur very frequently in many documents. Common terms such as *the* or *is* appear in many documents and are less informative, so they have lower IDF scores. Unique terms have higher IDF scores.

The **TF-IDF score**, which is obtained by multiplying the TF by the IDF, represents the importance of each term in a document, adjusted for its commonness across the collection. In sparse retrieval, each document is represented as a vector in a high-dimensional space, where each dimension corresponds to a unique term and the value is the TF-IDF score: `https://en.wikipedia.org/wiki/Tf%E2%80%93idf`.

We call it *sparse* because, in this high-dimensional vector space, most dimensions (terms) will have a value of zero for any given document, indicating that most terms in the collection do not appear in that document. If we were to visualize these vectors, this would result in a *sparse* representation, with many zeros, as most documents contain only a small subset of the total vocabulary of the collection.

During retrieval, a query is also converted into its TF-IDF vector representation. The relevance of each document to the query is calculated using measures such as cosine similarity, and the documents are ranked accordingly. The top-ranked documents with the highest similarity scores to the query are then returned as results.

Sparse retrieval methods such as TF-IDF are particularly effective for tasks where exact term matching is important. However, they may not capture the semantic meaning of the text or the context in which terms are used, which can be addressed by more advanced retrieval techniques such as dense retrieval methods.

As you've probably guessed, they have several advantages compared to dense retrieval:

- **Efficient handling of large datasets**: Sparse retrieval methods, such as TF-IDF, are generally more efficient at handling large datasets. The inverted index structure allows fast search and retrieval of documents based on keyword matching, making it suitable for large collections of text

- **High precision**: Sparse methods often provide high accuracy in scenarios where the exact matching of terms is critical. They excel at retrieving documents that contain specific keywords present in the user's query, which is beneficial in applications where keyword specificity is essential

- **Simplicity and interpretability**: Sparse retrieval methods are conceptually simpler and more interpretable than dense methods. The fact that they rely on explicit keyword frequencies makes it easier to understand why certain documents are retrieved in response to a query

- **Less resource intensive**: Unlike dense retrieval, sparse methods do not require complex neural network models to generate embeddings. This makes them less resource-intensive in terms of computing power and memory requirements. This means they're easier to deploy and maintain

- **Less dependence on model variability**: Because sparse retrieval doesn't depend on the nuances of machine learning models to the same extent as dense retrieval, it's generally more robust to variations in model quality. Performance is more predictable and consistent across different datasets

Sparse methods also have their limitations. Some of the most important are as follows:

- **Lack of semantic understanding**: Sparse methods may not capture the semantic relationships between words. They may miss documents that are contextually relevant but do not share exact keyword matches with the query.

- **Vulnerability to synonymy and polysemy**: These methods struggle with synonymy – different words with similar meanings – and polysemy – words with multiple meanings – leading to potential misses or irrelevant retrievals.

- **Failure to capture context and nuance**: Sparse retrieval does not effectively capture the broader context or nuances in language that can be critical to understanding the true intent behind a query.

Implementing sparse retrieval in LlamaIndex

At a core level, constructs such as `KeywordTableIndex` can already be considered a basic form of sparse retrieval. After all, they share most of the principles and methods described above. However, there are even more advanced sparse retrieval capabilities available in LlamaIndex.

A perfect example is `BM25Retriever`, which implements the **Best Matching 25 (BM25)** retrieval algorithm.

BM25, a refinement of the TF-IDF method, is a more sophisticated algorithm that's used for sparse retrieval. Unlike TF-IDF, BM25 takes into account both term frequency and document length, providing a more nuanced approach to document relevance scoring. With this retriever, nodes are ranked based on their BM25 scores relative to the query. The top-k nodes with the highest scores are returned as query results, providing users with the most relevant results.

Let's look at an example of how we can use `BM25Retriever`.

To use this particular retriever, you'll need to install the required Python package and the corresponding LlamaIndex integration package by running the following commands:

```
pip install rank-bm25
pip install llama-index-retrievers-bm25
```

After installing the `rank-bm25` package, you can test it with this sample code:

```
from llama_index.retrievers.bm25 import BM25Retriever
from llama_index.core.node_parser import SentenceSplitter
from llama_index.core import SimpleDirectoryReader
reader = SimpleDirectoryReader('files')
documents = reader.load_data()
splitter = SentenceSplitter.from_defaults(
    chunk_size=60,
    chunk_overlap=0,
    include_metadata=False
)
nodes = splitter.get_nodes_from_documents(
    documents
)
```

We're using the two initial sample files containing data about ancient Rome and different breeds of dogs. In this example, I've used `SentenceSplitter`, configured with a relatively small chunk size. That is because the sample file is small in size and I wanted to produce more granular nodes structured as sentences to better exemplify the workings of `BM25Retriever`. Next, let's implement the retriever:

```
retriever = BM25Retriever.from_defaults(
    nodes=nodes,
    similarity_top_k=2
)
response = retriever.retrieve("Who built the Colosseum? ")
for node_with_score in response:
    print('Text:'+node_with_score.node.text)
    print('Score: '+str(node_with_score.score))
```

After chunking the two documents, we use the retriever to apply the BM25 algorithm and retrieve the two most relevant chunks relative to our query about the Colosseum.

You can further experiment with this sample and try to adjust the `similarity_top_k` parameter, the query, or the chunking strategy to better understand how this retriever works.

When should we use sparse retrieval instead of dense retrieval?

Let's consider a practical example of when sparse retrieval might give better results than dense retrieval in an RAG application.

> **A practical use case for sparse retrieval**
>
> Suppose we've built a system for retrieving legal documents. In this scenario, user queries would likely include precise legal terms, citations, or specific phrases found in legal texts. Let's assume a user inputs a query such as, "*Article 45 of the GDPR regarding personal data transfers on the basis of an adequacy decision.*" This query contains specific phrases, such as "Article 45" and "GDPR," which are likely to be found in relevant legal documents exactly in this form.
>
> Sparse search is likely to provide very accurate results for such a query. It will accurately locate documents that contain the specific article from the GDPR, reducing noise and irrelevant retrievals. Given that legal documents often have a structured format, with different sections and articles, sparse retrieval methods can efficiently parse through this structured data and retrieve nodes based on direct references found in the query.

Because dense retrieval methods tend to prioritize general meaning over exact term matching, they may produce less accurate results in such a specialized, keyword-specific query.

Unless trained specifically on legal texts, an embedding model used for dense retrieval might struggle to accurately interpret and match the complex legal jargon and specific citation styles used in legal queries.

When would dense retrieval be a better choice?

Here's another practical example.

A typical use case where dense retrieval would most likely produce better results would be a customer support chatbot designed to understand and respond to a wide range of customer queries. Let's say the chatbot is tasked with assisting users with various issues related to technical products, such as hardware troubleshooting, software features, usage tips, and general inquiries about products and services.

A user might ask a question such as "*My laptop battery is draining really quickly, even when I'm not using it much. What can I do about it?*" Because dense search excels at understanding the semantic context of queries, in this case, it could understand the broader meaning behind phrases such as "battery drains really fast" and relate them to similar problems, even if the exact phrase isn't in the knowledge base.

Sparse methods, on the other hand, may not perform well if the query doesn't contain specific keywords that are present in the support documents. In our example, the user might describe a problem using different terms to those used in the technical manuals or FAQs.

Can we combine the two methods in a single retriever?

The short answer is yes. You've probably already guessed that I'm building a case along these lines. By combining them, we'd get the best of both worlds in terms of benefits and features. A few pages ago, we talked about using selectors and routers to implement more complex query behavior in our RAG application.

I'll leave it up to you to adapt the methods I've demonstrated there and implement a hybrid system that uses both dense and sparse retrieval methods. If you feel the need for an additional example, you can have a look at this one, which uses the Pinecone vector database to implement hybrid search: `https://docs.llamaindex.ai/en/stable/examples/vector_stores/PineconeIndexDemo-Hybrid.html`.

Dealing with empty results from the retrieval process

Sometimes, our retrievers may come up empty-handed, without finding any indexed content matching the current query. This typically means that there are no relevant nodes in the index for that particular query.

In such cases, the retriever may return an empty result set, indicating that no matching nodes were found. Depending on the type of index used, this situation can arise if the query keywords are very specific or rare, and none of the nodes in the index contain those exact keywords, or, in the case of embedding-based indexes, the similarity search that was performed during the search did not find any matching nodes with the current parameters used. To handle this scenario, we can consider various approaches:

- **Fallback mechanisms**: The search system can have fallback strategies in place, such as performing a more general search by adjusting the retriever's parameters or suggesting alternative query terms to the user.

- **Query expansion**: The query can be automatically expanded to include synonyms, related terms, or broader concepts to increase the chances of finding relevant nodes.

- **Relevance scoring**: Even if no exact keyword matches are found, the search system can employ relevance scoring algorithms to identify nodes that are semantically similar to the query or contain partial matches.

Discovering other advanced retrieval methods

In addition to the basic concepts just discussed, several other advanced retrieval methods are worth familiarizing yourself with. There is a special section in the official documentation where these methods are explained: `https://docs.llamaindex.ai/en/stable/optimizing/advanced_retrieval/advanced_retrieval.html`.

There, you will learn more about special techniques, such as *Small-to-Big retrieval*, *recursive retrieval*, *retrieval from embedded tables*, *multi-modal retrieval*, *auto-merging retrieval*, and others.

A detailed explanation of each retrieval strategy would go far beyond what I intend to cover in this book, but that doesn't mean they aren't important. After all, there is no point in ingesting and indexing the original documents if we cannot effectively extract the context we need in RAG.

> **Practical advice**
>
> Always read the latest version of the official documentation before starting a major project. Things move so fast, and new methods and techniques emerge so quickly, that it is a shame to waste time reinventing the wheel. As an anecdote, I can tell you from personal experience that I have spent hours *inventing* something very similar to the *small-to-big* method, only to discover a few days later that it was already a tested and documented technique.

That's enough information for one chapter. We'll skip the PITS coding practice now as we'll let more information accumulate in the next chapter before implementing additional features in our personal tutoring project.

Summary

In this chapter, we explored various querying strategies and architectures within LlamaIndex with a deep focus on retrievers. Retrievers provide essential capabilities for extracting relevant information from indexes to generate useful responses in RAG systems. Throughout this chapter, we looked at basic retriever types such as `VectorIndexRetriever` and `SummaryIndexRetriever`. We also gained an understanding of advanced concepts such as asynchronous retrieval, metadata filters, tools, selectors, and query transformations. These allow us to build more sophisticated retrieval logic.

Additionally, we covered fundamental paradigms such as dense retrieval and sparse retrieval and discussed their strengths and weaknesses. Implementations in LlamaIndex such as BM25Retriever were also introduced.

Overall, this chapter provided an overview of retrieval capabilities in LlamaIndex, laying the foundation for building high-performance and contextually-aware RAG applications.

We're now equipped with the necessary knowledge to effectively retrieve information from indexes. In the next chapter, we'll build on this knowledge by addressing the other important components of a query engine: post-processors and response synthesizers.

7

Querying Our Data, Part 2 – Postprocessing and Response Synthesis

Building on the knowledge acquired in the previous chapter, we will now explore various postprocessing techniques to refine the retrieved context before covering the final query response synthesis. Afterward, we will learn how to bring all these components together into powerful query engines so that we can perform end-to-end natural language querying over documents. We'll also get to practice our new skills by working on our tutoring project.

In this chapter, we're going to cover the following main topics:

- Re-ranking, transforming, and filtering nodes using postprocessors
- Understanding the response synthesizers
- Implementing output parsing techniques
- Building and using query engines
- Hands-on – building quizzes in PITS

Technical requirements

For this chapter, you will need to install the following packages in your environment:

- *spaCy*: https://spacy.io/
- *Guardrails-AI*: https://www.guardrailsai.com/
- *pandas*: https://pandas.pydata.org/

All the code samples in this chapter can be found in the `ch7` subfolder of this book's GitHub repository: `https://github.com/PacktPublishing/Building-Data-Driven-Applications-with-LlamaIndex`.

Re-ranking, transforming, and filtering nodes using postprocessors

In the previous chapter, we discussed the various retrieval methods that LlamaIndex offers. We extracted the necessary context to be able to enrich and improve the query we are now sending to the LLM. But is this enough?

As we have already discussed, *naive* retrieval methods are unlikely to produce ideal results in any scenario. There will probably be many situations where the returned nodes will perhaps contain irrelevant information or will not be sorted in chronological order. These kinds of situations could put the LLM in difficulty, adversely affecting the quality of the prompt that our RAG application builds.

> **A quick side notes**
>
> In case it wasn't already obvious, the main purpose of a RAG flow is to programmatically build prompts. Instead of manually building these prompts and then inputting them into a ChatGPT-like interface, LlamaIndex dynamically assembles the prompts from our documents, which are split into nodes and then indexed and selected using retrievers. Many things could go wrong in this process. Maybe we didn't ingest the original documents completely or correctly, or maybe we didn't choose the right `chunk_size` value and ended up with nodes that were too granular or too loaded with irrelevant information. Maybe we didn't index them correctly, or maybe the retriever we used simply didn't select the nodes in the correct order or brought in more information than we wanted.

There are many points where errors could creep into the whole process. That doesn't sound very encouraging, does it?

The good news is that we still have an opportunity to improve this context before the final step of sending the information to the LLM. This opportunity comes in the form of **node postprocessors** and **response synthesizers**.

But first, let's understand how postprocessors work.

Node postprocessors are critical in refining the results that are obtained from the retrieval process. That is because no matter how good the retrieval step is, there is always a chance of additional, unnecessary retrieved data *polluting* our context and confusing the LLM. In other cases, the retrieved nodes might be relevant but not necessarily in the correct order, and that can also affect the quality of the LLM's response.

Figure 7.1 depicts the role of the postprocessors in a RAG workflow:

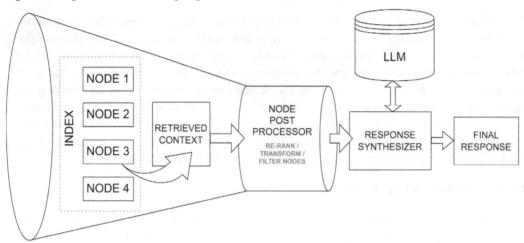

Figure 7.1 – The role of node postprocessors in RAG

These processors operate on a set of nodes, applying transformations or filters to enhance the relevance and quality of the information. They can be used on their own, to process a given set of nodes, but they are more commonly used within query engines, after the node retrieval step and before response synthesis. LlamaIndex provides various built-in processors but also the option of building custom postprocessing logic.

Let's begin by understanding the different purposes and operating modes of node postprocessors.

Exploring how postprocessors filter, transform, and re-rank nodes

At their core, all node postprocessors work by adjusting the retrieved context before that context gets injected into a prompt and sent to the LLM for response synthesis. They operate by either filtering, transforming, or re-ranking nodes. Let's have a look at these operating modes to get a better understanding.

Node filtering postprocessors

Node filtering postprocessors are designed to remove irrelevant or unnecessary nodes from the set of retrieved results. They work by applying specific criteria to each node and discarding those that don't meet the requirements. For example, SimilarityPostprocessor filters out nodes whose similarity score falls below a specified threshold, ensuring that only highly relevant nodes are passed to the language model for response generation. Similarly, KeywordNodePostprocessor keeps only the nodes that contain certain required keywords or excludes nodes with specific unwanted keywords. Node filtering helps to reduce information overload and improve the quality of the final response by focusing on the most pertinent information.

Node transforming postprocessors

Node transforming postprocessors modify the content of the retrieved nodes without necessarily removing any of them. These postprocessors aim to enhance the relevance and usefulness of the information within each node. One example is `MetadataReplacementPostprocessor`, which replaces the content of a node with a specific field from that node's metadata. This allows the text being used to be dynamically adjusted to represent a node based on its metadata rather than the original ingested content. Another example is `SentenceEmbeddingOptimizer`, which optimizes longer text passages by selecting the most relevant sentences within a node based on their semantic similarity to the query. By transforming the nodes' content, these postprocessors help align the information more closely with the user's query and improve the overall quality of the generated response.

Node re-ranking postprocessors

These postprocessors don't specifically remove or change the retrieved nodes. The purpose of a re-ranker is to take the initial set of nodes returned by the retriever and reorder them based on their relevance to the given query. This is particularly important when dealing with long-form queries or complex information needs as many LLMs struggle to effectively process and generate accurate responses when provided with lengthy or multi-faceted contexts. By employing a re-ranker, the RAG system can prioritize the most pertinent information and present it to the LLM in a more coherent format, thus leading to better responses.

Re-rankers often leverage advanced techniques such as deep learning, transformers, or LLMs themselves to assess the relevance of each retrieved document or passage. They may consider factors such as semantic similarity, context overlap, or query-document alignment to assign relevance scores to the retrieved nodes. The top-ranked nodes are then fed into the LLM, which generates the final response based on this refined context, enhancing the overall performance and utility of the RAG system. By incorporating a re-ranking step into the RAG pipeline, the system can overcome the limitations of LLMs in handling long or complex queries, ultimately providing more accurate, relevant, and useful responses to users.

Next, we'll explore the built-in LlamaIndex postprocessors in all three categories.

SimilarityPostprocessor

`SimilarityPostprocessor` filters nodes by comparing them to a similarity score threshold. Nodes that score below this threshold are removed, ensuring only relevant and similar content to the query remains. This is particularly useful because it ensures that the nodes that are passed to the language model for response generation are relevant by having a high degree of semantic correlation with the query.

> **A potential use cases**
>
> An e-commerce company has a customer support chatbot powered by an LLM. Let's assume that the chatbot retrieves nodes from `KeywordTableIndex` and tries to identify all contexts based on the keywords contained in the user query. For a query such as, *How do I return a damaged item I received yesterday?*, the retrieved nodes might include general return policies, product descriptions for items ordered by the customer, shipping information, and even irrelevant product advertisements or promotions. `SimilarityPostprocessor` could filter out nodes that are not closely related to the specific context of the query. In this case, it would prioritize nodes specifically discussing return policies for damaged items and recent orders by the customer, while discarding general product advertisements and unrelated shipping details. That would greatly increase the chance of the LLM producing a more meaningful response.

This postprocessor takes a list of nodes, typically fetched by a retriever, as input, each with an associated similarity score. The postprocessor can be configured with a `similarity_cutoff` parameter. This threshold determines the minimum score a node must have to be considered relevant. If a node's similarity score is `None` or if it's lower than `similarity_cutoff`, the node is considered not to meet the threshold and is therefore excluded from the final list. Essentially, this postprocessor filters out any nodes that have a similarity score below the set threshold. This ensures that only nodes closely related to the query are retained. The nodes meeting or exceeding the similarity score threshold is then passed on for further processing or response synthesis. Here's a simple example of how we can use it in practice:

```python
from llama_index.core.postprocessor import SimilarityPostprocessor
from llama_index.core import VectorStoreIndex, SimpleDirectoryReader
reader = SimpleDirectoryReader('files/other')
documents = reader.load_data()
index = VectorStoreIndex.from_documents(documents)
retriever = index.as_retriever(retriever_mode='default')
nodes = retriever.retrieve(
"What did Fluffy found in the gentle stream?"
)
```

In the first part of the code, we took care of the imports and then ingested a sample file into a document. Then, we created a `VectorStoreIndex` index and used the default retriever to fetch relevant nodes based on a query:

```python
Print('Initial nodes:')
for node in nodes:
print(f"Node: {node.node_id} - Score: {node.score}")
```

Here, we printed the original list of nodes since they were fetched by the retriever. Now, let's apply the postprocessor.

```
Pp = SimilarityPostprocessor(
    nodes=nodes,
    similarity_cutoff=0.86
)
remaining_nodes = pp.postprocess_nodes(nodes)
print('Remaining nodes:')
for node in remaining_nodes:
print(f"Node: {node.node_id} - Score: {node.score}")
```

After building and applying the postprocessor on the nodes, we print the remaining nodes. The output will be similar to the following:

```
Initial nodes:
Node: da51464d-e83f-4aec-a9db-8bd839ab3a4c - Score: 0.8516122822966049
Node: f839ec27-e487-4132-b139-79e3695d5500 - Score: 0.8368901228748273
Remaining nodes:
Node: da51464d-e83f-4aec-a9db-8bd839ab3a4c - Score: 0.8516122822966049
```

As we can see, the second node from the initial list was removed because it had a score below the threshold we defined – 0.85.

KeywordNodePostprocessor

KeywordNodePostprocessor is designed to refine the selection of nodes based on specific keywords. This postprocessor works by ensuring that the retrieved nodes either contain certain required keywords or exclude specific unwanted keywords. It's a great method for aligning the content of the nodes more closely with the user's query by focusing on keyword relevance.

Practical use case in a RAG scenario

Imagine a scenario in a corporate environment where the RAG system is used to retrieve information from a vast internal database for employee queries. However, there are certain confidential files or sections of files that should not be accessible to all employees. By configuring KeywordNodePostprocessor with keywords that indicate sensitive content (such as *confidential*, *restricted*, or specific project code names), the system can automatically exclude nodes containing these keywords from the retrieval results. This setup ensures that sensitive information is not inadvertently disclosed, maintaining the integrity and confidentiality of the corporate data.

It takes a list of nodes as input, typically fetched by a retriever, and is configured with parameters for required and excluded keywords. KeywordNodePostprocessor then processes these nodes, keeping only those that meet the keyword criteria. This ensures that the final set of nodes is highly relevant to the specific query, leading to more accurate and useful responses in a RAG system.

> **Quick note**
>
> The postprocessor relies on the spaCy library (https://pypi.org/project/spacy/), which you must install on your system before running the next example. This is a powerful Python library for advanced NLP. Its features include neural network models for various NLP tasks such as tagging, parsing, and NER. It's a piece of commercial open source software available under an MIT license.

To use `KeywordNodePostprocessor`, make sure you install spaCy in your environment by running the following command:

```
pip install spacy
```

Here's a basic example of how to use this postprocessor to filter out some log entries based on their classification label:

```
from llama_index.core.postprocessor import KeywordNodePostprocessor
from llama_index.core.schema import TextNode, NodeWithScore
nodes = [
    TextNode(
        text="Entry no: 1, <SECRET>, Attack at Dawn"
    ),
    TextNode(
        text="Entry no: 2, <RESTRICTED>, Go to point Bravo"
    ),
    TextNode(
        text="Entry no: 3, <PUBLIC>, text: Roses are Red"
    ),
]
```

In this example, we're manually defining the nodes instead of ingesting data from external files. After we define the nodes, we have to wrap them into `NodeWithScore` because that's the expected input of the postprocessor:

```
node_with_score_list = [
    NodeWithScore(node=node) for node in nodes
]
pp = KeywordNodePostprocessor(
    exclude_keywords=["SECRET", "RESTRICTED"]
)
remaining_nodes = pp.postprocess_nodes(
```

```
        node_with_score_list
    )
print('Remaining nodes:')
for node_with_score in remaining_nodes:
    node = node_with_score.node
    print(f"Text: {node.text}")
```

In this example, `KeywordNodePostprocessor` filters the nodes fetched by the retriever, excluding those that include `SECRET` and `RESTRICTED`.

Several parameters can be customized with this postprocessor. The most important ones are as follows:

- `required_keywords`: This is a list of strings, where each string represents a keyword that must be present in the node for it to be included in the final output. If this list is not empty, the postprocessor will filter out any nodes that do not contain these keywords.

- `exclude_keywords`: Similar to `required_keywords`, this is also a list of strings. However, in this case, any node containing a keyword from this list will be excluded from the final output. It's used for filtering out nodes based on unwanted content.

- `lang`: This argument specifies the language model to be used by the internal spaCy NLP library. The default value is *en* for English, but it can be set to other language codes supported by Spacy. The effectiveness and accuracy of keyword matching might depend on the language-specific processing of the text. For example, the way words are tokenized by Spacy can affect how keywords are identified.

Keep in mind that keywords – both required and excluded – are processed in a case-sensitive way. To ensure consistent behavior regardless of case, you might consider converting both the keywords and the text in the nodes into the same case (for example, all lowercase) before processing.

PrevNextNodePostprocessor

`PrevNextNodePostprocessor` is designed to enhance node retrieval by fetching additional nodes based on their relational context in the document. This postprocessor can operate in three modes – `previous`, `next`, or `both` – allowing users to retrieve nodes that are either preceding, succeeding, or both concerning the current set of nodes.

> **A potential use cases**
>
> Consider a legal research scenario where a user queries a RAG system about a specific legal case. `PrevNextNodePostprocessor` can be set in *both* modes to retrieve not only the nodes directly related to the case but also the preceding and succeeding nodes that might contain vital contextual information, such as related legal precedents or subsequent rulings. This ensures a comprehensive understanding of the case by providing a broader context, which is especially crucial in legal research where every detail matters.

The process begins by taking a list of nodes, typically fetched by a retriever. It then extends this list by adding nodes that are directly preceding, succeeding, or both, based on the configured mode. This results in a more contextually enriched set of nodes, leading to responses that are more nuanced and comprehensive in a RAG system. Here's a list of the parameters for this postprocessor:

- `docstore`: The actual document store storing the nodes.
- `num_nodes`: This sets the number of nodes to return. By default, it returns 1 node in the chosen direction.
- `mode`: Can be set to previous, next, or both.

Additionally, we have `AutoPrevNextNodePostprocessor`, which is an advanced variation of `PrevNextNodePostprocessor`. This one is intelligently inferring whether to fetch additional nodes based on the *previous*, *next*, or neither relationship in response to the query context.

In comparison to `PrevNextNodePostprocessor`, which requires manual setting for mode selection, `AutoPrevNextNodePostprocessor` automates this process. It utilizes specific prompts to infer the direction (previous, next, or none) based on the current context and the query.

This inference is particularly useful in scenarios where the direction of node retrieval isn't explicitly clear or when it needs to be dynamically determined based on the nature of the query and existing answers. For example, in a scenario where a RAG system is used for historical research, `AutoPrevNextNodePostprocessor` can automatically determine whether to fetch preceding or succeeding historical events or data points based on the query's context, enhancing the relevance and comprehensiveness of the response.

This capability makes it useful in applications where the sequence of information and its contextual relevance are essential for generating accurate and useful responses.

The prompts can be customized using the `infer_prev_next_tmpl` and `refine_prev_next_tmpl` arguments. There's also a `Verbose` argument, which provides more visibility on the selection process.

LongContextReorder

`LongContextReorder` is specifically designed to improve the performance of LLMs in handling long context scenarios. Research has shown that significant details in extended contexts are better utilized when positioned at the start or end of the input context *(Liu et al., Lost in the Middle: How Language Models Use Long Contexts (2023)* – `https://arxiv.org/abs/2307.03172`). The `LongContextReorder` postprocessor addresses this by reordering the nodes, placing crucial information where it's more accessible to the model.

> **A practical scenario**
>
> In a RAG system, particularly in academic or research-oriented queries where long, detailed documents are common, `LongContextReorder` can be very useful. For instance, if a user queries about detailed historical events, the system might retrieve lengthy nodes encompassing extensive details. `LongContextReorder` would rearrange these nodes, ensuring that the most relevant details are positioned at the beginning or end, thereby enhancing the model's ability to extract and utilize this crucial information effectively. This results in responses that are more coherent and contextually rich, significantly improving the overall quality of the output in cases involving lengthy contexts.

`LongContextReorder` takes a list of nodes, typically fetched by a retriever, and reorders them based on their relevance scores. The goal is to optimize the arrangement of information in a way that maximizes the language model's ability to access and process significant details, especially in cases where the context length might otherwise hinder performance.

This postprocessor is particularly effective in scenarios where detailed and comprehensive responses are required, ensuring that the most relevant information is presented in a way that is most accessible to the model.

PIINodePostprocessor and NERPIINodePostprocessor

These postprocessors mask **personally identifiable information** (PII) in nodes, improving privacy and security. `PIINodePostprocessor` is designed to use a local model, while `NERPIINodePostprocessor` relies on a NER model from Hugging Face. We saw an example of how this postprocessor works in *Chapter 4, Ingesting Data into Our RAG Workflow*, in the *Scrubbing personal data and other sensitive information* section.

`PIINodePostprocessor` takes the following arguments:

- `llm`: This object should contain a local model for processing.
- `pii_str_tmpl`: This can be used to customize the default prompt template used for masking personal data.
- `pii_node_info_key`: This string serves as a key in the node's metadata to store information related to PII processing. It's used to track and reference the PII data processed within each node. It can be used to later recompose the original information if required.

`NERPIINodePostprocessor` can be configured with the `pii_node_info_key` parameter. Similar to the previous postprocessor, this string key is used to store information related to PII processing in the node's metadata. It's a unique identifier within the node metadata for tracking the PII data that has been processed.

> **Best practice**
>
> As we discussed in *Chapter 4, Ingesting Data into Our RAG Workflow*, for maximum privacy, the best approach is to apply PII masking before the actual retrieval. This way, you ensure that no sensitive data is sent to any external LLM.

Let's see what other postprocessors we have.

MetadataReplacementPostprocessor

`MetadataReplacementPostProcessor` is designed to replace the content of a node with a specific field from that node's metadata. This allows us to dynamically switch the text that's used to represent a node based on metadata instead of the original ingested content.

> **A useful application for this postprocessor**
>
> Imagine a workflow where files are ingested via `SentenceWindowNodeParser`, which splits text into sentence-level nodes and captures the surrounding text in metadata. By configuring the processor to swap the node's content with the metadata field containing the *sentence window*, queries would retrieve full sentence context instead of sentence fragments. This allows the retriever to operate on sentences for higher accuracy while still exposing broader document context to the LLM. This technique can be very useful for processing large documents. You can find a complete example here: `https://docs.llamaindex.ai/en/stable/examples/node_postprocessor/MetadataReplacementDemo.html`.

This postprocessor takes a list of nodes as input and is configured with the `target_metadata_key` parameter, specifying which metadata field to use for the replacement. `MetadataReplacementPostProcessor` processes the nodes by replacing the `text` attribute of each node with the contents of the given metadata key. If the key is missing, the original text is kept. This provides flexibility to transform node content on the fly.

Here's another, simple example that will help you understand its functionality:

```
from llama_index.core.postprocessor import
    MetadataReplacementPostProcessor
from llama_index.core.schema import TextNode, NodeWithScore
nodes = [
    TextNode(
        text="Article 1",
        metadata={"summary": "Summary of article 1"}
    ),
    TextNode(
        text="Article 2",
        metadata={"summary": "Summary of article 2"}
```

```
    ),
]
```

First, we defined two sample nodes on which we'll now apply the postprocessor. We'll instruct it to replace the content of each node with the values stored in the summary metadata field:

```
node_with_score_list = [
    NodeWithScore(node=node) for node in nodes
]
pp = MetadataReplacementPostProcessor(
    target_metadata_key="summary"
)
processed_nodes = pp.postprocess_nodes(
    node_with_score_list
)
for node_with_score in processed_nodes:
    print(f"Replaced Text: {node_with_score.node.text}")
```

After processing takes place, the output should look like this:

```
Replaced Text: Summary of article 1
Replaced Text: Summary of article 2
```

Let's explore the other postprocessing options that LlamaIndex provides.

SentenceEmbeddingOptimizer

SentenceEmbeddingOptimizer is built to optimize longer text passages by selecting the most relevant sentences given a query based on semantic similarity. It uses advanced NLP techniques to score sentence relevance and discard less useful sentences.

> **Why and where should we use it?**
>
> In a workflow that's ingesting lengthy documents, retrieving full passages may exceed model context size limits. SentenceEmbeddingOptimizer allows us to send only the most important sentences to the LLM while preserving enough context. This prevents wasted tokens on irrelevant text by reducing noisy content. Removing irrelevant parts of the content also improves the response time and can greatly reduce the cost associated with the final LLM call.

The postprocessor takes a list of nodes as input and uses embeddings to analyze the semantic similarity of each sentence to the search query. Sentences closest to the query vector are retained while distant, unrelated sentences are stripped away.

This is how we use it in practice:

```
from llama_index.core.postprocessor.optimizer import
    SentenceEmbeddingOptimizer
optimizer = SentenceEmbeddingOptimizer(
    percentile_cutoff=0.8,
    threshold_cutoff=0.7
)
query_engine = index.as_query_engine(
    optimizer=optimizer
)
response = query_engine.query("<your_query_here>")
```

In this example, `SentenceEmbeddingOptimizer` uses a `percentile_cutoff` value of 0.8 and a `threshold_cutoff` value of 0.7 to select sentences. This means it aims to retain the top 80% of sentences by similarity score and further filters to include only those with similarity scores above 0.7. The main parameters that can be customized are as follows:

- `percentile_cutoff`: The percentage of top sentences above the similarity threshold to preserve. This allows us to compact nodes to the most relevant 75% of sentences, for example.

- `threshold_cutoff`: An absolute similarity score threshold where only sentences with similarity above this value are kept. This is useful for more stringent filtering.

- `context_before` and `context_after`: These allow us to keep several sentences before and after the matches for more context.

In a similar fashion to `KeywordNodePostprocessor`, the `SentenceEmbeddingOptimizer` postprocessor removes less relevant sentences from nodes. However, in this case, it does so use vector search rather than keywords.

This postprocessor is more about refining and shortening the content within each node for better alignment with the query. This allows for optimal information density tailored to the query while accounting for the LLM's limitations.

In contrast, processors such as `KeywordNodePostprocessor` and `SimilarityPostprocessor` operate at the node level, keeping or removing entire nodes based on keywords or similarity scores, respectively.

Time-based postprocessors

Time-based postprocessors are designed to prioritize recency and provide users with the latest, most up-to-date information. They achieve this goal through various techniques, such as sorting nodes by `date` metadata, filtering based on embedding similarity, or applying time-decay scoring models.

Let's get an overview of these processors.

FixedRecencyPostprocessor

This simple postprocessor focuses results on the most recent data by sorting nodes based on their date metadata and then returning the top_k nodes sorted by date. This ensures we get the latest data, which is critical for applications such as environmental monitoring, where having current information is vital. For example, when querying about recent air quality metrics, the postprocessor guarantees that only the most up-to-date readings are provided. They focus the results on the latest information.

The two configurable parameters for this processor are as follows:

- top_k: The number of top recent nodes to return
- date_key: The metadata key that's used to identify the date in each node

EmbeddingRecencyPostprocessor

This postprocessor further refines recency-sorted results by comparing node contents using embedding similarity and removing those too similar to earlier nodes. Nodes that are too similar to earlier ones are filtered out, ensuring that the content is both recent and diverse. The output it produces is not just recent but also diverse in terms of the information it contains.

EmbeddingRecencyPostprocessor sorts the nodes by date using the specified date_key metadata field. Then, it generates a query embedding for each node by inserting the node's content into the query_embedding_tmpl template. This query embedding is used to find similar documents.

> **Where could that be useful?**
>
> Let's think, for example, about a news aggregation service. When users query about a recent event, the system retrieves a set of nodes (news articles, in this case) sorted by date. However, many articles might cover the same event, leading to redundant information. EmbeddingRecencyPostprocessor examines these articles and filters out those that are too similar in content to more recent articles. This prevents us from presenting multiple redundant articles about the same event by eliminating those whose content significantly overlaps with more recent coverage.

Its configurable parameters are as follows:

- similarity_cutoff: The threshold for embedding similarity, above which nodes are considered too similar and filtered out
- date_key: This specifies the metadata key that's used for sorting nodes by date
- query_embedding_tmpl: This is the template that's used to generate query embeddings for each node

TimeWeightedPostprocessor

`TimeWeightedPostprocessor` prioritizes newer results by reranking nodes based on a **time-decay function** accounting for how recently they were accessed. This favors fresh, less repeated content, which is critical for use cases such as trending news aggregation, where users want the latest updates rather than the same information.

The scoring dynamically adapts to changing access patterns over time. `TimeWeightedPostprocessor` is engineered to re-rank nodes based on their recency and prior access history, applying a time-weighted scoring system. This postprocessor is particularly effective in scenarios where it's crucial to avoid repeatedly presenting the same information and where the freshness of content matters.

It works by adjusting the score of each node based on the last time it was accessed, applying a decay factor to prioritize less recently accessed content. This dynamic reranking ensures that the output is not just relevant but also timely and varied. This works great for applications where keeping the users updated with the most recent information is essential.

It also has several parameters that we can tweak:

- `time_decay`: The decay factor for the time-weighted scoring
- `last_accessed_key`: Metadata key for tracking when a node was last accessed
- `time_access_refresh`: A Boolean to determine if the last accessed time should be updated
- `now`: An optional parameter to set the current time. This is useful for testing
- `top_k`: The number of top nodes to return after reranking. The default value is 1

With these advanced time-aware postprocessors, our RAG system transforms into a dynamic information curator, adept at navigating the temporal aspects of data. They ensure that our system doesn't just retrieve information but smartly selects content that's not only recent but also varied and relevant.

This makes them indispensable for scenarios where timely and diverse information is crucial, offering us a consistently fresh and rich experience.

Re-ranking postprocessors

Along with the basic processors we've discussed so far, LlamaIndex provides several more sophisticated options that make use of LLMs or embedding models for re-ranking nodes. As a general principle, they work by re-ordering the nodes based on their relevance to the query, rather than removing them or altering their content. Some of these postprocessors, such as `SentenceTransformerRerank`, also update the relevance scores of the nodes to reflect their similarity to the query.

They all accept a `top_n` parameter, which specifies how many re-ordered nodes they should return. You can explore them in full detail by consulting the official docs: `https://docs.llamaindex.ai/en/stable/module_guides/querying/node_postprocessors/`.

This section provides a quick overview of the available LLM-based processors.

LLMRerank

This processor re-orders nodes by asking an LLM to assign relevance scores. It selects the `top_n` most relevant nodes from a given set based on the user's query. The prompt that's used by this postprocessor can be customized via the `choice_select_prompt` parameter.

To increase efficiency, it works in batches. The batch size can also be customized by using the `choice_batch_size` argument. It requires a `query_bundle` argument for processing and uses the model configured in `llm`. Its reranking process involves formatting node contents into prompts, using the LLM to assess relevance, and then reordering nodes based on their calculated relevance scores.

CohereRerank

This processor re-ranks nodes using Cohere's neural models (`https://cohere.com/rerank`) to sort nodes by relevance. The default model that's used is *rerank-english-v2.0*. The `top_n` nodes deemed most relevant by the Cohere model are selected and returned.

This processor allows us to leverage powerful relevance algorithms provided by Cohere but requires a Cohere API key and their libraries to be installed in the local environment.

SentenceTransformerRerank

`SentenceTransformerRerank` uses sentence transformer models to re-rank nodes based on their relevance to a given query.

This process involves scoring nodes using a sentence transformer model, with the default being *cross-encoder/stsb-distilroberta-base*, and then reordering them based on these scores. It selects the top-ranked nodes to return, up to the specified `top_n` limit. You can find more information here: `https://www.sbert.net/examples/applications/retrieve_rerank/README.html`.

RankGPTRerank

This re-ranking postprocessor is designed to improve retrieval results relevance using an LLM such as GPT-3.5. It involves a process where the user's query and content from nodes are formatted into prompts, guiding the language model to rank these nodes based on relevance.

The model's output is then used to re-order the nodes, ensuring that the most relevant ones appear at the top. When the context that's retrieved is too large for the LLM's context window, `RankGPTRerank` uses a sliding window approach to gradually re-rank a segment of chunks.

This method is based on a paper by Sun et al. (2023), *Is ChatGPT Good at Search? Investigating Large Language Models as Re-Ranking Agents* (`https://arxiv.org/abs/2304.09542v2`).

LongLLMLinguaPostprocessor

This very useful postprocessor is designed to optimize node texts concerning queries by compressing them. It's based on a method described in a paper by Jiang et al. (2023), *LLMLingua: Compressing Prompts for Accelerated Inference of Large Language Models* (`https://arxiv.org/abs/2310.05736v2`).

`LongLLMLinguaPostprocessor` addresses several issues associated with LLMs, such as increased API latency, context window limit overruns, and expensive API costs.

The key idea is to intelligently compress prompts in a way that they focus on the most relevant information, enabling more efficient and accurate processing by the LLM. It offers a balance between performance and efficiency, demonstrating that prompt compression – with up to 20x achievements – can lead to substantial improvements in model inference and cost-effectiveness without considerable loss in performance.

The processor is designed to work with a local, well-trained language model. This setup allows for the efficient compression of prompts for use with LLMs, supporting the optimization process locally without relying on external API calls.

You can find a complete demo here: `https://github.com/microsoft/LLMLingua/blob/main/examples/RAGLlamaIndex.ipynb`.

Measuring the effectiveness of LLM-based re-ranking

A common source of concern – especially when using LLM-based re-rankers – is the quality of their output. Because LLMs are trained on vast amounts of data, they can sometimes generate results that are biased, inconsistent, or even factually incorrect. This is particularly problematic when dealing with specialized domains or sensitive information. To verify that the LLM-based postprocessors are re-ranking the nodes well enough, it is important to properly evaluate their performance. Here are a few approaches you can use to gauge the quality of the re-ranking step:

- **Manual relevance assessment**: Manually examine the re-ranked results to check if the most relevant nodes are indeed appearing at the top. This qualitative evaluation depends on human judgment to determine if the re-ranking matches the query's intent. While not exactly very scientific, this simple approach may suffice for simple use cases, experiments, or non-production RAG applications.

- **Benchmark datasets**: Evaluate the re-ranking performance on standard **information retrieval** **(IR)** benchmarks that have pre-defined queries and relevance judgments. This process can be time-consuming and it may require a well-prepared evaluation dataset but it will save you from troubles later in the RAG workflow. By comparing the re-ranked results against the ground truth, you can calculate metrics such as precision, recall, and others to quantify the re-ranking quality. We'll cover the evaluation process in more detail in *Chapter 9, Customizing and Deploying Our LlamaIndex Project.*

- **User feedback:** In real-world applications, collect user feedback on the re-ranked search results. User satisfaction scores, click-through rates, or other engagement metrics can indicate if the re-ranking enhances the user experience and provides more relevant results. There's an inherent advantage to this method. Because it relies on human feedback directly collected in the live environment, it becomes a form of **continuous evaluation**. This makes it useful in detecting any potential **model drift**, thus enabling timely adjustments to our pipeline to help us avoid quality degradation over time.

- **A/B testing:** Another form of gathering user feedback would be by running controlled experiments where some users are shown the original ranking, while others see the LLM-based re-ranked results. Compare the performance metrics between the two groups to assess if the re-ranking leads to improved outcomes.

- **Domain expert evaluation:** For specialized domains, ask subject matter experts to review the re-ranked results and provide feedback on their relevance and quality. While more expensive and difficult than the other options, this method could be the best solution when dealing with highly technical or niche topics that require a deep understanding of the subject matter.

The evaluation method you choose will depend on your specific use case, available resources, and the level of rigor you need. Using a mix of qualitative and quantitative approaches can give you a thorough assessment of the LLM's re-ranking performance.

Understanding the model drift phenomenon

While not necessarily specific to re-ranking, model drift can significantly impact the quality of our RAG pipelines and it's an important factor to consider. Our models are static representations of the snapshot datasets that are used for their training. But in time, that data changes. For example, new concepts may emerge that were not included in the training data, or the data itself may shift in distribution. This phenomenon is known as *model drift*, and it can manifest in multiple forms:

- **Data drift:** This occurs when the statistical properties or distribution of the input data change over time. For instance, if a model was trained on a dataset of customer reviews from a specific period, it may not perform as well on newer reviews that contain different language patterns, sentiments, or topics.

- **Concept drift:** This happens when the relationships between the input features and the target variable evolve. In a RAG system designed to assist with medical queries, the introduction of new diseases, treatments, or medical terminology can lead to concept drift. The model's understanding of the domain becomes outdated, and its performance may degrade.

- **Upstream data changes:** This type of drift happens when the data used to train the model is different from the data used in production. For example, if a RAG system is trained on a curated dataset but then applied to raw, unprocessed data in production, the model's performance may suffer due to differences in data quality, format, or distribution.

- **Feedback loops:** In some cases, the outputs of a model can influence its future inputs, creating a feedback loop. For instance, if a RAG system is used to recommend articles to users, and those recommendations are then used to update the retrieval component, the model may become biased toward its previous outputs, leading to a narrowing of the information it provides over time.

- **Domain shift:** This occurs when a model is applied to a different domain or context than it was originally trained for. In a RAG workflow, if the retrieval component is trained on data from one domain (for example, legal documents) but then used to answer queries in another domain (for example, medical questions), the model's performance may suffer due to differences in language, terminology, or underlying concepts.

- **Temporal drift:** This type of drift is related to the passage of time and can encompass both data drift and concept drift. As time passes, the data and concepts relevant to a particular task may evolve, leading to a gradual decline in model performance if not addressed.

To mitigate these various types of model drift, it's important to continuously monitor the performance of a RAG system, regularly update its retrieval component with new data, and adapt it to changes in the underlying data distribution, concepts, or domain. Additionally, implementing feedback loops carefully and ensuring that the training data is representative of the production environment can help minimize the impact of upstream data changes and feedback-related drift. This helps ensure that our RAG system remains accurate, up-to-date, and aligned with the evolving needs of the users.

Final thoughts about node postprocessors

If the existing ones are not exactly fit for our particular use case, we have the option to build our own. **Custom postprocessors** can be built by extending `BaseNodePostprocessor`. You can find a complete example here: `https://docs.llamaindex.ai/en/stable/module_guides/ querying/node_postprocessors/root.html#custom-node-postprocessor`.

> **Important note**
>
> In more complex scenarios, postprocessors can also be chained to apply multiple transformations to the nodes before they're passed to the response synthesizer.

The key is applying the right processors to remove noise, improve relevance signal, inject diversity, and handle sensitive content – leading to higher quality and more reliable generated responses.

For now, let's shift our focus to the final piece of our puzzle: **response synthesizers**.

Understanding response synthesizers

The final step before sending our hard-worked contextual data to the LLM is the response synthesizer. It's the component that's responsible for generating responses from a language model using a user query and the retrieved context.

It simplifies the process of querying an LLM and synthesizing an answer across our proprietary data. Just like the other components of the framework, response synthesizers can be used on their own or configured in query engines to handle the final step of response generation after nodes have been retrieved and postprocessed.

Here's a simple example demonstrating how to use one directly on a given set of nodes:

```
from llama_index.core.schema import TextNode, NodeWithScore
from llama_index.core import get_response_synthesizer
nodes = [
    TextNode(text=
        "The town square clock was built in 1895"
    ),
    TextNode(text=
        "A turquoise parrot lives in the Amazon"
    ),
    TextNode(text=
        "A rare orchid blooms only at midnight"
    ),
]
node_with_score_list = [NodeWithScore(node=node) for node in nodes]
```

The first part of the code, we've defined some arbitrary nodes. That's going to be our *proprietary* context. Next, we'll use a response synthesizer to run an LLM query based on our context:

```
synth = get_response_synthesizer(
    response_mode="refine",
    use_async=False,
    streaming=False,
)
response = synth.synthesize(
    "When was the clock built?",
    nodes=node_with_score_list
)
print(response)
```

The output is as follows:

```
The clock was built in 1895.
```

Curious to take a peek under the hood? What happened in the background here? OK, bear with me for the next few lines – once you understand this example, you'll know exactly how a response synthesizer works. Let me show you a diagram first:

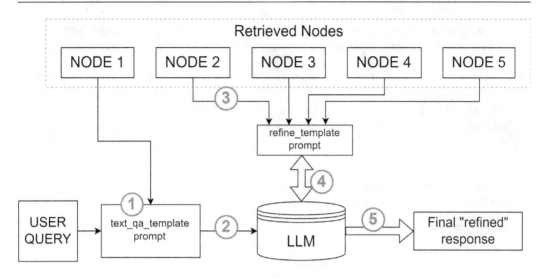

Figure 7.2 – The refine response synthesizer

Here's a description of the process:

1. The synthesizer begins by building a special-purpose prompt, starting with the first node in the list as context. This prompt includes the query, specific instructions, and the context – which in this case is our first node. It uses a default value but can be customized via the `text_qa_template` parameter:

    ```
    System: "You are an expert Q&A system that is trusted around
    the world. Always answer the query using the provided context
    information, and not prior knowledge. Some rules to follow:
    1. Never directly reference the given context in your answer.
    2. Avoid statements like 'Based on the context, ...' or 'The
    context information ...' or anything along those lines."

    User: "Context information is below. The town square clock
    was built in 1895. Given the context information and not prior
    knowledge, answer the query. Query: When was the clock built?
    Answer: "
    ```

2. The next step is to send this prompt to the LLM and wait for an answer.

3. After the initial answer comes back, it builds the prompt for the next node while also integrating the first answer in the prompt and refining the final answer using a prompt that can be customized with `refine_template`.

4. It then repeats this iterative process for all nodes while constantly refining the final answer.

5. Once the nodes are exhausted, it returns the *refined* final answer.

In this case, the behavior of the synthesizer is dictated by `response_mode="refine"`.

However, `refine` mode is just one of the several predefined synthesizers in LlamaIndex. Synthesizer mode can be specified using the `response_mode` parameter. Here's a list of the available response modes:

- `refine`: As we saw in the previous example, `refine` queries each node individually using `text_qa_template` and `refine_template` prompts to iteratively construct a detailed response. This mode is ideal for constructing detailed responses, ensuring that each piece of information is carefully considered. We can also set `Verbose` to `True` for more visibility on the inner workings of this synthesizer and use `output_cls` to specify a `pydantic` object to use as a response template.

- `compact`: This one is similar to `refine` but it concatenates nodes to reduce the number of required LLM queries, balancing detail, and efficiency.

- `tree_summarize`: This mode uses recursive summarization, processing each node with `summary_template`. It recursively summarizes and queries nodes, concatenating them in each iteration until a single final response remains. It's very useful for summarization and best suited for creating comprehensive summaries from multiple pieces of information.

- `simple_summarize`: This mode truncates nodes to fit in one LLM query for basic summarization. It's great for brief overviews as it's quick and cheap, but it may omit finer details.

- `accumulate`: This mode applies the query to each node individually and accumulates the responses. It's best suited for analyzing or comparing responses from multiple sources.

- `no_text`: In this operating mode, the response synthesizer fetches nodes without querying the LLM. This is mainly useful for debugging, analyzing raw data, or inspecting the retrieval or postprocessing outputs.

- `compact_accumulate`: A blend of compact and accumulate, this mode compacts prompts, similar to `compact` mode, and applies the query across nodes. This is especially suitable for efficiently processing multiple sources.

In addition to these predefined modes, custom response synthesizers can be created by subclassing `BaseSynthesizer` and implementing the `get_response` method. You can find a complete example in the official documentation: `https://docs.llamaindex.ai/en/stable/module_guides/querying/response_synthesizers/root.html#custom-response-synthesizers`. This provides you with the flexibility to design specialized response generation approaches.

Features such as `structured_answer_filtering` can also be enabled on the *refine* and *compact* synthesizers. It uses the LLM to filter out retrieved nodes that are irrelevant to the question, improving response quality.

Prompt templates such as `text_qa_template` and `refine_template` allow us to customize the prompts that are used at different stages of response synthesis. Additional variables can also be passed to influence response generation.

Overall, response synthesizers handle the critical task of querying nodes and producing a final response, providing options to balance performance, customizability, and accuracy.

But guess what? We're not out of the woods yet.

Let's talk about another challenge in our path.

Implementing output parsing techniques

Our next topic addresses a common problem that's encountered in RAG applications that rely on structured outputs produced by an LLM. When those outputs are to become inputs in the next processing steps of the application, their structure becomes very important.

> **A bit of background**
>
> Due to their non-deterministic nature, LLMs have the bad habit of sometimes producing responses in a format other than the requested one, adding unsolicited comments or descriptions – just like humans if you think about it. Simply relying on clever prompting techniques may not be enough to completely avoid this behavior.

Even models specifically trained to follow precise instructions occasionally deviate from the structure we've requested. In cases where that output is simply returned to the user, this doesn't matter much – it might even create a more natural experience.

The problems arise when the structure of the response matters – for example, when we are going to store that output in a set of variables and then send it to further processing. Have a look at *Figure 7.3* for a better understanding:

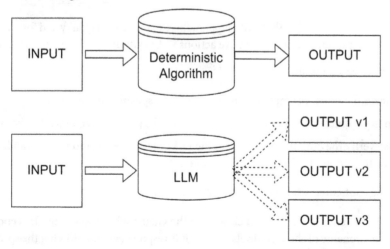

Figure 7.3 – LLMs may produce unpredictable outputs

So, how can we make sure that we receive a structured and predictable output from an LLM? As usual, LlamaIndex comes to our rescue – this time in the form of the **output parsers** and **Pydantic programs**. Here's an overview of the methods that are used to ensure a structured output.

Extracting structured outputs using output parsers

Output parsers are essential for managing the unpredictability of LLM responses. They ensure that outputs from LLMs are structured and formatted correctly for subsequent steps in an application. These parsers come in various forms, each with a unique approach to handling and refining the output.

GuardrailsOutputParser

This particular one is based on the **Guardrails** library provided by Guardrails AI: https://www.guardrailsai.com/. Guardrails ensures the outputs from LLMs adhere to specified structures and types. This is particularly useful in RAG applications, where outputs need to be consistent and structured for further processing.

Guardrails does this by validating the LLM outputs against a defined format and can take corrective actions such as re-asking the LLM if the outputs don't meet the specified standards. This feature is essential for maintaining the integrity and usability of LLM outputs in automated processes.

> **Under the hood**
>
> At the core of how Guardrails works, we find the notion of **rails**. In the Guardrails library, a rail serves as a specification tool for LLM outputs. It is used to enforce specific structures, types, and validation criteria on these outputs. Rails can be defined using either the **Reliable AI Markup Language** (**RAIL**) for structured outputs or directly in Python Pydantic structures.

The purpose of a rail is to ensure that the LLM outputs adhere to predefined quality and format standards, which includes setting validators and corrective actions if the output deviates from these standards.

This parser operates based on the following logic:

1. First, it takes the initial prompt and an output format specification as input.

2. Based on the output format specification, it re-formats the prompt, adapting it for the target LLM.

3. It can also verify the output received from the LLM. If the specification is not validated, it can regenerate the output until the structure is valid.

This parser can be configured with the following parameters:

- `guard`: An instance of the `Guard` class from the Guardrails library. This class encapsulates the core functionality of the Guardrails system. It is responsible for enforcing the specifications defined in a RAIL structure

- `llm`: This parameter is optional and is used to select the language model that's used in conjunction with the Guardrails parser

- `format_key`: This optional parameter is useful when you want to inject specific formatting instructions into the query based on the output format required

You can find a complete example of using this method here: `https://docs.llamaindex.ai/en/stable/module_guides/querying/structured_outputs/output_parser.html#guardrails`.

Once you've familiarized yourself with the RAIL language, the Guardrails library becomes an easy-to-use parsing solution for your apps.

Just make sure you install the Guardrails library in your environment first by running the following command:

```
pip install guardrails-ai
```

In case you're wondering how you could build an output parser and implement any custom guard rail logic in it, you can find a complete example here: `https://docs.llamaindex.ai/en/latest/examples/output_parsing/llm_program/#define-a-custom-output-parser`.

LangchainOutputParser

Apart from `GuardrailsOutputParser`, LlamaIndex also supports the output parsers provided by Langchain.

Instead of using the more complex RAIL language to define validation criteria and corrective actions, `LangchainOutputParser` relies on a simpler concept called a **response schema**.

Response schemas in Langchain are primarily used for structuring the output and focus on defining specific fields that the output should contain. These schemas guide the Langchain system to ensure that the output matches the expected format.

This approach is less about enforcing stringent validation rules or corrective actions and more about organizing the output data in a coherent and predictable structure.

Here's an example that implements a very simple quotation system based on this method:

```
from langchain.output_parsers import (
    StructuredOutputParser, ResponseSchema)
from llama_index.core.output_parsers import LangchainOutputParser
from llama_index.llms.openai import OpenAI
from llama_index.core.schema import TextNode
from llama_index.core import VectorStoreIndex
from pydantic import BaseModel
from typing import List
```

```
nodes = [
    TextNode(
        text="Roses have vibrant colors and smell nice."),
    TextNode(
        text="Oak trees are tall and have green leaves."),
]
```

In the first part of our code, we took care of the necessary imports and then defined some random *proprietary data* contained in two nodes. Next, we must define the response schemas that will be used to structure the LLM's output:

```
schemas = [
    ResponseSchema(
        name="answer",
        description=(
            "answer to the user's question"
        )
    ),
    ResponseSchema(
        name="source",
        description=(
            "the source text used to answer the user's question, "
            "should be a quote from the original prompt."
        )
    )
]
```

As you can see, the schema defines the expected output structure. Now, we can define the Langchain parser and an OpenAI `llm` object that's been configured to use it:

```
lc_parser = StructuredOutputParser.from_response_schemas(schemas)
output_parser = LangchainOutputParser(lc_parser)
llm = OpenAI(output_parser=output_parser)
```

Now, it's time to build an index and `QueryEngine` from our Nodes. `QueryEngine` will be configured to use the Langchain parser so that it can structure the output:

```
index = VectorStoreIndex(nodes=nodes)
query_engine = index.as_query_engine(llm=llm)
response = query_engine.query(
    "Are oak trees small? yes or no",
)
print(response)
```

The output is as follows:

```
{'answer': 'no', 'source': 'Oak trees are tall and have green
leaves.'}
```

Neat, isn't it?

Note that citations are useful in a RAG system as they increase transparency and allow the answers to be validated against our proprietary data.

The Langchain parser has two configurable parameters:

- `output_parser`: This parameter accepts an instance of a Langchain output parser (`LCOutputParser`). This is where the primary logic for parsing and structuring the output is defined. As seen in the previous example, the parser provided here determines how the output from the LLM is processed and formatted

- `format_key`: This is an optional parameter that, if provided, is used to insert additional format instructions into the query. This can be particularly useful when the query needs to be formatted with specific instructions that guide the output generation of the language model

While both `GuardrailsOutputParser` and `LangchainOutputParser` aim to structure and validate LLM outputs, their specific mechanisms and extent of control over the output format vary. The Langchain parser is more focused on processing the LLM output, while the Guardrails parser has a more proactive role in shaping the query and output format. We'll talk about the other method next.

Extracting structured outputs using Pydantic programs

Pydantic programs represent another way to generate structured outputs. Pydantic programs are a form of abstraction in LLM workflows that convert input strings into structured pydantic object types. They can either call functions or rely on text completions, along with output parsers.

They are highly versatile and can be used for various applications, being both composable and adaptable for general or specific use cases. There are multiple programs available for various use cases.

You can find an overview and working examples here: `https://docs.llamaindex.ai/en/ stable/module_guides/querying/structured_outputs/pydantic_program. html`.

You'll learn how to use a Pydantic program – in this case, `OpenAIPydanticProgram`, later in this chapter, when we continue working on our PITS tutoring app.

Building and using query engines

Our puzzle is now complete. Throughout the previous chapters, we've gradually learned about the key ingredients in a RAG setup. Now, it's time to bring everything together: the nodes, indexes, retrievers, postprocessors, response synthesizers, and output parsers.

In this chapter, we'll focus on blending these elements into a complex construct: the query engine. We'll learn about how query engines work and the neat tricks they have up their sleeves.

Exploring different methods of building query engines

At its core, QueryEngine is an interface that processes natural language queries to generate rich responses. It often relies on one or more indexes through retrievers and can also be combined with other query engines for enhanced capabilities.

The easiest way to define QueryEngine is using the **high-level API** provided by LlamaIndex, like this:

```
query_engine = index.as_query_engine()
```

With just a single line of code, we've built a simple query engine from an existing index. Although fast, this method uses RetrieverQueryEngine under the hood with the default settings and does not provide many opportunities for customization.

If we want to have complete control over its parameters and full customization options, we can use the **low-level API** to explicitly build the query engine.

Let's have a look at an example:

```
from llama_index.core.retrievers import SummaryIndexEmbeddingRetriever
from llama_index.core.postprocessor import SimilarityPostprocessor
from llama_index.core.query_engine import RetrieverQueryEngine
from llama_index.core import (
    SummaryIndex, SimpleDirectoryReader, get_response_synthesizer)
```

As usual, we start by handling the imports. Next, we ingest our demo files and build a simple SummaryIndex:

```
documents = SimpleDirectoryReader("files").load_data()
index = SummaryIndex.from_documents(documents)
```

Then, we throw in a retriever, a response synthesizer, and a node postprocessor. Building a query engine with this low-level API approach allows us to fully customize each component:

```
retriever = SummaryIndexEmbeddingRetriever(
    index=index,
    similarity_top_k=3,
```

```
)
response_synthesizer = get_response_synthesizer(
    response_mode="tree_summarize",
    verbose=True
)
pp = SimilarityPostprocessor(similarity_cutoff=0.7)
```

Now, it's time to bring them all together and assemble our `QueryEngine`:

```
query_engine = RetrieverQueryEngine(
    retriever=retriever,
    response_synthesizer=response_synthesizer,
    node_postprocessors=[pp]
)
response = query_engine.query(
    "Enumerate iconic buildings in ancient Rome"
)
print(response)
```

The output should look similar to the following:

```
The iconic buildings in ancient Rome included the Colosseum and the
Pantheon.
```

Now that we've built a simple query engine, let's take a look at some more advanced scenarios.

Advanced uses of the QueryEngine interface

The LlamaIndex community has gradually developed – and continues to develop – various advanced query methods while using `QueryEngine` as a main component.

Apart from the query engines that I'm already covering in this book, *Table 7.1* provides an overview of other available engines at the time of writing:

QueryEngine Class	Short Description and Use Cases
CitationQueryEngine	Designed for situations requiring citations from multiple sources to support answers. It is especially useful in academic research, legal analysis, or any context where validated, source-based information is important. When generating responses, this query engine incorporates and cites relevant sources, ensuring answers are not only accurate but also verifiably supported by documented evidence.

QueryEngine Class	Short Description and Use Cases
`CogniswitchQueryEngine`	Integrates with the Cogniswitch service (`https://www.cogniswitch.ai/`) to answer queries using a combination of Cogniswitch's knowledge processing capabilities and OpenAI's models.
`ComposableGraphQueryEngine`	Designed to operate within a composable graph structure, enabling flexible, modular querying across different data sources and indices. It is ideal for complex data ecosystems where different types of information are interconnected.
`QASummaryQueryEngineBuilder`	Combines `SummaryIndex` and `VectorStoreIndex`. This is useful both to retrieve specific information from documents and to get concise summaries of content.
`TransformQueryEngine`	Designed to preprocess queries using a specific transformation before they are submitted to an underlying query engine. When queries vary greatly in format or clarity, applying a transformation to normalize or enhance them can greatly improve retrieval.
`MultiStepQueryEngine`	Works by decomposing complex queries into simpler, sequential steps. It can be useful for handling complex or multi-faceted questions that require a series of logical steps.
`ToolRetrieverRouterQueryEngine`	Can dynamically choose from multiple candidate query engines based on the query's context. It uses the most appropriate query engine tool for each specific query.
`SQLJoinQueryEngine`	Designed for cases that require a combination of SQL database queries and additional information retrieval or processing. This is especially useful when the SQL query results need to be augmented or refined using further queries.
`SQLAutoVectorQueryEngine`	Integrates SQL database queries with vector-based retrieval, enabling a two-step process where a query can be executed against a SQL database. Based on those results, further information can be fetched from a vector store.
`RetryQueryEngine`	When the initial response to a query does not meet certain evaluation criteria, it automatically retries the query if it fails evaluation.

QueryEngine Class	Short Description and Use Cases
`RetrySourceQueryEngine`	Designed to perform retries on a query with different source nodes based on evaluation criteria. If the initial response from the query engine does not pass the evaluator's criteria, it attempts to find alternative source nodes that may yield a better response.
`RetryGuidelineQueryEngine`	Similar to `RetryQueryEngine`, this one also transforms the query on each retry, based on feedback from the evaluation process.
`PandasQueryEngine`	Converts natural language queries into executable pandas Python code, allowing for data manipulation and analysis over pandas DataFrames.
`JSONalyzeQueryEngine`	Designed to analyze JSON list-shaped data by converting natural language queries into SQL queries that are executed within an in-memory SQLite database.
`KnowledgeGraphQueryEngine`	Generates and processes queries for knowledge graphs, translating natural language queries into graph-specific queries and synthesizing responses based on graph query results. This is useful for applications requiring interaction with knowledge graphs.
`FLAREInstructQueryEngine`	Implementing the Forward-Looking Active REtrieval (FLARE) method, this query engine allows the model to continually access and incorporate external knowledge as it generates content. This is particularly useful for generating long, knowledge-intensive texts. By actively predicting future content needs and retrieving information accordingly, FLARE aims to reduce hallucinations and improve the factual accuracy of generated responses. It's based on a paper by Jiang et al. (2023), Active Retrieval Augmented Generation (https://arxiv.org/abs/2305.06983v2).
`SimpleMultiModalQueryEngine`	A multi-modal query engine that can process queries involving both text and images, assuming that the retrieved text and images can fit within the LLM's context window. It retrieves relevant text and images based on the query and then synthesizes a response using a multi-modal LLM.

QueryEngine Class	Short Description and Use Cases
SQLTableRetrieverQueryEngine	Converts natural language queries into SQL queries but also synthesizes responses from the query results, making the responses more understandable and relevant to the user's natural language query.
PGVectorSQLQueryEngine	Designed to work with PGvector (https://github.com/pgvector/pgvector), an extension for PostgreSQL that allows vectors to be stored and embedded directly within the database.

Table 7.1 – Different query engine modules available in LlamaIndex

The list of advanced implementations has already become so long that it could probably be the subject of a separate book. Consequently, I did not set out to give a detailed presentation of each method. Instead, I encourage you to consult the official project documentation on the subject and discover how these building blocks can be used in various scenarios: `https://docs.llamaindex.ai/en/stable/module_guides/deploying/query_engine/modules.html`.

There, you will find detailed explanations, use cases for each module, and, most importantly, code examples with which you can understand the operation and implementation of each method.

However, we cannot end this chapter without introducing you to at least a few essential modules in a RAG scenario. So, that's what we are going to cover next.

Implementing advanced routing with RouterQueryEngine

Remember when we talked about routing retrievers in *Chapter 6, Querying Our Data, Part 1 – Context Retrieval*? It's time to see a more advanced routing mechanism, this time implemented at the query engine level.

Figure 7.4 summarizes the operation of `RouterQueryEngine`:

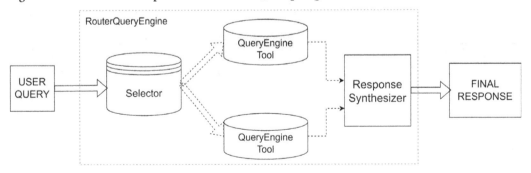

Figure 7.4 – How RouterQueryEngine works

`RouterQueryEngine` is capable of choosing between different tools it has available. Depending on the user query, the router will decide which `QueryEngineTool` should be used to generate an answer.

Just like in the case of retrievers, we can use `PydanticMultiSelector` or `PydanticSingleSelector` to configure its behavior. The multi-selector combines multiple options and can handle a broader spectrum of user queries.

> **Potential use case**
>
> Imagine a real-life scenario where an organization has its knowledge split into multiple individual documents. Such a router would allow for general queries over the entire knowledge base, while still enabling and precisely pinpointing the source data used to generate the answer.

In the following example, we're building a `RouterQueryEngine` engine that operates different query engine tools – each one built over a different document. Here's the code:

```
from llama_index.core.tools import QueryEngineTool
from llama_index.core.query_engine import RouterQueryEngine
from llama_index.core.selectors import PydanticMultiSelector
from llama_index.core import SummaryIndex, SimpleDirectoryReader
from llama_index.core.extractors import TitleExtractor
documents = SimpleDirectoryReader("files").load_data()
```

The first part of the code handles the imports and ingests our sample data. As before, we are using two simple text files: one containing information about ancient Rome and another containing a generic text about dogs. In the next part, we'll go through each document and use `TitleExtractor` to extract a title and store it as a `metadata` field:

```
title_extractor = TitleExtractor()
for doc in documents:
    title_metadata = title_extractor.extract([doc])
    doc.metadata.update(title_metadata[0])
```

Once the files have been ingested and we have generated document titles, we can define `SummaryIndex`, `QueryEngine`, and `QueryEngineTool` for each of the documents. We use the document title to provide the selector with a description of each tool:

```
indexes = []
query_engines = []
tools = []
for doc in documents:
    document_title = doc.metadata['document_title']
    index = SummaryIndex.from_documents([doc])
    query_engine = index.as_query_engine(
```

```
        response_mode="tree_summarize",
        use_async=True,
    )
    tool = QueryEngineTool.from_defaults(
        query_engine=query_engine,
        description=f"Contains data about {document_title}",
    )
    indexes.append(index)
    query_engines.append(query_engine)
    tools.append(tool)
```

Now that we have a list of available tools, we can build our `RouterQueryEngine` based on `PydanticMultiSelector`.

To do this, we must pass the query engine tools as an argument. These will be the options that are available for the selector:

```
qe = RouterQueryEngine(
    selector=PydanticMultiSelector.from_defaults(),
    query_engine_tools=tools
)
```

Depending on the query, the selector will decide which tools to use to gather responses. After each tool has responded, the query engine will synthesize and return a final response:

```
response = qe.query(
    "Tell me about Rome and dogs"
)
print(response)
```

For relatively small documents, this method will probably work just fine. So long as the text is short enough to be properly summarized into a title, this query engine will handle most user queries pretty well. In a real-life scenario, though, it's highly unlikely that we could fully summarize the whole content in a title. In that case, using a document summary instead of the title would be preferable.

Querying multiple documents with SubQuestionQueryEngine

In a real-life scenario involving multiple data sources, as in the previous example, users may come up with more complex queries – for example, they may ask for comparisons between different subjects documented in different files. For this kind of situation, we can use `SubQuestionQueryEngine`. It is designed to handle complex queries by breaking them down into smaller sub-questions.

Each sub-question is processed by its designated query engine and the individual responses are then combined. A response synthesizer is used to compile these into a coherent final response, effectively managing queries that require a multi-faceted approach. *Figure 7.5* describes its operation:

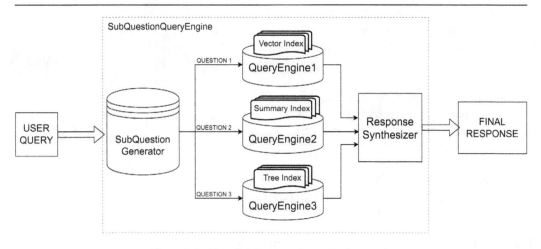

Figure 7.5 – How SubQuestionQueryEngine works

Let's have a look at the code. The first part is very similar to our previous example regarding RouterQueryEngine:

```
from llama_index.core.tools import QueryEngineTool
from llama_index.core.query_engine import RouterQueryEngine
from llama_index.core.query_engine import SubQuestionQueryEngine
from llama_index.core.selectors import PydanticMultiSelector
from llama_index.core.extractors import TitleExtractor
from llama_index.core import SummaryIndex, SimpleDirectoryReader
```

After importing the necessary modules, we load the files and extract their titles:

```
documents = SimpleDirectoryReader("files/sample").load_data()
title_extractor = TitleExtractor()
for doc in documents:
    title_metadata = title_extractor.extract([doc])
    doc.metadata.update(title_metadata[0])
indexes = []
query_engines = []
tools = []
```

So far, we have completed the same steps that we did for RouterQueryEngine. One notable change in the next part is that we also extract file_name from the metadata and use it as a name for the corresponding tool. This way, we'll be able to tell exactly where each answer is coming from:

```
for doc in documents:
    document_title = doc.metadata['document_title']
    file_name = doc.metadata['file_name']
    index = SummaryIndex.from_documents([doc])
```

```
    query_engine = index.as_query_engine(
        response_mode="tree_summarize",
        use_async=True,
    )
    tool = QueryEngineTool.from_defaults(
        query_engine=query_engine,
        name=file_name,
        description=f"Contains data about {document_title}",
    )
    indexes.append(index)
    query_engines.append(query_engine)
    tools.append(tool)
```

Next, let's build our `SubQuestionQueryEngine`:

```
qe = SubQuestionQueryEngine.from_defaults(
    query_engine_tools=tools,
    use_async=True
)
```

At this point, we're ready to generate the output:

```
response = qe.query(
    "Compare buildings from ancient Athens and ancient Rome"
)
print(response)
```

Along with the final response, we'll be able to see each sub-question generated and its corresponding query engine tool name. In our case, the tool name will correspond to the filename of each source text.

`SubQuestionQueryEngine` is particularly useful for complex queries that cannot be addressed directly in a single step. It produces great results in cases such as the following:

- **Comparative analysis**: For queries that require comparing and contrasting different subjects, the engine can divide the query into smaller, focused sub-questions to gather detailed information about each subject before synthesizing a comparative response. Here's a sample question: *Compare and contrast the economic policies of Country A and Country B in the last decade.*

- **Multi-faceted questions**: In cases where a query involves multiple aspects or criteria, this engine can break down the query into individual components, handle each separately, and then combine the results for a comprehensive answer. That means questions such as *What are the environmental, economic, and social impacts of deforestation in the Amazon rainforest?*

- **Complex research tasks**: For research-oriented queries that require information to be gathered from various sources or perspectives, this engine can efficiently handle the task by segmenting it into more manageable sub-questions. Here's the type of query it could answer: *Investigate the historical development of renewable energy technologies and their adoption across different continents.*

Now that you've got a general understanding of how query engines work, I'll let you explore the different possibilities and experiment with all the existing query engine modules.

In case you're wondering whether you can create custom ones, that option is also available.

You can find an example here: `https://docs.llamaindex.ai/en/stable/examples/query_engine/custom_query_engine.html#option-1-ragqueryengine`.

Now that we've got some fresh knowledge, it's about time we built some new components into our tutoring project.

Hands-on – building quizzes in PITS

One of the features we are building in our PITS project is the ability to generate quizzes based on the learning material uploaded by the user.

These quizzes will initially be used to gauge the overall knowledge of the user on the topic. Based on that assessment, the training slides and narration will be adjusted to the level of the learner.

The same mechanism can also be used to generate intermediate quizzes at the end of each section to test the user's current knowledge. Let's see how we can easily implement the quiz builder feature.

We'll be using one of the LlamaIndex pre-packaged pydantic programs: the DataFrame Pydantic extractor. This is designed to extract tabular DataFrames from raw text.

Let's have a look at the code in `quiz_builder.py`:

```
from llama_index.core import load_index_from_storage, StorageContext
from llama_index.program.evaporate.df import DFRowsProgram
from llama_index.program.openai import OpenAIPydanticProgram
from global_settings import INDEX_STORAGE, QUIZ_SIZE, QUIZ_FILE
import pandas as pd
```

First, we imported all the necessary modules, including our global variables defined in `global_settings.py`:

- `INDEX_STORAGE`: The index's storage location
- `QUIZ_SIZE`: The number of questions to be included in a quiz
- `QUIZ_FILE`: The path where the quiz will be saved as a CSV

We're also importing the `load_index_from_storage` function, which we will use to fetch our indexes from storage to avoid the cost and time of rebuilding them.

Because we're using DataFrames, we'll also need to import the pandas library. If you don't have it already installed in your environment, make sure you run this first:

```
pip install pandas
```

OK – let's build our main function. The `build_quiz` function will be responsible for generating the quiz and saving the questions in a CSV file for further use:

```python
def build_quiz(topic):
    df = pd.DataFrame({
        "Question_no": pd.Series(dtype="int"),
        "Question_text": pd.Series(dtype="str"),
        "Option1": pd.Series(dtype="str"),
        "Option2": pd.Series(dtype="str"),
        "Option3": pd.Series(dtype="str"),
        "Option4": pd.Series(dtype="str"),
        "Correct_answer": pd.Series(dtype="str"),
        "Rationale": pd.Series(dtype="str"),
    })
```

1. First, we set up a DataFrame to structure the quiz questions and their associated options and answers. This DataFrame will serve as the foundation for our quiz. It includes columns for the question number, question text, four answer options, the correct answer, and a rationale for the answer. The use of a pandas DataFrame will make handling and manipulating the quiz data much easier.

2. Next, we need to load our vector index from storage. To do this, we must define a `StorageContext` object while using the `INDEX_STORAGE` folder as a parameter:

```python
        storage_context = StorageContext.from_defaults(
            persist_dir=INDEX_STORAGE
        )
        vector_index = load_index_from_storage(
            storage_context, index_id="vector"
        )
```

3. Here, we used `index_id` to identify the *vector* index because there's also a `TreeIndex` index in that storage that we won't be using for now. It's time to initialize our `DataFrame` extractor:

```python
        df_rows_program = DFRowsProgram.from_defaults(
            pydantic_program_cls=OpenAIPydanticProgram,
            df=df
        )
```

4. Now, we can define our query engine and craft a prompt that will generate the quiz questions:

```python
        query_engine = vector_index.as_query_engine()
        quiz_query = (
            f"Create {QUIZ_SIZE} different quiz "
            "questions relevant for testing "
            "a candidate's knowledge about "
```

```
            f"{topic}. Each question will have 4 "
            "answer options. Questions must be "
            "general topic-related, not specific "
            "to the provided text. For each "
            "question, provide also the correct "
            "answer and the answer rationale. "
            "The rationale must not make any "
            "reference to the provided context, "
            "any exams or the topic name. Only "
            "one answer option should be correct."
        )
    response = query_engine.query(quiz_query)
```

5. Next, the prompt is passed to the query engine, and the response is then processed by DFRowsProgram to convert it into a structured DataFrame format:

```
    result_obj = df_rows_program(input_str=response)
    new_df = result_obj.to_df(existing_df=df)
    new_df.to_csv(QUIZ_FILE, index=False)
    return new_df
```

6. Finally, the new DataFrame containing the quiz questions is saved as a CSV file in the path defined by QUIZ_FILE. The function returns the new DataFrame for further use.

This serves as a simple demonstration of how to leverage a combination of LlamaIndex features, Pydantic programs, and DataFrame manipulation to create a dynamic quiz generator. We'll continue working on the rest of the features in future chapters.

Summary

This chapter explored how to refine search results with various postprocessors, generate responses using different synthesizers, and ensure structured outputs with specific parsers.

We also explored how to construct query engines while integrating the various components that we discussed in the previous chapters.

This chapter also covered handling diverse data sources with RouterQueryEngine and decomposing complex queries with SubQuestionQueryEngine, and also demonstrated quiz creation in our tutoring app.

See you in the next chapter, where we'll talk about chatbots, agents, and conversation tracking with LlamaIndex.

8

Building Chatbots and Agents with LlamaIndex

This chapter provides an in-depth look at implementing chatbots and intelligent agents using the capabilities of LlamaIndex. We will explore the various chat engine modes available, from simple chatbots to more advanced context-aware and question-**condensing engines**. Then, we'll dive into **agent architectures**, analyzing tools, **reasoning loops**, and parallel execution methods. You will gain practical knowledge so that you can build conversational interfaces powered by LLMs that can understand user needs and orchestrate responses or actions by utilizing tools and data sources.

Throughout this chapter, we're going to cover the following main topics:

- Understanding chatbots and agents
- Implementing agentic strategies in our apps
- Hands-on – implementing conversation tracking for PITS

Technical requirements

The following LlamaIndex integration packages will be required for the sample code:

- *Database Tool*: https://pypi.org/project/llama-index-tools-database/
- *OpenAI Agent*: https://pypi.org/project/llama-index-agent-openai/
- *Wikipedia Reader*: https://pypi.org/search/?q=llama-index-readers-wikipedia
- *LLM Compiler Agent*: https://pypi.org/project/llama-index-packs-agents-llm-compiler/

All the code samples in this chapter can be found in the `ch8` subfolder of this book's GitHub repository: `https://github.com/PacktPublishing/Building-Data-Driven-Applications-with-LlamaIndex`.

Understanding chatbots and agents

In the modern business ecosystem, the role of **chatbot systems** is increasingly important. First appearing in the 1960s (`https://en.wikipedia.org/wiki/ELIZA`), chatbots have always fascinated both developers and technology users alike. *Figure 8.1* shows the user interface of one of these early systems:

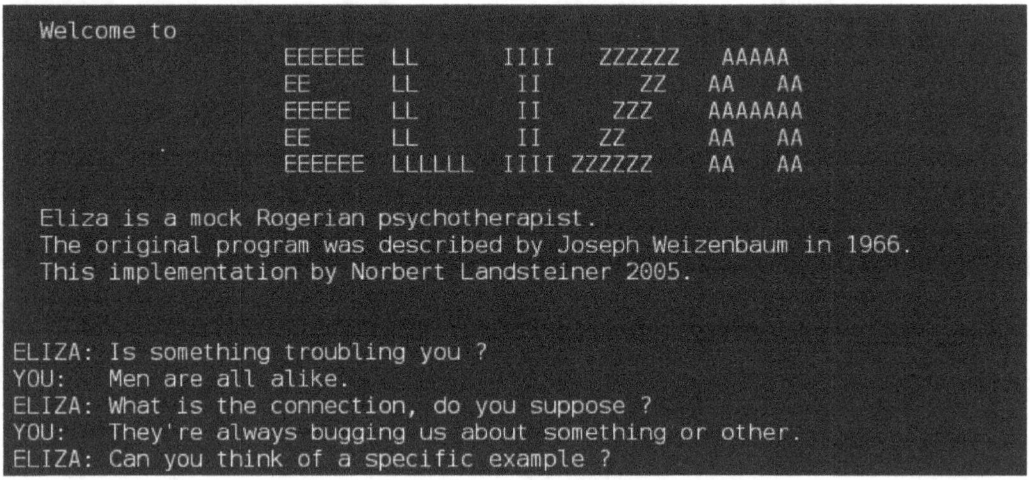

```
Welcome to
                    EEEEEE  LL      IIII   ZZZZZZ   AAAAA
                    EE      LL       II        ZZ   AA  AA
                    EEEEE   LL       II       ZZZ   AAAAAAA
                    EE      LL       II      ZZ     AA  AA
                    EEEEEE  LLLLLL  IIII  ZZZZZZ    AA  AA

  Eliza is a mock Rogerian psychotherapist.
  The original program was described by Joseph Weizenbaum in 1966.
  This implementation by Norbert Landsteiner 2005.


ELIZA: Is something troubling you ?
YOU:   Men are all alike.
ELIZA: What is the connection, do you suppose ?
YOU:   They're always bugging us about something or other.
ELIZA: Can you think of a specific example ?
```

Figure 8.1 – The ELIZA chatbot interface

While these systems were rudimentary initially and seen as more of an experiment, with the advancement of NLP technologies, the experience they offer has become increasingly interesting and valuable to users.

Chatbot-based support systems offer today's consumers a self-service experience. For users, self-service support services have two major advantages over human support:

- They are available 24/7, even outside normal working hours
- The user does not have to *hold the line* to access them

Even if there is some reluctance to use these systems at first, once they discover these advantages, users soon get used to interacting with them.

Don't necessarily think of chatbots as a technology designed to replace human support and interaction entirely. Although they have made enormous progress in recent years, these technologies, while getting more and more advanced, still have their shortcomings.

Lacking real empathy and the human touch, even under ideal operating conditions, chatbot-based services are unlikely to replace human support completely. But that doesn't mean they aren't extremely valuable, both for organizations and their users.

Perhaps the greatest value they bring is when they work in a blended experience, where users can receive both human support and access to self-service platforms that are interfaced with chatbot technologies. Implemented strategically, these systems can vastly improve not only the support offered to end consumers but also the internal interactions between an organization's employees.

ChatOps, for example, is a model increasingly used by modern organizations (`https://www.ibm.com/blog/benefits-of-chatops/`).

> **Definition**
>
> ChatOps refers to the ability to integrate chat platforms with operational workflows, facilitating transparent collaboration among team members, processes, tools, and automated bots to enhance service dependability, accelerate recovery, and boost collaborative productivity.

Based on the idea of **conversation-driven collaboration**, the ChatOps model combines **DevOps** principles (`https://en.wikipedia.org/wiki/DevOps`) by simplifying and accelerating interactions between team members using chatbots.

Whether we use them for internal communication or in interactions with our users, chatbots can only be useful to the extent that they can solve real problems. This depends on how well they can understand the context of the interaction and how relevant the answers they provide are.

Figure 8.2 provides a visual representation of the ChatOps model:

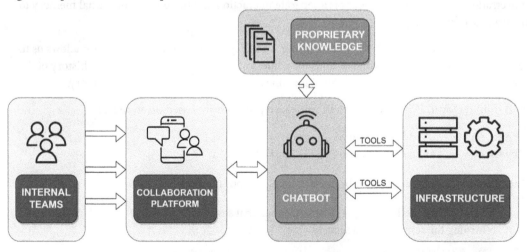

Figure 8.2 – The ChatOps paradigm

If, in the beginning, the main limitation of chatbots came from the *clumsy* way of interacting with the user, with the evolution of NLP technologies, the main shortcoming has become, more recently, the lack of integration with the organization's knowledge base.

After all, what good is a natural communication experience if the answers given by the system aren't useful in solving the user's requests?

This brings us to RAG.

By now, I think it has become obvious that without being connected to an organization's knowledge base, a chatbot can, at best, be considered a technology experiment. Even conversational engines based on powerful LLMs such as GPT-4 can, at best, provide generic answers that don't always address the specific problems of each organization. Perhaps worse, not being anchored in validated documentation, they can *hallucinate* very convincingly, creating unpleasant or even potentially dangerous experiences.

As you've probably guessed by now, LlamaIndex also offers RAG tools for implementing chatbot technologies. In this chapter, we will explore the options available to us and understand how we can implement very simple systems to advanced chatbot mechanisms.

But first, let's see how this functionality is built into LlamaIndex.

Discovering ChatEngine

In the previous chapters, we saw how we can build a query engine to run queries based on our data. This mechanism allows us to integrate multiple types of indexes, retrievers, node postprocessors, and response synthesizers at the same time, thus being able to access our proprietary data in multiple ways. Unfortunately, the `QueryEngine` class does not provide any mechanism to keep the history of a conversation. That means each query is a separate interaction and there is no contextual memory to allow a true *conversation*.

For that purpose, however, we have **ChatEngine**. Unlike query engines, `ChatEngine` allows us to have an actual conversation, giving us both the context of our proprietary data and the history of the chat. To simplify this concept even further, imagine a `QueryEngine` class with memory.

In its simplest form, a chat engine can be initialized just as easily, based on an index:

```
chat_engine = index.as_chat_engine()
response = chat_engine.chat("Hi, how are you?")
```

Once initialized, a chat engine can be queried using various methods:

- `chat()`: This method initiates a synchronous chat session, processing the user's message and returning the response immediately.

- `achat()`: This method is similar to `chat()` but executes the query asynchronously, allowing multiple requests to be processed simultaneously. This can be useful, for example, in a web or mobile application where we want to avoid blocking the main thread during server queries.

- `stream_chat()`: This method opens a streaming chat session, where responses can be returned as they are generated, for more dynamic interaction. This is particularly useful for long or complex responses that require significant processing time, allowing the user to start seeing parts of the response before all processing is complete.

- `astream_chat()`: This method is an asynchronous version of `stream_chat()` that allows us to handle streaming interactions in an asynchronous context.

Another option is to initiate a **Read-Eval-Print** (**REPL**) loop with `ChatEngine`:

```
chat_engine.chat_repl()
```

A REPL chat is akin to a ChatGPT interface, where a user sends a message or question, the LLM processes the input, generates a response, and then immediately displays it to the user. This loop continues for as long as the user keeps providing input, creating an interactive conversation.

To reset a chat conversation, you can use the following command:

```
chat_engine.reset()
```

This is useful when you want to clear the history and begin a new conversation thread.

So, the basics are very straightforward. Next, let's talk about the different **built-in chat modes** available in LlamaIndex.

Understanding the different chat modes

When initializing a chat engine, we can use the `chat_mode` argument to invoke various chat engine types predefined in LlamaIndex. I will show you how each of these engines works. We will discuss them one by one and get a good understanding of the advantages and use cases best suited for each of them.

But first, let's have a short introduction to how chat memory is managed within LlamaIndex.

Understanding how chat memory works

The `ChatMemoryBuffer` class is a specialized memory buffer that's designed to store chat history efficiently while also managing the token limit imposed by different LLMs. This structure is important because we can pass it as an argument when initializing chat engines using the `memory` parameter. By saving and restoring this buffer from one session to another, we can implement persistence for our conversations.

There are two different storage options for the chat store:

- The default `SimpleChatStore`, which stores the conversation in memory

- The more advanced `RedisChatStore`, which stores the chat history in a Redis database, eliminating the need to manually persist and load the chat history

The `chat_store` attribute, which is an instance of the `BaseChatStore` class, is used for the actual storage and retrieval of chat messages. This modular approach allows different storage implementations, such as a simple in-memory store or more complex database-backed stores.

We also have the `chat_store_key` parameter, which is used to uniquely identify the chat session or conversation within the chat store. This is useful for retrieving the correct conversation history when there are multiple conversations stored in the same chat store. Here's a basic example of **conversation history persistence** using `SimpleChatStore`:

```
from llama_index.core.storage.chat_store import SimpleChatStore
from llama_index.core.chat_engine import SimpleChatEngine
from llama_index.core.memory import ChatMemoryBuffer
```

After importing the necessary libraries, we can try to load the previous conversation. If there is no previous conversation save file, we simply initialize an empty `chat_store`:

```
try:
    chat_store = SimpleChatStore.from_persist_path(
        persist_path="chat_memory.json"
    )
except FileNotFoundError:
    chat_store = SimpleChatStore()
```

It's now time to initialize our memory buffer by using `chat_store` as an argument. Although not needed here, for a more detailed illustration, we will also customize `token_limit` and `chat_store_key`:

```
memory = ChatMemoryBuffer.from_defaults(
    token_limit=2000,
    chat_store=chat_store,
    chat_store_key="user_X"
)
```

OK; we have all the necessary pieces. Let's put them together into a `SimpleChatEngine` class and create a chat loop:

```
chat_engine = SimpleChatEngine.from_defaults(memory=memory)
while True:
    user_message = input("You: ")
    if user_message.lower() == 'exit':
        print("Exiting chat...")
        break
    response = chat_engine.chat(user_message)
    print(f"Chatbot: {response}")
```

Once the user types `exit` and we break the loop, we use the `persist()` method to store the current conversation for future sessions:

```
chat_store.persist(persist_path="chat_memory.json")
```

In case you're wondering why we haven't used the `chat_repl()` method shown previously and created a chat loop instead, the answer is in the following note.

> **Important note**
>
> While the `chat()`, `achat()`, `stream_chat()`, and `astream_chat()` methods can benefit from loading and resuming previous conversations, by design, the `chat_repl()` method will reset the conversation history during initialization.

`ChatMemoryBuffer` also plays an important role in ensuring that the conversation's context remains within the token limits of the model being used. Among other parameters available for `ChatMemoryBuffer`, the `token_limit` attribute specifies the maximum number of tokens that can be stored in the memory buffer. This limit is essential to ensure we stay within the maximum context window size of the current LLM we are using.

When the conversation exceeds the context limit, a sliding window method is applied. Older parts of the conversation are truncated to ensure that the most recent and relevant parts are retained and processed by the LLM within its token constraints.

> **An analogy to better understand the sliding window method**
>
> Imagine a conversation with an LLM as a train journey, where each piece of dialogue adds a carriage. However, the train can only be so long due to the tracks' length limit, representing the model's context window limit. To keep the journey going and add new carriages – in our case, messages – older ones need to be detached and left behind. This ensures the train can continue its journey, carrying the most recent and relevant parts of the conversation, while staying within the limits of the track. Just like in a train journey, where we might prioritize which carriages to keep based on their importance, the sliding window method prioritizes newer conversation parts, keeping the dialogue flowing smoothly.

Now that we understand how memory works, let's talk about the different available chat modes.

Simple mode

This is the most **basic chat engine** available. It allows for a simple, direct conversation with the LLM, without any connection to our proprietary data. *Figure 8.3* explains this chat mode visually:

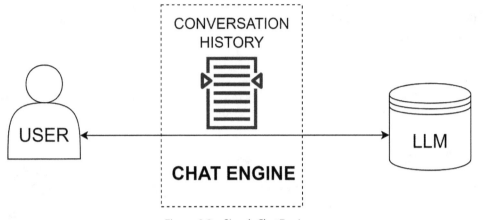

Figure 8.3 – SimpleChatEngine

The user's experience in this mode is defined by the inherent capabilities and limitations of the LLM, such as its context window size and overall performance.

To initialize this mode, we can use the following code:

```
from llama_index.core.chat_engine import SimpleChatEngine
chat_engine = SimpleChatEngine.from_defaults()
chat_engine.chat_repl()
```

If we want, we can customize the LLM using the llm argument:

```
from llama_index.llms.openai import OpenAI
llm = OpenAI(temperature=0.8, model="gpt-4")
chat_engine = SimpleChatEngine.from_defaults(llm=llm)
```

As you probably won't be using this mode too much in your RAG designs, let's talk about the more advanced options that are available.

Context mode

ContextChatEngine is designed to enhance chat interactions by leveraging our proprietary knowledge. It works by retrieving relevant text from an index based on the user's input, integrating this retrieved information into the system prompt to provide context, and then generating a response with the help of the LLM.

Have a look at *Figure 8.4* for a visual representation of this chat mode:

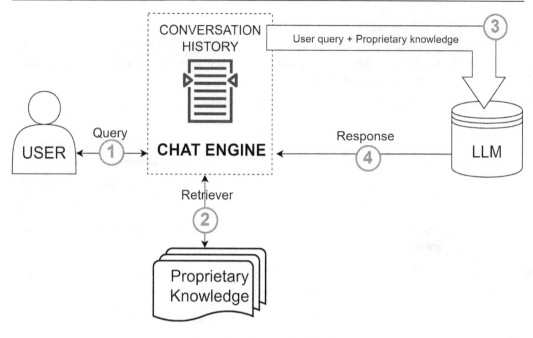

Figure 8.4 – ContextChatEngine

There are several parameters that we can customize for this chat engine:

- `retriever`: The actual retriever that's used to retrieve relevant text from the index based on the user's message. When the chat engine is initialized directly from the index, it will use the default retriever for that particular index type

- `llm`: An instance of an LLM, which will be used for generating responses

- `memory`: A `ChatMemoryBuffer` object, which is used to store and manage the chat history

- `chat_history`: This is an optional list of `ChatMessage` instances representing the history of the conversation. It can be used to maintain continuity in a conversation. This history includes all messages that have been exchanged in the chat session, including both user and chatbot messages. For instance, it can be used to continue a conversation from a certain point. A `ChatMessage` object contains three attributes:

  - `role`: This defaults to *user*

  - `content`: The actual message

  - Any optional arguments provided via `additional_kwargs`

- `prefix_messages`: A list of `ChatMessage` instances that may be used as predefined messages or prompts before the actual user message. This can be useful for setting a particular tone or context for the chat

- `node_postprocessors`: An optional list of `BaseNodePostprocessor` instances for further processing the nodes retrieved by the retriever. This can be used to implement guardrails, scrub sensitive information from the context, or make any other adjustments to the retrieved nodes if required

- `context_template`: A string template that can be used to format the prompt that feeds the context to the LLM

- `callback_manager`: An optional `CallbackManager` instance for managing callbacks during the chat process. This is useful for tracing and debugging purposes

- `system_prompt`: An optional string that's used as a system prompt, providing initial context or instructions for the chatbot

- `service_context`: An optional `ServiceContext` instance, which can be used to make additional customizations to the chat engine

To implement `ContextChatEngine`, we must load our data and build an index, then optionally configure the chat engine with different parameters as needed.

Here's a quick example based on our sample data files, which can be found in the `ch8/files` subfolder in this book's GitHub repository:

```
from llama_index.core import VectorStoreIndex, SimpleDirectoryReader
docs = SimpleDirectoryReader(input_dir="files").load_data()
index = VectorStoreIndex.from_documents(docs)
chat_engine = index.as_chat_engine(
    chat_mode="context",
    system_prompt=(
        "You're a chatbot, able to talk about "
        "general topics, as well as answering specific "
        "questions about ancient Rome."
    ),
)
chat_engine.chat_repl()
```

In this example, we initialized `chat_engine` from the index. Alternatively, we could have defined it standalone, providing a retriever as an argument, like this:

```
retriever = index.as_retriever(retriever_mode='default')
chat_engine = ContextChatEngine.from_defaults(
    retriever=retriever
    )
```

Overall, this chat mode is particularly effective for queries that relate to the knowledge contained within our data, supporting both general conversations and more specific discussions based on the indexed content.

Because the engine first retrieves context from the index and uses it to generate responses, this approach makes the chat experience a lot more useful and natural for users seeking specific information from the indexed data.

Condense question mode

`CondenseQuestionChatEngine` streamlines the user interaction by first **condensing the conversation** and the latest user message into a standalone question with the help of the LLM. This standalone question, which tries to capture the essential elements of the conversation, is then sent to a query engine built on our proprietary data to generate a response.

The main benefit of using this approach is that it maintains the conversation focused on the topic, preserving the essential points of the entire dialogue throughout every interaction. And it always responds in the context of our proprietary data.

Figure 8.5 describes the operation of this particular chat mode:

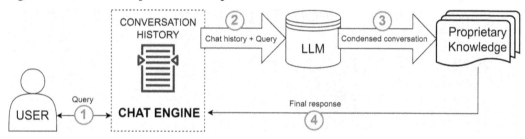

Figure 8.5 – CondenseQuestionChatEngine

The fact that the final response comes from our retrieved proprietary data and not directly from the LLM can also be a disadvantage sometimes. This chat mode may struggle with more general questions, such as inquiries about previous interactions, due to its reliance on querying the knowledge base for every response.

Let's look at some of the key parameters of `CondenseQuestionChatEngine`:

- `query_engine`: This is a `BaseQueryEngine` instance that's used to query the condensed question. Any type of query engine may be used here, including complex constructs with routing functionality
- `condense_question_prompt`: This is a `BasePromptTemplate` instance that's used for condensing the conversation and user message into a single, standalone question
- `Memory`: A `ChatMemoryBuffer` instance that's used to manage and store the chat history
- `llm`: A language model instance for generating the condensed question
- `verbose`: A Boolean flag for printing verbose logs during operation
- `callback_manager`: An optional `CallbackManager` instance for managing callbacks

To implement this chat engine, we typically initialize it with a query engine and, optionally, configure it with custom parameters. The conversation is condensed into a question using a predefined template that can be customized using the condense_question_prompt parameter. The resulting question is then sent to the query engine.

Here's a brief implementation example:

```python
from llama_index.core import VectorStoreIndex, SimpleDirectoryReader
from llama_index.core.chat_engine import CondenseQuestionChatEngine
from llama_index.core.llms import ChatMessage
documents = SimpleDirectoryReader("files").load_data()
index = VectorStoreIndex.from_documents(documents)
query_engine=index.as_query_engine()
chat_history = [
    ChatMessage(
        role="user",
        content="Arch of Constantine is a famous"
        "building in Rome"
    ),
    ChatMessage(
        role="user",
        content="The Pantheon should not be "
        "regarded as a famous building"
    ),
]
```

In the first part of the code, we ingested our sample files, created an index, and then created a simple query engine. Next, we introduced a previous conversation context by creating a chat history consisting of two ChatMessage objects. Specifically, we instructed the chat engine not to consider the Pantheon as a famous building.

Now, let's create our chat engine and query it:

```python
chat_engine = CondenseQuestionChatEngine.from_defaults(
    query_engine=query_engine,
    chat_history=chat_history
)
response = chat_engine.chat(
    "What are two of the most famous structures in ancient Rome?"
)
print(response)
```

Let's see what happened in the background:

1. `CondenseQuestionChatEngine` took the user's message, along with the provided chat history, and condensed them into a standalone question. This process involved using the LLM and `condense_question_prompt` to generate a question that encapsulates the essence of the conversation context and the user's latest query.

2. Then, the engine forwarded this condensed question to the query engine, which searched the indexed data for relevant information.

3. The query engine, having access to the information from `VectorStoreIndex`, processed the question and returned an answer. This answer reflects the collective context of the previous conversation and the specific query about famous structures in ancient Rome.

Without the added chat history, the output of the sample would have been similar to the following:

```
The Colosseum and the Pantheon.
```

This is because the two buildings are explicitly mentioned in our sample data.

However, once we add the new conversational context, the output looks like this:

```
The Colosseum and the Arch of Constantine are two famous buildings in
ancient Rome.
```

Another way of initializing this chat engine would be directly from the index, like this:

```
index.as_chat_engine(chat_mode="condense_question")
```

This chat mode is particularly useful for complex conversations where the context and nuances of previous exchanges play a crucial role in understanding and accurately responding to the latest query. It ensures that the chatbot remains aware of the conversation's history, thus making the interaction more coherent and contextually relevant.

The next chat mode we'll talk about uses a mix of two other approaches.

Condense and context mode

`CondensePlusContextChatEngine` offers an even more comprehensive chat interaction by combining the benefits of condensed questions and context retrieval.

While the previous chat engine we discussed is more straightforward and focuses on simplifying the conversation into a question for response generation, `CondensePlusContextChatEngine` takes an extra step to enrich the conversation with additional context from the indexed data, leading to more detailed and context-aware responses. The trade-off here is an increase in response generation time due to the additional step performed. Let's explore how it works under the hood by looking at *Figure 8.6*:

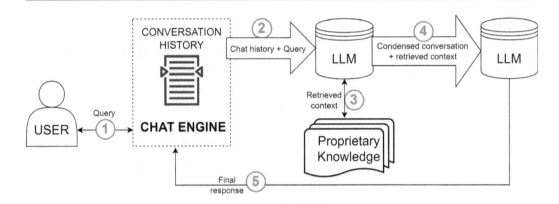

Figure 8.6 – CondensePlusContextChatEngine

First, this engine condenses a conversation and the latest user message into a standalone question. Then, it retrieves relevant context from the index using this condensed question. Finally, it uses both the retrieved context and the condensed question to generate a response with the LLM.

Here are some of the key parameters of `CondensePlusContextChatEngine`:

- `retriever`: Used to fetch context based on the condensed question
- `llm`: The LLM that's used to generate the condensed question and the final response
- `memory`: A `ChatMemoryBuffer` instance for storing and managing chat history
- `context_prompt`: A prompt template for formatting the context in the system prompt
- `condense_prompt`: A prompt for condensing the conversation into a standalone question
- `system_prompt`: A prompt with instructions for the chatbot
- `skip_condense`: A Boolean flag to bypass the condensation step if desired
- `node_postprocessors`: An optional list of `BaseNodePostprocessors` for additional processing of retrieved nodes
- `callback_manager`: As usual, this can be used for managing callbacks
- `verbose`: A Boolean flag for enabling verbose logging during operation

To build this particular chat engine from an index, we can use the following command:

```
index.as_chat_engine(chat_mode="condense_plus_context")
```

This chat mode is ideal in scenarios where both the context of the conversation and specific information from the indexed data are crucial for generating accurate and relevant responses. It enhances the chat experience by ensuring the responses are both contextually relevant and enriched with specific details from the indexed content.

OK. It's time to discover the more advanced chat modes.

Implementing agentic strategies in our apps

The name is Bot. Chat Bot.

At the beginning of this chapter, we talked about the growing popularity of the ChatOps model. This model is based on the interaction between groups of human operators and AI agents, who can understand the context of discussions to provide answers to questions but also to perform certain functions, thus playing the role of virtual assistants for the group they serve.

You probably realize, however, that the chat engine models we have discussed so far can only answer questions and cannot execute functions or interact in ways other than read-only with backend data.

For these use cases, we need **agents**.

The major difference between an agent and a simple chat engine is that an agent operates based on a **reasoning loop** and has several tools at its disposal. After all, who would be Bond without the gadgets that Q always provides?

Unlike a simple chatbot, which can – at best – answer questions, either directly with the help of an LLM or by extracting proprietary data from a knowledge base, agents are much more powerful and can handle far more complex scenarios. This gives them a lot more utility in a business context, where human interactions augmented by AI are becoming increasingly prevalent.

Let's understand the core components of an agent: the tools and the reasoning loop.

Building tools and ToolSpec classes for our agents

We briefly discussed tools in *Chapter 6, Querying Our Data, Part 1 – Context Retrieval*. However, because the main topic of *Chapter 6* was data querying, I only showed you how different query engines or retrievers can be wrapped in tools and then become components of a router. In many ways, you can think of a router as a very simple type of agent. It uses LLM reasoning to decide which query engine or retriever should be used, depending on their specified purpose and the actual user query.

But tools can be a lot more useful.

A tool can also be a wrapper for any kind of user-defined function, capable of reading or writing data, calling functions from external APIs, or executing any kind of code. This means that tools come in two different flavors:

- `QueryEngineTool`: This can encapsulate any existing query engine. This is the kind we covered during *Chapter 6* and it can only provide read-only access to our data
- `FunctionTool`: This enables any user-defined function to be transformed into a tool. This is a universal type of tool as it allows any type of operation to be executed

Because we have already seen examples of how `QueryEngineTool` works, let's focus on `FunctionTool` instead.

Here's an example of how we can define one:

```
from llama_index.core.tools import FunctionTool
def calculate_average(*values):
    """
    Calculates the average of the provided values.
    """
    return sum(values) / len(values)
average_tool = FunctionTool.from_defaults(
    fn=calculate_average)
```

To enable agents to assimilate our functions as tools, they must contain descriptive docstrings, just like in the previous example. LlamaIndex relies on these **docstrings** to provide agents with an *understanding* of the purpose and proper usage of a particular tool wrapping a user-defined function.

Definition

In Python, a docstring is a string literal that occurs as the first statement in a module, function, class, or method definition. It is used to document the purpose and usage of the code block it describes. Docstrings can be accessed from the code at runtime using the __doc__ attribute on the object they describe, and they are also the primary way that documentation is generated in Python.

This description will be used by the reasoning loop of an agent to determine which particular tool is fit for solving a specific task, allowing the agent to decide the execution path.

However, competent agents are usually able to handle more than just one tool.

For this purpose, LlamaIndex also provides the `ToolSpec` class. Akin to a collection of individual tools, `ToolSpec` specifies a full set of tools for a particular service. It's like equipping our agent with a complete API for a particular type of technology.

We can build custom `ToolSpec` classes but there is also a growing number of them already available on LlamaHub: `https://llamahub.ai/?tab=tools`. They cover different types of service integrations, such as Gmail, Slack, SalesForce, Shopify, and many others.

The LlamaHub agent tool repository

The LlamaHub agent tool repository is a key addition to LlamaHub, providing a curated collection of tool specs that enable agents to interact with and extend the functionality of a range of services. This repository simplifies the agent design process for various APIs and includes numerous practical examples in its notebooks for easy integration and use.

Let's take the `DatabaseToolSpec` class available on LlamaHub as an example.

This `ToolSpec` class can be found here: `https://llamahub.ai/l/tools-database?from=tools`. First, let's have a look at *Figure 8.7* to understand its structure:

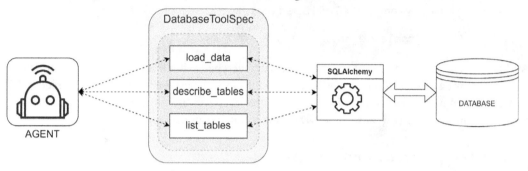

Figure 8.7 – DatabaseToolSpec

Built on top of the SQLAlchemy library (`https://www.sqlalchemy.org/`) this tool collection can access many types of databases while providing three simple tools:

- `list_tables`: A tool that lists the tables in the database schema

- `describe_tables`: A tool that describes the schema of a table

- `load_data`: A tool that accepts a SQL query as input and returns the resulting data

---

Quick note

SQLAlchemy is a powerful and versatile toolkit for Python that allows developers to work with various databases, such as Microsoft SQL Server, OracleDB, MySQL, and others, in a more Pythonic way, abstracting away many of the complexities of database interaction and query construction.

Because this is not a LlamaIndex core component but comes as an integration package instead, it must be installed in our environment first:

```
pip install llama-index-tools-database
```

Next, to initialize this `ToolSpec`, all we have to do is import it:

```
from llama_index.tools.database import DatabaseToolSpec
```

Then, we must configure our database access, like this:

```
db_tools = DatabaseToolSpec(<db_specific_configuration>)
```

Once the `ToolSpec` class has been built, if we want to initialize an agent with it, we have to convert it into a list of tools using the `to_tool_list()` method. This is because agents expect a list of tools as an argument.

Here's how we can easily convert the `ToolSpec` class into a list of tool objects:

```
tool_list = db_tools.to_tool_list()
```

At this point, we can pass `tool_list` as an argument when initializing any type of agent. Our agent will now be capable of *understanding* the schema of the database and extracting any required information from its tables. You can find a full example of how to use this `ToolSpec` class later in this chapter in the *OpenAIAgent* section. Next, let's see how reasoning loops work.

Understanding reasoning loops

Having so many specialized tools already available for our agents is a great advantage. But unfortunately, a box full of some of the best-quality instruments is not always enough. Our agents also need to know *when* to use each of these tools.

Specifically, the RAG applications we build need to decide – as autonomously as possible – which tool to use, depending on the specific user query and the dataset they are operating on. Any hard-coded solution will only deliver good results in a limited number of scenarios. This is where reasoning loops come in.

The reasoning loop is a fundamental aspect of agents, enabling them to intelligently decide which tools to use in different scenarios. This aspect is important because, in complex, real-world applications, the requirements can vary significantly and a static approach would limit the agent's effectiveness.

Figure 8.8 presents a visual representation of the reasoning loop concept:

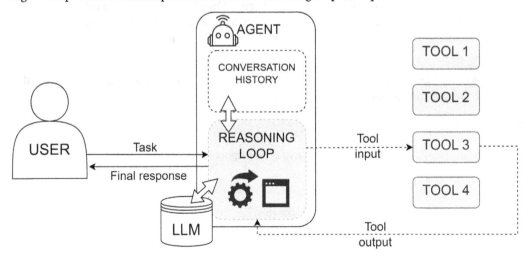

Figure 8.8 – The reasoning loop in an agent

The reasoning loop is responsible for the decision-making process. It evaluates the context, understands the requirements of the task at hand, and then selects the appropriate tools from its arsenal to accomplish the task. This dynamic approach allows agents to adapt to various scenarios, making them versatile and efficient.

In LlamaIndex, the implementation of the reasoning loop is tailored to the type of agent. For instance, `OpenAIAgent` uses the Function API to make decisions, while `ReActAgent` relies on chat or text completion endpoints for its reasoning process.

This loop is not just about selecting the right tool, though; it's also about determining the sequence in which the tools should be used and the specific parameters that should be applied. It's the brain of the agent, orchestrating the tools to work together seamlessly, much like a skilled craftsman uses a combination of tools to create something greater than the sum of its parts.

This ability to intelligently interact with various tools and data sources, and read and modify data dynamically, sets agents apart from simpler chat engines and makes them invaluable in a business context where adaptability and intelligence are key.

The remaining types of chat modes that I'm going to describe over the next few pages are not simple chat engines but agents at their core. They all operate using a list of tools but implement the reasoning loop in different ways.

OpenAIAgent

This specialized agent leverages the capabilities of OpenAI models, particularly those supporting the function calling API. It works with OpenAI models that have been designed to support the function calling API. They can interpret and execute function calls as part of their capabilities.

> **Quick note**
>
> These models are designed to interpret prompts and context to determine when a function call is appropriate. They respond with outputs that adhere to the defined structure of the function, based on the patterns they've learned during training. For more information on this topic and a list of supported models, you may consult the official OpenAI documentation: `https://platform.openai.com/docs/guides/function-calling`.

The key advantage of this agent type is that the tool selection logic is implemented directly on the model itself. When a task is provided by the user to **OpenAIAgent**, along with any previous chat history, the function API will analyze the context and decide whether another tool needs to be invoked or if a final response can be returned. If it determines that another tool is required, the function API will output the name of that tool. `OpenAIAgent` will then execute the tool, passing the tool's response back into the chat history. This cycle continues until the API returns a final message, indicating the reasoning loop is complete.

Figure 8.9 explains this process visually:

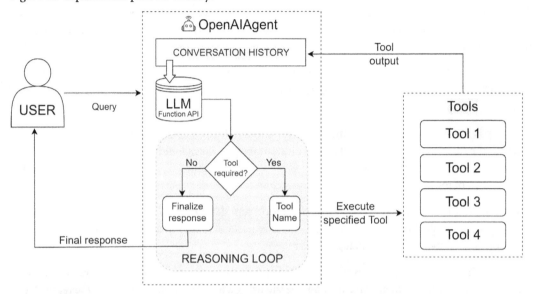

Figure 8.9 – The simplified workflow of OpenAIAgent

With the model handling the complex logic of tool selection and chaining, `OpenAIAgent` is a great solution for tool orchestration. One tradeoff is less flexibility compared to other architectures as the tool selection logic is hard-coded into the LLM.

However, for many use cases, the pre-trained capabilities of the function API model are sufficient to enable effective tool orchestration and task completion.

Before proceeding to the next example, make sure you install the required integration package:

```
pip install llama-index-agent-openai
```

To implement OpenAIAgent, we must define the available tools and then initialize the agent with these components, adding any other custom parameters we desire. The best way to explain how they work is through an example.

For the following example, we are using an SQLite database containing a single table called *Employees*. This table contains some randomly chosen salary data for 10 employees from different departments. *Table 8.1* displays the contents of the *Employees* table:

ID	Name	Department	Salary	Email
1	Alice	IT	36420.77	Alice_IT@org.com
2	Karen	Finance	57705.06	Alice_Finance@org.com
3	Helen	IT	52612.51	Helen_IT@org.com

ID	Name	Department	Salary	Email
4	Jackie	Finance	61374.58	Jack_Finance@org.com
5	David	Finance	32242.72	David_Finance@org.com
6	Cora	HR	62040.53	Alice_HR@org.com
7	Ingrid	IT	70821.96	Alice_IT@org.com
8	Jack	IT	57268.89	Jack_IT@org.com
9	Bob	Finance	76868.23	Bob_Finance@org.com
10	Bill	HR	74161.45	Bob_HR@org.com

Table 8.1 – The sample Employees table from the Employees.db file

The database file itself can be found in the ch8/files/database subfolder of this book's GitHub repository. Let's have a look at the code:

```
from llama_index.tools.database import DatabaseToolSpec
from llama_index.core.tools import FunctionTool
from llama_index.agent.openai import OpenAIAgent
from llama_index.llms.openai import OpenAI
```

The first part is responsible for the imports.

Next, it's time to define a simple function that's going to become a custom tool for our agent. This simple tool will allow us to save files in the local folder. Notice the detailed docstring that we are providing to the agent:

```
def write_text_to_file(text, filename):
    """
    Writes the text to a file with the specified filename.
    Args:
        text (str): The text to be written to the file.
        filename (str): File name to write the text into.
    Returns: None
    """
    with open(filename, 'w') as file:
        file.write(text)
```

Once the function has been defined, we must wrap it into a new tool called save_tool.

We also initialize an entire ToolSpec class from the imported DatabaseToolSpec. We need these tools because the agent will have to read data from our SQLite database to solve the task:

```
save_tool = FunctionTool.from_defaults(fn=write_text_to_file)
db_tools = DatabaseToolSpec(uri="sqlite:///files//database//employees.
```

```
db")
tools = [save_tool]+db_tools.to_tool_list()
```

Once we've created `db_tools`, we must join it with `save_tool` and put them into a single list called `tools`. We'll use this list as an argument for initializing the agent.

Now, let's build our agent. Notice that we're not using the default LLM in this case; instead, we're configuring our agent to use GPT-4 for more accuracy:

```
llm = OpenAI(model="gpt-4")
agent = OpenAIAgent.from_tools(
    tools=tools,
    llm=llm,
    verbose=True,
    max_function_calls=20
)
```

In the preceding code, we initialized our agent using the list of tools we prepared. The `verbose` argument will make the agent display every execution step for better visibility of the reasoning process. We also set `max_function_calls` to a larger value because, for complex tasks, the default value may not be enough to allow the agent to complete the task.

> **A quick note on the max_function_calls parameter**
>
> It may be tempting to simply set this to a very large value to avoid exhausting the function calls and increase the chances for the agent to solve the task. Keep in mind, however, that every function call incurs costs, and sometimes, agents have the bad habit of entering infinite loops. I call them *rogue agents* when they do that. Chances are that if your agent implementation requires a lot of LLM calls to solve even simple tasks, you're probably doing something wrong when defining or describing the underlying tools.

Let's continue with our code. It's time to dispatch the task to our agent:

```
response = agent.chat(
    "For each IT department employee with a salary lower "
    "than the average organization salary, write an email,"
    "announcing a 10% raise and then save all emails into "
    "a file called 'emails.txt'")
print(response)
```

As you can see, the task we provided is relatively complex. Multiple steps will be required to solve it. As we are not providing too many details in the query, our agent will have to figure out the structure of the database and then craft a SQL query to extract the average salary in the organization and the list of employees from the IT department who are paid below the average.

Since the `verbose` argument is set to `True`, running this sample will show you the entire reasoning logic and steps performed by the agent.

Notice how, in each step, the agent incorporates outputs from the tools into its ongoing reasoning process. Once it has the list of employees, it will compose an email for each one. The final step of the task is to use our custom-created tool and save the results in a local file.

This is just a simple example. In a more complex implementation, instead of saving the text locally, for example, we could import `GmailToolSpec` from LlamaHub and create email drafts that can be manually reviewed later and sent by the user. Unfortunately, that would have made the example much longer as `GmailToolSpec` requires stored credentials for the Google API, but I leave it to you to experiment with that `ToolSpec` class (`https://llamahub.ai/l/tools-gmail?from=tools`) and all the other tools available on LlamaHub.

The customizable parameters of `OpenAIAgent` are as follows:

- `tools`: A list of `BaseTool` instances that the agent can utilize during the chat session. These tools can range from specialized query engines to custom processing modules or collections of tools extracted from `ToolSpec` classes

- `llm`: Any OpenAI model that supports the function calling API. The default model that's used is `gpt-3.5-turbo-0613`

- `memory`: Just like with any chat engine, this is a `ChatMemoryBuffer` instance that can be used for storing and managing the chat history

- `prefix_messages`: A list of `ChatMessage` instances that serve as pre-configured messages or prompts at the start of the chat session

- `max_function_calls`: The maximum number of function calls that can be made to the OpenAI model during a single chat interaction. The default is 5

- `default_tool_choice`: A string indicating the default choice of tool to be used when multiple tools are available. This is useful for coercing the agent into using a specific tool

- `callback_manager`: An optional `CallbackManager` instance for managing callbacks during the chat process, aiding in tracing, and debugging

- `system_prompt`: An optional initial system prompt that provides context or instructions for the agent

- `verbose`: A Boolean flag to enable detailed logging during operation

Overall, `OpenAIAgent` stands out from other chat engines due to its ability to execute complex function calls, on top of contextually rich conversations. This makes it particularly suitable for scenarios where advanced functionalities, such as integrating external tools or processing user queries in more sophisticated ways, are required. `OpenAIAgent` provides a versatile and powerful platform for creating engaging and intelligent chat experiences.

But wait – there are other types of agents too.

ReActAgent

In contrast to `OpenAIAgent`, **ReActAgent** uses more generic text completion endpoints that can be driven by any LLM. It operates based on a **ReAct** loop within a chat mode built on top of a set of tools.

This loop involves deciding whether to use any of the available tools, potentially using it and observing its output, and then deciding whether to repeat the process or provide a final response. This flexibility allows it to choose between using tools or relying solely on the LLM. However, this also means that its performance is heavily dependent on the quality of the LLM, often requiring more nuanced prompting to ensure accurate knowledge base queries, rather than relying on potentially inaccurate model-generated responses.

The input prompt for `ReActAgent` is carefully designed to guide the model in tool selection, using a format inspired by the ReAct paper by Yao, S., et al. (2022), *ReAct: Synergizing Reasoning and Acting in Language Models* (`https://arxiv.org/abs/2210.03629`).

It presents a list of available tools and asks the model to select one and provide the required parameters in JSON format. This explicit prompt is critical to the agent's decision-making process. After selecting a tool, the agent executes it and integrates the response into the chat history. This cycle of prompting, execution, and response integration continues until a satisfactory response is achieved. For an overall visual representation of the workflow, you may review the diagram that was presented for `OpenAIAgent` in *Figure 8.9*.

Unlike `OpenAIAgent`, which uses a function calling API with a model capable of selecting and chaining together multiple tools, the `ReActAgent` class's logic must be fully encoded through its prompts.

`ReActAgent` uses a predefined loop with a maximum number of iterations, along with strategic prompting, to mimic a reasoning loop. Nevertheless, with strategic prompt engineering, `ReActAgent` can achieve effective tool orchestration and chained execution, similar to the output of the OpenAI Function API.

The key difference is that whereas the logic of the OpenAI Function API is embedded in the model, `ReActAgent` relies on the structure of its prompts to induce the desired tool selection behavior. This approach offers considerable flexibility as it can adapt to different language model backends, allowing for different implementations and applications.

In this case, we have the usual customizable parameters that we discussed for `OpenAIAgent`: `tools`, `llm`, `memory`, `callback_manager`, and `verbose`.

In addition, `ReActAgent` comes with a few specific parameters:

- `max_iterations`: Similar to `max_function_calls`, this parameter sets the maximum number of iterations the ReAct loop can execute. This limit ensures that the agent does not enter an endless loop of processing

- `react_chat_formatter`: This formats the chat history into a structured list of `ChatMessages`, alternating between user and assistant roles, based on the provided tools, chat history, and reasoning steps. This helps maintain clarity and consistency in the reasoning loop

- `output_parser`: An optional instance of the `ReActOutputParser` class. This parser processes the outputs generated by the agent, helping in interpreting, and formatting them appropriately

- `tool_retriever`: An optional instance of `ObjectRetriever` for `BaseTool`. This retriever can be used to dynamically fetch tools based on certain criteria. Similar to how we index nodes, there is also an option to create an `ObjectIndex` index to index a set of tools. This can be especially useful when we have to work with a large number of tools. You can find more information about this feature in the official documentation: `https://docs.llamaindex.ai/en/stable/module_guides/deploying/agents/usage_pattern.html#function-retrieval-agents`

- `context`: An optional string providing initial instructions for the agent

Initializing and using `ReActAgent` is done the same as with the OpenAI one, except this time, you won't need to install any integration packages first – this type of agent is part of the core LlamaIndex components:

```
from llama_index.agent.react import ReActAgent
agent = ReActAgent.from_tools(tools)
```

Overall, `ReActAgent` stands out for its flexibility as it can use any LLM to drive its unique ReAct loop, enabling it to smartly choose and use various tools. It's like having a virtual assistant that not only answers questions but also intelligently decides when to consult external sources, making the conversation more contextually relevant and improving the user experience.

How do we interact with agents?

There are two main methods that we can use to interact with an agent: `chat()` and `query()`. The first method utilizes stored conversation history to provide context-informed responses, making it suitable for ongoing dialogues.

On the other hand, the former method operates in a stateless mode, treating each call independently without reference to past interactions. This is better suited for standalone requests.

Enhancing our agents with the help of utility tools

To improve the capabilities of the existing tools, LlamaIndex also provides two very useful so-called *utility tools* – `OnDemandLoaderTool` and `LoadAndSearchToolSpec`. They are universal and can be used with any type of agent to augment the standard tool functionality in certain scenarios.

One common issue when interacting with an API is that we might receive a very long response in return. Our agents may not always be able to handle such large outputs.

Problems may arise because they may overflow the context window of the LLM or sometimes, key context may be diluted by a large amount of data, decreasing the accuracy of the agent's reasoning logic.

A good way to understand this issue is by looking at our previous example for OpenAIAgent. In that case, we used a collection of tools called DatabaseToolSpec to retrieve data from our sample *Employees* table. If you've run that particular agent with the Verbose parameter set to True, then you've probably noticed that the outputs produced by the load_data tool are in the form of LlamaIndex document objects, as we can see in *Figure 8.10*:

```
===========================
=== Calling Function ===
Calling function: load_data with args: {
  "query": "SELECT AVG(Salary) as average_salary FROM Employees"
}
Got output: [Document(id_='39577a59-47fd-4129-b03e-0a8cd3853f44', embedding=None, metadata={}, excluded_embed_metada
ta_keys=[], excluded_llm_metadata_keys=[], relationships={}, hash='1a75830c8999ee5f7f10ccd140fee952f10f2b2ecb7f1dbb7
151890ffc9e3419', text='58151.67', start_char_idx=None, end_char_idx=None, text_template='{metadata_str}\n\n{content
}', metadata_template='{key}: {value}', metadata_seperator='\n')]
===========================
```

Figure 8.10 – Sample output for the OpenAIAgent code example

This means that whenever the agent calls the load_data tool, using a SQL query to interrogate the database, instead of simply receiving the output of the query, it gets a whole document in return – along with a bunch of additional data, such as the ID of the document, metadata fields, hashes, and so on. The agent has to extract the actual query results from that data using the LLM, hence the aforementioned potential issues.

So, what if we want to extract *only* the result of the query, without all the additional data on top of it? That is the job of LoadAndSearchToolSpec.

Understanding the LoadAndSearchToolSpec utility

This utility tool is designed to help the agent handle large volumes of data from API endpoints, as demonstrated in *Figure 8.11*:

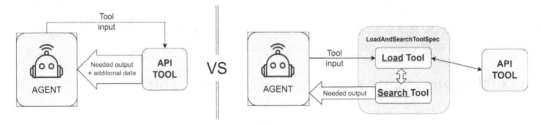

Figure 8.11 – Visualization of a direct API call versus interaction via LoadAndSearchToolSpec

It takes an existing tool and generates two separate tools: one for loading and indexing data – by default, using a vector index – and another for conducting searches on this indexed data. The agent will now use the *Load* tool to ingest the data, and, similar to a caching mechanism, it will store it in an index. In the next step, the agent will use the *Search* tool to extract only the needed information using a built-in query engine.

Let's see how that translates into code. We will adapt the previous `OpenAIAgent` example so that it uses `LoadAndSearchToolSpec`:

```
from llama_index.core.tools.tool_spec.load_and_search.base import (
    LoadAndSearchToolSpec)
from llama_index.tools.database import DatabaseToolSpec
from llama_index.agent.openai import OpenAIAgent
from llama_index.llms.openai import OpenAI
db_tools = DatabaseToolSpec(
    uri="sqlite:///files//database//employees.db")
tool_list = db_tools.to_tool_list()
tools=LoadAndSearchToolSpec.from_defaults(
tool_list[0]
).to_tool_list()
```

Once we finished with the imports, we initialized our `DatabaseToolSpec` utility, which points to the same sample SQLite database as in the previous example. However, this time, we didn't add any additional tools since we'll only run a simple query. For that reason, we only pass the first tool from `ToolSpec` – that is, `tool_list[0]` – as an argument to `LoadAndSearchToolSpec`. That's the `load_data` function, by the way. We don't need the other two functions available in the database's `ToolSpec` this time.

From this point on, the code is very much straightforward:

```
llm = OpenAI(model="gpt-4")
agent = OpenAIAgent.from_tools(
    tools=tools,
    llm=llm,
    verbose=True
)
response = agent.chat(
    "Who has the highest salary in the Employees table?'")
print(response)
```

If you look at the output – presented in *Figure 8.12* – you'll notice the reduced amount of data the agent has to deal with this time:

```
Added user message to memory: Who has the highest salary in the Employees table?'
=== Calling Function ===
Calling function: load_data with args: {
  "query": "SELECT * FROM Employees ORDER BY Salary DESC LIMIT 1"
}
Got output: Content loaded! You can now search the information using read_load_data
========================

=== Calling Function ===
Calling function: read_load_data with args: {
  "query": "Who has the highest salary?"
}
Got output: The person with the highest salary is Bob.
========================

The employee with the highest salary in the Employees table is Bob.
```

Figure 8.12 – Sample agent output when LoadAndSearchToolSpec is used

Instead of receiving an entire document as a response, the first call returns just a confirmation message that the data has been loaded and indexed, while the second extracts the final response using a query. We'll talk about another utility tool next.

Understanding OnDemandLoaderTool

Another important utility is OnDemandLoaderTool. This utility is designed to make the process of loading, indexing, and querying data seamless and efficient within an agent's workflow, particularly when dealing with large volumes of data from various sources.

It simplifies the process of using data loaders for agents by allowing them to trigger the loading, indexing, and querying of data through a single tool call.

The normal approach in a RAG workflow would be to ingest all data at the start of our application, then chunk it, index it, and build a query engine on it. But that may not always be the most efficient method.

Let's say we have a large number of data sources. Ingesting and indexing all of them during startup would take a very long time, negatively affecting the user experience. And what if the user asks a question that cannot be answered by the agent based on the ingested data sources alone? That's where a feature like this becomes useful.

OnDemandLoaderTool is especially useful in scenarios where data requirements are dynamic and unpredictable. Instead of pre-loading a vast amount of data at startup, which may not all be relevant to the user's current needs, this tool enables an agent to fetch, index, and query data on demand. This approach significantly enhances efficiency as it allows the agent to focus only on the relevant data at any given time, rather than handling large datasets that may not be immediately necessary.

How does it work? It takes any existing data loader and wraps it into a tool that can be used by the agent as required. Before running the code, make sure you install the Wikipedia integration package:

```
pip install llama-index-readers-wikipedia
```

Here's the sample code. We'll start with the imports:

```
from llama_index.agent.openai import OpenAIAgent
from llama_index.core.tools.ondemand_loader_tool import(
    OnDemandLoaderTool)
from llama_index.readers.wikipedia import WikipediaReader
```

Next, let's define an on-demand tool for our agent, based on `WikipediaReader`:

```
tool = OnDemandLoaderTool.from_defaults(
    WikipediaReader(),
    name="WikipediaReader",
    description="args: {'pages': [<list of pages>],
        'query_str': <query>}"
)
```

Notice how I provided usage instructions in the description argument. These should help the agent better *understand* how to properly use the tool, although it might still take a few tries to get it right. Now, it's time to initialize the agent:

```
agent = OpenAIAgent.from_tools(
    tools=[tool],
    verbose=True
)
response = agent.chat(
    "What were some famous buildings in ancient Rome?")
print(response)
```

> **Important side note**
>
> One big advantage of using this approach is that once data has been loaded into the index, it's also cached. Therefore, subsequent queries on the same topic will run faster.

In addition, `OnDemandLoaderTool` can be chained together with other, regular tools, allowing the agent to handle more complex scenarios.

With that, we've covered the basics. Now, let's have a look at more advanced types of agents.

Using the LLMCompiler agent for more advanced scenarios

I saved the best for last.

While they tend to perform well in many scenarios, both OpenAI and ReAct agents have some drawbacks. Because current LLMs are not very good at long-term planning, they can sometimes get stuck in an infinite loop without finding the desired solution. At other times, their attention can be distracted by certain outputs they receive during execution, and this can cause them to stop before solving the given task.

But probably the biggest drawback of these types of agents is their serialized way of working. In other words, the execution of the steps is done in sequence. These agents wait for the output generated by one step to trigger the next step. This is a very inefficient approach in many practical scenarios. Often, a series of steps can be executed in parallel, significantly improving application performance and user experience. Based on these premises, I will now present a more advanced form of agent.

Inspired by the paper by Kim, S., et al. (2023), *An LLM Compiler for Parallel Function Calling* (`https://arxiv.org/abs/2312.04511`), this agent implementation offers outstanding performance and scalability. The concept is based on the ability of LLMs to execute multiple functions in parallel and draws inspiration from classical compilers to efficiently orchestrate multi-function execution.

The **LLMCompiler agent** orchestrates these parallel function calls using a three-part system that plans, dispatches, and executes tasks, resulting in faster and more accurate multi-function calls compared to sequential methods. Just as compilers transform and optimize code to run efficiently, LLMCompiler transforms natural language queries into optimized sequences of function calls that can be executed in parallel when dependencies allow. This makes calling multiple tools with LLMs faster, cheaper, and potentially more accurate. An additional advantage is that it works with any kind of LLM, including both open source and closed source models.

Under the hood, an LLMCompileraAgent has three main components:

- **LLM planner**: Formulates execution strategies and dependencies from user input and examples
- **Task-fetching unit**: Sends and updates function-calling tasks based on the dependencies
- **Executor**: Executes tasks in parallel using associated tools

Figure 8.13 explains the structure of the LLMCompiler agent visually:

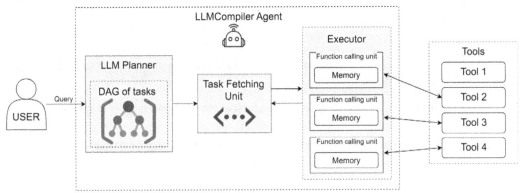

Figure 8.13 – An overview of the LLMCompiler agent's architecture

The *LLM planner* determines the order of function calls and their interdependencies according to user input. Next, the *task-fetching unit* initiates parallel execution of these functions, replacing variables with the outputs from prior tasks. The *executor* then carries out these function calls with the relevant tools. Combined, these elements enhance the efficiency of parallel function calling in LLMs.

The **directed acyclic graph (DAG)** of tasks is a key data structure created by the *LLM planner* from user inputs and examples. This planning graph captures task dependencies and enables optimized parallel execution (`https://en.wikipedia.org/wiki/Directed_acyclic_graph`).

The DAG facilitates the simultaneous execution of tasks that do not depend on each other. Should one task rely on the completion of another, the prerequisite task must finish before the dependent task can commence. Independent tasks, on the other hand, are capable of being executed concurrently without any dependency constraints.

> **Quick note**
>
> While OpenAI has already introduced parallel function calling into their API, the LLMCompiler is still superior in its approach because it manifests fault tolerance in case of wrong LLM decisions and can replan, depending on the outputs generated.

To understand how we can implement an agent using the LLMCompiler, let's have a look at a simple example. But first, to run the example, you'll need to install the necessary integration package:

```
pip install llama-index-packs-agents-llm-compiler
```

Here's the code:

```
from llama_index.tools.database import DatabaseToolSpec
from llama_index.packs.agents_llm_compiler import LLMCompilerAgentPack
db_tools = DatabaseToolSpec(
    uri="sqlite:///files//database//employees.db")
agent = LLMCompilerAgentPack(db_tools.to_tool_list())
```

After importing `LLMCompilerAgentPack` and `DatabaseToolSpec`, we initialized the database tools and used the tool list to initialize the agent. It's now time to interact with the agent, this time using the `run()` method:

```
response = agent.run(
    "Using only the available tools, "
    "List the HR department employee "
    "with the highest salary "
)
```

Figure 8.14 shows the output of the preceding code:

```
> Running step a9d76c4a-1db4-473a-bec1-b7cc22a00b4d for task 046b629b-6e5a-4cfd-9a03-6ffed7d2466e.
> Step count: 0
> Plan: 1. list_tables()
2. load_data("SELECT * FROM employees WHERE department = 'HR'")
3. join()
4. load_data("SELECT MAX(salary) FROM employees WHERE department = 'HR'")
5. join()<END_OF_PLAN>
Ran task: list_tables. Observation: ['Employees', 'sqlite_sequence']
Ran task: load_data. Observation: [Document(id_='a91e5066-c2bf-4a72-aff9-00df87df1859', embedding=None, metadata={}, exc
luded_embed_metadata_keys=[], excluded_llm_metadata_keys=[], relationships={}, text='6, Cora, HR, 62040.53, Alice_HR@org
.com', start_char_idx=None, end_char_idx=None, text_template='{metadata_str}\n\n{content}', metadata_template='{key}: {v
alue}', metadata_seperator='\n'), Document(id_='b3d22846-89e7-42dc-9323-adafa9f7a6f6', embedding=None, metadata={}, excl
uded_embed_metadata_keys=[], excluded_llm_metadata_keys=[], relationships={}, text='10, Bill, HR, 74161.45, Bob_HR@org.c
om', start_char_idx=None, end_char_idx=None, text_template='{metadata_str}\n\n{content}', metadata_template='{key}: {val
ue}', metadata_seperator='\n')]
Ran task: join. Observation: None
> Thought: The HR department has two employees with their salaries listed.
> Answer: Bill
```

Figure 8.14 – Sample output of the LLMCompiler agent

Looking at the output, we can see both the execution plan generated by the agent and the actual steps performed. Quite neat, isn't it?

In conclusion, LLMCompiler-based agents represent a leap forward in addressing the limitations of serial execution found in traditional agents, pushing the boundaries of what's possible in terms of chatbot implementations and user interaction.

Using the low-level Agent Protocol API

Taking inspiration from the **Agent Protocol** (https://agentprotocol.ai/) and several research papers, the LlamaIndex community also created a more granular way to control the agents. This provides enhanced control and flexibility for executing user queries. It enables users to manage the agent's actions with finer detail, facilitating the development of more sophisticated agentic systems.

The entire concept is based on two main components, AgentRunner and AgentWorker, and works as described in *Figure 8.15*:

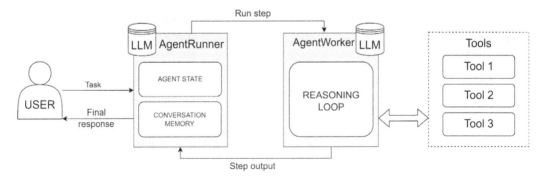

Figure 8.15 – The AgentRunner and AgentWorker orchestration model

We use **agent runners** to orchestrate tasks and store conversational memory. **Agent workers** control the execution of each task step by step without storing the state themselves. The agent runner manages the overall process and integrates the results.

In terms of benefits, there are multiple reasons to use agents like this. Firstly, it allows for a clear separation of concerns: agent runners manage the task's overall orchestration and memory, while agent workers focus only on executing specific steps of a task. This division enhances the maintainability and scalability of the system.

Moreover, the architecture promotes enhanced visibility and control over the agent's decision-making process. We can observe and intervene at each step, with very good insight into the agent's operation. This is particularly useful for debugging and refining our agent's behavior.

Another key benefit is the flexibility it provides. We can tailor the behavior of agents according to the specific needs of the application. We can modify or extend the functionality of agent workers, or integrate custom logic within the agent runner, making the system highly adaptable. This setup also supports modular development. We can build or update individual components without affecting the entire system, facilitating easier updates and iterations.

Here's a sample implementation that takes one of our previous examples and applies this more granular approach. We'll implement `OpenAIAgent` in a low-level fashion by using `AgentRunner` and `OpenAIAgentWorker`:

```
from llama_index.core.agent import AgentRunner
from llama_index.agent.openai import OpenAIAgentWorker
from llama_index.tools.database import DatabaseToolSpec
db_tools = DatabaseToolSpec(
    uri="sqlite:///files//database//employees.db"
)
tools = db_tools.to_tool_list()
```

Here, we've imported the necessary components and prepared the tool list for the agent. We're using the same `employees.db` database as before. Next, we'll define the agent worker:

```
step_engine = OpenAIAgentWorker.from_tools(
    tools,
    verbose=True
)
```

It's time to initialize our agent runner and prepare the input that will contain the task:

```
agent = AgentRunner(step_engine)
input = (
    "Find the highest paid HR employee and write "
    "them an email announcing a bonus"
)
```

There are two distinct methods to engage with our agent now. Let's take a look.

Option A – the end-to-end interaction, using the chat() method

The chat() method offers a seamless, end-to-end interaction, executing the task without requiring intervention at each reasoning step:

```
response = agent.chat(input)
print(response)
```

It's very straightforward: just two lines of code, at which point we wait for the agent to solve the task and provide a final response when all the steps are completed.

Option B – the step-by-step interaction, using the create_task() method

For more granular control, we could leverage the agent runner and use a step-by-step method that allows us to create a task, run each step individually, and then finalize the response:

```
task = agent.create_task(input)
step_output = agent.run_step(task.task_id)
```

In the first part, we created a new task for the agent runner and executed the first step of the task. Because this method provides manual control of the execution of each step, we have to manually implement a loop in our code. We will repeatedly call run_step() until the output indicates all steps are complete:

```
while not step_output.is_last:
    step_output = agent.run_step(task.task_id)
```

The previous loop will run until the last step is completed. Then, it's time to synthesize and display the final answer:

```
response = agent.finalize_response(task.task_id)
print(response)
```

This allows us to execute and observe each reasoning step individually. The create_task() method initializes a new task, run_step() executes each step, returning an output, and finalize_response() generates the final response once all steps are complete.

Overall, this option is particularly useful when you need to monitor the agent's decisions closely or when you want to step in at certain points to guide the process or to handle exceptions.

Now, it's time to apply this fresh knowledge and add some chat features to our PITS project.

Hands-on – implementing conversation tracking for PITS

In this practical section, we'll use some of our newfound knowledge to further improve our personal tutoring project. Like any professional tutor, eager to teach students and answer their questions, PITS should have a proper conversational engine at its core. It should be able to understand the topic, be aware of the current context, and keep track of the entire interaction with the student. Because the learning process will probably take place through multiple sessions, PITS must be able to persist the entire conversation and resume the interaction when a new session is initiated. We'll implement all these features in `coversation_engine.py`. This module is not meant to be used directly in our app architecture. Instead, it will provide three callable functions that we will later import and use in the `training_UI.py` module:

- `load_chat_store`: This function is responsible for retrieving the chatbot conversation from previous sessions. We're using a generic `chat_store_key="0"` key. In a multi-user scenario, this key could be used to store chat conversations for different users in the same chat store.

- `initialize_chatbot`: This function is responsible for loading the training material vector index from storage, defining a query engine tool on the index, and then initializing `OpenAIAgent` using this tool as an argument. It also provides the agent with a system prompt that contains context information describing the purpose of the agent, the username and study topic, as well as the current slide content. The function returns the initialized agent, which will then be used by `chat_interface` to implement the actual conversation.

- `chat_interface`: This function implements the ongoing conversation by taking the user input and generating an answer from the agent. It also persists the conversation after each interaction. If the user ends the current session, on resume, the conversation will be continued from that point.

Once implemented in the main training interface, this chat should look similar to what's shown in *Figure 8.16*:

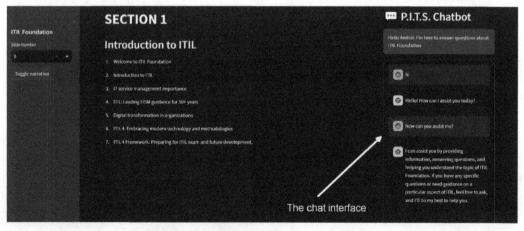

Figure 8.16 – Screenshot from the PITS training UI

Let's have a look at the code. The first part contains all the necessary imports:

```
import os
import json
import streamlit as st
from openai import OpenAI
from llama_index.core import load_index_from_storage
from llama_index.core import StorageContext
from llama_index.core.memory import ChatMemoryBuffer
from llama_index.core.tools import QueryEngineTool, ToolMetadata
from llama_index.agent.openai import OpenAIAgent
from llama_index.core.storage.chat_store import SimpleChatStore
from global_settings import INDEX_STORAGE, CONVERSATION_FILE
```

You'll notice that in the first part of the code, we imported a lot of components. The os and json modules will be used for the chat persistence feature. The specific LlamaIndex elements will be used to implement the agent with all its required components.

We also imported the INDEX_STORAGE and CONVERSATION_FILE locations from the global_settings.py module. Because the chat conversation will be implemented using Streamlit, we also have to import the streamlit library.

Next, let's have a look at the load_chat_store function, which is responsible for resuming the previous conversation by loading the chat history from the local storage file specified by CONVERSATION_FILE:

```
def load_chat_store():
    try:
        chat_store = SimpleChatStore.from_persist_path(
            CONVERSATION_FILE
        )
    except FileNotFoundError:
        chat_store = SimpleChatStore()
    return chat_store
```

As we can see, the load_chat_store function tries to retrieve the conversation history from the local storage file. If the storage file does not exist, a new empty chat_store is created. The function returns chat_store.

The next function is responsible for displaying the entire conversation history in the Streamlit interface:

```
def display_messages(chat_store, container):
    with container:
        for message in chat_store.get_messages(key="0"):
            with st.chat_message(message.role):
                st.markdown(message.content)
```

The `display_messages` function takes a chat store and a Streamlit container as arguments. It extracts all messages from the chat store using `get_messages()`. The function iterates over and displays each message from the chat store, assigning appropriate roles – *user* or *assistant* – to each.

The messages are displayed in the Streamlit container using Streamlit's `chat_message()` method, which has the advantage of automatically adding a corresponding icon for each role.

The next function is responsible for initializing the agent. This function takes five arguments:

- `user_name`: The name of the user – to enable a more personal experience.

- `study_subject`: The topic covered by the study materials.

- `chat_store`: Used to initialize the conversation history.

- `container`: This is the Streamlit container where the chat conversation will be displayed. It's not used by this function itself and instead passed further to the `display_messages` function.

- `context`: This is the content of the current slide being displayed in the training interface. This context will be fed into the agent's system prompt to ground any answer on the current context of the user.

Let's see the first part of the function:

```
def initialize_chatbot(user_name, study_subject,
                       chat_store, container, context):
    memory = ChatMemoryBuffer.from_defaults(
        token_limit=3000,
        chat_store=chat_store,
        chat_store_key="0"
    )
```

Here, we have defined a `ChatMemoryBuffer` object for the agent, specifying the `chat_store` attribute containing the conversation history. We used the same `chat_store_key` as before. This is important to allow the agent to correctly retrieve the chat history.

Next, we'll prepare the tools for the agent:

```
    storage_context = StorageContext.from_defaults(
        persist_dir=INDEX_STORAGE
    )
    index = load_index_from_storage(
        storage_context, index_id="vector"
    )
    study_materials_engine = index.as_query_engine(
        similarity_top_k=3
    )
    study_materials_tool = QueryEngineTool(
```

```
        query_engine=study_materials_engine,
        metadata=ToolMetadata(
            name="study_materials",
            description=(
                f"Provides official information about "
                f"{study_subject}. Use a detailed plain "
                f"text question as input to the tool."
            ),
        )
    )
```

Here, we first retrieved our vector index by using a `StorageContext` object and the `load_index_from_storage()` method. We had to specify the *ID* of the index – *vector* – because in our case, the storage contains more than one index.

After loading the index, we created a simple query engine configured with `similarity_top_k=3` and then created a `QueryEngineTool` utility, providing a proper description in its metadata so that the agent can *understand* its purpose and usage. The top-k similarity parameter is set to 3 to retrieve the three most relevant pieces of information from the index.

The next part will initialize `OpenAIAgent`:

```
    agent = OpenAIAgent.from_tools(
        tools=[study_materials_tool],
        memory=memory,
        system_prompt=(
            f"Your name is PITS, a personal tutor. Your "
            f"purpose is to help {user_name} study and "
            f"better understand the topic of: "
            f"{study_subject}. We are now discussing the "
            f"slide with the following content: {context}"
        )
    )
    display_messages(chat_store, container)
    return agent
```

In the preceding code, we initialized `OpenAIAgent` while providing `QueryEngineTool`, `memory`, and `system_prompt` as arguments. This prompt is used to provide the LLM with background information to contextualize its responses, ensuring they are relevant to the current discussion topic and the user's study needs.

As you can see, I've tried to keep the code as simple as possible. Many things could be improved in this implementation. After initializing the agent, we call `display_messages` to display the existing conversation.

Our last function is responsible for handling the actual conversation. It takes three arguments:

- `agent`: The agent engine that will be used to run the chat
- `chat_store`: The `chat_store` argument that will be used to persist the conversation
- `container`: The Streamlit container where the messages will be displayed

Let's have a look at the code:

```python
def chat_interface(agent, chat_store, container):
    prompt = st.chat_input("Type your question here:")
    if prompt:
        with container:
            with st.chat_message("user"):
                st.markdown(prompt)
            response = str(agent.chat(prompt))
            with st.chat_message("assistant"):
                st.markdown(response)
        chat_store.persist(CONVERSATION_FILE)
```

This `chat_interface` function displays a chat input widget using Streamlit's `chat_input()` method. Upon receiving input, it does the following:

- Adds the user's question to the chat interface in the specified container
- Calls the chat method of `OpenAIAgent` to process the question and generate a response
- Adds the chatbot's response to the chat interface in the specified container
- Persists the new conversation to `CONVERSATION_FILE` using the chat store's persist method to ensure continuity across sessions

That's it for now. We'll talk about more of the features of PITS in the next few chapters.

Summary

This chapter provided an in-depth exploration of building chatbots and agents with LlamaIndex. We covered `ChatEngine` for conversation tracking and different built-in chat modes, such as simple, context, condense question, and condense plus context.

Then, we explored different agent architectures and strategies using `OpenAIAgent`, `ReActAgent`, and the more advanced LLMCompiler agent. Key concepts such as tools, tool orchestration, reasoning loops, and parallel execution were explained.

We concluded this chapter with a hands-on implementation of conversation tracking for the PITS tutoring application.

Overall, you should now have a comprehensive understanding of leveraging LlamaIndex capabilities to create useful and engaging conversational interfaces.

Throughout the next chapter, we'll discover how to customize our RAG pipeline and provide a straightforward guide to deploying it with Streamlit. We'll also explore advanced tracing methods for seamless debugging and unravel strategies for evaluating our applications.

Part 4:
Customization, Prompt Engineering, and Final Words

In the final part of this book, we explore customizing RAG components for robust, production-ready applications, covering tracing and evaluation methods as well as deployment with platforms such as Streamlit. We also discover techniques for effective prompt engineering and understand how prompts can enhance a RAG workflow. We conclude with reflections on the transformative potential of RAG and AI, emphasizing continuous learning, community engagement, and ethical considerations, alongside a forward-looking perspective on the role of technology and responsible development in shaping the future.

This part has the following chapters:

- *Chapter 9, Customizing and Deploying Our LlamaIndex Project*
- *Chapter 10, Prompt Engineering Guidelines and Best Practices*
- *Chapter 11, Conclusion and Additional Resources*

9

Customizing and Deploying Our LlamaIndex Project

Customizing **Retrieval-Augmented Generation** (RAG) components and optimizing performance is critical to building robust, production-ready applications with LlamaIndex. This chapter explores methods for leveraging open source models, intelligent routing across **large language models** (LLMs), and using community-built modules to increase flexibility and cost-effectiveness. Advanced tracing, evaluation methods, and deployment options are explored to gain deep insight, ensure reliable operation, and streamline the development life cycle.

Throughout this chapter, we're going to cover the following main topics:

- Customizing our RAG components
- Using advanced tracing and evaluation techniques
- Introduction to deployment with Streamlit
- Hands-on – a step-by-step deployment guide

Technical requirements

For this chapter, you will need to install the following package in your environment:

- *Arize AI Phoenix*: `https://pypi.org/project/arize-phoenix/`

Three additional integration packages are required in order to run the sample code:

- *Hugging Face embeddings*: `https://pypi.org/project/llama-index-embeddings-huggingface/`

- *Zephyr query engine*: `https://pypi.org/project/llama-index-packs-zephyr-query-engine/`

- *Neutrino LLM*: `https://pypi.org/project/llama-index-llms-neutrino/`

All code samples from this chapter can be found in the `ch9` subfolder of the book's GitHub repository:

`https://github.com/PacktPublishing/Building-Data-Driven-Applications-with-LlamaIndex`

Customizing our RAG components

For starters, let's talk about which components of a RAG workflow can be customized in LlamaIndex. The short answer is *pretty much all of them, as we have seen already in the previous chapters*. The fact that the framework itself is flexible and allows customization of all the core components is a definite advantage. But leaving aside the framework itself, the core of a RAG workflow is actually the LLM and the embedding model it uses. In all the examples given so far, we have used the default configuration of LlamaIndex – which is based on OpenAI models. But, as we already briefly discussed in *Chapter 3, Kickstarting Your Journey with LlamaIndex*, there are both good reasons and enough options available to choose other models – both commercial variants offered by established companies in this market, and open source models, which can be hosted locally, offering private alternatives, and substantially reducing the costs of a large-scale implementation.

But first, some background.

How LLaMA and LLaMA 2 changed the open source landscape

In early 2023, Meta AI introduced the **Large Language Model Meta AI (LLaMA)** family, offering a notable leap in accessibility for LLMs by releasing model weights to the research community. Following this, LLaMA 2 was launched in July 2023, with improvements such as increased data for training and expanded model sizes, alongside models fine-tuned for dialogue under less restrictive commercial use conditions. Meta developed and launched three versions of LLaMA 2 with 7, 13, and 70 billion parameters, respectively. While the basic structure of these models stayed similar to the original LLaMA versions, they were trained with 40% additional data compared to the original models, in order to enhance their foundational capabilities.

Despite some controversy regarding its open source status, the initiative marked a significant contribution to the open source ecosystem, triggering a new wave of community-based research and application development. The model consistently showcased competitive performance in tests against other leading LLMs, proving its advanced capabilities.

Further down the line, these releases have led to the creation of tools such as *llama.cpp* by Georgi Gerganov (`https://github.com/ggerganov/llama.cpp`), enabling the operation of these sophisticated models on more modest hardware, thus democratizing access to cutting-edge AI technologies.

Quick note

llama.cpp is an efficient C/C++ implementation of Meta's LLaMA architecture for LLM inference. Hugely popular in the open source community, with more than 43,000 stars on GitHub and over 930 releases, this foundational framework has sparked the development of many other similar tools and services such as Ollama, Local.AI, and others. These updates and advances signaled that AI research was changing, focusing more on making information freely available and making sure AI models can run on simpler computers and other edge devices. This opened up more possibilities for using **generative AI (GenAI)** and encouraged new ideas and improvements everywhere.

I won't go into a detailed discussion of all the currently available tools for running local LLMs. This is because there is already a plethora of available methods by which various open source models can be run on the local system. And not just local LLMs: there's also an increasing number of service providers offering access either to their own proprietary AI models or providing cloud-hosted access to open source models, and the good news is that LlamaIndex already provides built-in support for many of them. You can always consult the official documentation of the framework for a detailed overview of the supported models, along with examples of how they can be used: `https://docs.llamaindex.ai/en/stable/module_guides/models/llms/modules.html`.

Instead, I will try to offer you an alternative that I personally find very convenient for two important reasons: it is very easy to implement, and your existing code can be reused with only a few minimal changes. For beginner coders and tinkerers wanting to quickly experiment with an idea or build simple prototypes, this may be one of the best solutions.

Running a local LLM using LM Studio

Built on top of the `llama.cpp` library, **LM Studio** (`https://lmstudio.ai/`) provides a very user-friendly graphical interface for LLMs. It allows us to download, configure, and locally run almost any open source model available on Hugging Face. A great resource, especially for non-technical users, LM Studio offers two ways of interacting with a local LLM: through a chat UI similar to OpenAI's ChatGPT or via an OpenAI-compatible local server. This second option makes it particularly useful because we can easily adapt any LlamaIndex application natively designed to use OpenAI's LLMs with very few modifications. We'll get to that in a moment, but first, let's see how to get things started with LM Studio.

To start using this tool, you'll first have to download and install the right version, depending on your operating system. Releases are available for Mac, Windows, and Linux. The installation steps are self-explanatory and well documented on their website.

Once installed, the LM Studio GUI starts with a **Model Discovery** screen where you can type any model or model family name and get a list of matching model builds available for download. We'll use the popular **Zephyr-7B** model for our example (`https://huggingface.co/HuggingFaceH4/zephyr-7b-beta`). I have specifically chosen Zephyr because, albeit a compact model, it demonstrates the effectiveness of distilling an LLM into a more manageable size. Derived from **Mistral-7B**, Zephyr-7B establishes a new benchmark for chat models with 7 billion parameters, surpassing the performance of **LLAMA2-CHAT-70B** on the Hugging Face *LMSYS Chatbot Arena Leaderboard* (`https://huggingface.co/spaces/lmsys/chatbot-arena-leaderboard`). *Figure 9.1* shows a typical output when searching for the `zephyr-7b` keyword:

Figure 9.1 – LM Studio screenshot displaying search results

In the search results screen, you'll see two panels:

- The one on the left contains all models that match your search query. In our case, these are different builds of the Zephyr-7B model

- The right panel lists all the **Generative Pre-trained Transformer-Generated Unified Format (GGUF)** file versions available for download

> **About GGUF files**
>
> GGUF is a specific file format used for storing models for inference. Enhancing model sharing and usage efficiency, this format has quickly become a popular way of storing and distributing models throughout the open source community.

For most models, you'll get an entire list of GGUF files available. Each one will have its own characteristics, but probably the most important characteristic is the **quantization** level.

Understanding LLM quantization

Running an open source LLM on typical consumer hardware can prove challenging mainly because of its large memory footprint and high computational requirements. While some consumer-grade GPUs can aid in this regard, they may not be as effective as enterprise-level hardware in handling the demands of LLMs. That's why we need quantization. The goal of applying quantization – a post-training optimization technique – to an AI model is to optimize it for better performance and efficiency, particularly in terms of speed and memory usage, without significantly compromising its accuracy or output quality.

The quantization process achieves this by converting the model's parameters – typically stored as 32-bit floating-point numbers – to lower-bit representations, such as **16-bit floating-point** (FP16), **8-bit integers** (INT8), or even lower. It's a kind of approximation process that works by reducing the numerical precision used to represent the model's parameters, combined with complex techniques to maintain as much accuracy as possible. Modern quantization techniques are designed to minimize accuracy loss, often resulting in models that are nearly as accurate as their full-precision counterparts.

> **A simple analogy to help you better understand the concept**
>
> Imagine you have a recipe that calls for very precise measurements, such as 1.4732 cups of flour. In practice, you might round this to 1.5 cups, as the difference is negligible in most cases and the difference will not affect the end result. This is similar to quantization, where we reduce the precision of the model's parameters to make the model more efficient while maintaining acceptable accuracy. But instead of cups of flour, we reduce the numerical precision of the model's parameters. Instead of using 16 bits to store a parameter as 23.7, we could quantize it into 8 bits as 23. This directly translates to less memory usage and faster processing times. However, there is a trade-off between model size, speed, and accuracy.

With an acceptable loss of accuracy, this process can significantly reduce the size of the model and the computational resources required for both training and inference phases, making it more feasible to deploy these models on consumer hardware. Generally, the lower the bit representation (such as INT4 or even binary), the smaller and faster the model becomes, but at a higher risk of accuracy loss.

Being built on top of llama.cpp, LM Studio can take advantage of any compatible GPUs that could be used during the inference process. This feature is commonly called *GPU offloading* and means that computing operations can be partially or even entirely transferred from the CPU to the GPU. Given the fact that a modern GPU is capable of handling highly parallel computing tasks more efficiently than CPUs, this can dramatically speed up the inference process. It also reduces the load on the CPU, thus providing an overall balanced improvement of system performance. The main limitation when attempting GPU offloading is the amount of video memory available on your GPU. In order to run efficiently, the GPU must load the model in the video memory first.

Because of this, apart from the quantization level, the GGUF files in the right panel will also have a flag showing three possible compatibility scenarios, each represented by a different color:

- **Green**: This means your GPU has enough video memory to load the model and execute the inference. In most cases, this is the ideal scenario

- **Blue**: Not ideal, but still provides a considerable uplift in performance

- **Gray**: This may or may not work depending on the model architecture

- **Red**: Unfortunately, this means you won't be able to run this version on your machine, the most probable reason being that its size exceeds your total system memory

> **Pro tip**
>
> A very handy tool for approximating the required VRAM for a particular model given a particular quantization level can be found on the Hugging Face website: `https://huggingface.co/spaces/hf-accelerate/model-memory-usage`

So, which model should you choose?

The general rule of thumb is that with a lower quantization level, less memory will be required and the inference process will be faster. The trade-off is decreased accuracy. For example, a 3-bit quantization will always result in less accuracy than a 6-bit quantization.

Once you've made a decision on the exact model version, the next step is to download the model on your machine. But first, make sure you have the necessary space on your hard drive. There's a handy status bar on the bottom of the UI to monitor the status of the download.

After the download is complete, moving to the **Chats** screen will display something similar to *Figure 9.2*:

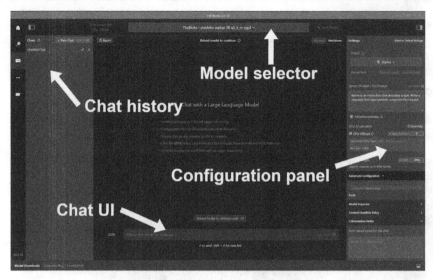

Figure 9.2 – LM Studio's chat UI

This is the interaction method that I mentioned at the beginning of this section – the one resembling the ChatGPT interface. In this screen, you'll be able to do the following:

1. Select the desired AI model from a list of all downloaded ones. To choose your model, use the *model selector* on top of the screen. You'll have to wait for a few moments until the model is loaded into memory.

2. Configure any available parameters of the model using the *configuration panel* on the right side. We'll talk in more detail about that in a moment.

3. See a list of previous chats on the left side.

4. Chat with the model using a familiar interface inspired by ChatGPT.

There are a number of parameters that you can tweak in the configuration panel. The most important ones are the following:

- **Preset**: Some models come with predefined configurations that you can load from presets. For an easy start, I would recommend selecting the model's specific preset from the list. For example, there is a Zephyr preset that can be used with all Zephyr-based models

- **System Prompt**: This prompt will set the initial context of the conversation

- **GPU Offload**: Allows you to configure the number of model layers to be offloaded to the GPU. Depending on the model you're using and your available GPU, you may want to gradually experiment with increasing values while checking for model stability. Higher values can sometimes produce errors. If you feel confident, use -1 to offload all the model's layers to the GPU

- **Context Length**: Allows you to define the maximum context window to be used

Changing some of these parameters may trigger a model reload, so you'll have to be patient until it completes the process. Once you have customized everything, the floor is yours – enjoy chatting with your local LLM.

So far, so good, but where's the RAG part in all this?

For that, we'll have to go to the **Local Inference Server** screen, which you can do by pressing the double-arrow icon on the left-side menu. You'll be presented with a UI similar to *Figure 9.3*:

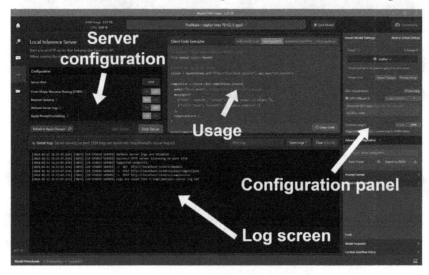

Figure 9.3 – The local Inference Server interface in LM Studio

The configuration options from the right-side panel are almost identical to the ones in the **Chat** screen. In the beginning, you can leave the *server configuration* options as default. The *usage* section tells you how to interact with the API. One of the great aspects of LM Studio is that it emulates the OpenAI API. That means your already existing code will need very few changes to work with a local LLM hosted through LM Studio.

All you have to do at this point is to click the **Start Server** button, and you're good to go.

> **Quick note**
> Please keep in mind that while the API server is running, the chat UI will be disabled, so you won't be able to use both at the same time.

Let's see exactly what we need to change in our code if we want to port it to a local LLM using this method. If we look at the recommendation in the *usage* section, we'll see that a single change is necessary:

```
client = OpenAI(base_url="http://localhost:1234/v1")
```

However, because LlamaIndex has its own implementation of the OpenAI API client, in our case, we'll have to use the `api_base` parameter like this:

```
from llama_index.llms.openai import OpenAI
llm = OpenAI(
    api_base='http://localhost:1234/v1',
    temperature=0.7
)
print(llm.complete('Who is Lionel Messi?'))
```

As you can see, the only real change we have to make is pointing the `llm` instance toward our local server instead of the OpenAI one. The rest of the code remains unchanged. After running this example, you'll see actual requests coming from our code and responses coming from the API in LM Studio's log screen. If you want to permanently reconfigure the LLM in the entire code, you'll have to define a `Settings` object and use it to configure global settings, as I showed you in *Chapter 3, Kickstarting Your Journey with LlamaIndex*, in the *Customizing the LLM used by LlamaIndex* section.

Neat, isn't it? Our data is now completely private, and we don't have to pay for using an AI model in our RAG workflows anymore. Of course, there's still a cost, albeit in electricity rather than tokens. The capability to run local models on modest hardware unlocks numerous possibilities that extend beyond mere text generation. This includes the opportunity to embrace fully multimodal experiences with models such as **LLaVa** (https://huggingface.co/docs/transformers/main/en/model_doc/llava), allowing for a wider range of applications: a wonderful tool that serves as an excellent resource for rapid prototyping or exploring diverse ideas.

However, keep in mind that LM Studio is governed by a licensing model, which restricts its use to personal, non-commercial purposes. To utilize LM Studio for commercial applications, obtaining permission from the developers is necessary.

Routing between LLMs using services such as Neutrino or OpenRouter

Sometimes, a single LLM may not be ideal for every single interaction. In complex RAG scenarios, finding the best mix between cost, latency, and precision could prove to be a difficult task when forced to choose a single LLM for everything. But what if we could find a way to mix different LLMs in the same app and dynamically choose which one to use for each individual interaction? That is the exact purpose of third-party services such as **Neutrino** (https://www.neutrinoapp.com/) and **OpenRouter** (https://openrouter.ai/). These types of services can significantly enhance a RAG workflow by providing intelligent routing capabilities for queries across different LLMs.

Neutrino's smart model router, for instance, allows you to intelligently route queries to the most suited LLM for the prompt, optimizing both response quality and cost efficiency. This can be particularly useful in a RAG workflow where different types of queries may require different LLM strengths or specialties. For example, one model might be more effective at understanding and parsing the initial user query, while another might be better suited for generating responses based on retrieved documents. By employing a router, we can dynamically select the most suitable model for each task without hardcoding model choices into our application, thus enhancing flexibility and potentially improving the overall performance of our RAG system. *Figure 9.4* describes the working mechanism of a Neutrino router:

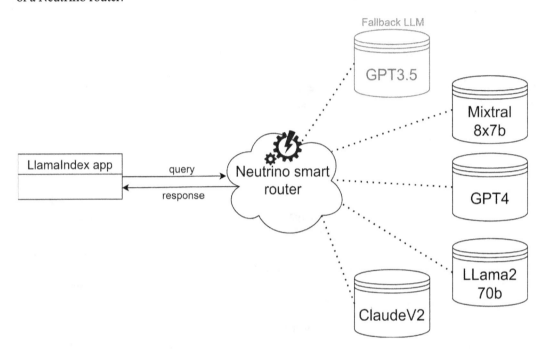

Figure 9.4 – A diagram of the Neutrino smart routing feature

The great news is that both Neutrino and OpenRouter are supported as integration packages in LlamaIndex. Let's have a look at a simple example that uses a custom Neutrino router to dynamically choose between different LLMs depending on the user query. To run this example, make sure you first install the Neutrino integration package by running the following command:

```
pip install llama-index-llms-neutrino
```

Once the package is installed, you should first sign up for an account and obtain an API key on the Neutrino website. The next step is to create an LLM router by selecting your desired LLMs as well as a *fallback* LLM. The fallback model will be used by default in case of errors or whenever the router cannot determine which LLM to use. During the router setup, you will also have the option of choosing to use Neutrino as a provider for the AI models or utilize your own API keys for each LLM. The last step in the router setup process requires you to provide a *router ID*. This ID will be used in the code to specify the router used by the service.

Here is how we can use the Neutrino router in LlamaIndex:

```
from llama_index.core.llms import ChatMessage
from llama_index.llms.neutrino import Neutrino
llm = Neutrino(
    api_key="<your-Neutrino_API_key>",
    router="<Neutrino-router_ID>"
)
```

The code first initializes the Neutrino router in the form of a LlamaIndex `llm` object, for which you'll need to provide your Neutrino API key and the ID of the router you have defined. Next, it runs in a loop, continually taking questions from the user until the `'exit'` keyword is received:

```
while True:
    user_message = input("Ask a question: ")
    if user_message.lower() == 'exit':
        print("Exiting chat...")
        break
    response = llm.complete(user_message)
    print(f"LLM answer: {response}")
    print(f"Answered by: {response.raw['model']}")
```

The questions are submitted to the Neutrino router, and, in return, the script not only prints the answer but also the name of the LLM that was chosen by the router to generate the answer. You can play around and experiment with different types of questions. Based on whichever models you selected when you defined the router, you'll see that it will send the questions to different LLMs, depending on their capabilities. Another, more general approach in using such a router would be to use the `Settings` class to create a global configuration using that `llm` object:

```
from llama_index.core import Settings
Settings.llm = llm
```

This has the advantage that it configures every subsequent LlamaIndex component in our code to use the Neutrino router.

Pro tip

If you're not entirely satisfied with the decisions made by the router, Neutrino also gives you the ability to fine-tune your defined router by uploading a list of examples on which the router can be trained: `https://platform.neutrinoapp.com/training-studio`

And Neutrino is just one example. OpenRouter works in a similar way, but it's mostly focused on optimizing the cost of LLM calls, not necessarily the quality.

There are also other providers offering similar services, and the concept is bound to become more and more popular as hundreds of new AI models emerge every week. The ability to use LLM routing services enhances the RAG workflow by abstracting the complexity of model selection and management. As a result, we can focus on building and optimizing our applications instead of managing the underlying AI models.

What about customizing embedding models?

Another important component that can be considered for customization in a RAG scenario is the underlying embedding model. Intensively used in scenarios where vector store indexes are employed, the embedding model can also be a source of concern regarding cost and privacy. That is why we may sometimes prefer using a local model in our RAG workflow. Again, the good news is that LlamaIndex provides out-of-the-box support for more than 30 embedding models. They can be used by installing embedding integration packages, documented on the *LlamaHub* website: `https://llamahub.ai/?tab=embeddings`.

You can find a very simple example of how to configure LlamaIndex to use a local embedding model from Hugging Face in *Chapter 5, Indexing with LlamaIndex*, in the *Understanding embeddings* section.

Leveraging the Plug and Play convenience of using Llama Packs

The fact that LlamaIndex offers us such a rich framework of low-level elements and methods for RAG is a double-edged sword. On the one hand, it is extremely useful to have a tool available for almost any practical problem you have to solve. On the other hand, to successfully implement these tools, we must first spend a fair amount of time familiarizing ourselves with each one. Then comes the fine-tuning and optimization phase for each component. We are already talking about a significant effort in the development and optimization process. Sometimes, in order to be able to test an idea with a rapid prototype, it would be preferable if we already had some advanced ready-made modules. Imagine some *Lego* pieces already structured into functional sub-assemblies: a roof, a window, a bus stop, and so on. Well, we have that to hand.

Created and continually improved by the flourishing LlamaIndex community, **Llama Packs** are pre-packaged modules that can be used to quickly build LLM applications. Just like some pre-built Lego structures, they provide reusable components such as LLMs, embedding models, and vector indexes that have been preconfigured to work together for various use cases in building a RAG pipeline. They are ready-to-use modules that can be downloaded and initialized with parameters to achieve a specific goal outside of the box.

> **Example**
> A pack could contain a full RAG pipeline to enable semantic search over text or an entire agent construct that could be immediately invoked in our app.

Llama Packs act as templates that can be inspected, customized, and extended as needed. The code for each pack is available, so developers can modify it or take inspiration to build their own applications. The beauty of this concept is that it provides **Plug and Play** (**PnP**) solutions without bloating the main code base of the framework. You can still use various integration packages together with the core components of LlamaIndex, and you can definitely customize any of these packs according to your needs.

You'll find a collection of all the published Llama Packs, together with all the other integration packages, available on LlamaHub (`https://llamahub.ai/?tab=llama_packs`). There's a *README* file for each pack that provides details about its usage, and most of them also have detailed examples that you can follow and experiment with.

Using them is very straightforward. Because, in this section, we talk about customizations in general and, among other options, moving our RAG workflows to local, open source models, I'm going to show you an example in the same line. We'll explore a Llama Pack that allows for the creation of a query engine that relies entirely on locally hosted AI models. The pack implements `HuggingFaceH4/zephyr-7b-beta` as the LLM used for inference and `BAAI/bge-base-en-v1.5` as the embedding model. The pack is called Zephyr Query Engine Pack, and you can find it here: `https://llamahub.ai/l/llama_packs-zephyr_query_engine`.

In a similar way to how LM Studio works, this pack can leverage existing GPUs to accelerate the inference process. Let's see how it works.

The first step in using any Llama Pack is to download the actual modules on your local environment. This can be accomplished in three different ways:

- By installing the corresponding integration package. In our example, that would be accomplished with the following command:

```
pip install llama-index-packs-zephyr-query-engine
```

This method is simple and permanently installs the required pack into your local environment. Its only disadvantage is that you cannot inspect and modify the pack code. For that purpose, the other two methods are recommended.

- By using the **command-line interface** (**CLI**). Here's an example:

```
llamaindex-cli download-llamapack ZephyrQueryEnginePack
--download-dir ./zephyr_pack
```

We'll discuss the CLI tool in more detail in the next section.

- Directly in the code, using the `download_llama_pack()` method and specifying a download location like this:

```
from llama_index.llama_pack import download_llama_pack
download_llama_pack(
    "ZephyrQueryEnginePack", "./zephyr_pack"
)
```

Once downloaded into your local environment, the pack contents will be stored in a subfolder called `zephyr_pack`. You can inspect and modify anything in the code, adjusting it to your own needs. You will also need to install the Hugging Face `embeddings` integration package before running the example:

```
pip install llama-index-embeddings-huggingface
```

Here's a simple example of how to use this pack after downloading:

```
from zephyr_pack.base import ZephyrQueryEnginePack
from llama_index.readers import SimpleDirectoryReader
reader = SimpleDirectoryReader('files')
documents = reader.load_data()
zephyr_qe = ZephyrQueryEnginePack(documents)
response=zephyr_qe.run(
    "Enumerate famous buildings in ancient Rome"
    )
print(response)
```

Notice that we're using the `run()` method, which, in this case, is a wrapper for the `query()` method used by the regular query engine.

This is just one of the more than 50 packs already available on LlamaHub at this moment. And the number keeps growing. The great news is that all of them are well documented and follow pretty much the same implementation model. So, next time you're faced with a practical scenario that needs combining low-level components into more advanced elements, instead of reinventing the wheel, I encourage you to spend some time browsing LlamaHub for a potential ready-made solution for your problem. Llama Packs accelerates LLM app development by letting developers tap into pre-built components tailored for common use cases. Both ready-made solutions and customizable templates are available to kickstart projects.

Using the Llama CLI

Another very useful tool in the LlamaIndex arsenal is the `llamaindex-cli` utility. Installed together with the LlamaIndex libraries, the tool can be accessed very easily from the command line and can be used for various purposes, including the following:

- Downloading Llama Packs, as seen in the previous section. The syntax to download a Llama Pack is given as follows:

```
llamaindex-cli download-llamapack <pack_name> --download-dir
<target_location>
```

- Upgrading source code from versions older than LlamaIndex v.0.10. Due to the fact that version 0.10 brought many changes related to the code structure and how to use certain modules in the framework, the authors of LlamaIndex provided developers with this automatic upgrade tool. Basically, it automatically modifies the code written on older versions and updates it to the new structure introduced with v0.10 for an easier transition. The syntax used for this feature is the following to process all sources in a given folder simultaneously:

```
llamaindex-cli upgrade <target_directory>
```

Or execute the following command to upgrade a single file:

```
llamaindex-cli upgrade-file <target_file>
```

- By far the most interesting capability is enabled by using the `rag` argument. This feature allows you to build a RAG workflow directly from the command line without having to write any code. By default, the command-line RAG mode uses local storage for embeddings based on a Chroma DB database and OpenAI's GPT-3.5 Turbo model as LLM. For privacy reasons, keep in mind that this means that all data we upload will be sent to OpenAI by default.

How RAG works in the command line

Before we can use the RAG mode from the command line, we must first install the ChromaDB library in our local environment:

```
pip install chromadb
```

The `llamaindex-cli` utility offers a variety of command-line parameters that enable users to interact with language models and manage local files efficiently. Here are descriptions of the most important command-line parameters:

- `--help`: Displays a help message, providing an overview of available commands and their usage.

- `--files <FILES>`: Defines the name of the file or directory from where the tool will ingest our proprietary data. The contents will be ingested and embedded into the local vector database, enabling the RAG CLI tool to index the specified files and later retrieve context from them at query time.

- `--question <QUESTION>`: Specifies the question you want to ask about the ingested files. Used for querying indexed content, leveraging the power of the LLM to extract information from our proprietary data.

- `--chat`: Opens a chat **read-eval-print loop** (**REPL**) for an interactive Q&A session within the terminal. This provides a conversational interface to query the ingested documents.

- `--verbose`: Enables verbose output during execution, offering detailed information about the tool's operations that can be useful for troubleshooting and understanding the tool's inner workings.

- `--clear`: Clears out all currently embedded data from the local vector database. Because a Chroma database is used to store the embeddings, these will persist across the sessions. The `--clear` command is the equivalent of a reset.

- `--create-llama`: Initiates the creation of a LlamaIndex application based on the selected files. This parameter extends the tool's functionality beyond simple Q&A, enabling the development of full-stack applications with a backend and frontend, leveraging the ingested data. You'll find a complete example of how to use it here: `https://www.npmjs.com/package/create-llama#example`.

Talking about examples, let's have a look at a simple way to have a conversation with our files using the CLI RAG feature. We'll use the contents of the `ch9\files` folder from our GitHub repository. So, make sure you're running this script from inside that folder, which should contain some sample files:

```
llamaindex-cli rag --files files -q "What can you tell me about
ancient Rome?" --verbose
```

Alternatively, once the files have been ingested, for an interactive chat session with the data, you can use the following command:

```
llamaindex-cli rag --chat
```

And just in case you need to customize the mechanics of the CLI RAG, a complete example can be found in the official documentation of the framework, here: `https://docs.llamaindex.ai/en/stable/use_cases/q_and_a/rag_cli.html`.

Next, it's time to dive deeper into the logic of our LlamaIndex applications.

Using advanced tracing and evaluation techniques

The process of building an LLM-based application using a tool such as LlamaIndex is very developer-friendly since the framework abstracts away a lot of technical stuff. But at the same time, this complicates things, for the very same reason. When things don't work as planned, developers need to have effective ways of understanding why. They have to peel back all these layers of abstraction in order to pinpoint the root causes. In other words, we need to be able to see the inner mechanics of our code, understand how different components interact, and be able to identify underlying issues. That's where tracing becomes a really important feature. On the other hand, because we have so many tools available and so many ways of building our solution, we need a way to benchmark different combinations and determine the best mix of tools and orchestrations. That's where evaluation comes into play. Evaluation is essential for comparing various tool and method combinations until we find the right configuration for our specific needs. Together, tracing and evaluation form the backbone of a successful RAG development process, ensuring both transparency and optimal performance.

In *Chapter 3*, *Kickstarting Your Journey with LlamaIndex*, we already discussed simple logging methods that we can use to better understand what's happening under the hood of our LlamaIndex apps. Now, it's time to discover a much more advanced way in which we can understand and evaluate RAG applications. In this section, I will explain advanced tracing and evaluation using the **Phoenix framework** developed by Arize AI (`https://phoenix.arize.com/`). Integrating LlamaIndex with specialized tracing and evaluation tools provides a sophisticated approach to understanding and optimizing RAG applications. Phoenix provides the necessary instrumentation together with a great visualization UI, making our RAG execution workflow really simple to understand.

To make use of the advanced capabilities of the Phoenix framework, we must first install some necessary libraries in our environment:

Tracing our RAG workflows using Phoenix

In Phoenix, tracing is built on the concept of **spans** and **traces**, which are fundamental for capturing the detailed execution flow of applications. A span represents a specific operation or unit of work within the application, tracking the start and end times, along with metadata that provides context about the operation. These spans are nested within traces, which aggregate multiple spans to depict the entire journey of a request through the application. This hierarchical structure allows developers to drill down into specific operations, understanding how each component contributes to the overall process. Phoenix's tracing capabilities are designed to seamlessly integrate with LlamaIndex, enabling developers to instrument their RAG applications with minimal effort.

Because it features a client-server architecture, Phoenix is able to gather traces both locally and remotely. We can automatically collect telemetry data about each operation, including data ingestion, indexing, retrieval, processing, and any subsequent LLM calls. In the background, this data is collected by the Phoenix server, where it can be visualized and analyzed in real time.

Once the necessary requirements have been installed, using Phoenix is really easy. There are many advanced capabilities that you can explore with this framework, but I will show you the most simple and straightforward way to use it for tracing the execution of a LlamaIndex application. We'll make use of a special method called `set_global_handler`, which conveniently configures LlamaIndex to use a certain tracing tool for every operation – in our case, the Phoenix framework.

Make sure you install the required packages before running the example:

```
pip install "arize-phoenix[llama-index]" llama-hub html2text
```

Here is the code:

```
from llama_index.core import (
    SimpleDirectoryReader,
    VectorStoreIndex,
    set_global_handler
)
import phoenix as px
```

Apart from the obvious imports that will provide our basic RAG functionality, we're also importing `set_global_handler` and the Phoenix library. The next part will be responsible for starting the Phoenix server and configuring LlamaIndex to use it as a global callback handler:

```
px.launch_app()
set_global_handler("arize_phoenix")
```

From now on, every single operation performed by our app will generate traces that will get collected by the Phoenix server. Let's build a simple query engine based on a `VectorStoreIndex` index and run a random query:

```
documents = SimpleDirectoryReader('files').load_data()
index = VectorStoreIndex.from_documents(documents)
qe = index.as_query_engine()
response = qe.query("Tell me about ancient Rome")
print(response)
```

Because we need the server to be live in order to visualize the trace, we keep the script running with this line:

```
input("Press <ENTER> to exit...")
```

Now, with the script still running in the background, we can access the Phoenix UI at this URL: `http://localhost:6006/`. *Figure 9.5* shows what you'll find in the Phoenix server UI:

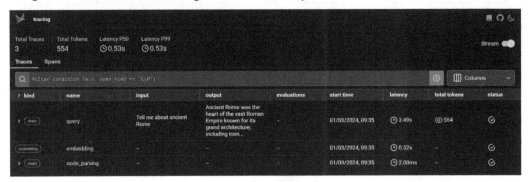

Figure 9.5 – A screenshot from the Phoenix server UI depicting our tracing output

Looking at this screenshot, we can see that the Phoenix server UI helps us visualize a complete trace of our code, divided into multiple spans. If you have successfully executed the previous sample code, our trace should consist of three different spans, each displayed on a separate line.

Let's talk about the columns in the screenshot:

- The first column, `kind`, contains the type of the span. It can be `chain`, `retriever`, `re-ranker`, `llm`, `embedding`, `tool`, or `agent`. We are already familiar with what these concepts represent in LlamaIndex, except for a chain. In Phoenix, a chain can be either the starting point for a series of operations in an LLM application or a connector linking different steps within the application workflow. In our example, the screenshot contains three spans: two chains and an embedding. They are displayed in the reverse order of their operation, beginning with the last one.

- The second column, *name*, provides a more detailed description of the span. We can see that in our example, the first span represents a *query*, the second one is an *embedding*, and the third is a *Node-parsing* operation. The logic of our code is now clear: it first parsed the ingested documents into Nodes, then created a vector index by embedding the Nodes, and the final step was to run a query against that index.

- The next two columns, *input,* and *output*, show exactly what went as an input into the span and what was the final output produced by it. In our example, we only have values in these fields for the query span as this does not apply to the other ones.

- The *evaluations* column displays the results of the evaluation for each span. For now, that column should be empty as we have not yet executed any evaluation. We'll cover this topic in the next section.

- *start time* provides an exact timestamp for each span.

- *latency* measures the total execution time for each span. This is really useful when trying to optimize our code for increased performance.

- As the name implies, *total tokens* count the total number of tokens used by the corresponding operation.

- The last column, *status*, indicates whether the operation was completed successfully or not.

Here comes the best part. If we now click on the *kind* column of the query span – the first one in our list – we'll get a detailed visualization, similar to the one depicted in *Figure 9.6*:

Figure 9.6 – Trace details visualized on the Phoenix server UI

As you can see, we can now get a detailed understanding of each individual step performed during this span. In this case, we see a decomposed view of the query engine operation: first, the retrieval part, and then the final response synthesis using the LLM. By clicking on each individual step, we can explore its attributes and underlying mechanics. And because Phoenix runs locally, all this data remains private.

> **Practical exercise**
>
> Here's a useful exercise you could attempt now. Try to reconfigure some of the samples discussed in the previous chapters to use the Phoenix framework. You'll get a better understanding of how different components work in LlamaIndex and also have a chance to familiarize yourself with this great tool.

And if you want to go deeper and explore more advanced tracing features of Phoenix, you'll find everything you need in their official documentation: `https://docs.arize.com/phoenix/`.

Next, let's talk about how we can use Phoenix to evaluate and optimize our RAG apps.

Evaluating our RAG system

When developing LLM-based systems, proper evaluation is essential for checking how well a RAG pipeline works. In general, LLM applications have to deal with very diverse inputs, and there is usually not a single, absolute answer they are supposed to return. That means evaluating them can prove to be a challenging task.

In general, evaluating a RAG pipeline involves assessing key aspects such as the following:

- **Retrieval quality**: Evaluating the relevance and effectiveness of the retrieved Nodes in providing the necessary information to answer the query

- **Generation quality**: Assessing the quality of the final output, including its correctness, coherence, and adherence to the provided context

- **Faithfulness**: Ensuring that the generated output is faithful to the retrieved information and does not introduce hallucinations or inconsistencies

- **Efficiency**: Measuring the computational efficiency and scalability of the RAG pipeline, especially in real-world scenarios with large-scale datasets

- **Robustness**: Testing the RAG system's ability to handle diverse queries, edge cases, and potential adversarial inputs

To address these evaluation challenges, several tools and frameworks have been developed to facilitate the evaluation process. These tools aim to provide automated metrics, reference-based comparisons, and also human-in-the-loop evaluation methodologies. By leveraging these evaluation frameworks, we can obtain insights into the strengths and weaknesses of our RAG pipelines, identify areas for improvement, and iterate on their designs to enhance overall performance.

Because in the previous section, we've seen how Phoenix can help us with its tracing functionality, I'd like to continue building on the previous example and first explore some of the evaluation features provided by this framework.

Using the Phoenix framework evaluation features

Since manual labeling and testing evaluation data can be very time-consuming, Phoenix uses GPT-4 as a reference to decide on the correctness of our RAG's answers. This framework provides out-of-the-box support for batch processing, custom datasets, and pre-tested evaluation templates. Unlike traditional, more basic evaluation libraries that lack rigor for production environments, Phoenix ensures data science rigor, high throughput, and flexibility across different environments, making it significantly faster and more adaptable for evaluating both the model and the context in which it is used. Phoenix can be used for evaluating two important dimensions of a RAG workflow: **retrieval** and **LLM inference**.

For retrieval, Phoenix evaluates the relevancy of the retrieved context. In other words, it verifies if the retrieved Nodes actually contain an answer to the query or not. When evaluating LLM inference, the framework checks three main attributes:

- **Correctness**: This verifies if the system has accurately answered a question

- **Hallucinations**: This aims to identify any unrealistic or fabricated responses by the LLM in relation to the context it was provided

- **Toxicity**: This checks for any harmful content in the AI's responses, including racism, bias, or general toxicity

Because a complex RAG scenario could sometimes rely on many individual spans, being able to individually evaluate each one becomes an essential feature. This way, we can isolate the source of errors and stop them from propagating further in the flow. Since it uses an LLM for running evaluations, Phoenix returns not just the test result but also an explanation provided by the model. This can be very useful for understanding the root cause of a failed evaluation and pinpointing the misbehaving component in our RAG application.

Let's have a look at a simple example to understand how Phoenix can be used for evaluation. In order to minimize costs and keep the code simple, we're going to use the previous approach we used for the tracing example. We're going to ingest the contents of our ch9/files folder, create a vector index, and run a simple query against the index. In a real scenario, you would probably run these evaluators against a much larger dataset in order to cover as many edge cases as possible and increase the probability of finding underlying issues in the pipeline. Here is an example:

```
from llama_index.core import (
    SimpleDirectoryReader,
    VectorStoreIndex,
    set_global_handler
)
import phoenix as px
px.launch_app()
set_global_handler("arize_phoenix")
documents = SimpleDirectoryReader('files').load_data()
index = VectorStoreIndex.from_documents(documents)
qe = index.as_query_engine()
response = qe.query("Tell me about ancient Rome")
print(response)
```

So far, the first part is identical to the previous example. It's time to add the part responsible for the evaluation. We'll begin by importing the necessary Phoenix components. Two functions, get_retrieved_documents() and get_qa_with_reference(), will be responsible for fetching the documents retrieved by queries and the queries with their reference answers for evaluation. We're also importing three of the Phoenix evaluators: HallucinationEvaluator, QAEvaluator, and RelevanceEvaluator. These evaluators will assess the hallucination in responses, the correctness of question-answer pairs, and the relevance of retrieved documents, respectively. We also need to import run_evals(), which will be responsible for performing the evaluation tasks and returning DataFrames containing the evaluation results. Finally, the DocumentEvaluations and SpanEvaluations classes will be used to encapsulate evaluation results and display these results in the Phoenix server UI:

```
from phoenix.session.evaluation import (
    get_qa_with_reference,
    get_retrieved_documents
)
```

```
from phoenix.experimental.evals import (
    HallucinationEvaluator,
    RelevanceEvaluator,
    QAEvaluator,
    OpenAIModel,
    run_evals
)
from phoenix.trace import DocumentEvaluations, SpanEvaluations
```

Now that the imports are complete, it's time to prepare our evaluations. First, we declare the LLM that will be used to perform evaluations. This should always be the best available model:

```
model = OpenAIModel(model="gpt-4-turbo-preview")
```

Once the evaluation model has been defined, it's time to prepare our data. We'll fetch the retrieved documents and queries in separate data frames. These data frames will later become the input for evaluator functions:

```
retrieved_documents_df = get_retrieved_documents(px.Client())
queries_df = get_qa_with_reference(px.Client())
```

Now that we have the data, we need to define evaluator functions and run the actual evaluations:

```
hallucination_evaluator = HallucinationEvaluator(model)
qa_correctness_evaluator = QAEvaluator(model)
relevance_evaluator = RelevanceEvaluator(model)
hallucination_eval_df, qa_correctness_eval_df = run_evals(
    dataframe=queries_df,
    evaluators=[hallucination_evaluator, qa_correctness_evaluator],
    provide_explanation=True,
)
relevance_eval_df = run_evals(
    dataframe=retrieved_documents_df,
    evaluators=[relevance_evaluator],
    provide_explanation=True,
)[0]
```

When running the evaluators, notice that I'm setting the `provide_explanation` argument to `True`. This ensures that explanations for the evaluation scores are included in the response from the LLM. The last part involves encapsulating the results in corresponding `SpanEvaluations` and `DocumentEvaluations` classes and sending them to the Phoenix server so that they can be properly displayed in the UI:

```
px.Client().log_evaluations(
    SpanEvaluations(
```

```
        eval_name="Hallucination",
        dataframe=hallucination_eval_df),
    SpanEvaluations(
        eval_name="QA Correctness",
        dataframe=qa_correctness_eval_df),
    DocumentEvaluations(
        eval_name="Relevance",
        dataframe=relevance_eval_df),
)
input("Press <ENTER> to exit...")
```

Just like in the previous example, the input at the end keeps the script running until the user decides to exit by pressing the *Enter* key. This allows us to view and interact with the Phoenix app before closing it. If everything went smoothly, accessing the UI at `http://localhost:6006/` should reveal an output similar to what we can see in *Figure 9.7*:

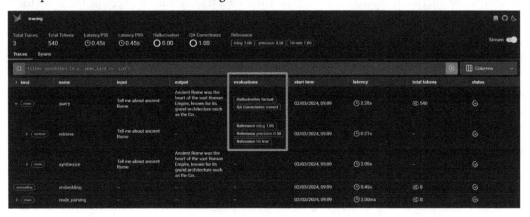

Figure 9.7 – Visualizing evaluation results in the Phoenix server UI

As you can see, the *evaluations* column has been updated with the values returned by the evaluators we just executed. We can now see the results, as well as the rationale for each individual score.

The topic of evaluating RAG apps is huge and could probably become the subject of an entirely separate book. There are many nuances and different approaches that could be considered regarding evaluation. I've only shown you a tool – Phoenix – but there are many other options for this purpose, including LlamaIndex's own instrumentation. If you're planning to explore this topic deeper, I encourage you to start by reading the LlamaIndex official documentation here: `https://docs.llamaindex.ai/en/stable/module_guides/evaluating/root.html`. Also, get a better understanding of the complete capabilities of the Phoenix framework by reading their official documentation here: `https://docs.arize.com/phoenix/`.

Other alternatives for evaluation – RAGAS

While Phoenix provides a comprehensive evaluation framework for RAG pipelines, there are other alternatives available. Another notable framework is **Retrieval-Augmented Generation Assessment (RAGAS)**, which is based on the techniques introduced by Es et al. (2023) in their paper, *RAGAS: Automated Evaluation of Retrieval Augmented Generation* (`https://doi.org/10.48550/arXiv.2309.15217`). The RAGAS framework provides a practical implementation of these evaluation methods, along with additional features and integrations.

RAGAS is specifically designed for evaluating and analyzing RAG systems. It offers a standardized approach to assess various aspects of a RAG pipeline, including retrieval quality, generation quality, and the interplay between the retrieval and generation components.

Key features of RAGAS include the following:

- **Retrieval evaluation**: RAGAS assesses the quality of the retrieval component by measuring the relevance of the retrieved Nodes to the given query using metrics such as **Recall@k** – the proportion of relevant Nodes retrieved within the top k results, where k is a user-defined parameter. Another metric that measures retrieval quality is the **Mean Reciprocal Rank (MRR)** – measuring how quickly the system finds the first relevant Node.

- **Generation evaluation**: RAGAS also evaluates the quality of the generated text using a combination of automatic metrics and human evaluation. The automatic metrics include **Bilingual Evaluation Understudy (BLEU)**, which measures the similarity between the generated text and a reference text by comparing overlapping word sequences, and **Recall-Oriented Understudy for Gisting Evaluation (ROUGE)**, which calculates the overlap of words and word sequences between the generated text and the reference text. To complement these automatic metrics, RAGAS also incorporates human evaluation to assess aspects such as fluency, coherence, and relevance of the generated output, providing a comprehensive assessment of the generation quality.

- **Retrieval-generation interplay**: The framework also analyzes the interplay between the retrieval and generation components by measuring how much the generated text relies on the retrieved Nodes. It introduces metrics such as **Retrieval Dependency (RD)**, which quantifies how much the generated text depends on the retrieved Nodes, and **Retrieval Relevance (RR)**, which measures the relevance of the retrieved Nodes to the generated text to quantify this relationship.

- **Simulation**: RAGAS includes a simulation component that allows us to simulate different retrieval scenarios and analyze their impact on the generation quality. This helps in understanding the robustness and generalization ability of RAG models under various retrieval conditions. By manipulating the retrieval results, users can test how the RAG model performs under scenarios such as retrieving irrelevant, partially relevant, or noisy data. The simulation feature provides insights into the interplay between the retrieval and generation components, enabling us to identify strengths and weaknesses and guide improvements in the RAG model.

- **Fine-grained analysis**: RAGAS enables fine-grained analysis of RAG pipelines by providing tools to visualize and interpret the retrieval-generation process, such as attention weights and individual Node contributions.

A key advantage of this framework is that it enables reference-free evaluation of RAG pipelines, meaning it does not rely on ground truth annotations. This allows for more efficient and scalable evaluation cycles.

Compared to Phoenix, RAGAS offers a more focused evaluation framework specifically tailored for RAG systems. While Phoenix provides a general-purpose evaluation platform with features such as tracing, hallucination detection, and relevance assessment, RAGAS goes deeper into the intricacies of retrieval-generation interplay and also offers simulation capabilities. The framework provides seamless integration with LlamaIndex, simplifying the evaluation of LlamaIndex-based RAG systems. To keep things simple, I have not included any code examples in this case, but you can find detailed examples and documentation on the official project's page, at this URL: `https://docs.ragas.io/en/stable/howtos/integrations/llamaindex.html`.

It's worth noting that RAGAS is a more recent framework compared to Phoenix, and while it shows great promise, it may take some time for it to see the same level of adoption in the research community.

> **Important note**
>
> One thing to always keep in mind in terms of evaluation is the concept of model drift, which we have already covered in *Chapter 7, Querying Our Data, Part 2 – Postprocessing and Response Synthesis* section. Model drift can impact our RAG pipeline when the LLM's behavior gradually deviates from its intended purpose or when the quality of the generated output deteriorates. Regular or even continuous evaluation can help detect and mitigate this phenomenon, ensuring the RAG system remains reliable and effective in production environments.

By mastering tracing and evaluation techniques, you'll be able to create a complete system for finding and fixing problems in an LLM application. Using evaluations and tracing together, you can spot where things go wrong, figure out why, and see which part of your application needs to be improved.

It's now time to focus our attention on our side project: the PITS tutor. In this chapter, we'll finally get to deploy its components and run it as a standalone application. But first, let's have a short introduction to the different deployment options provided by **Streamlit**.

Introduction to deployment with Streamlit

As I explained in *Chapter 2, LlamaIndex: The Hidden Jewel - An Introduction to the LlamaIndex Ecosystem*, I chose Streamlit as the backbone for our side project because of its simplicity and the many deployment options it provides. Streamlit offers an easy approach to deploying your applications, making it possible to share your work with a broader audience with minimal effort. If you successfully followed the installation steps in *Chapter 2*, your local environment should already be ready for the next steps. However, just in case, before proceeding, make sure you have completed the necessary installation mentioned in *Chapter 2*, in the *Discovering Streamlit – the perfect tool for quick build and deployment* section.

Now that we're all set up, let's explore the deployment options available for Streamlit applications. Beyond the simplest method of running apps on your local machine, Streamlit offers a variety of web deployment solutions to cater to different needs and preferences:

- **Streamlit Community Cloud**: This user-friendly platform is the most straightforward option for deploying Streamlit apps, enabling users to deploy directly from their GitHub repositories in just a few clicks. It requires minimal configuration, and once deployed, your app will be accessible via a unique URL on Streamlit Community Cloud, making it easy to share with others.

- **Custom cloud services**: For those seeking greater control over their deployment environment, Streamlit apps can be deployed on various cloud services, including **Amazon Web Services (AWS)**, **Google Cloud Platform (GCP)**, and Azure. Deployment on these platforms might involve additional steps such as containerizing your app with Docker and configuring cloud-specific services such as AWS Elastic Beanstalk, Google App Engine, or Azure App Service.

- **Self-hosting**: If you have your own servers, opting to self-host your Streamlit applications gives you maximum control over the deployment environment and resources. This method involves setting up a server environment capable of running Python applications, installing Streamlit, and configuring your network for Streamlit app access. The self-hosting option answers to specific requirements for security, performance, or customization that cloud platforms cannot meet.

- **Heroku**: Heroku (`https://www.heroku.com/`) is another well-known platform for deploying Streamlit apps due to its simplicity and a free tier suitable for small projects and prototypes.

- **Streamlit in Snowflake**: For use cases prioritizing security and **role-based access control** (RBAC), Streamlit's integration with Snowflake offers a secure coding and deployment environment within the Snowflake platform. You can easily sign up for a trial Snowflake account, create a warehouse and database for your apps, and deploy Streamlit applications directly within Snowflake.

Each of these deployment options offers unique benefits, with different advantages in terms of level of control, scalability, security requirements, and budget constraints. However, I have chosen to show you the simplest option and probably the most appropriate choice for our PITS application: deployment in Streamlit Community Cloud. However, for a commercial-ready solution, the other options would have been a better choice.

HANDS-ON – a step-by-step deployment guide

It's time to share our PITS tutoring application with the world. However, as a quick side note, keep in mind that the current version is far from being ready for use in a multi-user, real-world environment. To keep the code base small and the deployment steps simple, I have designed PITS as a pure experiment in LlamaIndex. After all, the purpose of this book was not to delve into the architectural intricacies of building a full-fledged Streamlit application but rather to explain the tools and features that are available in LlamaIndex. This is the main reason why some of the PITS source files are not explained in detail in this book. Rest assured, however, that you will find plenty of comments in these modules, and if the comments available in the GitHub code aren't enough, you can always explore the official

Streamlit documentation and get a better understanding of the framework here: `https://docs.streamlit.io/`.

However, a brief introduction to the way Streamlit applications is built is in order. We'll use one of the PITS UI files as an example, and I'll walk you through the code to give you a basic understanding of the principles of Streamlit applications. Here is the code for `app.py`, our main program in the PITS structure. This code is responsible for orchestrating the execution of the various components that make up the tutoring application. It acts as the central hub, routing users through the onboarding process, handling session management, and dynamically presenting the quiz and training interfaces based on user interactions and session data:

```
from user_onboarding import user_onboarding
from session_functions import load_session, delete_session, save_
session
from logging_functions import reset_log
from quiz_UI import show_quiz
from training_UI import show_training_UI
import streamlit as st
```

We start by importing the necessary modules and components, including Streamlit. We also import several custom functions from the other modules, such as `user_onboarding`, `load_session`, `delete_session`, `save_session`, `reset_log`, `show_quiz`, and `show_training_UI`, each serving a specific role in the application's flow. Following the imports, the `main()` function encapsulates the application's logic:

```
def main():
    st.set_page_config(layout="wide")
    st.sidebar.title('P.I.T.S.')
    st.sidebar.markdown('### Your Personalized Intelligent Tutoring
System')
```

The use of `st.set_page_config` at the beginning establishes the basic layout of our web application. Streamlit provides a sidebar feature, and we'll make use of that to streamline our UI. Next, the application's flow is primarily controlled through conditional statements that check for the presence of certain keys in Streamlit's (`st.session_state`) session state. This session state acts as persistent storage across reruns of the app within the same browser session, allowing the application to remember user choices, entered information, and other stateful data:

```
if 'show_quiz' in st.session_state and
st.session_state['show_quiz']:
    show_quiz(st.session_state['study_subject'])
elif 'resume_session' in st.session_state and
st.session_state['resume_session']:
    st.session_state['show_quiz'] = False
    show_training_UI(st.session_state['user_name'],
    st.session_state['study_subject'])
```

```
    elif not load_session(st.session_state):
        user_onboarding()
```

> **A quick note on Streamlit's session state**
>
> Web applications are inherently stateless, meaning each request and response between the client and server are independent. Streamlit's session state allows us to overcome this by providing a way to maintain state across reruns of the app within the same browser session. This is essential for creating an interactive and user-friendly experience, as it allows the application to remember user choices, inputs, and actions without requiring the user to re-enter data after every interaction.

I'll briefly explain what happens in the previous part of the code:

- **Quiz display logic:** If the user has opted to take a quiz (`'show_quiz'` in `st.session_state`), the quiz interface is displayed by calling `show_quiz()`.

- **Resuming sessions:** If the user has already chosen to resume an existing session (`st.session_state['resume_session']`=True), the app will take them directly to the training UI.

- **User onboarding and session management:** `load_session(st.session_state)` checks whether session data exists. If not, the user is directed to the onboarding process through `user_onboarding()`.

Next, let's see what happens when an existing session is found but `show quiz` is `False` and the user hasn't clicked on the **Resume session** button yet:

```
    else:
        st.write(f"Welcome back {st.session_state['user_name']}!")
        col1, col2 = st.columns(2)
        if col1.button(f"Resume your study of
        {st.session_state['study_subject']}"):
            st.session_state['resume_session'] = True
            st.rerun()
        if col2.button('Start a new session'):
            delete_session(st.session_state)
            reset_log()
            for key in list(st.session_state.keys()):
                del st.session_state[key]
            st.rerun()
```

The first operation in this `else` block is displaying a welcome back message. The app then displays two buttons, allowing the user to decide whether they want to resume the existing training session or start a fresh one. Choosing to start a new session will basically reset everything and rerun the entire code to start the application from the beginning. Resuming the session at this point will determine the app to run `show_training_UI` and continue the existing training session.

Deploying our PITS project on Streamlit Community Cloud

Because of the way the internal folder structure of the Streamlit Community Cloud environment is implemented, we'll have to make a few modifications to our PITS folder structure. The plan is to deploy the application straight from a GitHub repository. However, one of the requirements for deploying from GitHub into the Community Cloud environment is that the main `.py` file is hosted in the `root` folder of the repository. That is not the case for PITS as the folder structure is a bit different. `app.py`, which is the main file in our case, is currently found in the `Building-Data-Driven-Applications-with-LlamaIndex\PITS_APP` folder. To fix that, we'll first make a copy of the `PITS_APP` subfolder, and then we'll initiate a new GitHub repository from that new folder. To keep things simple and require minimum changes, I will guide you on how to create a new repository containing just the PITS app and then deploy it from your own GitHub account:

1. First, let's create a copy of our local `PITS_APP` subfolder. Open Command Prompt and navigate to the `Building-Data-Driven-Applications-with-LlamaIndex` folder of your cloned repository. From that folder, type the following command:

```
xcopy PITS_APP C:\PITS_APP /E /I
```

2. This will create a folder on your `C:` drive containing only the source files of the PITS application. If you navigate to the newly created folder and list its contents with the `dir` command, the output should look like *Figure 9.8*:

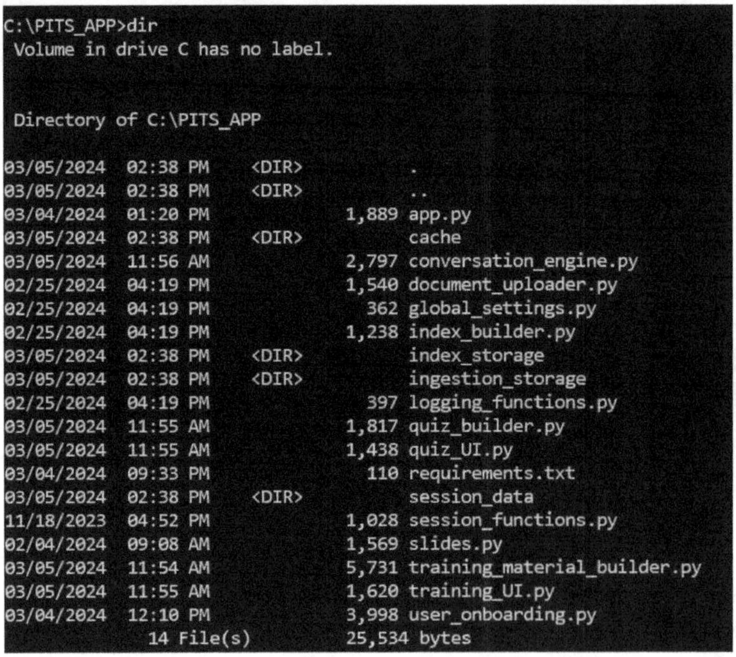

```
C:\PITS_APP>dir
 Volume in drive C has no label.


 Directory of C:\PITS_APP

03/05/2024  02:38 PM    <DIR>          .
03/05/2024  02:38 PM    <DIR>          ..
03/04/2024  01:20 PM             1,889 app.py
03/05/2024  02:38 PM    <DIR>          cache
03/05/2024  11:56 AM             2,797 conversation_engine.py
02/25/2024  04:19 PM             1,540 document_uploader.py
02/25/2024  04:19 PM               362 global_settings.py
02/25/2024  04:19 PM             1,238 index_builder.py
03/05/2024  02:38 PM    <DIR>          index_storage
03/05/2024  02:38 PM    <DIR>          ingestion_storage
02/25/2024  04:19 PM               397 logging_functions.py
03/05/2024  11:55 AM             1,817 quiz_builder.py
03/05/2024  11:55 AM             1,438 quiz_UI.py
03/04/2024  09:33 PM               110 requirements.txt
03/05/2024  02:38 PM    <DIR>          session_data
11/18/2023  04:52 PM             1,028 session_functions.py
02/04/2024  09:08 AM             1,569 slides.py
03/05/2024  11:54 AM             5,731 training_material_builder.py
03/05/2024  11:55 AM             1,620 training_UI.py
03/04/2024  12:10 PM             3,998 user_onboarding.py
              14 File(s)         25,534 bytes
```

Figure 9.8 – The contents of the C:\PITS_APP folder

3. The next step is to sign in to your GitHub account and create a new repository. Let's name it `PITS_ONLINE`, as in *Figure 9.9*:

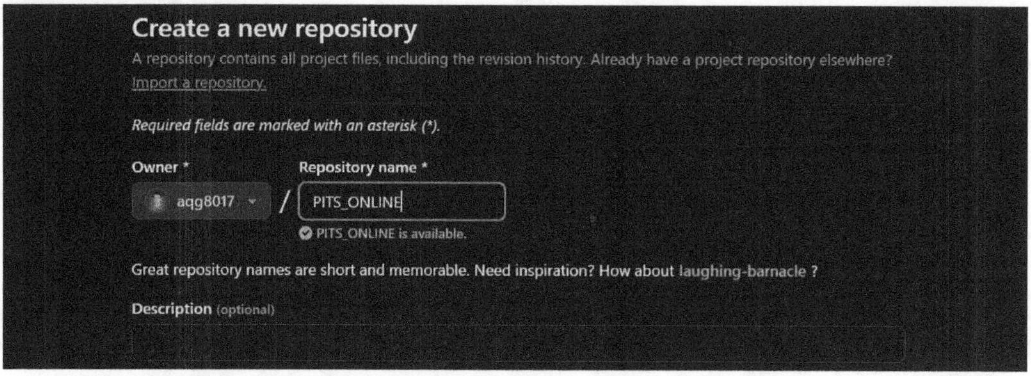

Figure 9.9 – Creating a new GitHub repository named PITS_ONLINE

4. Once created, note the repository URL for the next steps. Next, we'll initialize a new local repository in the desired folder. Open your CLI and navigate to the folder you want to turn into a separate repository – `C:\PITS_APP` – then execute the following command:

```
git init
```

5. Next, add and commit the existing files by running the following command:

```
Git add .
git commit -m "Initial commit for PITS_ONLINE repository"
```

6. It's now time to link your local repository to the GitHub repository you created. Replace the URL with your GitHub URL and append `.git` at the end in the following command:

```
git remote add origin <your_repository_URL>.git
```

7. And finally, we push the contents to the new online repository with the following command:

```
git branch -M main
git push -u origin main
```

If everything went smoothly you should now have a brand-new GitHub repository containing the PITS source code.

Let's handle the Community Cloud deployment next.

Deploying Streamlit applications into their Community Cloud environment is a fairly simple and straightforward process. To begin our deployment, the first step is to sign up for a free Streamlit account here: `https://share.streamlit.io/signup`. The best option is to use your GitHub account both for signing up and signing in to your Streamlit account. Once logged in, simply click on the **New app** button to begin the deployment process. You'll be taken to a screen similar to what you can see in *Figure 9.10*:

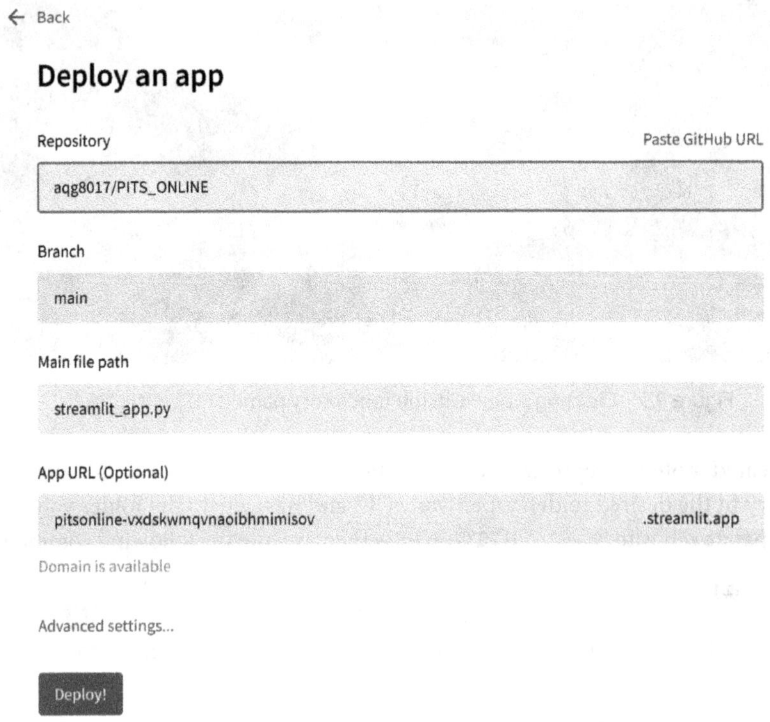

← Back

Deploy an app

Repository   Paste GitHub URL

aqg8017/PITS_ONLINE

Branch

main

Main file path

streamlit_app.py

App URL (Optional)

pitsonline-vxdskwmqvnaoibhmimisov   .streamlit.app

Domain is available

Advanced settings...

Deploy!

Figure 9.10 – Deploying an application into Streamlit Community Cloud

If you signed in to Streamlit using GitHub, you should already have the PITS_ONLINE repository listed as an option. Select it, then, under the **Main file path** field, change the default value to app. py and then click **Deploy**. From here, the Streamlit deployment service takes over and prepares the required environment for your application. This might take a while, but if you want to check on the progress, you can always expand the **Manage app** section on the bottom right of your screen. When everything is ready, the application should start automatically.

You can now ingest your existing training materials, have PITS generate slides and narrations about your desired study topic, and ask its chatbot any questions related to the contents.

> **Important note**
>
> Don't forget, you're using your own API key. To keep costs under control, you should first experiment on a limited scale by uploading some small training resources and always keeping an eye on the OpenAI API usage. The good news is that the majority of the cost is incurred during slides and narration generation. However, once that is completed, the resulting material is stored and reused in future sessions.

Simple, isn't it? Although offering an environment with limited resources, the Streamlit Community Cloud service makes it really easy to deploy simple apps and share quick prototypes. Your app is now online and can easily be shared with other users.

If anything went wrong, though, and you didn't manage to complete the deployment, head over to the official documentation, and look for a solution: `https://docs.streamlit.io/streamlit-community-cloud/deploy-your-app`. In the Streamlit documentation, you'll also find additional deployment options and configurations available that might be useful for your future projects.

Summary

In this chapter, we explored customizing and enhancing RAG workflows with LlamaIndex. We covered techniques to leverage open source LLMs such as Zephyr using tools such as LM Studio, offering cost-effective and privacy-focused alternatives to commercial models. The chapter discussed intelligent routing across multiple LLMs with services such as Neutrino and OpenRouter for optimized performance. Community-built Llama Packs were highlighted as powerful ways to rapidly prototype and build advanced components, and the chapter introduced the Llama CLI for streamlining RAG development and deployment workflows.

We talked about advanced tracing with Phoenix, allowing us to gain deep insight into application execution flows and pinpoint problems through visualization. The evaluation of RAG systems was covered using Phoenix's relevance, hallucination, and QA correctness evaluators, ensuring the robust performance of our LlamaIndex apps. Streamlit's deployment options, especially the Community Cloud service for easy application sharing, simplified the deployment process. A step-by-step guide demonstrated how to deploy the PITS tutoring application to the cloud.

With a strong grasp of customization, evaluation, and deployment techniques, developers can now build production-ready, optimized RAG applications tailored to their unique requirements.

Our journey continues with an exploration of the role of prompt engineering in enhancing the effectiveness of GenAI within the LlamaIndex framework.

Prompt Engineering Guidelines and Best Practices

In this chapter, we embark on an exploration of how the latest advancements in technology are reshaping our interaction with digital tools and applications. As the digital landscape evolves, the traditional interfaces we've relied upon for decades are being reimagined, paving the way for more intuitive and efficient forms of communication between humans and machines. At the heart of this transformation is the advent of conversational interfaces powered by **natural language** (**NL**). As a result, understanding how to write effective prompts to customize the behavior of our LlamaIndex components becomes a critical skill in building and improving RAG applications.

Therefore, in this chapter, we're going to cover the following main topics:

- Why prompts are your secret weapon
- Understanding how LlamaIndex uses prompts
- Customizing default prompts
- The golden rules of prompt engineering

Technical requirements

All code samples from this chapter can be found in the ch10 subfolder of the book's GitHub repository: https://github.com/PacktPublishing/Building-Data-Driven-Applications-with-LlamaIndex.

Why prompts are your secret weapon

I was 6 years old when I started writing my first lines of code using a ZX Spectrum computer. At the time, in the mid-1980s, computers were still a new thing in the world, and not many people understood the extraordinary impact they were going to have on human society. Today, we all live in a reality dominated, and in many ways, driven by technology. The way we relate to technology has also changed fundamentally in the last 40 years. Almost all human activities have come to be touched to a greater or lesser extent by technological progress.

What hasn't changed much is the way we interact with technology. With a few notable exceptions – such as the introduction of touch screens and voice interfaces – our interaction with technology has remained almost unchanged. We use, as we did 40 years ago, rudimentary methods to get computers to perform the functions we need.

> Clarification
>
> When I say rudimentary, I'm not necessarily referring to the sophistication of the interface itself – although functionally, if we were to compare a modern-day keyboard or mouse, we would find that even here, the advances are not fantastic. I'm referring rather to another aspect that unfortunately continues to stagnate: the bandwidth that our current interfaces can offer.

The way we currently interact with our technology is long due for replacement.

Let's go through a simple rationale together:

- The computing power offered by IT systems continues to grow at a rapid pace. Even if Moore's law – see *Figure 10.1* – is arguably no longer considered a valid benchmark, progress is far from slowing down (`https://en.wikipedia.org/wiki/Moore%27s_law`).

- We live in a world dominated almost entirely by applications. At the moment, applications are the layer between the user and the machine that makes our interaction with a computer possible – apps running on local systems, apps running on mobile devices, or apps running in the cloud. Each app offers a very specific set of functionalities.

- Many apps are designed to run only on specific platforms and cannot be easily ported to other platforms. This means a different app for each specific platform.

- Many applications overlap in terms of functionality. For a given task there are, in most cases, dozens of different applications that can perform it. So, there is a lot of duplication.

- Our interaction with technology has remained broadly the same bandwidth as 40 years ago. We use almost the same types of interfaces – keyboard, mouse, touchscreen, gesture- or voice-based – to control application logic.

- Almost every application comes with its own UI. There is a mandatory learning curve that users have to go through to learn how to operate each application. If we multiply this time by the number of applications that a typical user uses on a regular basis, we find that we actually spend a lot of time learning to use a tool effectively, and this eats into the actual time we spend using the tool to be productive.

- The number of software applications – including both publicly available applications and those used privately by organizations – is already huge. There are already more than 1 billion applications in the world. That's without taking into account the fact that an application very often exists in several different versions. And the number is growing.

- From an evolutionary point of view, the capacity of the human brain has remained unchanged throughout this time. Neuroplasticity gives us a remarkable ability to learn and adapt to new technologies, but unfortunately, evolution itself cannot keep up with technological progress.

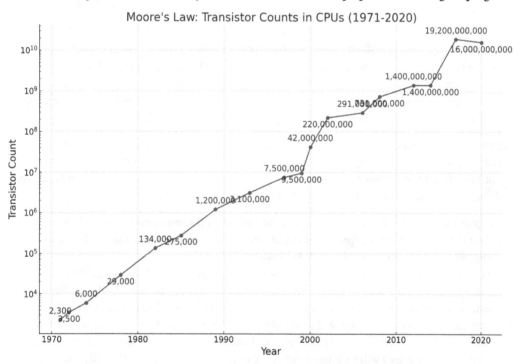

Figure 10.1 – According to Moore's law, the number of transistors roughly doubles every 2 years

See where I'm aiming? This very specific way of interacting with technology, combined with the rapid evolution of technology, is slowly making us victims of our own success. On the one hand, we have managed to build a huge number of specialized tools capable of solving a huge number of problems. But now, we have a bigger problem: we have so many tools that organizing and using them efficiently has become an extremely complicated process. A new paradigm is needed.

Conversational interfaces, based on **natural language processing** (**NLP**), present themselves as a promising alternative to the current way of interacting with technology. They represent a natural evolution in the way we communicate with our devices. Instead of relying on complex visual interfaces and input methods that require effort and time to learn, conversational interfaces allow us to use NL – the most fundamental and intuitive form of human communication.

This is where a new core competency in this new paradigm comes in.

> **Prompt engineering**
>
> As human-machine interaction becomes increasingly dependent on NL, the ability to formulate effective prompts that guide **artificial intelligence** (**AI**) algorithms toward desired responses or actions becomes essential. This skill involves not only formulating prompts clearly but also anticipating how different formulations may influence the interpretation and execution of commands by the AI.

Conversational interfaces transform the interaction with technology into a dialogue where linguistic precision and understanding of algorithmic subtleties become key factors in achieving desired outcomes. The ability to interact directly and effectively with computer systems using NL can significantly reduce the barrier between humans and technology. It offers a pathway to democratizing access to technology, making it accessible to a wider range of users, regardless of their technical expertise.

There are already indications that the intensive use of prompts in our everyday interactions with LLMs can improve even our interpersonal communication skills, as shown, for example, by this study: Liu et al. (2023), *Improving Interpersonal Communication by Simulating Audiences with Language Models* (`https://doi.org/10.48550/arXiv.2311.00687`).

Imagine computer systems that can replace the functionality of dozens or even hundreds of different applications but without the complexity of traditional interfaces. Language interaction: a form of technology where LLMs, augmented with RAG, take the place of applications and operating systems, giving us a universal and much simpler way to use computing power. Without getting too deep into the area of speculation, if I were to make a medium-to-long-term prediction, this is the direction I think we are heading in. In the short term, classical computing systems will continue to prevail. At first, conversational agent-based interfaces will gradually simplify user interaction with them, masking the complexity of the backend application layer. Then, as dedicated AI hardware becomes a commodity, a large part of the applications will be phased out of the ecosystem, and the functionality they provide will be taken over by AI models.

And I think this whole exposition justifies the title I have chosen for this section. Next, let's discover together how prompts are used by LlamaIndex for LLM interactions.

Understanding how LlamaIndex uses prompts

In terms of mechanics, a RAG-based application follows exactly the same rules and principles of interaction that a simple user would use in a chat session with an LLM. A major difference comes from the fact that RAG is actually a kind of prompt engineer on steroids. Behind the scenes, for almost every indexing, retrieval, metadata extraction, or final response synthesis operation, the RAG framework programmatically produces prompts. These prompts are enriched with context and then sent to the LLM.

In LlamaIndex, for each type of operation that requires an LLM, there is a default prompt that is used as a template. Take `TitleExtractor` as an example. This is one of the metadata extractors that we already talked about in *Chapter 4, Ingesting Data into Our RAG Workflow*. The `TitleExtractor` class uses two predefined prompt templates to get titles from text nodes inside documents. It does this in two steps:

1. It gets potential titles from individual text Nodes using the `node_template` argument, which creates prompts to generate appropriate titles

2. Combines the individual Node titles into one overall comprehensive title for the whole Document using the `combine_template` prompt

The default values for the `TitleExtractor` prompts are stored in two constants:

```
DEFAULT_TITLE_NODE_TEMPLATE = """\
Context: {context_str}. Give a title that summarizes all of \ the
unique entities, titles or themes found in the context. Title: """
DEFAULT_TITLE_COMBINE_TEMPLATE = """\
{context_str}. Based on the above candidate titles and content, \ what
is the comprehensive title for this document? Title: """
```

Looking at these two default templates used by `TitleExtractor`, we can easily understand how they work. Each template contains a *fixed* text part and a *dynamic* part, designated by `{context_str}` or other variables. That is where LlamaIndex will actually inject the text content of our Nodes during execution, as seen in *Figure 10.2*:

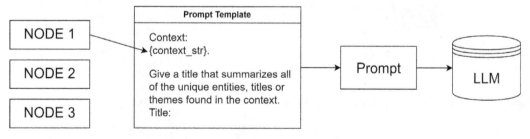

Figure 10.2 – How prompts are built by injecting variables into a prompt template

The prompt templates used by metadata extractors such as `TitleExtractor` are defined directly within the `metadata_extractors.py` module. The relative path of this module in the LlamaIndex GitHub repository is `llama-index-core/llama_index/core/extractors/metadata_extractors.py`. However, this is just an exception as the vast majority of the default templates are defined in two other key modules: `llama-index-core/llama_index/core/prompts/default_prompts.py` and `llama-index-core/llama_index/core/prompts/chat_prompts.py`.

Because a RAG workflow built with LlamaIndex can have so many different components that rely on LLM interactions and not all prompt templates can be easily located within the code base, the framework provides a simple method to identify the templates used by a specific component. That method is called `get_prompts()` and can be used with agents, retrievers, query engines, response synthesizers, and many other RAG components. Here is a simple example of how we can use it to obtain a list of prompt templates used by a query engine built on top of `SummaryIndex`:

```
from llama_index.core import SummaryIndex, SimpleDirectoryReader
documents = SimpleDirectoryReader("files").load_data()
summary_index = SummaryIndex.from_documents(documents)
qe = summary_index.as_query_engine()
```

The first part of the code should be very straightforward at this point. We import `SummaryIndex` and `SimpleDirectoryReader` and then ingest the two sample files that should have been cloned from our GitHub repository. Once the files have been ingested as Documents, we build an index and a query engine from that index. In this example, we won't run any queries because we don't need to. We just want to see the prompts. Therefore, the next step retrieves a dictionary containing the default prompts used within the query engine:

```
prompts = qe.get_prompts()
```

The dictionary returned by the `get_prompts()` method maps keys, which identify the different prompt types used by the query engine, to values that are the actual prompt templates. The last part of the code is responsible for iterating and displaying the keys and their corresponding templates:

```
for k, p in prompts.items():
    print(f"Prompt Key: {k}")
    print("Text:")
    print(p.get_template())
    print("\n")
```

Figure 10.3 shows the results after running this sample:

```
Prompt Key: response_synthesizer:text_qa_template
Text:
Context information is below.
---------------------
{context_str}
---------------------
Given the context information and not prior knowledge, answer the query.
Query: {query_str}
Answer:


Prompt Key: response_synthesizer:refine_template
Text:
The original query is as follows: {query_str}
We have provided an existing answer: {existing_answer}
We have the opportunity to refine the existing answer (only if needed) with some more context below.
------------
{context_msg}
------------
Given the new context, refine the original answer to better answer the query. If the context isn't useful, return the original answer.
Refined Answer:
```

Figure 10.3 – The two prompt templates used by the SummaryIndex query engine

Examining the output, we'll see the two templates used by the query engine: `text_qa_template` and `refine_template`. You'll notice that both keys begin with the text `response_synthesizer:`. This indicates the exact component of the query engine that actually uses the prompts – in our case, the response synthesizer. Following the same logic, we can use the `get_prompts()` method on many other types of RAG components in order to understand prompts used under the hood.

> **Pro tip**
>
> An alternative option to inspect the underlying prompts would be to use an advanced tracing method – such as the one using the Arize AI Phoenix framework, presented in *Chapter 9, Customizing and Deploying Our LlamaIndex Project*. Phoenix provides a visual representation of the execution flow, making it easier to understand how and when different prompts are used, in addition to displaying the final prompts with the inserted context. One caveat of using that method, though, is that instead of getting the original prompt templates, we'll see the final prompts – also including any context already inserted in the prompt.

Now that we have a reliable technique for inspecting prompts, the next step explores ways in which can customize them. Building on the title extractor and query engine examples, in the next section, we'll explore how to customize prompts used by various RAG components.

Customizing default prompts

While the default prompts provided by LlamaIndex are designed to work well in most scenarios, there may be instances where customization is necessary or desirable. For example, you might want to adjust prompts to do the following:

- Incorporate domain-specific knowledge or terminology
- Adapt prompts to a particular writing style or tone
- Modify prompts to prioritize certain types of information or outputs
- Experiment with different prompt structures to optimize performance or quality

By customizing prompts, we can fine-tune the interaction between the RAG components and the language model, potentially leading to improved accuracy, relevance, and overall effectiveness of our application.

The good news is that we can modify the behavior of various LlamaIndex components by supplying our own custom prompt templates. The not-so-good news is that contrary to common expectations, writing a good prompt template is not a trivial task. One would have to consider many intricacies such as accuracy, relevance, query formulation, prompt size, output formatting, and others. Because of the involved complexity, the recommended approach for customization is to start with the default prompts and use them as a foundation for making any desired modifications. Changes should be incremental and ideally followed by rigorous evaluation against a diverse set of edge cases. We will have a more detailed discussion about general principles and best practices for writing prompts in the next section. For now, let us focus on the methods used for prompt customization.

In LlamaIndex, every RAG component that exposes the `get_prompts()` method also provides an equivalent for modifying these prompt templates – the `update_prompts()` method. So, this is the easiest way to change a particular prompt template. Let's take our example from the previous section and experiment with a different prompt. This time, we will adapt the `text_qa_template` template to also rely on the LLM's own knowledge when answering the query. The default `text_qa_template` template would normally look like this:

```
Context information is below.
---------------------
{context_str}
---------------------
Given the context information and not prior knowledge, answer the
query.
Query: {query_str}
Answer:
```

In the following example, we'll make a very subtle change to this template and see how that will affect the behavior of our query engine. Let's have a look at the code:

```
from llama_index.core import SummaryIndex, SimpleDirectoryReader
from llama_index.core import PromptTemplate
documents = SimpleDirectoryReader("files").load_data()
summary_index = SummaryIndex.from_documents(documents)
qe = summary_index.as_query_engine()
```

So far, the code is identical to the previous example, with only one additional import that I will explain in a few moments. This time, though, we'll first run a query using the default template. We'll use this response as a reference later:

```
print(qe.query("Who burned Rome?"))
print("-----------------------")
```

It's now time to change the `prompt_template` template. We first define a string containing the new version:

```
new_qa_template = (
"Context information is below."
"--------------------"
"{context_str}"
"--------------------"
"Given the context information "
"and any of your prior knowledge, "
"answer the query."
"Query: {query_str}"
"Answer:")
```

If you carefully compare the new version with the original template, you'll notice a subtle but very important change. In this new version, I'm instructing the model to apply not just the knowledge provided in the retrieved context but also use its own knowledge on the matter. It's time to make use of that new import we added at the beginning of our code. Because the `update_prompts()` method requires the prompts to be in the `BasePromptTemplate` format, we must first make sure that our new prompt is structured like this:

```
template = PromptTemplate(new_qa_template)
```

We're now ready to rerun the query:

```
qe. Update_prompts(
    {"response_synthesizer: text_qa_template": template}
)
print(qe.query("Who burned Rome?"))
```

Let's have a look at the final output shown in *Figure 10.4*:

```
The query does not provide any information about who burned Rome.
------------------------
The city of Rome was famously burned during the reign of the Emperor Nero in 64 AD. While
Nero himself was not directly responsible for the fire, he was rumored to have played the
lyre and sung while the city burned, leading to the belief that he had orchestrated the fi
re for personal gain.
```

Figure 10.4 – The query output before and after updating the prompt templates

As you can see in the output, that slight modification in the `text_qa_template` template of the query engine completely changed its behavior. In a similar fashion, instead of changing the answering approach, we could have instructed the LLM to answer in a certain linguistic style, speak in rhymes, or anything else we might need. I think the value this feature provides for a RAG application is pretty clear by now.

Unfortunately, not all LlamaIndex components support the `update_prompts()` method. Take, for example, the `TitleExtractor` metadata extractor that I mentioned in the previous section. Although metadata extractors do not support the `update_prompts()` method, the good news is that we can still change their underlying prompt templates by using arguments. In particular, the two templates used by `TitleExtractor` can be customized with the `node_template` and `combine_template` arguments. Let's have a look at an example:

```
from llama_index.core import SimpleDirectoryReader
from llama_index.core.node_parser import SentenceSplitter
from llama_index.core.extractors import TitleExtractor
reader = SimpleDirectoryReader('files')
documents = reader.load_data()
parser = SentenceSplitter()
nodes = parser.get_nodes_from_documents(documents)
```

The first part of the example is responsible for ingesting our sample files as Documents and then chunking them into individual Nodes. Let's extract the titles, first by using the default prompt templates that we saw in the previous section:

```
title_extractor = TitleExtractor(summaries=["self"])
meta = title_extractor.extract(nodes)
print("\nFirst title: " +meta[0]['document_title'])
print("Second title: " +meta[1]['document_title'])
```

The output so far should be something similar to this:

```
First title: "The Enduring Influence of Ancient Rome: Architecture,
Engineering, Conquest, and Legacy"
Second title: "The Enduring Bond: Dogs as Loyal Companions - Exploring
the Unbreakable Connection Between Humans and Man's Best Friend"
```

Next, let's define a custom prompt template and pass it as an argument to `TitleExtractor` for the second run:

```
combine_template = (
    "{context_str}. Based on the above candidate titles "
    "and content, what is the comprehensive title for "
    "this document? Keep it under 6 words. Title: "
)
title_extractor = TitleExtractor(
    summaries=["self"],
    combine_template=combine_template
)
meta = title_extractor.extract(nodes)
print("\nFirst title: "+meta[0]['document_title'])
print("Second title: "+meta[1]['document_title']
```

Because we've added an extra instruction in this custom prompt, the extractor should now generate shorter titles. The output for the second run should be something along the lines of the following:

```
First title: "Roman Legacy: Architecture, Engineering, Conquest"
Second title: "Man's Best Friend: The Enduring Bond"
```

After seeing the basic mechanics of prompt customization, it's time to move on to more advanced methods.

Using advanced prompting techniques in LlamaIndex

LlamaIndex offers several advanced prompting techniques that enable you to create more customized and expressive prompts, reuse existing prompts, and express certain operations more concisely. These techniques include partial formatting, prompt template variable mappings, and prompt function mappings. *Table 10.1* breaks down the purpose and potential use cases for each method:

Method	Purpose
Partial formatting	Allows you to partially format a prompt by filling in some variables but leaving others to be filled in later. This is useful because it allows you to format variables as they become available, rather than maintaining all the required prompt variables until the end. The method is particularly useful in a multi-step RAG scenario that gradually builds the prompt by gathering different user inputs.
Prompt template variable mappings	They let you specify a mapping between some *expected* prompt keys and the keys actually used in your template, enabling you to reuse existing string templates without modifying the template variables. It is similar to creating an *alias* for template keys.
Prompt function mappings	This feature allows you to dynamically inject certain values, depending on other values or conditions, during query time by passing functions as template variables instead of fixed values.

Table 10.1 – An overview of the more advanced prompting techniques provided by LlamaIndex

You'll find detailed code examples for all three methods in the official LlamaIndex documentation here: `https://docs.llamaindex.ai/en/stable/examples/prompts/advanced_prompts.html`.

Having all these new cool gadgets in our knowledge inventory, we can now refine and tailor the dialogue between our application and the LLM, allowing us to customize the behavior of almost any RAG component of LlamaIndex.

For the final section of this chapter, we move our focus to an important aspect of maximizing our RAG setup's potential: the art and science of prompt engineering.

The golden rules of prompt engineering

This section is not intended to serve as a definitive guide to prompt engineering. In fact, the field is an ever-expanding one. Since many LLMs are demonstrating emerging capabilities that were not initially anticipated, it is only natural that our methods of interacting with these linguistic experts will also be refined over time. In other words, as LLMs evolve to better model and understand human nature, we in turn learn new ways of interacting with them. In this section, I aim to present some of the most commonly used techniques in prompt engineering, as well as the basic principles that govern the field. As stated in the previous section, writing a good prompt requires a fine balance between several parameters. Here are some of the most important aspects to consider when building prompts for a RAG application.

Accuracy and clarity in expression

The prompt should be clear and precise, avoiding ambiguity. The more clearly you state what you need, the more likely you are to get a relevant response. It's important to articulate the question or task in a way that leaves little room for misinterpretation. Make no assumptions about the model's ability to understand your message. These assumptions are usually biased and tend to produce hallucinations in return.

Directiveness

How directive the prompt is can significantly impact the response. A prompt can range from open-ended – encouraging creative or broad responses – to highly specific – requesting a very particular type of answer. The level of directiveness should match the intended outcome. Given that we're actually building prompt templates that mix a static part with dynamically retrieved content, consider exceptional scenarios and edge cases in which the model might misunderstand the prompt. Use clear instructions or commands (for example, `Summarize`, `Analyze`, and `Explain`) to guide the model on the desired task. Our prompts must be broad enough to accommodate varied inputs yet detailed enough to direct the model effectively.

Context quality

This is a major pain point for building an effective RAG system. Both the quality and structure of our proprietary knowledge base as well as the ability to retrieve the most relevant context from it are very important aspects. *Garbage in, garbage out* may be regarded as a general rule applicable to this subject. Try to remove any inconsistencies in the data, special characters that might derail the LLM, duplicate data, and even grammatical errors in the text. These types of quality issues will unfortunately affect both the retrieval and the final response synthesis. Experiment with different retrieval strategies, such as the ones discussed in *Chapter 6, Querying Our Data, Part 1 – Context Retrieval*. Try different values for `similarity_top_k`, `chunk_size`, and `chunk_overlap`, as discussed in *Chapter 4, Ingesting Data into Our RAG Workflow*. Employ re-rankers and Node postprocessors to increase the context quality, as we did in *Chapter 7, Querying Our Data, Part 2 – Postprocessing and Response Synthesis*.

Context quantity

There's a balance between being concise and offering sufficient detail. A prompt should be brief enough to maintain focus but detailed enough to convey the specific requirements of the task or question. Too little context may result in answers that lack depth or relevance, while too much may confuse the model or lead it off-topic.

In RAG scenarios, as the amount of context provided in a prompt increase, it's important to consider the potential impact on the alignment and accuracy of generated responses. While providing more context can be beneficial in many cases, as it gives the language model a broader understanding of the task at hand, there are also risks associated with excessively long prompts.

For example, when a prompt becomes too long, there is a higher chance of introducing irrelevant or contradictory information. This can lead to misalignment between the intended task and the model's understanding of it. The model may give too much attention to tangential details or lose focus on the core objective. Maintaining a clear and concise prompt helps ensure that the model stays aligned with the desired output.

Also, as the context grows, the model has to process and consider a larger amount of information. This increased **cognitive load** can lead to a decrease in accuracy. The model may struggle to identify the most relevant pieces of information or may give undue importance to less significant details. Additionally, longer prompts are more likely to contain ambiguities or inconsistencies, which can further degrade the accuracy of the responses.

> **Cognitive load in the context of LLMs**
>
> Cognitive load refers to the amount of processing effort and resources required by the language model to process, understand, and generate a response based on the provided context. In the case of RAG systems, the cognitive load is directly related to the quantity and complexity of the information present in the prompt.

Implementing Node postprocessors such as `SimilarityPostprocessor` or `SentenceEmbeddingOptimizer` can partially mitigate this issue by filtering less relevant Nodes or shortening their content, and therefore reducing the final prompt submitted to the LLM. We covered these methods in *Chapter 7, Querying Our Data, Part 2 – Postprocessing and Response Synthesis*. Moreover, if the retrieved context is inherently long, consider breaking it down into smaller, more manageable chunks.

Context ordering

The overall effectiveness of our RAG pipeline does not rely just on the quantity and quality of context. Especially when dealing with longer context, most LLMs may perform differently when trying to extract the key information from that context, depending on where exactly that key information is placed. A good approach is to structure the prompt hierarchically, with the most critical information at the beginning or at the end. This ensures that the model prioritizes the core instructions and context. That's where tools such as Node re-rankers or the `LongContextReorder` postprocessor may become useful.

> **Side note**
>
> There's an increasingly popular RAG evaluation technique called the *needle in a haystack test*, in which researchers gauge the model's ability to notice and recall a very specific piece of information from a larger context provided to the LLM. This specific information looks unsuspecting and is usually seamlessly blended into the overall context. In many ways, this method is similar to testing a human's ability to pay attention to a certain text and then recall key information in that text.

Required output format

In most cases, when building RAG workflows, we need LLMs to generate structured or semi-structured outputs. In almost all scenarios, we need the output to be predictable in terms of format, size, or language. Sometimes, providing a few examples in our prompt may lead to better responses, but that's not a silver bullet for all scenarios. That's were using output parsers and Pydantic programs becomes really important. We talked about these topics in *Chapter 7, Querying Our Data, Part 2 – Postprocessing and Response Synthesis*.

Inference cost

In most cases, we'll be running our applications within very specific cost constraints. Ignoring token usage would be a clear mistake. So, make sure you're doing cost estimations, and always keep track of token usage. In addition, you could use tools such as `LongLLMLinguaPostprocessor` for prompt compression. We talked about this Node postprocessor in *Chapter 7, Querying Our Data, Part 2 – Postprocessing and Response Synthesis*. Prompt compression techniques have the potential to improve not only cost efficiency but also the quality of the final response by eliminating redundant information from our context and keeping just key information.

Overall system latency

While this parameter depends on many factors, bloated, inefficient, or ambiguous prompts can also negatively affect system latency. It's just like talking to a real person. The longer and less efficient the query, the more processing will be required from the model in order to best understand the actual intent behind the query. Longer processing times will negatively impact the overall user experience.

Prompt engineering is a continuous process of experimentation and iteration. Regularly evaluate the performance of your prompts and refine them based on the results. Remember – this is a long game, and the rules are being constantly re-written. Try to keep your knowledge up to date with the latest advancements and techniques in prompt engineering, as the field is rapidly evolving.

Choosing the right LLM for the task

In the world of AI, not all LLMs are equal. In *Chapter 9, Customizing and Deploying Our LlamaIndex Project*, we already saw how easy is to customize different components of our RAG pipeline, including the underlying LLM. But there are actually many options available, so which one should we select for the job? Choosing the *wrong* LLM for a particular task will likely cancel many of the efforts we invested in crafting the actual prompts. It's pretty much like trying to get an answer from the wrong person. If you're persuasive enough, chances are you'll get an answer at some point. However, that may not be the answer you were looking for.

That's why understanding the different flavors of LLMs and knowing which one qualifies for a given task is essential. Several key characteristics should be useful for our model selection. Let's look at these next.

Model architecture

Models can have different underlying architectures, and these may determine their inherent capabilities. For example, encoder-only models are specialized in encoding and classifying input text, useful for categorizing text into defined categories, such as with **Bidirectional Encoder Representations from Transformers** (**BERT**), which excels in **next sentence prediction** (**NSP**) tasks (`https://en.wikipedia.org/wiki/BERT_(language_model)`).

Encoder-decoder models are capable of both understanding input text and generating responses, making them ideal for text generation and comprehension tasks, such as translation and summarizing articles. One example that fits in this category is **Bidirectional and Auto-Regressive Transformer** (**BART**) (`https://huggingface.co/docs/transformers/en/model_doc/bart`).

Decoder-only models can decode or generate subsequent words or tokens from a given prompt and are primarily used for text generation. Models such as **Generative Pre-trained Transformer** (**GPT**), Mistral, Claude, and LLaMa are superstars in this domain.

There are also more exotic architectures such as **Mixture-of-Experts** (**MoE**), which essentially leverage a *sparse MoE* framework to offer dynamic, token-specific processing – see Shazeer et al. (2017), *Outrageously Large Neural Networks: The Sparsely-Gated Mixture-of-Experts Layer* (`https://doi.org/10.48550/arXiv.1701.06538`). This approach can significantly enhance performance across a range of domains, including mathematics, code generation, and multilingual tasks, as demonstrated by **Mixtral 8x7B**.

Model size

Model size is another critical factor to consider when selecting an LLM, as it directly impacts both the potential computational cost and the model's capabilities. The number of parameters within an LLM, ranging from weights to biases adjusted during training, serves as a proxy for understanding the model's complexity and, by extension, its operational expense. Larger models, such as GPT-4 with its estimated 1.76 trillion parameters, offer profound capabilities but come with higher costs and requirements for computational resources. On the other hand, medium-sized models, typically under 10 billion parameters, strike a balance between affordability and performance, making them suitable for a wide array of applications without breaking the bank.

Inference speed

That's also a key parameter as it determines how quickly a model can process input and generate output. While larger models may offer enhanced performance in terms of output quality and depth, their inference speed tends to be slower due to the sheer volume of computations required. It's important to note that inference speed is influenced by various factors beyond just the number of parameters, including the efficiency of the model architecture and the computational infrastructure used. Techniques to reduce inference time, such as model pruning, quantization, and leveraging specialized hardware, can significantly improve the usability of LLMs in real-world applications.

To make things even more complex, apart from these characteristics, LLMs can be specialized for various tasks or domains, enhancing their performance in specific scenarios. This specialization arises from the type of data and the training objectives used to fine-tune the model. Let's look at some common specializations next.

Chat models

Chat models are optimized for conversational interactions. They are designed to engage users in dialogue, providing responses that mimic human-like conversation. These models are adept at back-and-forth exchanges and can maintain context over a series of interactions.

They are the ideal choice for building chatbots or virtual assistants where the interaction is more casual or conversational. These models are used in applications requiring natural, engaging dialogue with users, such as customer service bots, entertainment applications, or virtual companions. As a particular characteristic, they tend to be more open-ended in their responses, aiming to generate replies that are engaging, contextually relevant, and sometimes even entertaining.

Instruct models

Instruct models are fine-tuned to understand and execute specific instructions or queries. They prioritize executing the given task based on the instruction over engaging in a dialogue. That makes them suitable for scenarios where the user needs the model to perform a particular task, such as summarizing a document, generating code based on a prompt, or providing detailed explanations. These models are preferred in educational tools, productivity applications, and anywhere a direct, clear response to a query is needed, such as in the intricate workflow of a RAG application.

They are more focused on accuracy and relevance to the task at hand rather than maintaining a conversational tone. Their responses are tailored toward fulfilling the user's request as efficiently and effectively as possible.

Codex models

These models are optimized for understanding and generating code. They have been trained in a vast corpus of programming languages and can assist with coding tasks, debug code, explain code snippets, and even generate entire programs based on a description. This makes them the perfect candidates for integrating into development environments, coding education tools, and anywhere automated coding assistance is beneficial.

Summarization models

Specialized in condensing long texts into shorter summaries while retaining key information and context. These models focus on capturing the essence of the content and presenting it concisely. They are useful for news aggregation services, research, content creation, and any scenario where quick insights from long documents are needed.

Translation models

As the name implies these models are designed to translate text from one language to another. They have been trained on large multilingual datasets to understand and translate between languages with high accuracy, and they are best suited for global communication platforms, content localization, and educational tools aimed at language learners.

Question-answering models

Fine-tuned to understand questions posed in NL and provide accurate answers by referencing provided texts or their vast training data, these models are key in building intelligent search engines, educational aids, and interactive knowledge bases.

And the list could probably go on with other types of models, fine-tuned for specific domains or applications. Also, keep in mind that because these different specializations tend to enhance or diminish certain capabilities of the model, our carefully crafted prompts may yield inconsistent results. For one model, a prompt may lead to near-perfect responses, while for another it could barely hit an average mark.

When choosing your LLM, it's essential to weigh the trade-offs between all these characteristics and the specific requirements of your RAG application. Understanding these aspects helps in selecting a model that not only fits within your budget but also meets your performance and speed expectations. Whether you're deploying an LLM for real-time applications requiring quick responses or complex tasks demanding deep understanding and generation capabilities, the chosen model will have a profound impact on the outcomes of your LlamaIndex application. But keep in mind that you're never limited to using a single model for your entire RAG logic. As LlamaIndex gives you endless possibilities for customization, working with a suite of different models can also be an option. You just have to experiment and evaluate until you find the ideal mix and purpose for each one.

Common methods used for creating effective prompts

While simple prompts can be useful for many tasks, more advanced techniques are often required for complex reasoning or multi-step processes. While definitely not exhaustive, this section covers several powerful prompting techniques that can significantly enhance the performance of language models in our RAG applications. Since there's already an abundance of study materials, free courses, and plenty of examples available on the web, in case you're not yet familiar with these methods, take this list as a mere starting point for your future learning path.

Few-shot prompting, also known as k-shot prompting

As described in the paper by Brown et al. (2020), *Language Models are Few-Shot Learners* (`https://doi.org/10.48550/arXiv.2005.14165`), for complex tasks involving LLMs, few-shot prompting with demonstrations can enable in-context learning and improve performance. This method relies on providing a few examples of the task, along with the expected output, to condition the model. You can experiment with different numbers of examples (for example, one-shot, three-shot, and five-shot) to find the optimal balance, hence the *k-shot* alternative name.

> **What about zero-shot prompting?**
>
> For reference, *zero-shot prompting* involves presenting a model with a question without any preceding contextual question/answer pairs. This approach is more challenging for the model compared to one-shot or few-shot prompting, due to the absence of context.

When using few-shot prompting, keep in mind that the format you use for the examples and the distribution of the input text are important factors that can affect performance. While the few-shot prompting method increases the probability of a correct answer for simpler tasks, it may still struggle with more complex reasoning scenarios. Here's a practical prompt example using this technique:

```
Classify the following reviews as positive or negative sentiment:
<The food was delicious and the service was excellent!> // Positive
<I waited over an hour and my meal arrived cold.> // Negative
<The ambiance was nice but the dishes were overpriced.> //
Output:
```

Providing the model with a few examples in this style enables in-context learning and improves performance on the task without requiring fine-tuning.

Chain-of-Thought (CoT) prompting

First introduced in the paper by Wei et al. (2023), *Chain-of-Thought Prompting Elicits Reasoning in Large Language Models* (`https://doi.org/10.48550/arXiv.2201.11903`), this method provides impressive results for LLM tasks requiring reasoning or multi-step processes. We can use CoT prompting to encourage the model to break down the problem and show its thought process.

We can include examples in our prompts, demonstrating the step-by-step reasoning process in the prompt. Here is a practical prompt example:

```
There are 15 students in a class. 8 students have dogs as pets.
If 3 more students get a dog, how many of them would have a dog as a
pet then?
Step 1) Initially there are 15 students and 8 have dogs
Step 2) 3 more students will get dogs soon
Step 3) So the final number is the initial 8 students with dogs plus
the 3 new students = 8 + 3 = 11
Therefore, the number of students that would have a dog as a pet is
11.
A factory makes 100 items daily. On Tuesday, they boost production
by 40% for a special order. However, to adjust inventory, they cut
Thursday's output by 20% from Tuesday's high. Then, expecting a sales
increase, Friday's output rises by 10% over the day before. Calculate
the production numbers for Tuesday, Thursday, and Friday.
```

The first part of the prompt demonstrates the reasoning process, guiding the LLM to better answer the second part – which represents the actual task.

Self-consistency

Self-consistency aims to improve the performance of CoT prompting by sampling multiple, diverse reasoning paths and using the generations to select the most consistent answer. First introduced in the paper by Wang et al. (2023), *Self-Consistency Improves Chain of Thought Reasoning in Language Models* (`https://doi.org/10.48550/arXiv.2203.11171`), the self-consistency method helps boost performance on tasks involving arithmetic and commonsense reasoning by replacing the more traditional CoT prompting. Self-consistency involves providing few-shot CoT examples, generating multiple reasoning paths, and then selecting the most consistent answer based on these paths.

This approach acknowledges that language models, like humans, may sometimes make mistakes or take incorrect reasoning steps. However, by leveraging the diversity of reasoning paths and selecting the most consistent answer, self-consistency can potentially provide better answers than CoT prompting.

Tree of Thoughts (ToT) prompting

ToT is a framework that generalizes over CoT prompting and encourages the exploration of thoughts that serve as intermediate steps for general problem-solving with language models. Under the hood, it maintains a *tree of thoughts*, where thoughts represent coherent language sequences that serve as intermediate steps toward solving a problem. The language model's ability to generate and evaluate thoughts is combined with specialized search algorithms to enable systematic exploration of thoughts. ToT prompting involves prompting the language model to evaluate intermediate thoughts as *sure/maybe/impossible* with regard to reaching the desired solution and then using search algorithms to explore the most promising paths. The method was presented for the first time in the following papers: Yao et al. (2023), *Tree of Thoughts: Deliberate Problem Solving with Large Language Models* (`https://doi.`

org/10.48550/arXiv.2305.10601), and Long et al. (2023), *Large Language Model Guided Tree-of-Thought* (https://doi.org/10.48550/arXiv.2305.08291).

Here's a sample prompt:

```
Let's simulate a verbal conversation between three experts who tackle
a complex puzzle.
Each expert outlines one step in their thought process before
exchanging insights with the others, without adding any unnecessary
remarks. As they progress, any expert who identifies a flaw in their
reasoning exits the discussion. The process continues until a solution
is found or all available options have been exhausted. The problem
they need to solve is:
"Using only numbers 3, 3, 7, 7 and basic arithmetic operations, is it
possible to obtain the value 25?"
```

Prompt chaining

This method relies on breaking down complex tasks into subtasks and using a chain of prompts, where each prompt's output serves as an input for the next. Similar to the approach I used for the PITS application in the `training_material_builder.py` module, prompt chaining can improve the reliability, transparency, and controllability of the application. By default, in RAG applications, we use separate prompts for retrieving relevant information and generating a final output based on the retrieved context.

By following these golden rules and methods, you can develop more effective and reliable RAG applications using LlamaIndex and leverage the full potential of LLMs.

Summary

This chapter explored the importance of prompt engineering in building effective RAG applications with LlamaIndex. We learned how to inspect and customize the default prompts used by various components.

The chapter provided an overview of key principles and best practices for crafting high-quality prompts, as well as advanced prompting techniques. Additionally, it emphasized the significance of choosing the right language model for the task at hand and understanding their different architectures, capabilities, and trade-offs.

Finally, we talked about some simple yet powerful prompting methods, such as few-shot prompting, CoT prompting, self-consistency, ToT, and prompt chaining to enhance the reasoning and problem-solving abilities of language models. Mastering prompt engineering is crucial for unlocking the full potential of LLMs in RAG applications.

As we prepare to wrap up our journey, I invite you to join me in the final chapter of this book, where I will do my best to equip you with some additional learning tools and provide you with a bit of guidance on your future learning path.

Conclusion and
Additional Resources

In this final chapter, we'll reflect on the key takeaways from our exploration of RAG and its potential to revolutionize the field of AI. We'll discuss the importance of staying updated with the latest developments, highlight valuable resources such as Replit bounties and the LlamaIndex community, and emphasize the need for responsible AI development.

As we look to the future, we'll consider the impact of specialized AI hardware and the ethical considerations that must guide our progress. This chapter serves as a call to action for you to continue learning, contributing, and shaping the exciting world of RAG and AI, while always keeping the well-being of humanity at the forefront of our endeavors.

In this chapter, we're going to cover the following main topics:

- Other projects and further learning
- Key takeaways and final words and encouragement

Other projects and further learning

As we approach the end of this book, it becomes clear that our journey toward mastering the LlamaIndex framework is only just beginning. I believe that theoretical knowledge can only take us so far. Practical applications are the key to having a real understanding of the information and its application to real-world problems. For this reason, I strongly encourage you to practice and experiment with the tools described in this book. The best way to practice is by studying and building actual RAG applications.

The LlamaIndex examples collection

A great starting point for solidifying your knowledge is the plethora of examples and cookbooks available on the official LlamaIndex documentation page: `https://docs.llamaindex.ai/en/stable/examples/`. By examining and experimenting with the examples and cookbooks available there, you will gain practical insights into how to use nearly every component of the framework. Additionally, you will learn how to construct more complex RAG workflows by combining these components. This resource provides valuable code snippets, best practices, and real-world use cases that can help you understand the intricacies of building RAG applications.

Although some examples were also covered in this book, I had to be concise and therefore took some shortcuts. As a result, I have simplified the code in many cases. So, even if you're already familiar with the topic, it's worth having a look at some of the most interesting ones in there. Hundreds of examples are included, but to help you get started, I've noted a few very useful ones that you could begin with.

Slack chat data connector

This simple example demonstrates how to use the LlamaIndex Slack data connector to perform question-answering over Slack chat data: `https://docs.llamaindex.ai/en/stable/examples/data_connectors/SlackDemo/`.

It showcases how to integrate the Slack API to retrieve chat history and build an index for efficient information retrieval. This basic example is the perfect starting point for organizations that heavily rely on Slack for communication and want to extract valuable insights from their chat data, build a chatbot, or implement a ChatOps model. Together with many other examples provided, the data connectors section provides a very useful learning resource. You can expand your knowledge about ingesting data from different sources into your RAG workflow.

Discord thread management

Similar to the Slack data connector example, this Discord thread management example showcases the use of LlamaIndex to ingest, manage, and query Discord chat data: `https://docs.llamaindex.ai/en/stable/examples/discover_llamaindex/document_management/Discord_Thread_Management/`.

It demonstrates the process of indexing Discord threads and refreshing the index with new data as it comes in. Following the approach demonstrated in this example, you can build applications that efficiently search and retrieve information from your Discord chat history. This opens up possibilities for building chatbots and virtual assistants or simply providing a way to quickly access important discussions and decisions made within Discord. For communities and organizations that use Discord as their primary communication platform, this example could provide a simple boilerplate for building a more complex RAG solution.

A multi-modal retrieval application that uses GPT4-V

This more advanced example showcases the use of LlamaIndex with GPT4-V to build a multi-modal retrieval system that uses both text and image data: `https://docs.llamaindex.ai/en/stable/examples/multi_modal/gpt4v_multi_modal_retrieval/`.

> **Side note about multi-modal RAG**
>
> Multi-modal RAG combines information retrieval across multiple modalities – such as text and images – with the reasoning and generation capabilities of LLMs. Potential use cases for multi-modal RAG are vast, ranging from building knowledge bases and question-answering systems that can handle both text and visual queries, to powering engaging multi-modal conversational agents, to enabling new types of creative and analytical applications that blend language and vision.

Because we didn't cover multi-modal RAG in this book, I strongly encourage you to study this demonstration. Armed with the knowledge gained from this book and the explanations provided in this example, you'll soon realize that extending your apps with multi-modal features does not represent such a big challenge at this point.

Multi-tenancy RAG example

This example walks through the process of setting up a multi-user RAG system, including configuring the vector databases, indexing tenant-specific data, and handling user queries: `https://docs.llamaindex.ai/en/stable/examples/multi_tenancy/multi_tenancy_rag/`.

It explains a similar but more detailed approach than the one I used in the *Implementing metadata filters* section in *Chapter 6, Querying Our Data, Part 1 – Context Retrieval*. By utilizing separate vector databases for each tenant, group, or user, the example demonstrates how to ensure data isolation and privacy while providing basic RAG functions such as question-answering and content generation.

It shows a viable method for managing multiple tenants within a single application, making it a great starting point for production-ready RAG systems that must accommodate various clients or user groups.

> **Wondering where this may be useful?**
>
> Imagine a company that provides a chatbot service to multiple clients. Each client wants their own customized chatbot trained on their specific knowledge base and FAQs. With a multi-tenancy RAG system, the company can maintain separate indexes for each client, ensuring that queries to one client's chatbot only retrieve information from that client's knowledge base. This ensures data privacy and provides a personalized experience for each client.

By exploring this multi-tenancy RAG implementation, you can better understand how to design secure and efficient RAG systems that accommodate the needs of multiple tenants without compromising performance or user experience.

Prompt engineering techniques for RAG

This example builds on the topic of customizing the prompts that are used in the RAG pipeline – a topic we covered in *Chapter 10, Prompt Engineering Guidelines and Best Practices*: `https://docs.llamaindex.ai/en/stable/examples/prompts/prompts_rag/`.

The sample code illustrates how to use prompt engineering techniques to enhance the performance of different LlamaIndex RAG components. It explains strategies such as adding few-shot examples to the prompts to improve performance on various tasks. It also demonstrates techniques such as variable mapping and functions and gives an example of using prompt customization to handle context transformations, such as filtering personal data. This example, combined with the other examples available in the prompts section, represents a big step toward understanding how effective prompts can improve the quality and performance of RAG in specific use cases.

CitationQueryEngine implementation

This example is similar to the example discussed in *Chapter 7, Querying Our Data, Part 2 – Postprocessing and Response Synthesis* in the *Extracting structured outputs using output parsers* section. There, I showcased a simple method that not only answers a user question using their proprietary data but also points to the exact chunk of data that was used to generate the answer. Providing the source is an essential feature for a RAG system where transparency and traceability are important requirements. Here is a more advanced example: `https://docs.llamaindex.ai/en/stable/examples/ query_engine/citation_query_engine/`.

This sample demonstrates a more advanced querying technique that enhances the context and traceability of retrieved information. By leveraging the power of citations, users can easily track the sources of the retrieved text, providing a clear and transparent way to verify the authenticity and reliability of the information. This example demonstrates how to set up `CitationQueryEngine` with customizable settings, allowing us to fine-tune the behavior of the engine according to our specific needs. It also provides guidance on inspecting the actual source of the retrieved information, enabling a detailed examination of the original context when necessary.

`CitationQueryEngine` is particularly useful for researchers, journalists, auditors, compliance clerks, or anyone who requires a high level of transparency and accountability in their information retrieval process. By integrating this powerful tool into our RAG workflow, we can ensure that the information we rely on is well-documented and easily traceable to its sources.

Another very useful section in the LlamaIndex official documentation website is the **Open-Source Community** tab.

Available at `https://docs.llamaindex.ai/en/stable/community/full_stack_ projects/`, this section contains a collection of full-stack applications created by the LlamaIndex team. The main benefit here is that all the sample applications included have been open sourced under an MIT license, which means that you can freely use them out of the box to kickstart your projects.

Exploring these examples will strengthen the theoretical knowledge gained from this book and empower you to build robust, efficient, and innovative RAG applications. So, dive in, experiment, and let your creativity guide you in solving real-life problems using intelligent retrieval systems.

Moving forward – Replit bounties

Applying theoretical concepts in solving real problems is probably one of the best ways to further develop your skillset. As a potential next step, once you gain confidence in your RAG and LlamaIndex skills, you might be interested in taking on coding challenges or working on small, potentially profitable projects. Replit, an online coding platform, can be an excellent resource for this purpose. Replit offers a browser-based development environment that allows you to write, run, and share code in various programming languages. It provides a collaborative and interactive space for developers to work on projects, learn from one another, and even earn money through **Replit bounties**: `https://docs. replit.com/bounties/faq`.

How bounties work

One of the unique features of Replit is its bounties system, which encourages users to participate in coding challenges and contribute to open source projects while being rewarded for their efforts. Project maintainers or individuals who require assistance in solving specific problems or implementing new features create these bounties. Developers can explore the available bounties, select those that align with their skills and interests, and start working on them.

By participating in Replit bounties, you can gain practical experience in developing RAG solutions and applying the concepts covered in this book. These bounties often present real-world scenarios and requirements, providing you with the opportunity to tackle hands-on problems and enhance your problem-solving abilities.

Furthermore, the Replit platform nurtures a supportive and collaborative community. You can engage with other developers, learn from their approaches, and receive constructive feedback on your code. This interaction with the community can help your growth as a developer, broaden your knowledge, and keep you informed about the latest trends and best practices in the field.

To explore LlamaIndex-related content on Replit, you can go to `https://replit.com/ search?query=llamaindex`. This search will help you discover relevant projects, code snippets, and discussions related to LlamaIndex, enabling you to apply your RAG skills in practical contexts and potentially uncover lucrative opportunities.

The power of many – the LlamaIndex community

One of the most valuable resources available to any developer working with LlamaIndex is the vibrant and supportive community that has grown around the framework. With tens of thousands of developers actively participating, the LlamaIndex community offers a wealth of knowledge, experience, and inspiration. Joining this thriving community provides numerous benefits for developers at all skill levels. Whether you're a beginner just starting with LlamaIndex or an experienced developer looking to take your projects to the next level, engaging with the community can help you achieve your goals.

The LlamaIndex community is full of developers who have worked on a wide range of projects, from simple proof-of-concepts to complex, real-world applications. By engaging with the community, you can learn from their experiences, discover best practices, and gain valuable insights that can help you improve your projects. You can ask questions, share your projects, and learn from the experiences of others who are also building on the framework.

The community is also a great place to showcase your LlamaIndex projects and get feedback from other developers. Sharing your work can help you refine your skills, gather new ideas, and even inspire others who are working on similar projects. Also, being a part of the LlamaIndex community allows you to contribute to the ongoing development and improvement of the framework itself. Whether by providing feedback, reporting bugs, or even contributing code, you can help shape the future of LlamaIndex and make it an even more powerful tool for developers around the world.

To get started, you can sign up for the project's newsletter, join the official LlamaIndex Discord server, participate in discussions on the GitHub repository, or attend community events and webinars. The **LlamaIndex Blog**, which is available at `https://www.llamaindex.ai/blog`, is another great resource that can help you stay up-to-date with the latest developments in the LlamaIndex ecosystem. The blog features a wide range of articles, tutorials, and case studies that showcase how developers are using LlamaIndex to build innovative applications across various domains.

Key takeaways, final words, and encouragement

The future of generative AI is a complex and rapidly evolving landscape with immense potential for transforming industries, augmenting human capabilities, and driving economic growth. In other words, the future looks bright. However, this future also brings significant technical, ethical, and societal challenges that must be carefully managed to ensure the responsible use of these powerful technologies. As it already happened numerous times in our history, innovation can foster progress and improvement but it can also lead to unintended consequences and disruptions that ripple through society. The rise of generative AI is no exception to this pattern.

While not being a direct contributor to the evolution of generative AI, RAG is definitely a catalyst for accelerating the progress of LLMs. It amplifies the capabilities of even the simplest models, creating new possibilities but also bigger challenges and risks. The software we develop has an increasingly significant impact on our society, and as our everyday lives become more influenced by software, we must exercise greater caution.

In many use cases for implementing RAG in combination with generative AI, what a single, proficient developer can produce today used to be the work of an entire company just a few years ago. And this is not entirely good news for us. While most companies are driven by profits and market success, they also have more checks and bounds in place and governance that guides them in their operations. This governance often includes ethical considerations, compliance with regulations, and a level of accountability that might not be as stringent or easily enforceable for individual developers or smaller teams. As computational costs decline and AI expertise becomes more widespread, smaller entities such as startups, local governments, and community groups may increasingly develop their own customized, RAG-infused LLMs to address niche requirements. This shift could erode the centralized dominance of big tech firms and foster a more diverse and dynamic ecosystem of AI innovation. The agility and innovation that smaller entities can bring to the table with tools such as RAG combined with generative AI are indeed remarkable, but this also opens up Pandora's box of potential misuse and ethical dilemmas.

> **Just to clarify my message**
>
> I'm not suggesting that all hope is lost. I'm simply aiming to highlight and raise awareness of this risk. As these technologies evolve, the importance of integrating ethical considerations into the development process cannot be overstated. The democratization of AI technology means that the responsibility for its impact spreads across a wider array of stakeholders.

It's not just about *what we can create*, but also about *what we should create*. This includes considering the long-term implications of our work and ensuring that we're not inadvertently creating tools that can be used for harmful purposes. That being said, for starters, the Stanford Encyclopedia of Philosophy *Guideline on the Ethics of Artificial Intelligence and Robotics* should be considered a mandatory starting point for any aspiring AI developer: `https://plato.stanford.edu/entries/ethics-ai`.

Because developers are not the only ones who should bear responsibility for the ethical use of AI technologies, several guidelines for organizations have also been published. A notable example is the *AI and the Role of the Board of Directors* article published at the Harvard Law School Forum on Corporate Governance by Holly J. Gregory and Sidley Austin LLP. This particular article provides a comprehensive governance guideline for corporate boards that want to improve internal controls and their oversight over the company's AI-related activities: `https://corpgov.law.harvard.edu/2023/10/07/ai-and-the-role-of-the-board-of-directors/`.

Other useful resources providing ethical guidance for developing AI systems include the *Ethically Aligned Design*, written by the Institute of Electrical and Electronics Engineers (`https://standards.ieee.org/industry-connections/ec/ead-v1/`), and the *OECD AI Principles*, available at `https://oecd.ai/en/ai-principles`.

On the future of RAG in the larger context of generative AI

In many ways, writing this book felt like a race against the clock. The field is progressing so fast that keeping up with the latest developments and ensuring the content remains relevant is a constant challenge. Each chapter seemed to beckon for updates, even before the *ink was dry* on the previous one. As I navigated the latest research, breakthroughs, and debates, I was acutely aware of the need to present information that was not only accurate but also anticipated future trends. The aim was not only to depict the present situation but also to offer ideas that would be relevant and valuable in the long run. In particular, I'd like to highlight a few significant updates in the field that have led me to consider how RAG will be impacted in the long run.

Long-context LLMs are becoming something common

The advent of LLMs such as **Google's Gemini 1.5**, which can process up to 1 million tokens, has sparked a debate about the future of RAG: `https://blog.google/technology/ai/google-gemini-next-generation-model-february-2024/`. With such a huge capacity for context ingestion, a legitimate question arises: *Do we still need RAG with these models?*

Despite the impressive capabilities of these models, they still have limitations, such as high cost, latency, and potential accuracy issues with large context windows. In contrast, RAG offers advantages in terms of cost, better control of information flow, and easier troubleshooting, making it a strong contender in the LLM space. The expanding capacity of models to ingest more data is exciting, but it does not guarantee proper understanding since accuracy can decline for content in the middle sections of lengthy text. RAG's complementary strengths, such as filtration of irrelevant information, handling rapidly evolving knowledge, modular architectures, and specialized functionality, make it relevant even in the face of massively scaled models.

Therefore, in my opinion, even as the LLM context windows continue to increase in size, RAG will continue to play a crucial role in harnessing their potential while mitigating their limitations.

The emergence of specialized and highly efficient hardware for AI

Hardware innovations such as Groq's **GroqChip**™, specifically designed for running AI models with extremely low latency, could significantly impact the landscape of AI and the role of RAG. Built from the ground up to accelerate AI, ML, and HPC workloads, the GroqChip™ reduces data movement for predictable low-latency performance, bottleneck-free. This could make cloud-based AI more accessible and powerful, allowing for the development of more sophisticated applications. By focusing on inference speed and efficient data processing and having a fully deterministic architecture, this technology can enable real-time generation of text, images, audio, and even video, potentially reducing the need for local AI hardware. This could make cloud-based AI more accessible and powerful, allowing for the development of more sophisticated applications.

Combined with RAG, Groq's chips could help mitigate some of the limitations of LLMs by providing faster access to relevant information and even reducing the need for extensive context windows. The ability to process data rapidly and efficiently could also enhance RAG's strengths, such as handling rapidly evolving knowledge and enabling modular architectures. A mix of such advanced hardware and RAG techniques could lead to more powerful, efficient, and adaptable AI systems that can better serve users' needs while maintaining the benefits of information filtration and augmentation. Less latency means better user experience. A better user experience usually leads to faster adoption.

If this technology proves viable, traditional players in the hardware field such as NVIDIA, Intel and AMD will most probably follow through with similar products in the near future.

Multimodal is becoming the new norm

Lately, all major players in the LLM field seem to converge on the adoption of multi-modal features. The mixture of RAG and multimodal AI represents a leap forward in creating systems that can comprehend and interact with the world in ways more similar to humans. This synergy could revolutionize how we access information, make decisions, and communicate, making AI more intuitive and aligned with our natural ways of processing information. Going beyond text and NLP capabilities, the fusion of RAG with multimodal AI promises to enhance the relevance and precision of generated content. For instance, in educational applications, it could provide tailored learning materials that combine textual explanations with illustrative diagrams, audio explanations, and interactive simulations. In healthcare, it might analyze medical reports, patient history, and imaging together to support diagnostic processes. The potential for creating more immersive and interactive entertainment experiences is also vast, from video games to virtual reality.

The AI regulation landscape is gradually taking shape

As so often in recent history, the rapid advance of technology has left governments and institutions off-side. It's a new field, one that abounds with opportunities but also risks. It is almost certain that in the near future, laws and regulations will be updated to cover this area and to ensure the safe and harmonious use of AI. The European Union has already set the tone by recently passing the so-called **EU Artificial Intelligence Act** (**EU AI Act**): `https://artificialintelligenceact.eu/`.

This landmark legislation classifies AI applications based on risk and strictly regulates or outright bans those deemed harmful, such as non-consensual biometric surveillance and social scoring systems. It emphasizes the need for transparency, accountability, and human oversight of high-risk applications, and strengthens the rights of individuals to understand and challenge AI-driven decisions. The EU AI Act marks the EU as a leader in AI governance and could set a precedent for other countries to follow, similar to the impact of the EU's **General Data Protection Regulation** (**GDPR**) on data privacy laws worldwide.

Our future RAG solutions should be built considering these trends in regulations. They'll need flexibility in terms of underlying models being used – as new rules could potentially restrict or outright ban the usage of a certain LLM, our apps should be redundant and portable in such scenarios. Also, to maximize compliance and stakeholder value, we should aim for several objectives:

- **Transparency**: RAG systems should be designed with transparency in mind, allowing users to understand how the AI model generates its outputs. This includes providing clear information about the data sources used, the logic of the retrieval process, and any potential limitations that could reduce the overall trust that users can place in the output.

- **Human oversight**: On top of comprehensive evaluation, high-risk RAG applications should incorporate human oversight and control mechanisms. This allows for human intervention when necessary and ensures that the AI system's decisions can be challenged or overridden if needed.

- **Data privacy and security**: RAG workflows should be developed with strong data privacy and security measures in place. This includes adhering to data protection regulations, ensuring secure storage and processing of user data, and implementing measures to prevent unauthorized access or abuse. Implementing guardrails and misuse case testing (`https://en.wikipedia.org/wiki/Misuse_case`) should be mandatory in case of applications that handle high-value data.

- **Fairness and non-discrimination**: RAG systems should be designed to avoid unfair bias and discrimination. This involves carefully curating our data sources, testing for biases, and implementing measures to mitigate any identified biases in the RAG outputs.

- **Accountability**: From a governance perspective, RAG applications should have clear accountability mechanisms in place. This includes designating responsible parties for the AI system's actions, establishing processes for auditing and monitoring the system's performance, and providing channels for users to report issues or concerns.

- **Continuous monitoring and improvement**: RAG pipelines should be subject to ongoing monitoring and evaluation to ensure they continue to operate as intended and comply with relevant regulations. This involves regularly assessing the system's performance, addressing any identified issues, and updating any components as needed to improve its accuracy and reliability.

- **Stakeholder engagement**: Ideally, developers of RAG applications should engage with relevant stakeholders, including users, regulators, and civil society groups, to understand their needs and concerns. This feedback should be incorporated into the design and development process to ensure the system provides maximum value while adhering to ethical and legal standards.

By keeping these ideas in mind when creating and using RAG applications, developers can make sure their solutions remain compliant and at the same time, they provide solutions that are reliable, effective, and deliver value.

A small philosophical nugget for you to consider

Lastly, I'd like to share with you a beautiful analogy extracted from an article written by John Nosta – founder of NostaLab. A visionary innovator, observing the future at the intersection of technology, science, and humanity, Mr. Nosta speaks about a less obvious effect that LLMs have on human society. Here's a quick summary of his concept:

"Large language models are changing the way we think. They contain vast amounts of knowledge and are increasingly evolving toward human-like intelligence and probably beyond. As they grow in size and complexity, LLMs resemble a cognitive black hole, blurring the line between human and machine intelligence, potentially leading to their convergence. In the article, the idea of human escape velocity is a wonderful metaphor describing the difficulty of preserving human independence in the era of AI. The goal is to use AI to improve our cognitive abilities, creativity, and ethical reasoning. As LLMs become more integrated into human thinking and behavior, it is important to approach this new territory with care. To foster a symbiotic relationship that promotes a shared cognitive evolution, it is important to actively engage with AI's capabilities rather than passively benefiting from them. The use of LLMs represents a transformative moment in AI, challenging our understanding of intelligence, consciousness, and what it means to be human in a digital universe."

If you find these ideas intriguing, you can read the full article here: `https://www.psychologytoday.com/us/blog/the-digital-self/202403/llms-and-the-specter-of-the-cognitive-black-hole`.

Summary

This is a final encouragement for the road ahead. Alas, our time together has come to an end, but this is not a conclusion; rather, it is the beginning of a new journey. As you embark on this exciting path, it may initially appear that the road ahead is full of obstacles. However, remember that where there is a will, there is always a way. The knowledge and insights you have gained from this book will serve as essential items in your toolbox, empowering you to navigate the complexities that lie ahead. These concepts and techniques will provide a solid foundation upon which you can build, adapt, and innovate as you encounter new problems and opportunities in the ever-evolving landscape of AI. As you progress on this journey, I urge you to cultivate and maintain a curious mindset.

Curiosity is the fuel that propels us forward, driving us to ask questions, seek answers, and explore uncharted territories. It is through curiosity that we discover new possibilities, uncover hidden insights, and push the boundaries of what is achievable.

Above all, *never stop learning*, for knowledge is a lifelong pursuit.

Index

packtpub.com

Subscribe to our online digital library for full access to over 7,000 books and videos, as well as industry leading tools to help you plan your personal development and advance your career. For more information, please visit our website.

Why subscribe?

- Spend less time learning and more time coding with practical eBooks and Videos from over 4,000 industry professionals

- Improve your learning with Skill Plans built especially for you

- Get a free eBook or video every month

- Fully searchable for easy access to vital information

- Copy and paste, print, and bookmark content

Did you know that Packt offers eBook versions of every book published, with PDF and ePub files available? You can upgrade to the eBook version at packtpub.com and as a print book customer, you are entitled to a discount on the eBook copy. Get in touch with us at customercare@packtpub.com for more details.

At www.packtpub.com, you can also read a collection of free technical articles, sign up for a range of free newsletters, and receive exclusive discounts and offers on Packt books and eBooks.

Other Books You May Enjoy

If you enjoyed this book, you may be interested in these other books by Packt:

Unlocking the Secrets of Prompt Engineering

Gilbert Mizrahi

ISBN: 978-1-83508-383-3

- Explore the different types of prompts, their strengths, and weaknesses
- Understand the AI agent's knowledge and mental model
- Enhance your creative writing with AI insights for fiction and poetry
- Develop advanced skills in AI chatbot creation and deployment
- Discover how AI will transform industries such as education, legal, and others
- Integrate LLMs with various tools to boost productivity
- Understand AI ethics and best practices, and navigate limitations effectively
- Experiment and optimize AI techniques for best results

Generating Creative Images With DALL-E 3

Holly Picano

ISBN: 978-1-83508-771-8

- Master DALL-E 3's architecture and training methods
- Create fine prints and other AI-generated art with precision
- Seamlessly blend AI with traditional artistry
- Address ethical dilemmas in AI art
- Explore the future of digital creativity
- Implement practical optimization techniques for your artistic endeavors

Packt is searching for authors like you

If you're interested in becoming an author for Packt, please visit authors.packtpub.com and apply today. We have worked with thousands of developers and tech professionals, just like you, to help them share their insight with the global tech community. You can make a general application, apply for a specific hot topic that we are recruiting an author for, or submit your own idea.

Share Your Thoughts

Now you've finished *Building Data-Driven Applications with LlamaIndex*, we'd love to hear your thoughts! Scan the QR code below to go straight to the Amazon review page for this book and share your feedback or leave a review on the site that you purchased it from.

https://packt.link/r/1-835-08950-X

Your review is important to us and the tech community and will help us make sure we're delivering excellent quality content.

Download a free PDF copy of this book

Thanks for purchasing this book!

Do you like to read on the go but are unable to carry your print books everywhere?

Is your eBook purchase not compatible with the device of your choice?

Don't worry, now with every Packt book you get a DRM-free PDF version of that book at no cost.

Read anywhere, any place, on any device. Search, copy, and paste code from your favorite technical books directly into your application.

The perks don't stop there, you can get exclusive access to discounts, newsletters, and great free content in your inbox daily

Follow these simple steps to get the benefits:

1. Scan the QR code or visit the link below

https://packt.link/free-ebook/9781835089507

2. Submit your proof of purchase
3. That's it! We'll send your free PDF and other benefits to your email directly

www.ingramcontent.com/pod-product-compliance
Lightning Source LLC
Chambersburg PA
CBHW080614060326
40690CB00021B/4687